To –

John W. and Lorena Sublett

With best wishes –

Cordially –

[signature]

June 1, 1970

Thomas Gilcrease

Also by the author:

An Appreciation of Will Rogers

Before My Night

The Cherokee Kid

Thomas Gilcrease

by David Randolph Milsten

The Naylor Company
Book Publishers of the Southwest
San Antonio, Texas

Library of Congress Catalog Card No. 74-84447

Printed in the United States of America

SBN 8111-0291-2

This book is dedicated to the everlasting memory of

THOMAS GILCREASE

who left his imprint upon the land he loved and who said:

"EVERY MAN MUST LEAVE A TRACK
AND IT MIGHT AS WELL BE A GOOD ONE."

Contents

List of Illustrations

Preface

It is regrettable that Thomas Gilcrease did not write his autobiography. Had he done so, he would have without doubt imparted to his readers the events in his life which motivated him to do what few men have done. He would have bared many of his intimate thoughts and in doing so endeavored to rationalize his eventful career.

Thomas Gilcrease, while not a full-blood Indian, possessed sufficient Indian blood to make him conscious of his heritage. His hereditary traits were imprinted upon his mind by what he called the "sufferings of his people" at the hands of the white man. He was a highly prejudiced individual, and his efforts at rationalization would have been a difficult task for him.

The story of the life of Thomas Gilcrease does not fall into that class of biographies which takes the subject from rags to riches, and yet, had it not been for his perseverance, his native ability, and the era in which he lived, he could have gone from riches to rags.

How much can man learn about his fellowman? Will his friends and contemporaries color their opinions? Who talks and who remains silent? Who knows, but hesitates to reveal? Who speaks the truth and who indulges in plaudits instead of critical expressions?

The life of Thomas Gilcrease covered a complicated span of years. The events which captivated him are closely associated with his accomplishments and are therefore inseparable. There is romance to be found in this biographical essay, because the career of Thomas Gilcrease was so very real.

I have recorded what I believe to be an authentic summation, and I hope, created the image of a most ingenious individual.

David Randolph Milsten

A Mural of Discernment

If the talent of an artist had been my lot, I would paint an enormous mural upon which the countenances of those who exemplified their faith in this biography would be depicted. The legend would include the names of those whose unselfish contributions of fact, data, and memorabilia were so useful in developing and chronicling the events, accomplishments, heartbreaks, inspirations, and aspirations in the life of Thomas Gilcrease.

Special segments of the canvas would be reserved for: Thomas Gilcrease, Jr.,* Barton Gilcrease, and Des Cygne Gilcrease Denney,* sons and daughter of Thomas Gilcrease — to each of them I extend my gratitude for their blessings and acquiescence in permitting me to meet the challenge.

Eudotia Teenor, secretary of the Gilcrease Foundation, for her counsel, her patience and her genuine desire to see this work come to fruition; without her this volume may never have been adequately presented or authenticated. A more efficient and loyal liaison with Gilcrease immediates does not exist.

Bruce Wear, former Curator of Art of the Thomas Gilcrease Institute of American History and Art — with whom I conferred so often and whose judgment and talents assisted me in overcoming some of the early indecisions.

---

* Deceased

Paul Rossi, Director of the Institute — who expressed a constant willingness to facilitate my efforts.

W. E. "Dode" McIntosh, Principal Chief of the Creek Nation; George H. Bowen, E. Fred Johnson, Otha H. Grimes, William S. Bailey, Jr., all of Tulsa; Dr. Oliver S. Willham, former President of Oklahoma State University, Stillwater; Wolf Robe Hunt, Willard Stone, Gregory Perino, Woodrow Crumbo, Dr. David Harner, Charlien Sanditen; Mrs. Emmet Pugh and Mrs. Burton Logan; Lester and Louise Whipple, San Antonio, Texas; L. Karlton Mosteller, deceased, Oklahoma City, Oklahoma; Robert H. Welch, Postmaster, and Andrew Lynch, E. E. Dees, and Charlie Howell of Robeline, Louisiana; Mrs. E. W. Morris, Vowell's Mill, Louisiana; Raymond Sandler, Beverly Hills, California; Samuel J. Friedman, Natchitoches, Louisiana; Dr. Roger W. Getz, President, Bacone College, Bacone, Oklahoma; Dr. John E. King, President, Kansas State College, Emporia, Kansas; Robert W. Kelly, Pawhuska, Oklahoma; James Kennedy, Tulsa, Oklahoma; Rudolf G. Wunderlich, Kennedy Galleries, New York; Al Stendall, Stendall Galleries, Hollywood, California; John F. Fleming, Fleming Galleries, New York; W. F. Davidson, M. Knoedler Company, New York; Philip and Lionel Robinson, London, England; Wanita "Belle" Gilcrease, San Antonio, Texas; Jim Stevenson, Reference Department, Tulsa City County Library; Ray Pierce, and Marie L. Wadley, Department of the Interior, Muskogee, Oklahoma; Dr. Logan Wilson, President, American Council on Education, Washington, D.C., former President, University of Texas; Leon Wall, Superintendent, Chilocco Indian School, Chilocco, Oklahoma; Martin A. Wenger, Norman, Oklahoma, former Librarian, Gilcrease Institute; B. A. Schrod, Acting Superintendent, Osage Agency, Pawhuska, Oklahoma; D. Hays Solis-Cohen, Philadelphia, Pa.; H. L. "Red" Branscum, Alice, Texas; Dr. Alexandre Hogue, Tulsa University, Tulsa, Oklahoma; Dean Krakel, Director, National Cowboy Hall and Western Heritage Center, Oklahoma City, Oklahoma; Charles Banks Wilson, Miami, Oklahoma; Mrs. George H. Bruce, deceased; formerly Norma Smallwood, Wichita, Kansas; James T. Forrest,

Director, Bradford Brintony Memorial, Big Horn, Wyoming; Thomas L. Lewis, Taos, New Mexico; Robert O. Lindneux, Evergreen, Colorado; Dudley Dobie, San Marcos, Texas; Monsieur G. Bouttier, Versailles, France; Everett W. Leighton, Riverdale, California; Dr. George L. Cross, President, University of Oklahoma, Norman, Oklahoma; S. Morton Rutherford, Cephas Stout, Ludie Lazarus, George Stanley, Martin Wiesendanger and Marie Keene, all of Tulsa, Oklahoma; Robert Lee Humber, Greenville, North Carolina; and Morton R. Harrison, for the loyalty he demonstrated to his friend, Thomas Gilcrease. Mr. Harrison gave of his time, talents, and material assistance to prevent the creditors of Mr. Gilcrease from involving the treasured art collection in what might have been endless litigation. The segment of this volume which details this civic service is indispensible to this biography.

To Alfred E. Aaronson belongs the salute of success. His inspirations and aspirations for the arts and for mankind must become a permanent record in the Gilcrease story. He proved to be a leader of men and purpose, and his founding of the Keep Gilcrease Committee is carved deeply into the annals of Tulsa history and into the hearts and minds of all those who labored with him.

A very special expression of gratitude to my son, Dr. Donald Ellis Milsten, Professor of Political Science, University of Maryland, Baltimore Campus, for his critical reading of the manuscript and to Dr. Oliver S. Willham, former President of Oklahoma State University of Stillwater, Oklahoma, for his invaluable review of the manuscript, his frank comments, and his constructive suggestions.

The interest which James C. Leake expressed and manifested in the publication of this book will ever be a demonstration of genuine friendship.

And finally — in the center of the vast mural would be the portrait of my devoted Minnie who encountered and indulged the lonely hours while the ribbons of my typewriter turned into silken strings.

Introduction

The simple words, "Every man must leave a track," which appear in the dedicatory portion of this book, are somewhat indicative of the accomplishments of the man who coined the expression. These six words formed the keystone of the artistic structure upon which he built a repository for the handiwork of men of talent and for the preservation of their products.

Charles M. Russell might have said of Thomas Gilcrease, "He wasn't given much for talkin' but when he said what he had to say he said somethin'."

His small hands never knew the feel of a painter's brush and he did not write out or detail for posterity the facts of his long and exciting life. His body housed a heart which pumped life to a mind which stimulated a brain where homey thoughts were executed quietly, unobtrusively — but with certainty.

Those who knew him better never heard him quote from the scriptures, but the literature of the greats was not a stranger to his mental or physical library. His philosophy encompassed a full and definite belief in the dignity of man and what he called "nature's work."

He sought, he explored, he challenged, he fought, he won, and he lost and then tried again. He preserved and he exhibited, that others might observe and remember.

Biography is an independent branch of literature, and it has been wisely stated that there is no formula for the biographer. He is free to seek individual form and expression with the same license as that accorded the poet, novelist, painter, or sculptor.

In this biography of Thomas Gilcrease it has been almost herculean to avoid the panegyric. I embarked upon this labor of love knowing that in the realm of biography there is a place for the work that is not intended as creation but rather as chronicle. The facts of a man's life are found in his letters if he was prolific in the written form of expression. They are taken from the thoughts of his contemporaries if they are willing to part with them. They are deciphered from public records and newsprint if the individual's trails blazed in that direction. They are gleaned from family repositories if such previous sources are available. It becomes the decision of the biographer whether he seeks to dangle skeletons if they come to light or to let them reside in their immortal abodes.

If biography is an art and not a science, as I believe it to be, then I have elected to write the biography of Thomas Gilcrease because I firmly harbor the thought and conviction that he was an artist who lived in a world where he ingathered the kind of art he felt would enhance the plight of history. There are those who advocate that biographies fail when they do not give pleasure to the reader. It is my hope that this work will not be lacking in that aspect.

Thomas Gilcrease is not to be numbered among those who fall into the classification of letter writers. He was only an occasional correspondent. Where letters were discovered they have been utilized. It is regrettable that there were not more of them, because he possessed a delightful humor and delicate manner of expression. The intimate friendships of Thomas Gilcrease were few; J. Frank Dobie was the exception and their correspondence so reflects. Dr. Robert L. Humber was, without question, his closest friend and associate; yet few, if any, letters passed between them. H. L. "Red" Branscom was an employee and later a business associate; but they never wrote to each other.

A definite hiatus exists in his oil company operations as compared to his life as a collector. As clearly demonstrated, he held to the proposition that "wealth could hire brains," and that is what he did. The enlightenment about some of his early years might have been furnished by his sisters and brothers, but he was their senior and only two sisters were knowledgeable enough of his youth to be of assistance. His daughter frankly admitted that she did not really know her father in the sense of being able to recall his philosophy of life or his commercial ventures. All of his colleagues who were directors of his oil company have been deceased for many years and their memories are stilled. Countless individuals have been subjected to interview. From the composite came the comparisons. His sons belabored their memories to contribute the personal episodes of their youth. The total recall was far from satisfactory. The lawyers who represented him in early litigation involving the usual run of oil lease conflicts have long since crossed the bar, and even had they lived, their ethics would have locked the door to the intrigue which laymen might have found appealing. Through the eyes and comments of his living colleagues and protégés, some of the working tools of the mind of Thomas Gilcrease have been ferreted out; others were abandoned as repetitiously undesirable.

To apply the chronoscope to seventy-two years of a man's life could, with all honesty, be an impossible task. The biographer, unlike the author of fiction, cannot lay his plans on the trestle board and adjust the events so that each chosen character will die at will or fade from the pages to accommodate imaginative narration which has either been borrowed, feigned, or invented. Thomas Gilcrease was a pioneer of the West and his youth in many respects parallels the times in which he lived. His purchase of the painting *Rural Courtship* from Ridgway Knight, his first acquisition of art, is reminiscent of his adolescence and could have been the inspiration for many of his incentives to purchase objects of art.

His youth passed quickly due to the opportunities which came to him by reason of territorial laws. His early business experiences were rapid. Circumstances of his heritage made it possible for him to do what others could not or did not do. He married too soon, without knowing the significance of domestic responsibility. He traveled and did not record or keep a diary. He fell the victim of irreconcilable marital pangs. He broke away from encrusted life he did not cherish and found a purpose for living. His intellectual curiosity annihilated consistency in his allotted days.

David Randolph Milsten

Portrait of Thomas Gilcrease by Charles Banks Wilson

Thomas Gilcrease, Will Rogers, Jr., and David Randolph Milsten, 1954,
at Will Rogers High School in Tulsa, Oklahoma

Thomas Gilcrease holding *The Shepherd of the Hills* by Robert Lindneux; Acee Blue Eagle and Willard Stone

Norma Des Cygne Gilcrease, Miss America of 1926

Rural Courtship by Ridgway Knight

Belle Harlow Gilcrease

William R. Leigh studio as simulated in the Thomas Gilcrease Institute of American History and Art Exhibit, 1965

Lester Whipple

Des Cygne Gilcrease Denny and Thomas Gilcrease, 1959

Thomas Gilcrease Institute of American History and Art

George H. Bowen, W. E. "Dode" McIntosh, Principal Chief, Creek Nation, and David Randolp Milsten at dedication of bronze bust of Thomas Gilcrease by Margaret Taylor Dry

Barton Gilcrease, Thomas Gilcrease, and Thomas Gilcrease, Jr., 1958

Pierce Larkin, C. H. Lamb, Frank G. Walling, Thomas Gilcrease,
G. B. Bancroft, and Ed Gilcrease, 1947

Otha H. Grimes, Thomas Gilcrease, William S. Bailey, Jr., Alfred E. Aaronson,
David Randolph Milsten, and Morton R. Harrison, 1959

Thomas Gilcrease, age fifteen

The Thomas Gilcrease Trophy Room

Robert Lee Humber and Thomas Gilcrease, 1949

The first "Thomas Gilcrease Museum," San Antonio, Texas, 1945

GILCREASE OIL COMPANY
MILAM BUILDING
SAN ANTONIO, TEXAS

OFFICE OF THE PRESIDENT

1940

May she go fast. 9 day done gone.

Friend mine Parsons-Whipple,

Send you copy letter come from Newell This letter let you no him and his figures.

Send you copy Cablegram she come from Robert Lee Humber on other side big water We no answer his talk in Cablegram.

We got 40 acres north orange Same one big well offsettin sunnyside one bigger well settin other side way from sun. She look mighty good We go drill him good in few days.

She rained agua this morning 1½ inche Ben she gone home Bellyache heap much.

Everything come easy go easy.
New things she no come — No body nos nothin — Me too. Injun Tom

A humorous letter written in Indian jargon by Thomas Gilcrease to his attorney, Lester Whipple

Book 1
Indian Tom

Prologue

Tribal Trials and Trails

> The Creeks were warriors and native diplomats. Piece by piece their land was wrested from them . . . one has but to look upon the Great Seal of the Muskogee Nation, Indian Territory, to see that the Sheaves of Wheat and plow represent them as "Tillers of the Soil" and not as a migratory tribe.

"You will be my executioner!"[1]

"Duke" Berryhill looked Timmie Jack right square in the eye. He did not welcome being selected to kill a friend.

The trial docket in the office of the Superintendent of the Five Civilized Tribes in Muskogee, Oklahoma, records one of the most fantastic events in the romantic history of the land of the red man. Timmie Jack, well liked in his community, had gone to a dance near his home on Duck Creek, east of the Half-Circle-S Ranch. James Brown lived at Sapulpa. He was the grandson of W. H. Brown who built the old log cabin Council House at Okmulgee. The mother of James was an Euchee Indian. Too much fire water, a drunken brawl, an argument, and James Brown was dead. He was murdered by Timmie Jack. The crime was committed on the night of January 1, 1896. After two trials, the jury failing to agree at the first trial, Timmie Jack was sentenced to be shot. The execution was to be between the hours of 9:00 A.M. and 4:00 P.M. on May 1, and Timmie was told that he could go home with his family, but he was admonished to be back at the Council House in Okmulgee where he had been tried. In accordance with tribal custom he could select his own executioner. He chose the captain of the Light Horsemen. Timmie was also a member of the Light Horsemen and wanted an expert to carry out the orders of the court. Having completed his business affairs, Timmie stayed with his wife until the appointed time and then, with her at his side, he came back to be sent to the death he had brought upon himself by the crime he had committed.

Samuel J. Haynes, one of the attorneys for the prosecution at the time of the trial, was an eyewitness to the execution and recounts the following austere incident: "This trial occurred at the courthouse in the Okmulgee District which was then located not far from the home of Chief Isparhecher, West of Beggs, Oklahoma. Silas Smith was then operating a blacksmith and woodwork shop on the corner of what is now Sixth and Morton avenues where the Okmulgee Building now stands. Silas Smith made the coffin in which Timmie was to be buried but the fact was not to be disclosed to Timmie. However, he learned of it and went to the shop of Silas Smith, inspected the coffin, got into it and lay down, then announced to Silas that it was all right."

Only one shot was fired. Timmie was seated on a box facing the Council House; his eyes were not covered. A small piece of white paper was pinned to his shirt over his heart. The bullet did not pierce the heart but was so near that Timmie expired in ten minutes. Pleasant "Duke" L. Berryhill had carried out Timmie's request. Many of Timmie's friends and total strangers had assembled to witness this strange case which came to be known as the trial where justice was carried out without the benefit of a jail.

They called it law and order. There was no custody and no bail to be made. Timmie just rode out of town and then when the time came he rode back and joined his fathers at the happy hunting ground when the smoke had disappeared from the Winchester aimed at him by the marksman he had selected.

And that is how the Creeks did it. They were men of honor who followed the instructions of the Light Horsemen for the Okmulgee District, the law enforcement branch of the tribal law.

What manner of men were the Creeks? Or, as Robert Louis Stevenson, the profound philosophical poet, wrote:

> Keep your fears to yourself
> But share your courage with others.[2]

It was not always thus, and to understand the heritage of Thomas Gilcrease, to appreciate more fully what he represented, we must know something of what his people were in their day and what he was in his day, who he was and what he made himself become to so many.

Oklahoma gives much to the pages of yesteryear, including a history of her own that is word after word distinctive, creative and romantic. The delicate art of introducing charm into a philosophical work is not an easy task. Philosophy and history stand and fall together. The people who make a given era in the vast scheme of life blend many bloods, become pragmatic procreants, and then weave their fabrics into a design of human endeavor.

The Indian held dominion over a part of the United States which has been referred to as the "Aboriginal Country."[3] These primitive inhabitants knew every stream and path in a land which was virgin to the spoils of those who invaded their hunting grounds. The removal of the Indian tribes from the homes of their fathers east of the Mississippi extinguished their ancient council fires and altered their position in regard to each other. By the solemn pledge of man-made treaties they were assured, by the government of the United States, that the land they possessed would remain their home forever.

To preserve the brotherhood, if this modern term can be used to implement their native relations, they agreed that peace and friendship would forever be maintained between the nations and their respective citizens — and there were many and varied nations which made up their community. They agreed that revenge would not be cherished, that retaliation would not be practiced for offenses committed by individuals. They vowed to use their native skills and the acquired customs of the white man to improve their people in agriculture, industry, and domestic arts, to promote the comfort and happiness of their women and children. It was indeed a hard decision to make but they felt that their compact would assure them of security and prevent future removal, that the documents signed by their respective representatives would transmit to their posterity an unimpaired title to the lands guaranteed to their respective nations by the United States. They pledged in solemn ceremony to each other that no nation which was a party to the compact would, without the consent of all other signatories, cede, or in any manner alienate, to the United States, any of the precious territory occupied by them.

And so it was that the compact was made between the Cherokees, the Creeks, and the Osages — in General Council, around the Great Council Fire at Tahlequah, Cherokee Nation, on the third day of July, 1843; and today when one stands in the rotunda of the Thomas Gilcrease Institute of American History and Art, he can look out to the most beautiful sunset anywhere in the world and watch the rays point to where there are still sacred memories and shrines of the Cherokees, the Creeks, and the Osages.

A third of the western tribes reside in Oklahoma and that is why this great state has been and will ever be known as Indian country, sometimes called "The Land of the Red Man," derived from two Choctaw words, *Okla* meaning "people," and *humma,* meaning "red." Historians venture that the word *Oklahoma,* which has been immortalized in song by Rodgers and Hammerstein, was proposed in 1866 by the Reverend Allen Wright, governor of the Choctaws, as a name for the western Choctaw Territory which was ceded to the United States following the Civil War and was used in the Choctaw-Chickasaw Treaty in 1866.[4]

The southeastern half of what is now Oklahoma comprised the majority of the lands which made up the old Indian Territory.

Here, then, was the home of the Five Civilized Tribes; namely, the Creeks, Seminoles, Chickasaws, Choctaws, and the Cherokees. In other parts of the state were some twenty-three other tribes. Thomas Gilcrease possessed a percentage of Creek blood and, therefore, since it is his heritage with which we are concerned, it should be remembered that the first contingent of the Creek Indians came from Alabama to the Indian Territory in 1829 under the leadership of Roley McIntosh, chief of the "Loyal Creeks." Other migrations started from Georgia after the War of 1812 and continued until the year 1836.[5] The majority of the Creek tribe were transported under a contract made in 1835 and carried out in 1836. The pertinent language of the agreement read: "The Creek Indians, occupants of the Creek Nation in the State of Alabama, from said nation to a point in the new country allotted to the Creeks, within twenty miles of Fort Gibson, men, women, children and their slaves and goods and chattels."

There was to be one six-horse wagon with a weight limit of fifteen pounds of baggage to every group of approximately eighty persons. The daily travel was not to exceed twelve miles. The long trek was to be accomplished on foot by the able-bodied. It was a brutal assignment to the men, women, and children. Into the unbroken wilderness they were forced to march for over five hundred miles and left blood-stained paths along the route. The removal has been justly called a spectacle of a nation of people forced from their ancestral homes, sacred to them by all the traditions and memories that belonged to a romantic race. This last contingent, some twenty thousand who survived the "Trail of Tears," reached their destination in the fall of 1836.[6]

The foregoing movements did not just happen by the shot of an arrow. It was in 1824 that President Monroe's message to the Congress of the United States contained a recommendation that a tract of land west of Missouri and Arkansas be set aside for the colonization of the Indians from the states east of the Mississippi River. This was actually the beginning of Indian Territory. There were many missionaries in the untouched and untamed regions, which stretched as far as man's vision and endurance could carry him by foot and on horseback. These brave missionaries are credited with the original idea of colonization. Their desire to further the true spirit of the red man had prompted them to grasp their newly acquired friends and learn more about the pipe of peace.

As pointed out, some of the Creeks had moved across the Mississippi before the official authorization, and they had already met the whites and had been exposed to the ways of the great white fathers. The government officials were doubtful about the results of the migrations, and they were in a measure correct, because the price of progress was high. Conflicts continued and Indian wars were not uncommon.

In 1824, the now famous Fort Gibson was established.[7] The post was located on the Neosho, or Grand, River, astride the Arkansas near its confluence with the Grand. It afforded a unique and appealing site as a regimental headquarters and became the center of official and social life. The Creeks were settled in the hilly land where the water was plentiful. The great oak trees nodded their branches in welcome to the new citizens. They occupied the territory west on the tributaries of the Arkansas River for approximately seventy-five to eighty miles. The northeast boundary was provided by the fort at Three Forks, situated where the Grand, Verdigris and Arkansas were neighbors and where their respective river beds were abundant with fish and the game came to water at their shores. This area comprised what is now the greater part of Wagoner, Muskogee, McIntosh, Okfuskee, Creek, Tulsa, Okmulgee, and Hughes counties.

With Fort Gibson firmly rooted, another post was established in the valley of the Kiamichi a few miles above where it empties into the Red River. This was Fort Towson, and each of the forts was named for famous military men of the day – Fort Gibson in honor of Colonel George Gibson, and Fort Towson after General Nathan Towson.

In 1890 it was determined by congressional decree that

all adult Creeks, regardless of sex, as well as their issue, would be allotted land within the Creek Nation. As a result of an earlier treaty signed in 1866 the Creeks reluctantly agreed to grant tribal citizenship to their slaves and, therefore, all who fell into this classification were designated as Creek freedmen and shared in the land allotments. In 1893, a former senator, Henry L. Dawes of Massachusetts, Meredith H. Kidd of Indiana, and Archibald S. McKennon of Arkansas were appointed by President Grover Cleveland as members of the commission to administer to the Indians of the Five Civilized Tribes. They performed the task of obtaining agreements to take the land in severalty and surrender the privilege of continuing their independent tribal governments.[8]

Two years later the surveyors of the government sectionalized the lands in the Indian Territory and Creek Nation. The intricate job of the survey was completed in 1897 and the apportionment to each Creek Indian and to each Creek freedman of 160 acres of land was begun. Eligibility consisted of positive proof of identity with the Creek tribe. The names of the allottees were entered on census cards, numbers were assigned, and the completed index was forever thereafter to be designated as the Creek Roll.

After the Indian Territory and Oklahoma Territory were merged into the state of Oklahoma, part of the restrictions against alienation were removed. The restrictions were retained when the government or Federal Indian Department concluded that the individual was not competent to handle his own affairs.

Part of the allotted land of the Creeks was blessed with fertile soil. Other sections proved to be properly structured for the drilling of oil and gas wells.

The Santa Fe Trail, the Trail of Tears, the Battle of the Horseshoe, the age of the Great Iron Horse, the numerous treaties, the hardships, the visits to Fort Gibson by such men of history as Washington Irving, John Howard Payne, the artist George Catlin, "The Organic Act" which provided territorial government for the land, the romance of the run when the settlers came, the "Sooners," the

"Boomers," the land allotments, and other events all added up to form a part of the heritage of the Creek Indian.[9]

Typical of the times was "The Crazy Snake Uprising." Many of the illiterate and conservative members of the Creek Nation refused to select their allotments and clung to their native customs. The substitution of United States courts for their own tribal courts was not the least of their protests. In 1901, such dissatisfied members of the Creeks, mainly the full bloods, proclaimed Chitto Harjo, or Crazy Snake, their hereditary chief, because of his background and for the reason that he was a direct descendant of the royal line. Harjo lost little time in calling into session the National Council; consisting of the House of Kings, the lawmaking branch of the Creek Nation similar to the United States Senate; and the House of Warriors, equivalent to the United States House of Representatives, and proclaimed the reestablishment of the ancient laws, courts, and customs of the Creek Nation. This action provided a field day for the journalists of the era and the important newspapers quickly capitalized upon the sensational aspect of the action of "Crazy Snake."[10] The public reaction was instantaneous and cries went out to stop the "uprising." Government troops were mustered for action and Chitto Harjo and many of his followers were arrested and temporarily confined.

These then were the Indians of the Creek Nation who had ceded to the United States the western half of its reservation, amounting to 3,250,560 acres, at thirty cents per acre, or the sum of $975,168. The signing of the various treaties marked the dawning of a great change for the Indian Territory, and particularly the Creek whom the English colonists had so named because their country abounded in creeks and small streams and who later came to be known as the Muskogee, the origin and meaning of which is subject to much conjecture.

Such was the heritage of the Creek Indian Thomas Gilcrease, allottee under Roll Number 1505, whose 160 acres of land became the basis of his wealth and placed his name in the index of the history books of Oklahoma.[11]

Chapter 1

From Pelican Soil to Indian Territory

To be born the first child in a family of fourteen, carries with the distinction a multitude of obligations which are not always complemented by the advantages. To become a wealthy individual before reaching the twenty-first birthday is fraught with many problems. To be the recipient of such wealth without having had to earn it by the sweat of the brow can be frustrating. To retain such wealth and make it work for you is a challenge any man would welcome but might not accomplish. To find a place in the sun and be bathed in the rays of achievement is an even greater satisfaction. To be blessed with all of these possibilities creates temptations, opens many portals, and becomes a daring experience wherein survival can not only be questionable, but with a majority of men — disastrous.

Thomas Gilcrease was such a man. He was born William Thomas Gilcrease on February 8, 1890, the son of William Lee Gilcrease and Mary Elizabeth Vowell. For some unexplained reason he was twice baptized "William Thomas," but as soon as he was old enough to write he dropped the "William" and never used the name again.

A cursory examination of Tom's lineal ancestry would provide the writer of fiction with some basic facts upon which to launch a story of the early day settlers in Louisiana and Alabama; however, biography does not lend itself to a departure from authentic data. A few family records literally epitomize the available descent of the man who doted upon calling himself "Indian Tom."[1]

The genealogy is capsuled quickly. Hampton G. Vowell was the father of Mary Elizabeth Vowell, and Martha Ann Self was her mother. Enos Gilcrease was the father of William Lee Gilcrease, and Mary Elizabeth Bean was his mother. William Lee was born on the eighth day of January, 1868, at Winnfield, Louisiana, and died in Bixby, Oklahoma, near the City of Tulsa, on November 23, 1913. Mary Elizabeth Vowell was born on the twenty-fifth day of November in Natchitoches Parish, Louisiana, and died June 12, 1935, in Tulsa, Oklahoma. William Lee Gilcrease and Mary Elizabeth Vowell had fourteen children.*

Measured by the mores of the era, there was not anything especially unusual about the infant years of the life of Thomas Gilcrease. The short time he lived in Louisiana was hardly subject to recall, except as the incidents were planted in his mind by the anecdotes and experiences he heard from his parents – mostly from his mother since his father was not very verbose about Tom's plight as a child. William Lee Gilcrease was too busy keeping the pangs of hunger from striking the stomachs of his children. He was a hard man, made so by hard times.

When the parents of Hampton G. Vowell migrated to

---

* William Thomas who married Belle Harlow and, later, Norma Smallwood. Both of these marriages ended in divorce. Edward, who married Jennie Myles; Ben, who married Grace Covert; Wade, twin of Ben, who died in infancy; Lena, who married Burton Logan; Florence, who married Emmett C. Pugh; May, who died in infancy; Elmer, who married Mary McCartney, divorced her and later married Frona Williams; Mabel, twin of Elmer, who married James Milton Craven; Bessie, who married Hugh Hawkins; Marabel, who remained single; Connie, who married Euna Ione Key; Perry, who married Mary Ellen Lane; and Jewell, who married James Page, divorced him, and married Alva L. Willard.

the United States of America and settled in the state of Georgia, it is presumed that they changed their name. Where they started their journey, when they sailed, the length of the voyage, when they landed, what route they took, or how long they traveled to reach the southern state of Georgia, has been lost to the ages.

The ancestors of the Vowell and Gilcrease families were God-fearing stalwarts whose occupations were those which were necessary to preservation of life and everyday existence. They were woodworkers, blacksmiths, wheelrights and tillers of the soil. Their crops depended upon the seasons, and the fertilizers which fed the plants were provided by the ingenious conservation of barnyard waste.[2]

Their industry was largely confined to the operation of grist mills which were propelled by water power. Their medical needs came from the use of herbs which prevented disease. The women worked at the looms and made garments which were not to be purchased in the settlement stores. The underwear, nightgowns, gloves, head coverings, plowlines, clotheslines, and diapers for the young were all the handicraft of well-trained and dependable mates of the male. The thread was manufactured from home grown cotton by what was known as one-stand gins, which pressed the cotton into bales.

Mary Elizabeth Vowell inherited many of her traits from her Indian mother, who was a one-half blood Creek, none the less of which was the characteristic superstition which stemmed from tribal custom, namely that family history was not to be preserved. This concept was anchored in the fact that their aboriginal background was not conducive to formal recordation. They merely buried their dead with dignity and ritual, leaving them to the Great Spirit. This philosophy accounts for the statement attributed to Mary Elizabeth Vowell that she would "skin her children alive" if she ever heard them talking about the past.

Hampton G. Vowell, according to young Tom, was just about the most colorful grandfather that a boy ever had. Hamp, as he was known to his family and friends, had been a mail carrier at Vowell's Mill. He was a superb horseman and made two trips each week between the Mill and Robeline, Louisiana, over a ten-mile route, for which he received seventy-five cents a month. The town of Robeline was eleven miles from Natchitoches, Louisiana, the latter having had its beginning in 1714 when the French soldiers established a trading post on the banks of the Red River. Natchitoches had many traditions. The architecture of the buildings resembled those of New Orleans with their iron grillwork and enclosed patios. This accounts for the French and Spanish customs which are still in evidence in the area.

The significant historic sites are evidenced by markers, and near Robeline one can stand at the crest of a hill where once stood Fort Los Adais. This fort was considered old when George Washington went into winter quarters at Valley Forge. The ravages of time have removed all physical recognition of this page of history, where for over fifty years there resided Spanish soldiers and priests who knew what it meant to fight and die for a cause.

All of this was virgin country in the eighteenth century, with the old trail being the Camino de Natchitoches (later known as the "Camino Real" and the "San Antonio Trail"), leading from the settlement of Natchitoches on the Colorado (Red River) westward through the Adais country to where Robeline is now located.[3]

There can be no question but that the old trails held a sentimental attachment for the Vowell and Gilcrease families and that they indoctrinated their children with the customs they practiced and hoped that the gods would some day bless them with a better life.

The exact date of the marriage between William Lee Gilcrease and Mary Elizabeth Vowell cannot be reconciled, but it was presumed to have been either in 1888 or 1889. William Lee Gilcrease was of French, Scots, and Irish descent and apparently was more literate than other members of his family, and as such he was an avid reader of the posters and bulletins which were released by the government concerning the treaties which were being made with the Indians. Through this media he learned that the members of the Creek Tribe were going to be enrolled, and allotments of land made, and with his wife, Elizabeth, and his son, Tom, he joined the wagon train when the Vowells and Selfs left Louisiana in 1890.

It was a long and difficult journey. Their provisions and supplies depended largely upon their own ingenuity. They encountered all of the hardships which are so often described in the wagon train epics of the cinema, and Mary Elizabeth Gilcrease falls into the category of unforgettable characters. She had learned how to use firearms when she was barely old enough to hold a gun in her petite but strong hands. An excellent marksman, she taught her children to take accurate aim and then shoot to kill. Ammunition was expensive and far from plentiful, so every shot had to count. Young Tom was an apt student and learned to excel in everything he learned from his parents. His mother was a favorite on the wagon train because of her ability to trap animals and fowl when others failed in the effort.

When the wagon train reached the banks of the Red River, there was reason to celebrate, and that is exactly what they did. They had arrived in the territory when they reached Paris, Texas. As Tom grew older his mother related the events to him, and each chapter of adventure became welded to his heart and mind: the building of the log cabins, the search for game, the ever present danger of snakes which found perfect hiding places in the spaces between the logs where the mud washed away and left unplugged cracks. There was romance in the air as these pioneers realized they were headed for a new country. They pressed forward until they reached the Creek Nation, and camped for a spell at Eufaula, Indian Territory – moving on to a community called Twin Mounds where they became a part of the established settlement.

In 1904, they moved to Wealaka. William Lee Gilcrease was determined to make a stake. He was an extrovert in the full meaning of the word. Mary Elizabeth was just the opposite, and their son, Tom, somehow managed to strike a happy medium from these paternal and maternal influences. If anything, he leaned toward his mother's characteristics. Whether his apparent modesty came from avoiding the discipline meted out by his father or from seeking the shelter of his mother's gingham apron is debatable. Tom was born with club feet and this handicap contributed somewhat to his shyness when strangers to the family were present.* His grandfather, Hampton Vowell, designed a pair of leather protectors which made is possible for young Tom to do just about everything any other child could do or attempt.[4]

Young Tom's business career actually started when he regained his majority rights in a lawsuit instituted in the District Court of Wagoner County, Oklahoma. When his land allotment was made by the government, his father had been appointed his legal guardian. The action to terminate the guardianship came as a result of the poor judgment exercised by his parents in entering into certain oil and gas lease agreements on his behalf.

When his funds were released from the transactions, he opened a general store at Wealaka, Oklahoma, a mile south of the Wealaka Mission and near the Midland Valley railroad line. This acquisition was the only commercial enterprise in the small community. His motive became apparent when he later gave the store to his father and told him that the success of the store from then on would depend upon others than himself. His father had tried, to some extent, to engage in the retail business before Tom opened the store. He would often gather up some of his choice vegetables, load a wagon, and send Tom and his brother Ed on a selling trip. The boys were admonished not to return until they had disposed of all of their wares for cash. He had sold groceries at a place called Red Tank Farm, south of the town of Jenks, Oklahoma. This gift

---

* While Tom was still very young he underwent an operation to correct his deformity. The operation was performed in Mounds, Oklahoma, and was partially successful. The doctor was not equipped with anesthetic facilities and Tom's grandmother placed a pillow over the head of Tom's mother to keep her from fainting. Young Tom managed to stand the pain. When Tom reached his maturity he was again operated on by a skilled New York surgeon in New York City, who inserted kangaroo sinews into the deformed feet. The second operation left him somewhat lame and accounted for the forward-leaning stride which was so characteristic of his gait.

from his son gave William Lee Gilcrease a new challenge. Up to that date he had tried a number of ventures and had managed to keep his family clothed by operating a cotton gin, by farming, and by trading in varied products.

As the business expanded, Tom's father sought and obtained an appointment as postmaster and was later elected a justice of the peace.

The independence which came to Tom Gilcrease at the age of sixteen, accounts for much of the self-reliance which was evident throughout his life. It also provided a stubborn streak in him which burned slowly when his ambition conflicted with those he loved. His was a constant fight against selfishness, often mistaken for modesty. Few things resisted his will to do that which pleased him most.

The frugal streak possessed by Tom's father took root in his offspring and accounted for a venture which could have proved most embarrassing to his parents. Two enterprising young women had heard about the influx of oil men into the area and decided to pitch a tent near some drilling operations. They covered the ground with two large blankets and opened for business. Young Tom opened a hamburger stand under a tent he pitched next door to the female entrepreneurs. In later years, when recounting this commercial venture, Tom remarked, "I made money: the men always emerged from the girls' tent with a healthy appetite." This was one of the bright buckles on his youthful belt.

The better values of human endeavor came to Tom during his tender years.

There was the occasion when several outlaws stopped at the isolated Gilcrease home on the prairie and told his mother to prepare food for them. Mrs. Gilcrease was alone with her children and, though highly disturbed by the invasion of the highwaymen, she obeyed rather than incite their anger. Tom was delegated to catch some of the chickens which his mother soon cooked for the frugal repast of the unwanted guests. Before departing, the men wanted to know how much they owed for the food, and Mrs. Gilcrease responded by assuring them that there would be not a charge. The men thanked her but insisted upon paying what they felt was a fair price for the meal. The offer by the bandits and the acceptance by his mother of the money taught Tom that all people have their moral standards, even such intruders, who displayed their code of ethics which permitted them to rob a bank but not to steal from a woman who supplied them with sustenance.

Some of the stories which are said to have originated during these pioneer days are fantastic. Old settlers recall the occasion when William Lee Gilcrease was determined to have a railroad run through his town. The officials of the road did not agree with him and said that there was not enough business to warrant extension of their tracks into the community of Wealaka. The resentment was acute. To make his point, Bill Gilcrease chained one of the wheels of the steam engine to the tracks, and when the train started, the track was disconnected from the ties for several feet before the startled engineer could bring the old wood burner under control. Before long, the track was extended and they all lived happily ever after.

To roam the woods was Tom's greatest delight, and he would take his sisters and brothers with him on long walks while he explored the countryside. He taught them how to walk safely along the trails and urged them to put their footprints into those he made along the paths. Even then he must have felt that man should make good tracks.

The approach of the winter season made it necessary for Tom's father to increase the inventory of his store. New items were on the market, and the increased activity, both in agriculture and building, demanded his attention. He habitually slept on a bunk on one of the counters in his store when he contemplated a long ride to the wholesale suppliers. At 2:30 A.M. on November 23, 1913, he had secured the front door to the store and had fallen asleep. He was awakened by a heavy pounding on the door and yelled to see who the intruder was and what he wanted. The voice replied, "Me want cigars, you open up!" Whether William Lee Gilcrease recognized the voice or did not desire to lose a sale will never be known. He pulled on his trousers and opened the door. It was a dark night. As the door opened, a shot pierced the body of Bixby's beloved storekeeper. He did not fall immediately but grappled with his assassin. The struggle continued outside the store; a second shot broke the silence, and then a third. The first shot struck him in the shoulder, the second in the left arm, and the third in the back of the head. He died instantly. Within minutes after the shooting, a large crowd ran to the store where the murder had occurred and soon turned into a mob calling for vengeance, since Mr. Gilcrease was justice of the peace and well known in the community. The Bays Detective Agency dispatched two of its best agents to the scene when it was learned that the slayer had fled into the mountains, pursued by bloodhounds. Late Sunday evening he was captured when boarding a Frisco train named "The Governor." The arrest took place as the train passed between Haskell and Muskogee, Oklahoma.

The *Tulsa Daily Democrat* of Monday evening, November 24, 1913, carried the account of the tragedy, asserting that a young barber, Ernest Melton, twenty years of age, admitted the slaying, claimed self-defense, and indicated that the quarrel had resulted from a card game in which he and Mr. Gilcrease had been engaged several days before.

The murderer was convicted and sentenced to serve eight years in prison, but was finally paroled.

The death of Tom's father created a void which had to be filled. Being the oldest of the brothers and sisters, the burden came suddenly and with a demanding force. Incidents of early childhood flashed before young Tom's memory. He recalled the antics of his sister, Lena, who had earned the title of "tomboy" of the family, and how he had on one occasion urged her to ride an old sow when she begged him to let her ride his horse. How he had rolled on the ground with laughter when she fell off of the animal! He remembered the time Lena had closed the barn door on his fingers, and for a while it was thought they would have to be amputated, and yet he would not tell his parents how the accident happened.

He could draw into his mind a clear picture of Snake Creek, his favorite stream where he used the boat he had made and of which he acclaimed himself the captain. That was the same boat in which he took his schoolteacher for an outing on Sunday and in his youthful fashion had courted her with fervor. And there were the jaunts in the old surrey from Mounds to Eufaula, Oklahoma, when he watched with envy how his father controlled the horse with his handmade whip, as the feet of his brothers and sisters dangled over the edge of the rough bed of the vehicle, and the ground passed before their popping eyes and they imagined they were on a race track.

Although all of Tom's brothers and sisters did not heed his counsel, he had his favorites who relied upon him to guide them when the going was rough.

After his father was killed, he moved his sister, Florence, and several members of the family to Winfield, Kansas, so they could and would further their education. He had hoped they would follow the example he had tried to instill by his own experience in attending the country schools. He was an avid reader and read every book he could find in the school library.

The childhood of Thomas Gilcrease had been consumed by the relentless time which comes to all boys, and it was not long until the homesteads of the Gilcrease and Vowell families were completely destroyed by fire. The actual sites where the homes once existed are not now known. Landmarks left by the ancestors of "Indian Tom" are gone forever.

One memory stood out more than all the rest. That was the one which recaptured the voice of his mother when she would call to him, "Tom, what would you like for supper?" The answer was, "Fried chicken and turnip greens!"

Among the personal papers of Tom was found one handwritten note.[5]

> As a baby I used to slip away while my mother cooked, washed, ironed, cleaned house and gardened; I would go to the field where my father ploughed, planted and harvested. As soon as I had reached the age of some understanding my career began. When I was four my father taught me how to build fires,

carry water and feed the livestock. At the age of six I was taken to the corn fields where I hoed. When the work in the field was done for the day, I would return to the house and help my mother churn, wash the clothes and cook. I might have been in the way some but I helped her. When I reached my eighth birthday I was given the opportunity to plow, plant and harvest. When my tenth year came around I helped with the milling. When I was a dozen years my father took me to the cotton gin and I assisted him in running it. At fourteen I worked in the general store and two years later I helped with the buying of cotton and merchandise for the store. Seventeen found me going to school. I married at eighteen and became a farmer and rancher before my nineteenth birthday. All this before that wonderful age of twenty-one.

Tom Gilcrease had learned to live in a man's world. The small boy from the pelican soil had found his place in the Indian Territory.

carry water and feed the livestock. At the age of six I was taken to the corn fields where I lived. When the work in the field was done for the day I would return [illegible]

Chapter 2

The Country Schools

The history of education in the Indian Territory and Oklahoma is filled with strange tales of the missionaries and teachers who had labored among the tribes and accompanied them to the territory from their old stomping grounds east of the Mississippi. These early educators established new missions, schools, and churches. The Creeks did not manifest an interest in education as quickly as some of the other tribes. They were reluctant to provide the facilities for academies; however, they did make appropriations for the building of manual training schools in 1848, and one of the first Creek schools was established at Tullahasee, north of the Arkansas and west of the Verdigris. The mission press at Parkhill in the Cherokee Nation was much in demand. Besides tracts, hymns, catechisms, and portions of the Bible; almanacs and school books, such as primers, readers, spellers, and arithmetics were printed in the Cherokee, Choctaw, and Creek languages. Later other printing offices sprang up in the Indian nations where books and pamphlets were printed in the languages of the tribes.[1]

When Tom Gilcrease was old enough to start to school, the educational systems were still in their infancy. The common school system and the establishment of consolidated or township schools in the rural districts, as well as the secondary school for instruction in agriculture and industrial arts, were few indeed.

How much schooling did Tom Gilcrease have? What was the extent of his education? Both questions are appropriate and, although similar in context, they have a different connotation. The simple approach would be to merely conjure up a factual premise from the remnants of thought which generally follows biographical research, but why sacrifice accuracy when the actual record is available? Tom's formal schooling was limited. His formative mind, receptive. His forte was determination.

When Tom Gilcrease instituted a lawsuit against G. R. McCullough, H. B. Martin, A. E. Bradshaw, and Al Brown in the District Court in and for Tulsa County, state of Oklahoma, on the sixteenth day of February, 1912, little did he know that one day his testimony would provide the facts about his schooling which would otherwise have been outside the realm of discovery.[2]

While on the witness stand in his own behalf, his attorney, Mr. P. C. West of the law firm of Biddison and Campbell of Tulsa, Oklahoma, brought forth the following recitation of events:

> Question: Tom, how much schooling have you had in your lifetime, and what kind of school have you gone to?
>
> Answer: I went to country school, I never went to any school with the exception of four months at Muskogee besides going to country school.
>
> Question: You went to Country Schools, where did you live before you came to Tulsa?
>
> Answer: I lived in Wealaka.
>
> Question: Where did you live before you lived in Wealaka?

Answer: I had lived near Mounds.

Question: You grew up in the Creek Nation here?

Answer: Yes, sir, I was raised in the Creek Nation.

Question: And you attended the schools that were accessible to you in those places?

Answer: Yes, sir.

Question: Did you go to all the schools you could go to all the time; did you go every year the whole term?

Answer: No. I just went whenever I could go.

Question: About how much do you suppose—

Answer: Sometimes I would go to school for three or four months, and then maybe I would work for six months and maybe I would go to school six months and maybe I wouldn't go again for a year or so.

Question: Were there some years you didn't go to school at all?

Answer: Yes, sir.

Question: And some years you went to school three months?

Answer: Yes, sir.

Question: And some you went to school six months?

Answer: Yes, sir.

Question: What school did you go to at Muskogee four months?

Answer: Went to the Indian School out there, Bacone.

Question: Outside of that, have you had any other schooling?

Answer: No, sir.

Tom was twenty-two years old when the above testimony was given; consequently all the facts were fresh in his mind and provide the base for the embellishments remembered by a few of his extant contemporaries.

Damon Runyon, as his last words, is alleged to have said, "You can keep the things of bronze and stone, and give me one man to remember me just once a year." It is obvious that during the life of Thomas Gilcrease he remembered Alexander Lawrence Posey more than once a year. When talking of his education he never omitted to comment, "I started to school in a one-room log cabin which was conducted by Alex Posey, the Creek poet.[3] He was intelligent, had a keen insight into people and all things around him. He was a lover of nature, a good shot with the bow and arrow and he taught me how to make them and to shoot straight. I was the first student of Alex on the first day he taught and it was in his father's log cabin that the school was founded. I will always hold him in my memory as a kindly and helpful man and hope that I have in some measure followed in his ways." It was from Posey's lips that Thomas Gilcrease first heard about the "Trail of Tears," over which the Creeks and the Cherokees made the long trek from Georgia and Alabama to Oklahoma. He learned how hundreds of them died from exposure and mistreatment. All of this was history then, just as it is history today, but it fired the imagination of young Tom and caused him to wonder about his great-grandparents who had come from Georgia. How many tears had they shed to reach the land where they had been told the waters run and the grass grows tall? It was from the fertile mind of Alex Posey that he learned of the "Indian House of Warriors and House of Kings," who held their sessions in the Creek capital at Okmulgee. Is it any wonder that William Thomas Gilcrease was destined to become a strange kind of benefactor to the Indians of all tribes; that he would one day do through the medium of the collection of paintings and artifacts, through rare books and archaeological discoveries, what his first teacher, Alexander Lawrence Posey, had been able to do in poetry?*

One of the most captivating poems of Alex Posey was "The Homestead of Empire." The assimilation which was occurring among his people, and the fact that most of the Indians felt that their land was being appropriated by aliens, no doubt created the following lines of the poet, set forth in part as follows:

> Lo! plain and sky are brothers, peak
> And cloud confer; the rivers spread
> At length to mighty seas!
> The soul is lifted up
> In room whose walls are God's! wherein
> Empire has staked off a homestead.
>
> Roll on, ye rivers of the West,
> Roll on, through canyons to the sea!
> Ye chant a harmony
> Where to free People march!
> Roll on, O Oregon, roll on!
> Roll on, O thunderous Yosemite!

Alex Posey knew that all education is affected through the experiences of the educated, but that it did not follow that all experiences are educative. One cannot read the poems of Posey without concluding that they were inspired by the community in which he lived. He knew

---

* Alexander Posey, known as the Creek Poet, was born August 3, 1873, in the Creek Nation. Learned the Creek legends, tribal history and Indian lore from his mother. Attended public school at Eufaula. At age of 17, matriculated in Bacone College and became a member of the faculty. Always well-groomed and was said to be the epitome of grace and kindness. Served as Creek interpreter of the Creek Enrollment Field Party of the Commission of the Five Civilized Tribes. Was a professor, editor, superintendent of Creek Orphan Asylum at Okmulgee, superintendent of Public Instruction of Creek (or Muskogee) Nation. Met death by drowning May 27, 1908, in North Canadian River following a railroad washout during a flood.

that education is aimed at conserving and perfecting the life of the community, but that life is nothing other than the life of its individual members. The impressions he made upon the mind of young Tom were lasting. His appearance, as indicated, was appealing to Tom's eyes; his voice penetrated Tom's ears, which had been trained to listen to the sounds of nature as he roamed about in the woods — all of these things sharpened his mind and made his heart take on a more rapid beat. The instruction of Posey went far beyond the three classical R's — "readin', 'ritin', and 'rithmetic," — as is commonly supposed by some careless reviewers of rustic life in the early days of the territory. Tom Gilcrease was able to liberate himself from the useless things and to comprehend the order of nature. But perhaps the greatest lesson he learned was not from Alex Posey but from his mother. She taught him that truth is only possible when one has knowledge. Tom Gilcrease was determined to become educated to the best of his ability and his opportunities, and then go beyond those opportunities and make more paths through the wooded areas in which he was destined to find a parting with the inferior. He did not want to be known as a conceited man, and so he more or less went his own way and as quickly as possible severed his relationship with the children of the sharecroppers who did not evince a desire for education.

As he slipped from childhood to adolescence, he found that maturity was not easily attained or achieved. He discovered that devotion does not express itself all at once. He developed an introversion which clung to him for the remainder of his life, but somehow he managed to spark his personality with a friendly attitude which would eventually see him through many difficult times. His humor was of a homey, yet topical, type, and whenever he found himself in need of a metaphor, he could reach into his basket of nature's beauty and come up with a figurative expression which would often end debate and disarm the contestants.

Bacone, to which Tom referred in his court testimony, was his first and only school of higher education — that is, above the so-called common school level.[4]* This history of the early day schools is difficult to trace with any accuracy. In 1874, at the forks of the Canadian, an important and badly needed mission school was erected and was known as Asbury Mission. After the Civil War, the Eufaula Boarding School was established on the Asbury site, the old mission having been destroyed by fire. A second fire is alleged to have consumed the building, and another school was erected and remained in use until the 1950's. By this time the majority of the Creek children were enrolled in the public schools. The National High School at Eufaula, Oklahoma, and the *Wetumpka* National School were also typical of the area. Tom Gilcrease probably enrolled in some of them. All of the early day records of Bacone College were destroyed by fire and no one knows what courses Tom took, what grades he made, or what status he attained as a student. His name does appear in the *Baconian.* His address is shown as Wealaka, Oklahoma, and he attended the session from 1907 to 1908. The grade is not shown. So, if we are to accept Tom's own version of his education at Bacone, we must limit it to a four-month term; we must also assume that he attended Bacone in or about 1907, because he made Tulsa his home in December of 1908 and by that time he had married.

Just when the transition took place in Tom's life — that is, when he acquired the polish and culture which made it possible for him to know and associate with society with the same ease as he could fraternize with an oil field worker — is difficult to determine. There is little doubt that his business experiences, the early litigation

---

* Founded by Almon C. Bacone, February 9, 1880, and had its beginning at Tahlequah in the Indian Territory as Indian University. Started with a faculty of one teacher and three students in a small room in the Cherokee Baptist Mission. Bacone had migrated West from New York in 1878 and served as superintendent of the Cherokee Male Seminary at Tahlequah. To train more teachers he prevailed upon the Creek Tribal Council at Muskogee, the location of the Federal Agency for the Five Civilized Tribes, to favor him with a land grant; this he accomplished on October 29, 1881, but it was not until 1885 that Indian University was moved from Tahlequah to Muskogee and became known as Bacone College in honor of its founder and first president.

in which he became involved, and his association with lawyers and oil men, did much to keep him in touch with books.

The reading which counts is the reading which makes a man think, and that is precisely what Thomas Gilcrease did. With the coming of his fortune from the oil discovered on his allotted land, he traveled whenever he could and began to see the world.

In later years he wrote: "In order to have a beautiful, delicate and fragrant rose it is necessary to cultivate and care for it in a thoughtful and careful manner and the more it is cultivated and protected the more beautiful, delicate and fragrant it becomes, so it is with love."[5]

His travels and business took him to Europe, and while in France he studied French, Spanish, and history. He mastered the languages and became a prolific reader of French and Spanish literature. He was proficient in both languages, and his knowledge of French made it possible for him to acquire many fine paintings and rare books when he became imbued with the desire to collect art.[6]

He was considered well versed in the science of geology by reason of his many oil wells and the leases he acquired. If there was one trait he possessed, it was the recognition that the next man cannot be outsmarted in his own business or profession. With this realization and the wealth to do so, he managed to employ talent wherever and whenever he was faced with a new challenge. He learned from those he paid, and they were not aware that they were his teachers.

Tom Gilcrease possessed the capacity, whenever he desired to use it, for keeping silent when in the company of others. He could ignore questions which he considered irrelevant and perform the act with such innocence that personal embarrassment could be neither detected nor reflected in his facial expressions.

Tom Gilcrease had been a farmer; a banker; an oil man; a storekeeper; a collector of art, of good books, rare books, artifacts and, unlike the rolling stone, he gathered moss. His harvest came with age in his recollections and the blessings which he enjoyed despite a heart which was broken more than once. He drilled; he discovered. He acquired. He gave. He loved life. He made it possible for others to see what he sought and left it all behind for the generations to follow. His zeal for learning and his appreciation for education remained with him in all his endeavors.*

---

* In May, 1956, the University of Tulsa conferred an honorary degree of Doctor of Arts and Letters upon Tom Gilcrease. Later he received a citation from the University of Oklahoma. These honors could not be reflected in the face of Mr. Gilcrease since he accepted them with his usual stoicism and modesty. It is doubtful that he knew why he was the recipient of such accolades, and if he could have controlled the sponsors, the occasions would never have occurred. He was gracious, however, in his acceptance remarks, but never mentioned the subject again.

Chapter 3

The Oil Man Takes a Wife

Belle M. Harlow was the daughter of Susan and Warren W. Harlow. The Harlows had lived in Osage County, and Belle was a citizen of the Osage tribe of Indians. Her maternal grandparents were Peter Perrier and Katherine Chadwick Perrier. Her paternal grandparents were William and Margaret Harlow. She grew to maturity without any vivid memory of either of them. She was registered on the rolls as a quarter blood. She was born in Osage County near Skiatook, Oklahoma, in Indian Territory on the twenty-fifth day of September, 1893.

On July 28, 1906, the Congress of the United States approved an act which provided for the division of the lands and funds of the Osage Indians in Oklahoma Territory.* The act provided for proper registration of allottees;

---

* This well-known tribe had begun ceding their lands to the United States by treaty in 1808, their last cession being in 1870. They usually made good bargains, leaving the purchase price on deposit with the

however, no name was included of any person or his descendents that was placed on the roll prior to the thirty-first day of December, 1881, the date of the adoption of the Osage Constitution; and the secretary of the interior was ordered to make careful investigations to be sure that the spirit and letter of the law was observed. This was to prevent fraud in the process of the enrollments.[1] There were to be, in all, three selections made by each allottee, of 160 acres each. There was a further provision that after each member had made the authorized number of selections, the remaining lands of said tribe in Oklahoma Territory were to be divided as equally as practicable among the members by a commission so appointed, subject to some exceptions. The portion designated as "homestead" was to remain inalienable and nontaxable for a period of twenty-five years, or during the life of the homestead allottee if the person were proven competent within the definitions provided.

Belle Harlow was within the time limits by birth and was, therefore, registered or enrolled as number 1307. Her father, Warren Harlow, was a "non-Indian," but her mother, Susan Harlow, née Perrier, was an Osage allottee and enrolled as number 1305. Belle received 160 acres on her first selection, the same number of acres on her second, and her third selection was made up of 152.9 acres. The surplus allotment was 185 acres.

Warren and Susan Harlow were determined that their children would have good schooling. As soon as Belle entered her teens they took her to one of the mission schools, the Sacred Heart College, operated by Roman Catholic missionaries in the southern part of Pottawatomie County, Oklahoma, where she attended the lower grades of classroom instruction. When Belle and her sister Susan were

---

United States Treasury, the Osage drawing only the interest on the fund. Their Oklahoma reservation, to which the Osage moved in 1872, proved to be rich in oil and natural gas, the royalties from which added to the wealth of the tribe. The Osage derived their name from *Ouasage* the French form of *Washashe* or *Wasash,* the name by which they were known to Indians of other tribes.

old enough, they enrolled in Bacone College, at Bacone, Oklahoma, near the city of Muskogee.

Belle Harlow was most attractive, and while she was attending the convent she was entered as a candidate for the popularity contest. The participant who received the most votes was declared the victor. Belle won, and the fact that her brother bought a book of chances for the sum of five dollars did not take away from the honor. Her prize was a large, handsome doll which she treasured for many years and kept until it was lost in a fire.[2]

The Midland Valley Railroad ran a regular train from Tulsa to Muskogee, and the students attending Bacone were dependent upon the line for their transportation. Those who lived in Tulsa came home as often as their parents would grant them permission to do so. The seating arrangement of the old line coaches was adjustable and the seats could be made to face each other, thereby providing a rather intimate section for the passengers. Tom Gilcrease was a student at Bacone, and on the weekend he would board the train at Wealaka. Tom and a friend were always on the lookout for female company, and one day in September of 1907 they took their seats opposite two most attractive young girls. "I'm Tom Gilcrease and this is my friend," said the young Creek.

"Pleased to meet you," responded Susan Harlow. And then she added, "This is my sister, Belle!" When the train reached its destination, Tom Gilcrease assisted Belle Harlow off of the train and held on to her arm as she stepped from the vestibule platform to the station stool. Tom had been on the train so frequently that he knew the conductor, and the wink of assurance he received from the train official conveyed the message he needed—"Boy, you've got yourself a real pretty gal." From that day forward the courtship began. They went to the ice cream socials and the country dances. Tom was not much of a dancer, but he always managed to see that Belle had a good time. Within a few weeks Belle was visiting Tom in Wealaka and Tom was visiting Belle in Osage County. Tom would spend hours grooming his horse, polishing the harness, and shining the silver on the bridle, and then take Belle for long rides in his rubber-tired buggy. When he visited Belle's home, she would take him riding in the family surrey with the fringe on the top. They knew the trails and the country roads and where best to let the horse graze while they courted in the shade of secluded trees — or fished in some of the streams which were so plentiful in the area.

Belle would often remark to her mother, "Tom is going to be a real smart man because he reads all the time, and some of the books he reads twice. I guess he does not want to miss anything." For a young lady of fourteen years, she was most observant and, although she manifested an attitude of self-assurance around Tom, she was apprehensive because she could not match his scholastic record even though the subjects she took were elementary. The tongues of the gossip-mongers started to wag. The members of the Gilcrease and Harlow families heard rumors — "When is that Tom Gilcrease going to hitch up with the Harlow girl?" And then one day Tom had a long heart-to-heart talk with Pete Akers who had married Belle's sister, Grace. Tom told Pete that he was going to marry Belle.

After a few serious talks Tom said, "Pete, I want you and Grace to go with Belle and me to Harrisonville, Missouri. We are going to get married!" Tom was so anxious to consummate the marriage that he did not inquire whether he could buy a license — and his selection of Harrisonville as the site for the event remains unexplained. Pete, Grace, Tom, and Belle took the "Frisco" train to Harrisonville and upon their arrival they went directly to the courthouse. Tom walked boldly up to the clerk's office, asked for an application and filled it out. He stated that he was from Wealaka in the county of Wagoner, state of Oklahoma, and under the age of twenty-one years. He listed his bride-to-be as Belle Harlow of Tulsa County, Oklahoma and stated that she was under the age of eighteen years. When the clerk read the application he cast a suspicious glance at the youngsters and said, "Sorry young man, you will have to have written consent from your parents!" This was a stunning blow to Tom. He registered Belle and the Akers in a local hotel and immediately returned to Wealaka where he obtained the written consent from his mother. His ride back to Harrisonville on the Frisco was an eternity to the young lover. The license authorized any judge of a court of record, justice of the peace, or any licensed or ordained preacher of the Gospel who was a citizen of the United States to solemnize the marriage.* The ceremony was uneventful and as soon as it was over, the wedding party returned to Wealaka on the first available train.

Upon reaching Tom's home in Wealaka, the bride and groom were honored with a reception where ice cream and cake were served to the assembled guests.

The Gilcrease house had nine rooms. It was a square-shaped structure of wood siding with a veranda running in the front of the lower level as well as the upper story. It was composed of four large bedrooms on the second floor, and there was one large bedroom on the first floor which today would be called the "master bedroom." Tom's mother and father gave the big bedroom to Tom and Belle and it served as the abode for the bridal night and for many nights thereafter until the newlyweds moved to a farm north of Tulsa.

Referring to the Gilcrease home, Belle has said, "I have a vivid memory of the old house. It was considered a mansion then. Mother Gilcrease was a good cook and she always kept her fruits, potatoes, turnips, and corn in the outside cellar where they remained fresh and cool. We did not have any ice boxes in those days. There was a large walk-in pantry in the spacious kitchen and it was always filled with canned goods from the Gilcrease garden. We did not have plumbing and it was really a test of courage to venture to the little outhouse on cold nights. Especially for a young bride."

When Tom and Belle moved to their farm their child-

---

* The marriage was performed on the twenty-second day of August, 1908, by Reverend Lester Clark of the M. E. Church South and recorded in Book 7, Page 115 of the records of the Recorder of Deeds of Cass County, Harrisonville, Missouri.

hood days were left behind and the good times they had in Wealaka, Mounds, and the other small communities became a memory. Life on the farm afforded them many pleasures. When they caught up with their chores they would often ride the Frisco train to Galena, Kansas, where they would rent a small flat-top boat and float down the James River, which ran into the White River. At night they would make camp on the gravel shore. The following morning they would start out again until they reached Branson, in Taney County, Missouri, where they would put the boat on the first train which came by and return to Galena. They often went horseback riding. Tom gave Belle a pinto pony and another horse, a beautiful sorrel with a long black tail, which she named "Chimes."

In the month of December of the same year of their marriage, Thomas Gilcrease realized for the first time that he had taken on the obligations of a man, and even though he was still under legal age, his business career was budding.

Their son, Thomas Obed Gilcrease, later to be called Tom Gilcrease, Jr., was born on July 23, 1909, and they continued to live on a farm until the spring of 1914. Tom had started home from Tulsa one afternoon with his young son. He noticed that a stone house was being built on a hill in Osage County which he had always admired. The foundation was about completed and part of the walls were erected. This was in December of 1913, and on the twenty-sixth of that month he acquired the property from Flowers and Carrie Nelson, a casual acquaintance. Grover and Pearl Mackey had sold the property to the Nelsons on December 13, 1909, since it had been allotted to Grover Mackey, Allottee No. 1499. It is important to trace this bit of history because this is the land where the Thomas Gilcrease Institute of American History and Art now stands. It has come to be known as the historic south one-half of the southeast quarter of Section 28, Township 20, Range 12, and is still located in Osage County, although it is contiguous with the county line of Tulsa.

Tom's first automobile was a Chalmers which he used for social purposes, and then he decided to acquire a

Model "T" Ford for his daily use. He wanted Belle to have a vehicle which would befit her station in life, so he bought her a Detroit Electric Car. It had the appearance of a short funeral hearse, all black, adorned with lamps on either side, and in place of a steering wheel it was guided by a crossbar which extended in front of the driver just about lap high. Belle Gilcrease has some very vivid memories of the electric vehicle and recalls: "I had a most harrowing experience one day. I was at that time carrying our second son, who was momentarily due to arrive. My pregnant state did not permit much room between my body and the steering bar. I had driven to a place called Standpipe Hill in the north part of Tulsa, just beyond where we lived, and the car stalled with a dead battery. I became frantic when I started to have labor pains and did not know what to do. I managed to let the car coast down the hill where I was finally able to summon assistance and get the car to the charging station* Our son Barton was born the following morning. The date was April 12, 1911."

The road to the hill was always filled with adventure because it was the only way to town and back. Thomas Gilcrease, Jr., recounted an incident from which he learned a seldom-seen side to the personality of his famous father. "One hot day Dad and I were returning home from Tulsa in the Model 'T' Ford and when we reached the hill, the car just would not negotiate it. We were about even with the place where the old rock house now stands when the engine died. Dad cranked it up again and after a few yards it stopped. At that moment a young man could be seen walking up the hill toward us. Dad got out of the automobile, waved to the lad to come to him and said, 'Son, how much money have you got in your pocket?' The boy was afraid to talk. 'Don't be scared, son, just reach into your pocket and show me how much you have on you.' The chap agreed and pulled out a five dollar bill. My Dad reached out, took the five dollars, put it into his billfold and

---

* There were only three Electric Cars in Tulsa at the time and one "recharge station."

said, 'Congratulations, son, you have just bought yourself a new car!' He handed the still frightened boy the key, took hold of my hand and said, 'Come on Thomas, we are walking the rest of the way home.' I will never forget the expression on that lad's face as we left him in the middle of the road with a new Ford for which my father had paid $400 only hours before. From that time on he never owned anything but a Packard."[3]

The foregoing incident is an illustration of the determination possessed by Tom Gilcrease and is also indicative of his selfishness which came with his wealth. It was this trait which ripened into unrest and caused him to find fault with his wife and his family life.

There were times when he punished his sons severely, but never, in his opinion, without adequate reason. He was slow to anger, but once he reached the climax of his inflamed feeling he would become sullen and pout for hours.

His business interests were expanding and with each new venture he found himself on the fringe of social entanglements. His wealth made him attractive to ambitious women and there were times when he was unable to cope with the attention and flattery which was heaped upon him. Belle became suspicious of his periodic absences from home, and arguments followed. The Gilcrease tranquility erupted into a domestic holocaust.

On April 4, 1911, he was sued for divorce by his wife, Belle, but the case never came to a hearing and was eventually dismissed when Tom agreed to an adequate property settlement.[4] Belle Gilcrease was still a minor when she entered the suit, and it was prosecuted for her by Warren D. Abbott, a Tulsa attorney who had to be appointed her guardian for the purpose of maintaining the action. Whether the allegations made were well-founded will never be known, but it is reasonable to assume that both parties were still young and grossly inexperienced.

Numerous incidents in Belle's marriage to Tom could be related but some were more vivid than others. There was the venture into the banking business which proved unsuccessful. In the early days of his career he engaged the professional services of Frank G. Walling, a lawyer from the small community of Medford, Oklahoma. Young Walling was ambitious and thought there were great possibilities in opening a new bank at Bixby, Oklahoma. He convinced Tom that it was worth the gamble, and Tom very promptly put in some of his own money and then prevailed upon Belle to invest the sum of $18,000 in the capital stock of the institution. Belle's parents were against the proposition but Tom's persistent manner won out, and the investment was made. Walling was later instrumental in the organization of the Gilcrease Oil Company, but the bank failed and Belle lost her entire investment.

When Belle and Tom went to the World's Fair in San Francisco in 1915 they took Tom's mother with them. Tom insisted upon purchasing a bronze elephant and a bronze lion. The two items of uncertain value are still among the family heirlooms of Belle Gilcrease, and she feels that the purchase of the lion and elephant sparked Tom's desire to collect artifacts.

She often alludes to their visits to New York. Tom would insist upon her going with him to the art galleries and they would walk until she was ready to collapse, but Tom kept going. He would move from painting to painting to painting and finally, in desperation, she would leave him and return to their hotel.

They continued to reside in Tulsa for several years until the varied interests of Tom made it apparent that a change of residence might strengthen the marriage ties between himself and his wife, Belle. They moved to San Diego, California, and established a new residence. The novelty of the West did not change their feelings. Tom found his restless nature had to be satisfied. He became frustrated and unhappy. Belle's love for Tom was not compensated by the economic security he offered her. She did not like living in California and maintaining a residence which had become only an address instead of a home. She was slow to reach a decision, but once it was made there was no retreat. She again brought suit for divorce.

Tom and Belle separated on August 29, 1922. During the fourteen years and seven days of their marriage their union had been an uncertain experience. Belle Gilcrease remained the dutiful wife she had always been and devoted herself to rearing and educating their two sons. William Thomas, Jr. was fifteen and Eugene Barton thirteen, when the divorce became inevitable. Tom Gilcrease had reached the economic level where he wanted to possess and not be possessed.*

On August 29, 1924, Tom and a friend, George P. Taubman, embarked upon a hunting trip — going by way of the inside passage from Seattle, Washington, to Seward, Alaska, at the head of Resurrection Bay. The incidents of the trip were written by Tom in an article he penned for the magazine "Outdoor Life" and which he entitled, "Fires and Misfires on the Kenai Peninsula."[5] This was the only attempt he ever made to record his travels. He wrote in part:

> We left Long Beach, California, and joined our guide, Jack Lean, and one packer, Wallace McCreary on September 8th. After getting provisions, we waited for the train to leave Saturday morning on the 11th which took us to Kenai Lake, twenty miles northwest. There we loaded our row boat and had a small gas boat to tow us across the lake to its outlet, about twenty-five miles. On the way we passed another gas boat towing a barge with a horse on board. The boat had an accident, drowning the owner. We saw black bear on the mountain side eating berries. One mile below the outlet on the river we camped for the night and picked up another packer, Andrew Norlin, and our cook, Bud Williams. The morning of the 12th we started down Kenai River and had a fast and wild ride down to where it empties into Skilak Lake.

The trip was concluded October 10, 1924, and was filled with excitement and adventure. They made camera studies and observations of Kenai moose and other game. Another big-game hunt was over. It was during this trip

---

* A second divorce action was filed in the Superior Court of the State of California, County of Los Angeles on November 27, 1924, as case number D-33728.

that Tom learned a lesson he never forgot. He was engaged in tracking down big game in the heavily forested country when his attention was diverted by a sudden noise — and before he could readjust his footing he saw a mother bear with her cubs. They were unaware that nearby was an invader of their wooded sanctuary. The antics of the unsuspecting animals amused Tom and, in a moment of reversion to the hunter's instinct, he triggered his gun. The huge bear turned her head toward her assailant with what must have been a searching query of "Why, Mr. Hunter, did you do it? I was only playing with my young and now you have made orphans out of them. Why?" Before the stunned hunter had time to reflect upon his act, the cubs disappeared into the wilds in a state of bewilderment. Tom could not overcome his regret and the incident was cause for him to critically judge himself and to try to justify such sport. His fervor for the hunt had lessened.

The hunting trip did not add to the tranquility of his domestic life, and in his heart he knew that before long he, too, would leave his "cubs." He was a restless man and going on big-game hunts did not solve anything. He found that he could not run away from his troubles on the home front.

His burning desire for culture, as he defined the term, made his marriage a status of convenience and Belle Gilcrease determined that a second reconciliation could never be accomplished. The principal allegation of her complaint alleged that Tom had lived separate and apart from her without her consent and without cause, justification, or excuse. She requested custody of their minor sons. An interlocutory judgment was entered on the third day of April, 1925, and the final judgment filed on the fifth day of April, 1926. Their parting was not a bitter tragedy in the sense that communications were broken. They remained friendly to each other, and Tom provided for her in an agreed property settlement and support for the children. They realized that the most important consideration was to teach their sons to love and respect their parents. The maturity of Tom, Jr. and Barton gave them an understanding which was, to say the least, unusual. They found devotion for each of their parents and respected them within the limits of their divided allegiance.

A new life was ahead of Belle Gilcrease. She moved to Long Beach where Tom had acquired a house for her and the children.

Belle Gilcrease is a remarkable woman. At the age of seventy-four she drives her own automobile and often travels alone from Texas to Oklahoma. She resides in San Antonio where she divides her time visiting friends and relatives. While the loss of her son, Tom Gilcrease, Jr., has left a definite void in her life, she remains philosophical about the fate of mankind and finds comfort in her grandchildren and great-grandchildren.* She is the last of the pioneers in the immediate Gilcrease family, with the exception of Tom's sisters and brothers. She has survived those who in past years pierced her heart with arrows of deception and envy, and in her maturity she has found the reward of forgiveness.

When she speaks of her life with Thomas Gilcrease there is an evident pride in his accomplishment and the monument of museum history which he started and brought to fruition. She effervesces a charm which finds its origin in her Indian heritage and diffuses into her maternal instincts. She is alert to all about her — she has seen the storm clouds gather and watched them disperse into the heavens where tender memories are stored.

If her "Indian Tom" had survived, he would have recognized all of these attributes in his "Belle of the Osage Nation," but it would be too late for him to recapture the fulfillment of the love he never really abandoned.

When Belle Gilcrease visits the old home where Tom's mother lived until her demise, she sits in front of the large picture window where she can look to the east and to the west and to the north. She can see the house on the hill and recapture dreams of her life with Tom. She can see the Osage Country where her allotments were made. She

---

* Thomas Gilcrease, Jr., died March 11, 1967. The details appear in a later chapter.

can see the Thomas Gilcrease Institute of American History and Art. She can somehow conjure a vision of the man who was so many things to so many people and could have been so much to her. She can see the birds in the tall oak trees and wonders if they, too, remember their benefactor.

Book 2
Crude Oil and Refinement

Chapter 1

Land, Leases, and Law

In the dedication issue of *The American Indian* magazine published in October of 1926, the editor, the late Lee Harkins, wrote these lasting lines:

> In the makeup of the citizenship of Oklahoma there is blending of blood of the Puritan and the Cavalier, the Patroon and the Covenanter, while many of its people trace descent from the American Indian as well. Oklahoma may claim a part in the history of other states as a matter of right, but she need beg none as a matter of favor. She gives to the world a history of her own that is at once distinctive and romantic. Every Indian's heart should swell with pride at the mention of the word Oklahoma. It is truly an Indian state, named by an Indian, the seals of the Five Civilized Tribes make up the seal of this great state and some of the fairest counties and most prosperous cities have been named after prominent Indian families. Oklahoma is a typical Indian state.[1]

The words of Editor Harkins are just as convincing today, and the life of Thomas Gilcrease is tied to the history of Oklahoma with a firmness since the remnants or descendants of not less than fifty different tribes and nations of Indians came within its confines.

The allotment of land, while born in the minds of the lawmakers and implemented by congressional decree, merged into the lives of the Indians whose names were entered on census cards, assigned numbers and were thus enrolled. Their allotments became their patents in the nature of government grant, thereby conveying to them the legal fee simple title to the land. It spelled out their patrimony, which ripened into a heritage for their children and their children's children.

All of the foregoing was the preface to the fortune which awaited young Thomas Gilcrease. The Creek blood which entitled some of the members of the family of William Lee Gilcrease to tribal enrollment was both a blessing and an invitation for a complicated experience. The Dawes Roll reflects that six members of the Gilcrease family were admitted by the Colbert Citizenship Commission. Although Hampton G. Vowell was a non-citizen, his wife Martha Ann Self was of Creek blood and this entitled their daughter, Mary Elizabeth Vowell, to enrollment. She was listed as "Lizzie," age 25, one-quarter blood. William Lee Gilcrease was also a non-citizen; however, since his wife, Mary Elizabeth, possessed Creek Indian blood, five of their children were enrolled and she was recognized as having a one-quarter blood status. The enrollment record is as follows:

Residence: Leonard. Creek Nation. Creek Roll.
Post Office: Mounds, Ind. Ter.

Dawes' Roll No.	Name	Relationship to person first named	Age	Sex	Blood
1504	1 Gilcrease, Lizzie		25	F.	1/4
1505	2 " , Thomas	Son	9	M.	1/8
1506	3 " , Eddie	"	7	"	1/8
1507	4 " , Ben	"	5	"	1/8
1508	5 " , Lena	Daughter	3	F.	1/8
1509	6 " , Florence	"	1	"	1/8
Citizenship certificate issued-June 9th, 1899.			June 9/99.		

Tom's enrollment was just nine years after his birth.* A patent for the land was executed by the principal chief of the Creek Nation, and Thomas Gilcrease thereby became vested with an absolute title in and to the land.**

Before receiving his allotment, young Tom had already demonstrated his individualism. Each year took him further and further away from his childhood friends and intimate association with his brothers and sisters. His allotment was made when he was eighteen years old and, being a minor, he was restricted from many areas of activity and was under the thumb of his father who served as his legal guardian. He was still residing with his parents at Wealaka when he decided to inspect his land. It must be remembered that to one of Tom's background, the land was just so much property and he could not even begin to comprehend either the significance or the value of his government legacy.

One beautiful Sunday morning Tom arose early, saddled his horse, and rode to the location of his allotment, which was south of the Arkansas River and about two and one-half miles from Kiefer. We can only indulge in speculation as to the reaction which came over him as he surveyed the land which was to touch off the spark of his financial career.

The acreage was situated in the Glenn Pool area and contained a rich deposit of petroleum. The Glenn Pool

---

* As a citizen and member of the Creek Nation or tribe of Indians, he was entitled under agreement between the United States of America and the Creek or Muskogee Nation of Indians, embraced in the Act of Congress, approved March 1, 1901, and ratified by the Creek Nation on May 25, 1901, and the Supplemental Agreement between the United States of America and the Creek Nation, approved June 20, 1902, ratified by the Creek Nation on July 26, 1902, and proclaimed by the president on August 8, 1902, to an allotment of land out of the lands of said Creek Nation, consisting of 120 acres of surplus and 40 acres of homestead, and there was duly selected as the surplus allotment the south one-half of the northwest quarter, and the northeast quarter of the southwest quarter of Section 22, Township 17 North, Range 12 East . . . and the homestead allotment of the northwest quarter of the southeast quarter of the same section, township and range.

** The patent is dated August 25, 1902; approved by the secretary of the interior of the United States of America on December 15, 1902, and recorded in the office of the Commission to the Five Civilized Tribes at Muskogee, Oklahoma, in Record Book 2 at page 35.

discovery has storybook implications and to better understand the *get rich quick epidemic* which prevailed in the then baby state of the nation, it is necessary that this history be briefly reviewed.

A rugged citizen named Robert F. "Bob" Galbreath was making oil deals, leasing from the unsuspecting owners, drilling wildcat wells and bringing in paying production. Galbreath had studied the oil fields and knew that the first oil was discovered in the territory in Chelsea in 1889, and that new fields had been opened in Bartlesville and Muskogee. But it was the Glenn Pool which attracted national attention.[2]

Ida Glenn was the original allottee of acreage which was located in Section 22, Township 19 North, Range 12 East, in the Creek Nation. She and her husband had improved their farm, were cultivating good crops and were not too concerned about leasing their land for mining oil and gas. Robert F. Galbreath had his eye on the Glenn property and, in company with his business associate, Frank Chessley, he drove to the Glenn farm. Bob Galbreath winked at his friend Frank as he knocked on the door of the Glenn house.

"My name is Robert F. Galbreath, but just call me Bob."

"Glad to know you, Bob, and who is your friend?"

"Meet Frank Chessley. We came out to talk with you about your land," said Galbreath with a side glance to Chessley.

"Well now I am mighty glad you came, but it ain't for sale," remarked Robert Glenn and then he said, "This is my wife, Ida, and we would be proud to have you stay for dinner, wouldn't we, Ida?"

"Been out here long?" asked Bob Glenn.

"No," responded Bob Galbreath. "We camped last night over at Eck Brook's place in his horse lot and sort of walked around his property and looked it over. What we came out to ask you is whether you would give us an oil and gas lease on your land. We think there is oil in these parts and you could come out well off."

"We will talk about it after dinner," said Glenn.

Galbreath and Chessley left the Glenn farm with the oil and gas lease they sought, and the very next day Bob Galbreath had his friend Ray Dodd move his standard rig to the farm. They liked what they saw and were impressed with the formation of the mounds. There was a good chance that the structures were potential oil deposits. Bob Galbreath, Frank Chessley, and Ray Dodd formed a partnership. They did not have formal training in the science of geology but they looked about the farm to determine a drill site. Chessley's eyes settled on a piece of exposed rock; he broke off part of it and found that it had an oil stain. They decided to drill their first wildcat well.

Recalling the experience, the late Robert F. Galbreath said, "We hit the sand the morning of November 22, 1905. We did not have any casing in the hole but just some pinewood conductor pipe . . . but how that well headed and flowed."

The partnership was badly in need of casing so they enlisted the financial assistance of John O. Mitchell, who later became one of the early mayors of the city of Tulsa. The Glenn Pool was on its way. The wildcat well was completed and put into production. The Texas Company bought the oil and ran the pipeline. They hauled their equipment to the lease by rail.

The high production in Glenn Pool was in late 1907, the same year Oklahoma became a state. It produced 120,000 barrels each day, and the oil records show that from November 22, 1905 until September 1, 1955, the pool was estimated to have produced 251,382,045 barrels of oil.

The Galbreath and Chessley No. 1 commanded the attention of such men as Charles F. Colcord of Oklahoma City and hundreds of others. With the opening of the Glenn Pool the news spread like a Klondike gold rush and the town of Sapulpa began to boom. The red lights went on and the high lights were installed. Hotel rooms were at a premium, and since Sapulpa was not large enough to take care of the black-gold hunters, they forded the Arkansas River and came to Tulsa.

Galbreath had first arrived in Tulsa when the Red

Fork discovery was made, but at that time the government compelled the drillers and lease owners to close off their wells until after enrollment of the Indians. As early as 1903 Galbreath had opened another pool in the Red Fork area but was forced to abandon his venture.

Tom Gilcrease was not as yet of legal age when oil became the most sought after product in the territory. The drilling activities of Robert F. Galbreath and his partners were conversational subjects in all the places where the landowners and lease hounds kept vigil on developments. Because of Tom's legal disability, his father had appointed himself as his guardian.

On the nineteenth day of September, 1906, William L. Gilcrease, acting in his fiduciary capacity, leased Tom's tract of land to William H. Milliken of Bowling Green, Ohio. The instrument was a departmental lease for the purpose of drilling for oil and gas. The transaction called for a consideration of $17,000 as a bonus and a royalty of one-eighth of the oil and gas production. Milliken did not lose any time with his drilling operations, and between the fall of 1906 and the summer of 1909 some forty-nine oil wells were completed. By August of 1909, there were forty-two wells producing more than twenty-five thousand barrels of oil each month. Neither young Tom nor his father fully comprehended the extent of the potential production, and their appetites for the black gold had not been stimulated to the fullest.

The Milliken lease was to expire February 8, 1911, in accordance with its terms, and it was estimated that the property would by then be valued in excess of $300,000. This increased worth and the fervor for wealth which began to take hold of Tom Gilcrease caused him to seek majority rights. In February, 1909, he caused suit to be filed in Wagoner County, Oklahoma. The district judge rendered and entered a decree purporting to remove Tom's disability of minority and conferred upon him rights of majority. His father was promptly discharged as guardian and young Tom started to manage his own business affairs. This same year he moved to Tulsa.

In the meantime, on the eighteenth day of September,

1908, just after statehood, Tom had executed a warranty deed, from the lands he had been allotted, to his mother, "Lizzie" Gilcrease, and it was assumed and understood that the conveyance was in fact a declaration of trust for Tom. In the summer of 1909, anticipating the expiration of the Milliken lease, Tom wanted to sell another lease on the land, to take effect upon the expiration of the Milliken lease and run for a term of fifteen years. He would have accepted $10,000 as a bonus. His negotiations were with A. E. Bradshaw, of Tulsa, who said to Tom, "What bonus are you receiving from Milliken?"

Tom replied, "Seventeen thousand dollars."

Bradshaw then said, "I suppose you will take the same amount for another lease?" Tom answered in the affirmative.

This conversation actually took place on the tract of land involved, since Tom Gilcrease and Bradshaw had gone to the property to inspect the leasehold. The following day they returned to the Bank of Oklahoma in Tulsa where Bradshaw was then the cashier and one G. R. McCullough was president. The lease was prepared and dated August 24, 1909 for a recited cash bonus of $17,000 and one-eighth royalty, to commence at the expiration of the Milliken lease and to run for a term of fifteen years or for so long as oil or gas was found in paying quantities. As to the $17,000, it was agreed between Tom and McCullough that $2,000 be paid in cash, which was done, and $500 every ninety days thereafter until McCullough took possession of the leasehold, at which time the balance of the bonus was to be due and payable.

Subsequent to the execution of the legal papers, and after the sum of $2,000 had been paid on the obligation, it was discovered that Tom had conveyed the land in trust to his mother. McCullough demanded that the title be cleared, and this resulted in Tom's attorney securing a duplicate lease from Tom's mother to McCullough.

Speculation began. Rumors were running wild as to whether the lease was a pure gamble and therefore not a marketable proposition. McCullough was worried. Tom was restless: he seemed to possess a sixth sense that the lease would prove very valuable, and so he approached McCullough and offered to buy back from him a one-fourth interest in the lease. Negotiations followed with the result that on October 22, 1910, McCullough did assign a one-fourth interest to Tom for $15,000. McCullough also disposed of a one-fourth interest to one H. B. Martin, an attorney, for a like amount, and an interest was acquired by one Al Brown, who was associated in the bank. The financial arrangements between the parties is not essential for this narrative; however, on February 8, 1911, the day the Milliken lease expired, Tom Gilcrease reached his majority and McCullough and Martin entered into a contract with him.

The foregoing events formed the basis for the lawsuit which Tom instituted on February 12, 1912, in the District Court of Tulsa County, when he sued G. R. McCullough, H. B. Martin, A. E. Bradshaw and Al Brown, to set aside the oil and gas mining lease made, executed, and delivered by Tom to McCullough and which was dated August 24, 1909.* The petition alleged not only fraud on the part of all the defendants in its procurement, but that Tom Gilcrease was a minor at the time, and hence the lease was void. He also alleged that all the defendants, except Bradshaw, while he was yet a minor, conspired to defraud him on February 8, 1911; that they procured from him a contract in writing to explore the desired premises for oil and gas, which he assailed as fraud. He requested that both the lease and the contract be set aside and held for naught, and he asked for an accounting.

The record of the testimony given by Tom establishes certain facts which are worth reviewing. The questions and answers as they appear in the transcript are:

Question: Do you know how many wells there were on the premises when Mr. Milliken gave up the lease in February of 1911?

---

* *Gilcrease* v. *McCullough et al.*, 162 Pacific Reporter 178.

Answer: I think there was 41 producing wells and one dry one.

Question: What was the other time you had been on that allotment before you and Bradshaw went down there?

Answer: I just happened to go out there on Sunday, drove out from where I lived at Wealaka.

Question: Prior to your coming to Tulsa to live, did you live at Wealaka?

Answer: Yes, I lived at Wealaka.

Question: This tract of land is south of the Arkansas River?

Answer: Yes, sir, about two miles and one half east of Kiefer.

Question: And in what is known as Glenn Pool?

Answer: Yes, sir.

Question: Did you know anything about the value of that property at that time?

Answer: No, sir.

Question: That was in August of 1907?

Answer: No, I didn't know anything about it at all.

The case attracted attention in all of the oil circles in and out of the state of Oklahoma and the name of Tom Gilcrease was heard in financial institutions, in hotel lobbies, and on the street.

The oil reporters filed daily reports with their editors and the courtrooms became a gathering place for the curious and the interested.

The lawsuit ripened into a hard fought contest and the

testimony covered several hundreds of pages. During the trial, Tom testified in part:

Question: After you had consulted attorneys about this matter and before you filed this suit, did you have any conference with Mr. Martin and Mr. Bradshaw and Mr. McCullough with reference to the matter, and did you make any demand on them for a reconveyance to you of your property without a lawsuit?

Answer: Before I talked to you?

Question: No, sir, after you had consulted attorneys and before you filed this suit?

Answer: Yes, sir.

Question: Where did that take place?

Answer: In Mr. Martin's office.

Question: Who was present?

Answer: Mr. Martin and Mr. Bradshaw.

Question: Was Mr. McCullough there?

Answer: No, sir.

Question: He didn't come?

Answer: No, sir.

Question: Tell us as near as you can give it now what you said and did there that day?

Answer: Well, I told Mr. Bradshaw and Mr. McCullough what I had found out, they had beat me out of this lease and that Mr. Martin hadn't paid for his interest in it at all and that Mr. Brown had gotten an interest in it and he had always denied having any interest in it.

Question: Go ahead and tell us what else was said?

Answer: I believe that is about what I told them, and I told them that I wanted to see if I couldn't have a settlement with them, that I didn't want to sue them but I was going to sue them unless we could come to some settlement and so Mr. Bradshaw and Mr. Martin they just tried to talk me out of it and said that – I forget just what they said, anyway they said they hadn't beat me out of it, and so on, and so I finally told them they couldn't talk me out of it, and I told them they were either going to settle with me or I was going to sue them, I told them, says, "I will give you people all the money you have taken out of this lease, Mr. Martin can keep the property he taken," if they would just assign me back the nine-sixteenth interest. So when I told them that, Mr. Bradshaw said "I wouldn't give you a damned dime," Mr. Martin said he wouldn't either, but just before that Mr. Martin said, "Tom," says "If you think I have beaten you out of anything," says "I will give it back to you," says "I don't want to beat you," and so after Mr. Bradshaw he got mad, after he said what he did, Mr. Martin he got mad and said well, he looked at me and says "Tom, ——— damn you, you file this suit against me," he says "And you won't have a dime in twelve months." So I just picked up my coat then and walked out.

Question: And proceeded to file the suit, did you?

Answer: Yes, sir.

While the case was pending it was rumored that the defendants offered to pay Tom Gilcrease the sum of $500,000 to dismiss the action and settle all accounts between them but that Tom refused the offer. The case was tried before Judge A. H. Huston, who held, in effect, that Thomas Gilcrease was a minor at the time he executed the lease sought to be set aside, but, whether void or voidable on that account, the lease was expressly adopted by Gilcrease after he reached his majority, by signing of the contract of February 8, 1911, and he entered judgment for the defendants in the case.

The decision was appealed to the Supreme Court of the State of Oklahoma and the holding of the lower court was affirmed on October 10, 1916. A rehearing in the case was denied January 9, 1917.

There were other important questions raised in the lawsuit, such as the proof of Tom's quantum of Indian blood, and the probative force of the certified copy of the approved rolls of the Creek citizens to establish proper age. The trial judge had found that there was no fraud in the procurement of the second lease, but did hold that the lease executed by Tom during his minority without intervention of the county court, and in contravention of the applicable government act, was not voidable *but void.*

Approximately two years after the rehearing was denied in the Supreme Court of the State of Oklahoma, the case was argued before the Supreme Court of the United States where it had been taken on a writ of certiorari.* The opinion was delivered by the celebrated Mr. Justice Louis Dembitz Brandeis.

Justice Brandeis stated that the only substantial question submitted to the Supreme Court was: "Did the entry concerning Gilcrease's age made in the enrollment record of Creek citizenship preclude Tom Gilcrease from showing that he was actually of age when the lease was executed?"

He then continued: "Gilcrease insists that the entry 'June 9/99,' near the right-hand corner of the enrollment card, signifies that the application for his enrollment was made on June 9, 1899; that in giving his age as '9,' the roll declared him to be exactly nine years old on June 9, 1899; and that consequently, in the absence of other evidence to the contrary in the enrollment record, he must be deemed

* *Gilcrease* v. *McCullough et al.*, 249 United States Reports 178.

to have been under age on February 8, 1911. But there was no declaration or finding of fact by the Commission that Gilcrease was exactly 9 years old on June 9, 1899. The declaration that a person is 9 years of age signifies, in the absence of conditions requiring exact specifications merely that he has reached or passed the ninth anniversary of his birth and is still less than ten years old . . . is the court expected to believe that the Commission found, that the six members of the family were all born on the ninth day of June?"

Justice Brandeis then went on to state that the enrollment record was conclusive as to that which it in terms recites or which is necessarily implied from the words and figures used. That the purpose of Section three of the Act of May 27, 1908, seems to have been simply to make the record conclusive as to age insofar as it purports to state age — that the cases in the lower federal courts, the decisions in the Supreme Court of Oklahoma, and the great weight of all the authorities supported the proposition that, when the age is simply stated in years or whenever the age is not stated definitely by the addition of months or days, other evidence may be introduced to supplement the record by proving these and thus establish the exact date of birth.

The affirmation of the case by the Supreme Court of the United States settled the lawsuit. The decision has become a landmark in such litigations and has never been upset.

On March 6, 1911, Tom's mother had executed a quit claim deed to the property he had previously deeded to her in trust and thereafter there was never any question about the title being vested in Tom Gilcrease.

Subsequent dealings in oil and gas leases on Tom's property were negotiated with more caution. He had started to mature and the price was high.

The tenacity demonstrated by Tom Gilcrease in pursuing what he conscientiously deemed to be his legal rights and the prosecution of the litigation to the highest court is indicative of his character. While he did not emerge as the victor, he did prove to his opposition that he would survive the ordeal financially.

The oil lease contest was not the only brush Tom Gilcrease had with the courts. Subsequent to Belle's marriage to Tom, she sold her allotment of land, which was a part of her Osage headright, to the Gilcrease Oil Company. To accomplish this alienation, she applied for, and was issued, a certificate of competency. This procedure removed her restrictions against conveying title, and she was free to dispose of her land. She could not sell that part of her headright which was her interest in the pro rata distribution of tribal mineral income and other tribal revenues. This was one of the many advantages bestowed upon her by reason of her Indian extraction. The sale was made at the insistence of Tom, who felt it was the proper thing for her to do, and it is said that the price paid for the land was in excess of $50,000.

Thomas Gilcrease was not a stranger to litigation in later years. In the days that followed the McCullough case, he was destined to be either a defendant or a plaintiff in many civil cases involving lease cancellations and kindred subjects.

Tom Gilcrease was headed for a career in the petroleum industry. The potential had been handed to him by a roll number, and the same government which had appropriated the land from his people had designated his allotment. The industry was young and so was Tom. He was soon to learn that men would litigate, fight, and die over oil leases; they would become rich and prosper until greed overtook them and dry holes consumed them. Men would watch the black gold gush out of the ground and flow over the tops of derricks. Tom Gilcrease was to be a part of the new way of living, and the future would drill his image into the yet unexplored leases of Oklahoma's wealthy tycoons.

He did not know that one day the men of the petroleum world would name an oil discovery sand after him or that thousands of dollars would be spent in the future by other prospectors penetrating the "Gilcrease Sand" searching for the illusive oil. Other members of Tom's family had an equal opportunity, but they did not possess the native ability for money making. What Tom Gilcrease did not understand he sought to learn; what he learned he retained for the next "wildcat"; what he acquired he kept until good business dictated that profit time had come; when the drill stem came up dry he had the courage to move to a new location. Tom was to know many locations in his life which had just begun — but drill he would and drill he did — until he became a man of fortune instead of a fortune hunter.

Chapter 2

The Gilcrease Oil Company

The life of Thomas Gilcrease became more and more complicated with each new oil venture. He was living in an age when the independent oil man was still able to make deals with drilling contractors and, in the parlance of the oil business, carry the driller for an interest in exchange for rig and the labor. Pipe and supply yards were springing up on every empty lot in the community, and they were willing to provide the string of pipe for a carried interest. The time had come for Tom Gilcrease to expand his operations and seek shelter under corporate organization to avoid personal liability, since oil field accidents were prevalent in the industry. He consulted with his attorneys and asked them to explain the "limited liability" doctrine of the law. They went further and told him the advantages of obtaining a corporate charter and the possibilities of procuring additional capital without invading his individual holdings. The idea appealed to him, if for no other reason than to rid himself of the lease hounds who were beating a path to his office and his home.

The oil men of the area were generally those who had become investors in the speculations of others, or drillers who had teamed up with the men who were engaged in such commercial ventures. One by one Tom began to survey the field to determine the kind of men he wanted as associates. As in all other things he did, he moved slowly but with certainty. He had by this time met a number of professionals in the banking business and, because of his experience in the courts, he was cautious. He was also stubborn and selective. Actually, he had been exposed to very few investments with "outsiders." If there was one thing he hated bitterly, it was orientation and dictation, and he was determined to avoid further involvement with the so-called "high financiers."

The immediate members of his family caused him grave concern. They had learned to depend upon him in many ways, and he knew that eventually he would have to break away from the shackles of those to whom he supplied the necessities of everyday living. It was time they learned to ride alone. This was wishful thinking.

The inner drive of his physical demands was confronted with the outward force of a practical world. There were cultural dykes which he wanted to cross.

The destination was unknown and the road unmarked. Suddenly he knew he had the answer. He was a man of wealth and wealth could hire brains. He put his formula to work for him and it became a part of his philosophy for the remainder of his business career.

The Gilcrease Oil Company was organized under the laws of the state of Oklahoma with an authorized capital of $100,000 represented by 1,000 shares of common stock at the par value of $100 per share. The original investors had begun as a partnership or unincorporated association in 1918. They had engaged in leasing and drilling; but limited resources, other than the holdings of Thomas Gilcrease, led to the need for more working capital.[1]

The charter was issued on January 5, 1922, and the purpose clause defined as "oil and gas production." The officers were Thomas Gilcrease, president; F. G. Walling and W. Z. Dozier, vice-presidents; Pierce Larkin, treasurer; G. B. Bancroft, secretary; and C. H. Steel, assistant secretary. Gilcrease, Walling, Larkin, and Bancroft composed the directorate. Mr. Gilcrease was cautious in his selection of the professionals. Larkin was to be the geologist; Bancroft, his superintendent; and Charles Lamb was employed as the land man.

F. G. Walling was a happy-go-lucky individual and his quick wit was credited with exploding arguments when tensions ran high in board meetings. His legal training was a valuable asset to the corporation. Pierce Larkin, the geologist, was by contrast a quiet man. His personality was similar to that of Thomas Gilcrease. He was not, however, socially inclined, although he would go along with the crowd when business contacts were necessary. His ability to explore for oil was recognized and respected. G. B. Bancroft was the most likable of the lot; he was given to expounding philosophical gems, his favorite being: "One religion is as good as another and a whole lot better!" In modern terminology he was considered the "spokesman" of the board and resorted to his ingenious mind to always make a point, even though he sometimes strained at the bit to be logically correct. C. H. Steel was Charlien Steel (now Sanditen), who later became personal secretary of Mr. Gilcrease.

Such, then, were the pioneers of the Gilcrease Oil Company, who have all gone to their eternal resting places, with the exception of C. H. Steel (Sanditen), and left for posterity the logs of their careers as oil men with the same historical significance as the logs which recorded the discoveries they made in the fields. They did not all "spud in," but they drilled through the romantic days when it took stalwart men to walk away from a dry hole and say, "Okay, boys, we will move the rig over to the next location and start again."

As the incorporators, they were each aware that Thomas Gilcrease was to be reimbursed to the extent of the capital invested in the company, and thereafter they would each retain ten percent of the stock, with Mr. Gilcrease holding the controlling interest of sixty percent. By their joint efforts the company prospered and in due time the investment made by Mr. Gilcrease was completely reimbursed to him.

All of these hard-fisted oil men were aware that the petroleum industry had a fascinating history. It was in 1859 in Titusville, Pennsylvania, that oil had been produced for the first time.[2] The well was drilled to a depth of 69½ feet. The newly discovered liquid had a medicinal value. Seeking the origin of oil was one problem, but its accumulation into economic deposits was an entirely different one. As the commercial uses for oil were recognized, the oil business grew to meet the demand.

Thomas Gilcrease was not a novice when he formed his company. He had already learned much about the undeveloped properties, petroleum geology, and oil and gas rights. He had absorbed the terminology of the oil man and knew about the so-called "hot oil" regulations and cold dealing of the lease hounds, otherwise known as the men who found the deals for the men with the money to invest. He had already fought his way through the courts and gained costly knowledge about drilling contracts, easements, depletion, deeds, and damages. He possessed an uncanny knowledge of petroleum valuations and on one occasion. while testifying in court, he said:

> Well, the engineer has attempted to determine the amount of oil which underlies each piece in the field, and he assumes that it will require about thirty years to get that oil out of the sand, and he estimates the price at about, I think, 98¢ per barrel. Now, of course, I don't think that there is any man in the world that can tell anyone how much oil there is in the ground, nor how much can be recovered, or whether or not those wells will last ten years or twenty years or thirty years. I don't think that they can determine the value that we will receive for it per barrel. It may be fifteen cents or it may be fifty cents, or a dollar or two dollars, and no one can determine, I don't believe, the amount of gas that is there, that is, I mean the life of the gas, nor what these wells will produce when

> the gas pressure goes off. I don't think they can determine when the water will encroach upon these wells, each well individually, and it is very doubtful now, more so than ever, that they can determine what it will cost up per barrel to produce that oil. You don't know whether the labor will cost what it does now or two or three times more, but the tendency is that it is going to cost more.[3]

He was aware of the clouds on the title but never lost his appreciation for the clouds in the sky. He had been assignee and assignor. The word *abandonment* was as familiar to him as the meaning of the duty to plug a well. He sold and bought natural gas and could quickly disarm a sharpie who took him for a softie when negotiating for leases. He sold and bought oil and gas leases with the same confidence that early day ranchers traded in livestock. His sixth sense made him suspicious of the high binders and promoters who always knocked at his office door with the "best deal" in the country.

Thomas Gilcrease would have found much in common with Colonel Edwin L. Drake, who drilled the first well in 1859. Those were the days when the virgin lands were giving way to the individuals of the gold rush ilk. They pressed forward, rose to power, and were indeed the crude who needed refinement.

Thomas Gilcrease as an oil man was unique in one outstanding respect. He did not have to seek his fortune the hard way. His ready-made wealth was a segment of the oil fraternity history and has been recited down through the ages when Oklahoma and Texas discoveries were discussed.

Wealth can breed waste and lead men into idle and dissolute lives. Riches can provide the stimulus for the love and wisdom and turn man toward a life of culture and good deeds. Thomas Gilcrease had an aversion to ignorance and knew that unless he threw off the fetters of his primitive background he would fall by the paths which had been taken by so many of his contemporaries. He did not have any positive proof of his ancestry, and the plight of his direct line of forefathers was only incidental to him.

He looked upon the history of the Indian as something he had to explore and appreciate more fully. Every hour which added to his longevity meant that he possessed less time to capture the truths of the sufferings of his people. Oil was the means to the end.

The men of the Gilcrease Oil Company knew something of the talents of their founder. The corporation was to be a part of their lives and they were determined to make it so. It became the topic of conversation in oil circles, and, as the company expanded, new fields were explored, wildcat wells were drilled, gas wells were discovered, and the holdings of the corporation were increased. They concluded that they could not concentrate their production to limited areas and, lease by lease, the oil was converted into dollars.

On several occasions the wisdom of Thomas Gilcrease was discounted by his associates with painful results and regrets. The cardinal example was the incident relating to the now famous Signal Hill in Long Beach, California. Mr. Gilcrease had personally explored the possibility of acquiring the entire 85,000 acres. He provided a special account for closing the transaction but made the mistake of delegating the consummation of the transaction to others. This action was to prove the most costly error of his career as an oil man. He accepted an invitation to go on a hunting trip to Alaska and while he was engaged in shooting wild game his associates were engaged in shooting holes in his plans for the acquisition of Signal Hill. The deal was neglected.[4]

The next time Thomas Gilcrease looked at Signal Hill he was under the impression that the derricks belonged to the Gilcrease Oil Company, and he remained with such thoughts in his busy mind until he suddenly discovered that another company, in his absence, had beat him to the draw while he was beating his hunting companions to the draw in killing wild game.

Another unforgettable experience has application to the now well-known East Texas oil field. The industrious Tom wanted to lease 5,000 acres and told his associates to conclude the transaction. He never informed them that it was his opinion that there was oil strata just waiting to feel the drill bit. Again, he made a mistake. He had journeyed to Europe because he felt the urge to travel. Speaking of this and other events when the brilliance of his father would have made the Gilcrease Oil Company one of the major corporations in the nation, his son, Thomas, Jr., has said, "If my father had given the same attention to the oil business as he did to collecting art, he would have been among the wealthiest men in the nation!" Perhaps young Tom did not enlarge his remarks sufficiently, because there are numerous measurements of wealth and if Thomas Gilcrease had devoted as much attention to the oil business as he had to collecting art, his material wealth would have increased but his cultural wealth may never have developed.

At one point in the career of Thomas Gilcrease, he was the principal owner of several banks in Oklahoma. The state bank examiner often enlisted his cooperation in making a study of a bank which he suspected of being in financial difficulty. This contact made it possible for Tom to acquire bank stock at bargain prices. The story is told that one of the banks in which he was a minority stockholder made a demand that a personal note of Tom's be renewed. The obligation was for $75,000 and it was nearing the due date. The principal stockholder endeavored to block the renewal of the note but other officers were unanimous in their approval. Mr. Gilcrease was silent throughout the deliberations, but when the meeting adjourned he walked into the office of the dissenting stockholder and said, "How much do you want for your stock?"

The surprised gentleman, thinking that Tom was joking, said, "I'll take $100,000 in cash."

"Good," said Mr. Gilcrease, as he wrote out a check for the entire amount and walked out with the newly acquired stock in his possession.

He acquired stock holdings in the Rogan Oil Company and the Waterside Oil Company. Both of these companies were not long in existence and like many such corporate entities they fell by the wayside as the oil fraternity grew to mature proportions.

The virgin days of the oil fraternity saw many changes in the personnel of oil companies. The smaller, or independent, operators were constantly on the lookout for good men and experienced workers. The friendship with H. L. "Red" Branscum came about because of the ever-present desire on the part of Thomas Gilcrease to put good men on the derrick platform.[5] When Red was eighteen he went to work for an oil pioneer named S. P. Smith in Okfuskee County, Oklahoma, as a tool pusher. It has been said of Red that at one time his hands were so calloused that he could handle a sucker rod and let it slide through his palms with the same ease as a fireman descends an emergency pole. Red Branscum was born in the town of Searcy, Arkansas, on November 25, 1904, and his introduction to derricks, slush ponds, drill stems, and oil casing came quickly, and it was not long until his talents were noticed by other lease owners in the area. He earned the reputation of being a worker who gave his boss an honest tour of duty for every dollar he received.

One sweltering day when he was assisting the crew in running some pipe, a rather slight-of-build man came up to him and introduced himself. This man had been watching him work and remarked to one of the drillers, "Now, there is a real worker. I could use a man like that." Less than a year later Red Branscum received word from G. B. Bancroft that Thomas Gilcrease wanted to hire him. The date was December 1923.

Thirty-nine years and six months is a long time to most men, but to Red Branscum it was just a span of time during which he became vice-president and later general superintendent of production of the Gilcrease Oil Company. He witnessed fortunes made and lost in the oil industry; he saw gushers come in and directed the plugging of many dry holes. He remembers the Chapman discovery well near the town of Wetumka, Oklahoma where "The Gilcrease Sand" was discovered at 3,200 feet. He pulls back into his memory the activities of the Independent Oil and Gas Company which Tom Gilcrease acquired and which resulted in a recoupment of dry hole losses on other leases. But most of all he likes to let his mind dwell in retrospect on his association with Tom Gilcrease, the best boss a man ever had — Tom Gilcrease, who refused to run hot oil in East Texas; who always had time to listen to the private troubles of his employees; who liked to cook his own meals when out on a lease; and whose personal habits were constant and whose life was as oriented as a preacher on a holiday.

A bit of twinkle came into the eyes of the now thin-haired Red Branscum — often referred to as Tom's closest friend — and his ruddy face became ever more tinted with a manly blush as he said: "I'll never forget the time when we were drilling a well west of Wetumka in the winter and it was so cold in our tent that the flaps cracked when we opened them. Well, it was such a morning; I still had on my heavy underwear, in which I had slept, and I heard a noise outside the tent and thought it was raining. I peeked out and there was Tom taking a sponge bath out of an old washbasin. He would not let a day go by without his bath. The rest of us waited until Saturday night when we could get to town."

Red Branscum's appraisal of his friend, Tom Gilcrease, is best expressed by his simple statement, "Tom was okay." Red leaves much to be desired in the realm of reminiscent episodes which he shared with Thomas Gilcrease. He remarked, "Tom never did discuss his art life with me and I never got into that kind of conversation with him. I knew him for the man he was and I think he felt the same way about most of the Gilcrease boys. He never talked fancy words with us so long as we did our jobs, and when I was promoted to vice-president he treated me with the same attention as he did when I was a tool pusher on an oil rig. Others may have known more sides of him than I did, but they all knew one side — he was a friend, and when a man has a friend he has something no one can take away, so I reckon they did not take Tom away from any of us who knew him — you can't destroy that kind of friendship."

Thomas Gilcrease knew that petroleum, being a natural concentration procured from the ground, was not reproduceable except in terms of geological areas. He, likewise, knew that controlling the output of petroleum production was one of the industry's greatest problems. He was, by nature, an oil man who wanted to eliminate waste and extravagance. The Glenn Pool operation, which has so often been connected with the name of Thomas Gilcrease, had thirty-eight wells, thirty-two of which were in operation. The geologists had predicted that twenty-six of the wells would constitute a fair average of expectation of production throughout the life of the property. This prognostication, however, did not deter Thomas Gilcrease or his colleagues from being ever alert to the necessity of new discoveries.

The inimitable Tom never lost his enthusiastic and passionate attitude for drilling oil wells, especially when he had the opportunity of being present when they "blew in." Even in the more formative years of his company operations, he maintained a constant vigil every time a new location was determined. His announcement to his associates of a discovery well generally took the form of a quick telephone call. When he resorted to telegrams, his messages were brief but generally humorous. In April of 1932, following the "bringing in" of the second well on what was known as the Adams lease, he sent a telegraphic message to one of the company officials, reading:

> Just returned from Texas after drilling in number two Adams. She roared like number one, kind remembrances. Tom

And subsequently he wired again:

> Boy! North Number Three is a Bear. Tom.

There is a rather dramatic story told about one of the Gilcrease properties known as the "Sanders Lease," which is still producing and has yielded over one-half million barrels of crude oil. I. K. Crow, an independent oil operator of Corpus Christi, Texas, is authentically credited with guiding the Gilcrease Oil Company into the South Texas oil fields. The incident unfolds as follows: Thomas Gilcrease and G. B. Bancroft had gone to the Rio Grande Valley to observe some wells on a forty-acre tract. En route home, they had checked into the Plaza Hotel and the following morning Mr. Bancroft, while walking out on one of the piers, was noticed by Mr. Crow, whose office was on the second floor of the Jones building facing the Nueces Hotel. The sign over Crow's office read "Oil and Gas Leases." Crow was expecting a Mr. Sanders to meet him at seven o'clock; however, Sanders was a stranger to Crow and when he saw Bancroft he mistook him for Sanders, called to him, and invited him into his office. In the words of Mr. Crow, he soon discovered that "he had the wrong sow by the ears." Mr. Bancroft good-naturedly responded, "I see you handle oil leases and that Mr. Gilcrease and I passed a well being brought in about seven or eight miles west of here last night. What do you have in that area in the way of a lease?" This exchange of remarks resulted in the Gilcrease Oil Company acquiring leases from Mr. Crow.

The Crow story is perhaps only one of many which could be recited as a part of the history of the Gilcrease Oil Company, but more important is the fact that the economic situation throughout the world and particularly in the United States had not improved, and by 1929 much of the undeveloped acreage was surrendered and production dropped sharply. Prior to 1929 Thomas Gilcrease had gone to Paris, France, not only to continue the cultural pursuit, but in quest for funds with which to replenish the diminishing coffers of the Gilcrease Oil Company. The major stockholders had embarked upon a program of borrowing money to such an extent that their personal loans were jeopardizing the ability of the corporation to meet its obligations. The state of Oklahoma had initiated a tax program cutting into the profits of the company and this fact, coupled with the tremendous drain upon the company's treasury, eventually led to the determination on the part of the directors of the Gilcrease Oil Company to dissolve the Oklahoma corporation and organize under the laws of the state of Texas. This was accomplished on the seventeenth day of April, 1940.

Thereafter, the Gilcrease Oil Company of Texas and the Gilcrease Production Company came into being.[6]

But the simple words dedicated to Thomas Gilcrease on September 1, 1950, by Robert Lee Humber, Frank G. Walling, Pierce Larkin, Charles H. Lamb, G. B. Bancroft, Lester Whipple, and Eugene L. Ames are even more potent.

> It is a rare thing to know a man who has the gift to study human needs, to work for their fulfillment and to feel the call of duty where no one looks on.
>
> We know such a man who started life on the prairies, who plowed the soil in his childhood to reap Nature's harvest, who later explored her bowers to yield the wealth hidden in her chambers of liquid gold, and who amassed a fortune through the fructifying power of his industry, intelligence and dreams.
>
> This man understands the laughter of children, the sound of the mockingbird, the scent of flowers, the neighing of horses and the companionship of trees. He loves Nature: the call of the wild on lonely trails, the rustling of the elk in forests primeval, the sportive pleasures of bears near crystal streams, and the long flight of wild ducks in autumn en route to southern climes. Before the break of day, he has climbed mountain peaks to witness the miracle of dawn, and at eventide, beside placid lakes, he has gazed in solitude upon the glory of sunset, and the light of the ageless stars.
>
> Those close to him cherish his smile, his refreshing sense of humor and his keen human sympathy. Never is he an alien where the good of humanity is concerned. His credentials are his implicit faith in God and man, and his capacity for endless good works. He never fails a friend.
>
> This man has lived in many worlds and has cultivated many pastures. He has had possessions but they have never possessed him. He has regarded them as a trust for generations unborn.

> One day he laid his treasures upon an altar and consecrated them to the service of mankind. He created a great shrine of culture—one filled with the undying splendors of art; with historic scenes, transfigured on canvas with lasting beauty and fame; with the handicraft of a vanishing race, whose forebears roamed the prairies and were at home in the hills; with precious manuscripts, documents and tomes, which preserve for all time the knowledge of how a great nation was born. His Foundation has become a storehouse of things rare and priceless, a workshop of research and learning and a source of inspiration for all men everywhere.
>
> This man, humble in spirit, firm in purpose and selfless in service, continues to grow. Some day he will reach the Happy Hunting Ground, which will immortalize his work and make him a part of the ages to come.[7]

The accolades contained in the eulogistic words of Tom's colleagues, business associates, and some of the former stockholders of the Gilcrease Oil Company, while sincerely expressed, were probably accepted with the proverbial grain of salt. Lodged deeply into the mind of Thomas Gilcrease was the shadow of financial stress, which came to the company bearing his name when certain stockholders were accorded loans totaling approximately $188,833.41 from the period of 1930 to 1933. He knew only too well that such obligations, combined with the undeveloped leases which were held in the name of the company, would eventually bring about a chaotic condition and new organizational ventures.

While it is difficult to estimate with complete accuracy the financial worth of Thomas Gilcrease in 1922 when the Gilcrease Oil Company was organized, there is evidence that in 1928 certain financial statements were filed with a local bank which reflected that the personal assets of Mr. Gilcrease amounted to $2,333,212.20, against which there were notes payable in the approximate sum of $38,005.00, leaving a net worth of $2,295,207.20. Mr. Gilcrease owned 65% of the stock in the Gilcrease Oil Company, or 650 shares, and in 1930 the company's estimate of the value of the stock was $1,509,933.85. A statement of the Gilcrease Oil Company, January 1, 1929, reflected total assets of $869,619.11, with accounts payable of $14,840.58, and notes payable of $81,102.87, leaving a net worth of $772,675.66. However, another statement, dated January 1, 1931, shows total assets of $741,534.43, notes payable of $40,000.00 and accounts payable of $23,153.03, or a net worth of $678,381.40. The foregoing figures were based upon cost value. The estimated value of proven acreage amounted to 1020 barrels of settled production based upon $1,500.00 per barrel or $1,530,000.00. The company at that time had undeveloped leases estimated at $355,820.00, making a total estimated value of $2,232,171-.05. By December 31, 1932, the value of developed leases belonging to the Gilcrease Oil Company in Oklahoma, as estimated by engineers, was $1,007,275.66.

The recitation of these figures provides a fair comprehension of the growth of the Gilcrease Oil Company. In October, 1933, Thomas Gilcrease conveyed seven-sixteenths of the working interest in the lease on the S/2 of the NW and the N/2 of the SW of Section 22 in Township 17, Range 12 in the Glenn Pool District, to the Gilcrease Oil Company, for which no actual consideration was paid for the conveyance. This conveyance was to satisfy requirements of a local bank as additional security for obligations of the company. The Gilcrease Oil Company held valuable interests in the state of Texas.

The personal assets of Thomas Gilcrease at the time of the organization of the Gilcrease Oil Company were composed of real property in Country Club Heights in California, and real estate holdings in the city of Tulsa and in Winfield, Kansas. The 13-acre tract on the hill located in Osage County, where the Thomas Gilcrease Institute of American History and Art now stands, is alleged to have cost approximately $83,382.96, but was valued at $50,000.00 as of December 31, 1932. In addition to all of this property, Thomas Gilcrease owned 894.10 acres of good land in Osage County, of which 360 acres were located one and a quarter miles west of the hill property. He possessed stock and farm equipment and owned 1,440 acres of land in Pittsburg County, Oklahoma. There was on record in his name 317.72 acres of land in Teton County, Wyoming, which was rough land along the river and used for fishing. At that time Mr. Gilcrease had built one cabin on the property.

In the light of the limited formal education of Thomas Gilcrease, the financial empire, which was developed largely through his own industry, is little short of phenomenal. Bearing in mind the personal assets which he was endeavoring to protect, it is understandable that corporate organization was inevitable and was to play a tremendous part in the development of the oil leases which came under the thumb of Thomas Gilcrease and laid the groundwork for his wealth.

Chapter 3

Creating a Foundation

The modern concept for endowed institutions would appear to be the establishment of legal entities which serve as a tax-saving vehicle for the benefactors, regardless of whether the organizers or founders spring from individual wealth or collective fortunes.

While it is not the purpose of the author to engage in pedantry with respect to museums and galleries of art, it is vital to a better understanding of the reasons why Thomas Gilcrease embarked upon his career as a collector with such assurance and absorbing or controlling possession of mind that his overextensions almost resulted in the shattering of his creation.

The origin of museums, as they are identified today, came with the great revival of art, letters, and learning in Europe during the fourteenth to and including the sixteenth century, marking the transition from the medieval to the modern world. We know the period now as the Renaissance. The revival of interest in the classics led to an interest in the relics of classical antiquity, and individuals felt the compulsion to collect them. There are historians who feel that this impelling influence was rooted in curiosity, while others hold fast to the theory that preservation was the basis for their impulse. In the collections made by members of the nobility and others of the centuries referred to hereinabove may be found, not merely the models, but the actual beginnings of many of the recognized museums of this century. The great museums of Europe, for the most part, owe their origin to royal and princely collections which in the course of political changes became the property of the state.

Thomas Gilcrease may not have said it in so many words, but his intimates — few as they were — knew that he tenaciously embraced the belief that the creations of men must be living things and not destined for obscurity in a mausoleum.

The museums as they are known in this century found their origin in the last century when the people of at least parts of the world suddenly became conscious of the arts in a more generalized fashion. There was a breaking out of the musty morgues of conglomerated objects of art and the innovation of individual exhibits so that the work of a given artist could be studied, enjoyed, and interpreted.

In the nineteenth century, a new middleman of the business of "oil and canvas" appeared on the scene. For want of a more efficient title he emerged in the economic jungle as the "art dealer," or the benefactor for starving artists. Their ambition for profits actually stimulated the novice, whose gullible mind was in partnership with an empty stomach.

Little by little and painting by painting the art dealer gathered a variety of art objects and swelled his inventories. Recognition of genius matures slowly and often withers on the shelf or awaits the death of the artist before a critique of favor declares to the masses that a new star is in the galaxy. With the appearance of the "art dealer" came the antithesis of the trade — "the collector," a habit which is alleged to have started with the Romans. The rich bought from the dealer who acquired from the destitute men of talent. They were covetous for the curiosities, and their determination to outdo their social equals soon cluttered the halls of their mansions. Men who have researched the tomes of authentic information tell us that in the year 1682, an Englishman, Elias Ashmole, an antiquarian and son of a saddler, presented to the University of Oxford the Ashmolean Museum, the first public museum of curiosities in the kingdom. He had inherited the larger part of his collection, known as Tradescant's Ark, from a friend, John Tradescant, and stipulated that a suitable edifice be built for its reception; the installation of the collection was made in 1683.

In the United States the growth of art museums was motivated by the generosity of private donors, increased public interest, and the support by the public generally of museums for colleges and schools. Most such enterprises are understaffed, underfinanced, or look to legacies, endowments, and tax-free contributions for the necessary implementation to inadequate funds.

This lack of sufficient finance, coupled with the inability of most such institutions to acquire original objects, has led to many closed doors. When situations such as this develop there is a tendency to pursue one phase of art.

Thomas Gilcrease Collection Incorporated

Twenty-seven years have passed since Thomas Gilcrease caused a corporation to be organized under the laws of the state of Texas. Three of the subscribers were citizens of Texas, to wit, Lena Gilcrease Logan (sister of Thomas Gilcrease), Frank Burton Logan (her husband), and Eudotia Teenor (secretary to Thomas Gilcrease). The remaining subscribers were the sons of Mr. Gilcrease, Thomas, Jr., and Barton.

This was the actual beginning of what is now the Thomas Gilcrease Institute of American History and Art, because it provided the legal machinery with which many of the first acquisitions were made. The purposes of the corporation as set forth in its charter were:

To establish, maintain, and support any educational, scientific, historical, or literary undertaking by means of collecting, assorting, classifying, and exhibiting antiques, relics, objects and specimens having scientific, historical, cultural, or educational value of this or past periods, epochs, or ages, with authority to collect, receive as donations, purchase, or import any and all objects which may have educational, literary, scientific, historical, or cultural value, and to classify, assort, study, and exhibit the same, with authority to receive donations; and to rent, lease, or own such buildings and property as is necessary or incidental to the main purpose for which this corporation is formed; and with express authority to receive gifts and donations in furtherance of the purposes for which this corporation is formed.

The charter for this foundation was filed with the secretary of state, state of Texas on December 18, 1939. Thomas Gilcrease had taken his first step toward his career as a collector. He purchased the Casino Club building at Crockett and Presa streets in San Antonio and renamed it the "Gilcrease Building." The entire sixth floor was converted into a museum and the Thomas Gilcrease Collection was under way.[1]

Worthy of comment is the fact that while the actual name of the corporation was "Thomas Gilcrease Collection," it was never used publicly. The activities were conducted under the name of the "Thomas Gilcrease Foundation." After the formal opening on March 18, 1943, officials of the new organization published the first magazine, or pamphlet, which was titled "The American Indian," described as "An Exhibition of Paintings, Drawings, Books, Manuscripts and Sculptures." A special note was imprinted on the back cover which read: "This Foundation is not restricted to Indian children but is open to children of all races." The foreword of the brochure, which is now as rare as some of the documents in the collection it described, is not only a timetable for the events which occurred later, but embodies language of explanation which is essential to the overall intentions of Thomas Gilcrease.

The Thomas Gilcrease Foundation welcomes you to the Thomas Gilcrease Collection. The purpose of the Foundation is to provide education and proper environment for Indian boys and girls. The actual home for the Foundation is in Tulsa, Oklahoma, and the collection has been assembled for the purpose of shaping and supplementing the educational background of our charges.

We are opening the collection to visitors in San Antonio for a period of time. We have selected from the collection an exhibition of American paintings, sculpture and prints with emphasis on the life of the American Indian and his relation to the cultural development of our nation. The Indian has exerted a powerful influence on American sculptors, painters, and writers. Geographically and historically, the Indian is memorialized. There is hardly a locality that has not got its Indian associations. The spirit of the Indian is an engrossing human document. His courage in the face of insurmountable odds, his stoicism in the face of disaster, and his willingness to help in the maintenance of our country in spite of the many wrongs that he has suffered, have made his qualities an important part of our national heritage.

In conclusion we would like to point out the purely American character of this exhibition. No learned interpretation is necessary. European mannerism is encouragingly absent.

The peculiar twists of some of the thoughts expressed in the foregoing language must be measured against the philosophy of Thomas Gilcrease in later years. While the basic concepts did not change, he grew up and the collection expanded accordingly.

It was not until four years after the procurement of the charter for Thomas Gilcrease Collection, Incorporated, that the museum in the Gilcrease Building was opened to the public. San Antonians did not flock to the museum in large numbers. For reasons which were never sufficiently apparent to Mr. Gilcrease, the project suffered from lack of proper publicity and it may well be that the location discouraged visitors. The Gilcrease Oil Company occupied the fifth floor of the same building and it is understandable that confusion and suspicion could have been deterrents to many citizens who did not comprehend the motives of the founder or who did not grasp what he hoped to accomplish. Regardless of reason, the experiment — and it was little else — did not function as anticipated, and two years after the formal opening there was a most informal closing. The Thomas Gilcrease Collection, Incorporated, became an empty shell and, while it is still a duly authorized corporation under the laws of the state of Texas, it is dormant insofar as being utilized for any positive purpose.

The orbituary of the San Antonio offspring was best expressed in the *San Antonio Evening News* of June 22, 1949. The alert and no doubt disappointed reporter put his heart into the farewell message and, at the same time, aimed a spear of retribution into the hearts of a host of Texans. It was headlined:

> San Antonio Loses Valuable Collection
> of Indian Lore
>
> What San Antonio could have had, but showed no interest in, was opened as the Gilcrease Foundation in Tulsa, Oklahoma. Thomas Gilcrease, a quarter Creek Indian, who lives at 302 W. Mulberry Ave., has perhaps the greatest collection of American Indian lore in the world.
>
> Up until three years ago Gilcrease housed his collection on the top floor of the Gilcrease Building and hoped to make it permanent. Public apathy changed that desire, according to Mrs. Lester Whipple, wife of the Gilcrease Oil Company attorney.
>
> The collection was begun 30 to 40 years ago. The purpose behind it was to prove that the Indian was not merely a savage, but had a culture all his own. To make his point stronger Gilcrease set about finding any kind of material faithful to the preservation of the red man's way of life.

He collected, starting in 1912 when few persons had the same thought, paintings, drawings, carvings, relics. Gilcrease went back to the homes and sources to get authentic material. He strayed to New York, London, and Paris and to old libraries and family collections. He has specialized in everything having to do with the original man on this continent.

"Parson's Cherokee Chief," a painting put to canvas in 1762, is the oldest in the collection. Hick's "Penn's Treaty," drawn in 1810, is the next oldest painting.

Indians who left their names in painting are represented, among them, Crumbo, Acee Blue Eagle, Wilson, Kabotie and Herrea. The Taos, N.M. group has not been left out.

In the display are depicted the life, habits, modes of travel, fighting, hunting, dances, burial, ceremonial and religious rites, the hardship of the plains, Indian life in winter, the way they cared for their papooses. All these tales are told in the visual stories of our earliest native people.

Special manuscripts, folios, journals, pictures and books, are there for the looking. Latrobe's journal of early Western travels in 1882, even Columbus' letter, written and printed in Latin in 1494 which gave Europe its first written impression of the Indian, is there.

The Indian jewelry is said to be exceptional.

The Thomas Gilcrease Foundation

On the twenty-first day of September, 1942, Thomas Gilcrease and eight other individuals became the original incorporators and trustees of the Thomas Gilcrease Foundation. They were: Thomas Gilcrease, San Antonio, Texas;

Frank G. Walling, Tulsa, Oklahoma; G. B. Bancroft, San Antonio, Texas; C. H. Lamb, Tulsa, Oklahoma; Pierce Larkin, Tulsa, Oklahoma; Thomas Gilcrease, Jr., San Antonio, Texas; Barton Gilcrease, San Antonio, Texas; Lester Whipple, San Antonio, Texas; and Gene Ames, San Antonio, Texas.

Mr. Gilcrease was elected to the office of president and Thomas, Jr. became secretary. The Articles of Incorporation were filed with the secretary of state, state of Oklahoma on the seventeenth day of November, 1942, and thus came into being the foundation which has had the principal role in the development of the institute.

Mr. Gilcrease knew that his first foundation could not meet the requirements of his personal desires, although it was a good legal entity. The recitation of any legal document is without glamour or even reader interest to the lay person; nevertheless, a quick reference to the purpose clause is desirable. "The purpose for which this corporation is formed is to provide, maintain and operate a home for deserving boys and girls, who are descendants of members of any of the Indian tribes, together with such boys and girls of the White race as the Trustees may determine." It is noted here that any veiled language which might have been restrictive is removed by the use of the words "White race." While the record is not clear, it is doubtful if there was ever an instance when it was necessary to resort to the exception. An appraisal of the deeds of its founder fails to disclose positive prejudice which would have violated the avowed intention of the trustees.

The Articles of Incorporation are lengthy, wordy, repetitious and, in some instances, redundant. Paragraph 2 (g) and 2 (h) are, however, towers of strength in the framework of the artificially created creature, as reference is often made to such organizations.

Paragraph 2 (g)

> Own and maintain a library or libraries and art collection or collections, the same not being limited to any particular books or art objects, but with the principal

end in view of collecting and exhibiting free to the public and for the particular use of those boys and girls for which this foundation is established, books, literature and histories, art objects, objects of scientific and historical value and articles of special interest to the Indians.

Paragraph 2 (h)

Provide such moral and religious training as may advance the well being of society and reverence for God and lead to a virtuous and religious life for said boys and girls.

There were twenty-one separate paragraphs as sub-headings to paragraph two, and it was obvious that the author of the document was protecting against any *ultra vires* acts by the trustees. While the charter of the corporation was obtained by the law firm of Duff, Manatt, & Hardy of Tulsa, Oklahoma, it was actually written by Mr. Lester Whipple, of San Antonio, who in 1938 became general counsel to Thomas Gilcrease and to the Gilcrease Oil Company. The by-laws of the Thomas Gilcrease Foundation provided that during the lifetime of Mr. Gilcrease, he, as the founder, was to be vested with the exclusive management of the affairs of the corporation and to have exclusive power to direct and control its functions. He was also to determine the nature, scope and extent of the charities and benefactions contemplated; to determine the persons to be received into any home, school, clinic, hospital, or other institution maintained at the time of the incorporation or later; to employ and discharge at will all employees or servants, and to do any and all things not in conflict with the articles or the laws of the state of Oklahoma.

The powers he reserved unto himself were lifetime rights with respect to every provision of the articles and after his death everything would be under or within the discretion of the trustees and no appeal or review was to be had except for abuse of such discretion.

In excess of fifteen pages make up the by-laws. The foundation, except for legal qualifications, covered a multitude of situations, and if the corporate cloak had ever been lifted, only one person would have been standing solidly on the throne of the corporate castle: Thomas Gilcrease.

Probably the most comprehensive article written about the Thomas Gilcrease Foundation came from the declarative pen of Martin Wiesendanger, who served as the first curator of the Gilcrease Museum in San Antonio, Texas. In the autumn of 1946 in the *Southwest Review,* he authored a very authoritative analysis which he appropriately called "An Indian Foundation."[2] Mr. Wiesendanger defined the foundation as the embodiment of a man's dream tenaciously held for twenty years. He dubbed the founder as a philanthropist who was determined to create a repository of Indian life and culture. He reasoned that the steady encroachment on Indian lands, in the days before territorial government, tended to make those of Indian or part-Indian descent an underprivileged group; that the great absorption process and its attendant ferment and misery made a lasting impression upon the mind of Thomas Gilcrease, youthful as he was. His sudden wealth gave him the impetus to put his hopes to work, and this financial ability, coupled with his inborn humanitarianism, became uppermost in his ambitions. "Any other individual, especially one of Indian ancestry, might have been understandingly misanthropic. The chicanery to which the Indians had been continuously subjected had run like a never ceasing fire through his consciousness in his early years. But he did not allow this to impair the essential sureness and fineness of his vision for the Indian's welfare."

Thomas Gilcrease felt that if the Indian could be given the same opportunities as the white man he could eventually reach the same level. The Indian needed the equipment to compete with the white man and on the same terms, especially the children who would otherwise be denied the opportunity. The foundation was capable of becoming a sociological experiment in the field of education. It could serve to bring about a semblance of solidarity among Indians by making them aware of second-class status and thereby stimulating their pride to improve their plight. The foundation would also assist in the preservation of certain traditions and the art of the tribes. All this was reason enough for the formation and placing it into positive operation.

Mr. Lester Whipple recalls with pride:

> I became associated with Mr. Gilcrease professionally early in the year of 1938. I never had a written contract with him. His memory was practically infallible. When he first sought my professional services it was in relation to his oil interests, but alas, I became an assistant to an art collector. During our long association I must have devoted at least fifteen of those precious years to assisting him with the collection. I did not have any influence upon his choice of art objects and it was crystal clear to me that he was a lone hunter in that field. My job was to plan methods of collecting and counsel with him on the subject of ways and means. There was hardly a day when he did not discuss methods of extricating funds from his oil interests to pay for his acquisitions. He read the catalogues with the same regularity as a railroad man would read timetables, only I knew that he had already selected the route before he opened the pamphlets. Thomas Gilcrease was a difficult individual to really know. Many folks thought they knew him. He would spend $250,000 with the same ease that he would part with a $5 bill – if he had the funds, and many times when he was not sure if his canoe would make it to shore. When the collection had to be relocated, he considered Wyoming, Arizona, New Mexico and other western states, but Oklahoma became the victor of his decision.

The eighty acres of Black Dog Township, located in Osage County, Oklahoma, two and one-half miles northwest of Tulsa, on a ridge which commands a wide view across the city to the south and east and another of the Osage Hills on the west and north, is described in legal terms as the south one-half of the southeast quarter of section twenty-eight, township twenty north, range twelve east.

One February 4, 1924, Mr. Gilcrease entered into an agreement with W. O Ligon, Jr. and Ada Blanche Ligon, his wife, by which he sold thirteen acres of the eighty-acre tract; the transaction was apparently by contract for deed because a deed was never actually recorded. The purchase price was $60,000 and Mr. Gilcrease took back a mortgage for $39,000, which was recorded in Book 40 of Mortgages, at page 595. In February, 1928, W. O. Ligon conveyed the thirteen acres to his wife Blanche, subject to the mortgage, this instrument being recorded in Book 63 of Warranty Deeds at page 617. In the same year, Mr. and Mrs. Ligon defaulted on the payments due under the note and mortgage which they had given to Mr. Gilcrease, and a foreclosure proceeding was instituted in the District Court of Osage County as case number 11870. Mr. Gilcrease owned a town lot in Tulsa and the matter was finally concluded by compromise by a trade for the town property and a surrender of the thirteen acres to Mr. Gilcrease. On April 9, 1928, the Ligons deeded the land back to Mr. Gilcrease and the instrument was placed on record on April 13, 1928, in Book 63, page 617 of the registry of deeds in Osage County. During the four years that the title was in the name of the Ligons they occupied the stone house on the hill. This transaction is very significant; if the Ligons had retained title to the thirteen acres, the probability of the institute being located where it now stands is exremely remote and, in retrospect, it can be safely assumed that Thomas Gilcrease might never have established the museum in Tulsa. This is a twist of fate worthy of historical note and proves once again that despite all of the frustrations and happenstances, the institute was destined to become a part of the cultural addition to Tulsa from which the world of arts has benefited.

This is the tract where the Thomas Gilcrease Institute of American History and Art is located. This is the land Thomas Gilcrease acquired from attorney Flowers Nelson on December 26, 1913, and it remained in his name throughout the years, except as stated above, until he conveyed it to the Thomas Gilcrease Foundation on December 15, 1942, just one month after the foundation was organized.

Book 3
Culture and the Call to Art

Chapter 1

Foreign Intrigue and Travel

This chapter in the life of Thomas Gilcrease will be treated with a vastly different approach than all of the other episodes in his long and varied career. Assuming that it is an author's license to discover an appropriate title for each segment of his work, the title "Foreign Intrigue and Travel" has been selected merely for want of a better label for the unopened package which promised reward and resulted in a most ungratifying trophy.

When and where, or even in what manner Thomas Gilcrease became acquainted with Numa Bouttier in France may never be adequately disclosed.[1] When Edgar Allen Poe wrote his beautiful story about Ligeia, he opened with these lines: "I cannot, for my soul, remember how, when or even precisely where I first became acquainted with the lady Ligeia." Thomas Gilcrease might have been tempted to paraphrase Poe's words by a like observation with respect to Numa Bouttier. Suffice—we must let the speculation become intrigue for the actual facts are entombed with the mortal remains of these two travelers of long ago – Thomas Gilcrease, the Oklahoman, who was running away from domestic involvement, seeking the end of the rainbow with gold in his pockets, and Numa Bouttier, the Frenchman, who was destined to be his teacher, fellow companion, and keeper of the diary.

Bouttier doubtless looked upon Thomas Gilcrease with a sympathetic eye and a native compassion, for is it not said that Frenchmen are great lovers? Tom admired the devotion displayed by the Bouttier family and wondered why he had been unable to steady his own ship of matrimony. The realm of imagination can be employed to determine that Thomas Gilcrease disclosed to his French friend that all was not well with his homelife in the United States and that domestic tranquility was a pearl he sought rather than a pearl possessed. Two men could not have shared four months of journey and abstained from frank discussions of their private lives.

Thomas Gilcrease recognized a charm in Bouttier which was not present in the majority of men with whom he had been associated socially or with whom he fraternized in the oil business. He liked the musical language of the French people. Bouttier was a student of literature. He was at home in the social swing of Paris. Thomas Gilcrease had presumably read and heeded the classic statement of Benjamin Franklin, "Being ignorant is not such a shame, as being unwilling to learn." He was willing to learn and for what it was worth he would have Numa Bouttier at his side for a venture into the world of the Mediterranean. He would be the student and the benefactor, a rare combination. Bouttier would be the interpreter and the cultural walking stick upon which he would lean.

Regrettable it is that Thomas Gilcrease depended so completely upon Bouttier to record the daily events of their travels. The impressions of the Oklahoman would have been written in a homely fashion and with descriptions couched in his western manner. He would have pointed up in well-phrased sentences an appreciation for the historical sites and no doubt for the repositories of art which came to his attention. Bouttier was not a total stranger to the cities they visited, and the diary which he kept was not flavored with the kind of animation of which the virgin traveler is capable. Nevertheless, there is indication that "Tom and Numa" complemented each other in their approach to the journey. What a tragedy that Bouttier failed to record the reactions of Gilcrease to the landmarks they visited or to even comment upon the impressions he received from his exchange of thoughts with Gilcrease. The language barrier was hurdled in a passable fashion because Gilcrease knew a sufficient amount of French to make his likes and dislikes known. There were times when the Oklahoman would have found himself in extremely awkward positions, because he could not and did not resist exploration or mild aberration when forbearance would have been by far the more comfortable course to take. Bouttier often extricated his friend, "Indian Tom," from the hidden traps of foreign fortune hunters, not that Gilcrease was gullible. He was too trusting, and the feigned destitution of foreigners generally brought American money to the spurious as well as to the genuine seeker of alms.

The Europe of forty-two years ago is a different delineation than one would find in a Mediterranean cruise of today. Bouttier's notes of the journey lay untouched and untranslated in the files of the office of the Thomas Gilcrease Foundation from 1925 until 1967. When they were discovered or retrieved from their forgotten abode it was felt that a new kind of "Gilcrease sand" had been uncovered, to revert to the terminology of the oil fraternity, but, alas and alack — some seventy pages of writing, partly typewritten and partly in the hand of Bouttier, proved to be nothing more than a chronological travelogue filled with notes evidently made when the day was done or aboard ship or train. When on occasion there is reference to Mr. Gilcrease, the loquacious Frenchman called him "Mr. G." and then opined his own expressions of thought to such an extent that the reader gains the feeling that Bouttier was making the cruise alone.

Their journey commenced on November 30, 1925, one year following Tom's divorce from Belle Gilcrease. As they embarked from Nice, France, they took the coastal route along the Mediterranean between Toulon and Menton. The climate was somewhat Nordic and, due to the dislike of "Mr. G." to the cold air, their route was altered. They found lodging in the most expensive hotels, indulged in the finest foods, and there is evidence that Bouttier tasted a rare vintage now and then. Typical of some of the notes of Bouttier — "We registered at the Hotel de la Paix near the Canebierre, when we reached Marseille. We walked to the post office, somewhat dull except for a few shady Oriental girls who were strolling, and we concluded it was safer to return to our rooms. The promenade was worth while but the dirty streets and the suspicious Arabs in the area were not an appealing sight for thoughts of safety. I had a difficult time falling asleep and kept thinking about the trip we would take in the morning." It should be noted that the use of the first person is the common denominator in which Bouttier indulged almost with uniformity throughout his writings. When the sea was rough and the passengers became ill, he comments, "I feel disturbing sensations and choose to go to my cabin without delay. Mr. G. is no exception. Everyone seems to be so engaged. Sleep was truly welcome."

There is a constant mention of the desire of Mr. Gilcrease to sit in the sun and enjoy the fresh air of the ocean. On the lighter side, Bouttier records that in Algiers it was too bad that only the older women abstained from wearing veils. But here again — it was the comment of Bouttier and not a word which would suggest that Gilcrease shared this "veiled regret."

Bouttier suggests that it was the custom of the natives in almost every port to beg for pennies, all of which became rather obnoxious to himself and Mr. Gilcrease; however, when his observations concern the balconies of the "Kasbah" he does not give any hint of whether his friend from Oklahoma was interested or even impressed.

Bouttier and Gilcrease devoted several days of their

journey to visiting in Algiers and Biskra. When they reached Tunis, they had already visited Batna, Timgad, Constantine, and indulged in a few trips to the various countrysides. By December 18 they were in Carthage. Upon departing from Carthage the diary of Bouttier was no longer kept by daily dates. The end of December found them in Rome where they remained until the first days of January. The remainder of the month of January took them to Naples, Port Said, and Luxor, a town of Upper Egypt, on the east bank of the Nile, 450 miles above Cairo by river and 418 miles by rail — and here they visited the temple of Luxor, one of the greatest monuments of Thebes. Their next stop was Karnak, a village in Upper Egypt which has given its name to the northern half of the ruins of Thebes on the east bank of the Nile. The Karnak ruins comprise three great enclosures built of crude brick. The third and largest enclosure is of vast dimensions, forming approximately a square of 1,500 feet, and it contains the Karnak temple of Amen, said to be one of the historical wonders.

February was devoted to visiting Assuan, a town of Upper Egypt on the east bank of the Nile, the capital of a province of the same name, the southernmost province in Egypt. Bouttier and Gilcrease were far more interested in viewing the remains of Egypt's remote past than in exploring her modern cities. They discovered, to the utter amazement of Mr. Gilcrease, that the larger towns of that day were in many instances built on the sites of ancient cities. They were completely captivated by Memphis, the Pharaonic capital, on the west bank of the Nile — and with the Pyramids of Giza or Gizeh on the edge of the desert, the largest of the many pyramids and other monuments, including the famous Sphinx. Their travels through Egypt were rewarded because they were able to see, side by side, the activities of the century in which they lived, the memorial of every race and civilization which had flourished in the valley of the Nile.

They followed their planned route visiting Jerusalem, Alexandria, Athens, Dardanelles, and Constantinople. By the time the month of March arrived their travels found them in Venice, Florence, and other cities in Italy.

The temptation to abandon the Bouttier notes and relegate them to the musty files from whence they were discovered was tantalizing. It was like opening a bag of popcorn with the intention of eating one small portion, only to find that the delectable morsels had captured the taste buds. Perhaps the next page, or the next, would reveal events which could be conformed with the purpose of the search and thereby discover the roots of the aspirations of "Mr. G." It was Erich Fromm who so pointedly said, "Assumption is the very fallacy which has led to so many mistaken conclusions concerning our problems." We dare not assume that Bouttier's notes were prophetic or even so intended, yet they have provided the kernels which, when subjected to retrospect, become the "bag of popcorn."

A note written in Blidah merits consideration. Bouttier recalled:

> We are now in Blidah after crossing the Oued Kebir on a little bridge crowded with sheep. It is market day in Blidah. After a while we leave again to go to a public garden called "The Sacred Wood," because a Moslem monk is praying there. We watch him squatted there with his face toward the east and mumbling prayers while dropping amber beads similar to our rosary. In the center of his very tiny house there is a strange piece of furniture, his coffin covered with white and pink gauze. This is his only possession, with a little rug and some verses of the Koran on the wall. The faithfuls bring him food until the end of his life. In a way, this is similar to the life of a Buddhist priest or fakir in India — we leave and walk along a road where we meet a young Arab who offers to take us to a cave. His fingers are red with henna. His family lives in the mountains and he earns his living guiding tourists to his famous cave. We consent to go down into a rather shallow excavation where we see a few stalactites. We go back to the car which takes us to Kolea where the cafes are in abundance. We follow the road along the beautiful Turquoise Coast admiring the form on the red rocks, then back to Algiers.

Mr. Gilcrease and his friend then visited the Rue de la Kasbah by making the endless climb among the small and dirty shops of the local merchants. The streets were narrow and the balconies seemed to touch each other. Upon reaching "Devil Street," they heard the chatter and arguing of Arab women. Bouttier wrote:

> They are heavily made up, are sitting on a wooden balcony slightly above a small square. They send provocative winks in our direction. We leave hastily.
>
> We go in the afternoon to the marvelous Botanical Gardens. There we see the variety of species of palm trees, rubber trees, banana trees and other tropical plants. There is a charming corner, a bench surrounded by reeds near a pond where waterlilies are floating. An ideal refuge for lovers. There are wide paths bordered with bamboo two stories high, and in the center of the park there is a beautiful lawn and English garden. The season is not right for flowers, but it must be gorgeous in the spring.

What are the deductions from the foregoing notes? The visit to the cave would indicate the intense interest of Tom Gilcrease in exploration which eventually emerged into a full scale venture into archaeological studies. Their visits to the gardens can certainly be attributed to the profound admiration of Mr. G. for the beauty spots of nature created by the hand of man. In later years and in subsequent travels his interest in gardens was repeated again and again. The allusion by Bouttier to the "refuge for lovers" and the "winking women" probably furnished the distracted Mr. G. with moments of frustration — but one cannot help but speculate upon the end result of Bouttier's constant observations on the subjects.

When they arrived in Biskra, a town in Algeria, near the railhead for the desert, lying in the Sahara 410 feet above the sea at the exit from the gorges of El-Kantara on the right bank of the Wad Biskra, they were delighted with the climate, the genial temperature and the clear skies which made Biskra a famous winter resort. They could hardly appreciate the fact that they had reached the middle of the Sahara. Upon the evening of their arrival they registered at the Hotel Transatlantic. One paragraph of Bouttier's comments merits reproduction:

> That evening we are alone in the dining room. In spite of the suggestion of the guide to take us to the quarters with women under the pretext that a caravan has brought a fresh load of wavering dancing girls for the entertainment of a pacha, we limit ourselves to the Casino swarming with a colonial crowd, officers in uniforms red and blue, Greek croupiers and a small orchestra composed of three oriental musicians led by a Turk. A few Arabs wrapped in their floating burnouses are sipping their black coffee waiting for the showing of an American movie.

While in Biskra they visited Allah's Garden which Bouttier described with detail, even commenting upon the irrigation feat which he credited to a Frenchman. He called it a real paradise with little brooks running here and there to keep the temperature cool. Wonderment beguiles the reader — did Mr. G. share his impressions? Of one fact there can be no mistake, the able Frenchman never failed to include the native women in his writings — "We strolled through the Ouled-Nails Quarters. The local courtesans were not veiled. They wait for their customers on the threshold, very heavily made-up and dressed loudly. The Arabs treat them with contempt. Some are very young, with beautiful black eyes, thick lips and a tendency to be fat. They have tattoos of their tribe's colors on their chins and cheeks."

In Timgad, a city twenty-three miles southeast of Batna in the department of Constantine, Algeria, they explored the ruins and apparently Bouttier endeavored to encompass the thoughts of his fellow traveler in his notes because he dropped the first person approach. The ruins of the capital, which occupy a prominent position in the southwest of the city, were of particular interest. Here there is evidence in the Frenchman's notes that Mr. Gilcrease became inspired by the "ruins" and probably planted the seed for his venture into the Indian mounds in later years. Bouttier wrote:

> Besides numerous thermal baths, the town had a beautiful amphitheater made on a hillside—beyond it was the Forum very well preserved and near which they had public facilities with running water. We visited the Temple of Gods, of which only columns remain, but considered one of the best by archaeologists. Farther on we see another smaller one with the inscription "Enter good, exit better." From there we visit a most interesting museum. Outside large mosaics describe varied scenes. Sarcophagi are placed all around.

This paragraph discloses the first mention of *archaeology* or *museums.*

Historians have written that the birth of Italy, which began with the *Risorgimento,* or "resurrection," was an event full of hope of peace and the promise of progress for a new nation. Italy has weathered the inclemency of man-made obstacles and emerged with miraculous results. It is little wonder that Thomas Gilcrease and Numa Bouttier discovered these "miracles" as they traversed and visited the land of the Italians for the first time.

Italy has been called the "country of the human heart," and, having just emerged from the rapid tour of Constantine, Tunis, and Carthage, it was a determined duo of foreigners who were ready for a new venture. Both Bouttier and Gilcrease had read of the profound culture of Italy—now they were to brush shoulders with the arts—observe the religious aspects of the citizens and marvel at the preservation of antiquity in the cities of history.

It was the latter days of December when they reached Rome. They set out to crowd as many hours into the days as their tired legs would permit. Tom Gilcrease was not as much concerned about the people as he was with the architectural surprises which met his eager eyes. By contrast, Bouttier was prone to explore the habits of the peasants and their manner of dress and to observe the distinctive garb of the priests and nuns of the manifold orders of the church. His notes are replete with the mental images of the *Bersaglieri,* the men who made up the rifle battalions of the Italian army, and of the mounted troops with Lohengrin-type helmets and those who wore the "black shirts." A typical comment of Bouttier: "Mr. Mussolini is well guarded." He was likewise impressed by the dearth of beggars on the streets — streets which teemed with military personnel.

The ancient mausoleums of the early Christians, dating back to the second century, and which lined the passages in the lower Vatican grottoes, commanded the attention of Tom Gilcrease, and he was enthralled with the beauty of the sculptured treasures of man's genius.

The ruined Colosseum near the site of Nero's palace left the hungry mind of the Oklahoman in an almost hypnotic state and, even then, he must have harbored a burning desire to explore beyond what the eye could see. The discussions of the huge arena resulted in this comment by Bouttier:

> From the Colosseum we go to the Triclinium of the Palace of Flavian. There endless feasts took place in the large halls of marble and mosaics. Then we visit the house of Livia, the best preserved building of its kind. The rooms are intact and decorated with paintings, the colors are still fresh. Pottery and specimen of the pipes used for water are on display here.

The paintings and major sculpture of Michelangelo revealed a whole new world to Gilcrease and Bouttier. Surely, if this was the Italian's native land and his art, thought Tom, some day he would give the world a chance to see the American Indian's native land in much the same fashion. He did not then know or appreciate fully the extent to which some artists had gone to pave the avenues for him. He was not acquainted with the master products of the intrepid Thomas Moran, the genius of Frederic Remington, the delicate art of John James Audubon, the precision and natural ability of Charles M. Russell, the capacity or spirit brought to life on the canvas by Albert Bierstadt or Thomas

Eakins. He was yet to discover the style of a Woody Crumbo, Acee Blue Eagle, or Willard Stone. He was consumed by the glory of Italian art and stood close enough to touch the Moses by Michelangelo in the Church of St. Peter in Chains. He viewed with awe the domed St. Peter's, largest of all churches. Tom Gilcrease grew taller and his imagination matured.

Christmas day of 1925 was upon them. To be present in the Holy City on such a day was, according to Bouttier, an opportunity to witness a holy spectacle in all of its dignity and glory. They did not miss a function where they could gain entrance. The hours went by and the day was done.

December 26, they saw their first opera in Rome at the Theatre Constanzi; *Francesca di Rimini* by Gabriele d'Annunzio. Bouttier wrote: "Magnificent interpretation. Queen Helen was present." On the twenty-seventh they saw Giacomo Puccini's *La Boheme*. Too bad he did not record the names of the artists who sang the principal roles. A new kind of introduction to Italian culture had greeted the travelers.

December 28, 1925, Bouttier wrote:

> Early in the morning, guided by a Swiss guard, we visit the Museum and the Mosaic shop of the Vatican. Artists are making copies of some of the pictures of the Vatican. Most exacting work and quite beneficial to the Treasury of the Vatican.

He continued:

> We visit the library of the Vatican which contains manuscripts by Virgio, Michaelangelo and Dante. It measures 900 feet long and has more than 250,000 volumes. It is decorated with portraits of all the Popes and art treasures donated by royalty from all over the world. After that we see a most interesting museum of arms and armors of the XV and XVI centuries. We visit the museums of sculptors, the best of its kind in the world. Then to the gallery of tapestries and the room where the maps are kept. On display in a case by itself is an enormous cup, 15 feet in

> diameter, made of porphyry which was found in the ruins of Nero's Palace. The next gallery— the Rafael rooms with paintings commissioned by Julius II. After that we come to the famous Sistine Chapel with frescoes by Michaelangelo and the famous painting "The Last Judgment" done when the master was 66 years old.

Before leaving the Vatican they attended a pontifical mass. Bouttier's recitation of the event is comparable to what most travelers and visitors would see and it is unfortunate that he did not make notes on the reaction of Tom Gilcrease to the experience. The comments might have cast some light on the feeling of Mr. Gilcrease about ritual and religion, a subject which he infrequently discussed with his family and friends.

In Naples they toured every museum and building where they were directed to go and some which were not on their agenda. Upon seeing Mt. Vesuvius, which was inaccessible to them, Numa wrote, "It leaves us with a feeling of the weakness of mankind against the foes of nature."

Their visit to Jerusalem was taken in stride—but here again, the notes are definitely those of Bouttier and, aside from the use of the word *we*, they offer but little which is applicable to biographical study in the life of Thomas Gilcrease. Historically the following paragraph bears preservation. Bouttier said:

> From Mount Olive and Gethsemane we went to the gate of Jaffa, one of the two gates of the town. Some high walls are all that are left of the palace of David. At the same gate, Christ is said to have made his entrance into Jerusalem riding a donkey while the population waved olive branches.

Bouttier then describes with tourist-guide terminology the garden of Gethsemane, the Valley of Kidron, the barren mountains where shepherds tended their flocks, impressions of the basin by the Dead Sea and then concludes:

> The country is very plain, there isn't a soul around.

The Frenchman and the Oklahoman continued traveling until they reached the seashore situated 1800 feet below the Mediterranean Sea level on the banks of the Jordan.

"It is there that Christ would have received the baptism by John," noted Bouttier. On they went – reaching Jericho.

> This is the city where Joshua overcame the unfaithful and where the trumpets made the high wall crumble down as if it were made of paper mache. Behind, on the hillside is a most rugged site, the convent of Temptation, kept by monks. It is here, it is said, that Christ has been tempted by the devil after forty days of fast and prayer.

The remainder of their tour of the Holy Land took them to Bethlehem where they visited the Church of the Nativity. They made some pictures of the natives, listened to the ringing of the bells, heard the calls to prayer and followed some of the ancient paths as described in biblical commentaries. They found the Zionist villages and walked through the streets of Haifa, the big city on the edge of the Mediterranean, a town almost exclusively Jewish – as Bouttier observed. From Mount Carmel they would see the anchored ships and wonder what strange ports would welcome them when they steamed away.

By April 2, 1926, they arrived in Venice, having spent a few days in Alexandria, Athens, and other ports. Bouttier's narration of Venice is wordy and suggestive of a travel folder. One has the impression that he grew weary of writing; however, he does mention their visitations to museums and art markets. He concludes with a rather potent statement: "The Renaissance was glowing under our eyes."

While Thomas Gilcrease and Numa Bouttier had some mutual business interest, the written evidence of their endeavors adds only a minute segment to their association and friendship. Bouttier conducted a company bearing the name of "Neumaticos Michelin," with its home base in France and allied operations in Spain. Bouttier made some investments in the Gilcrease companies, and from time to time he sought the assistance of Mr. Gilcrease in obtaining information about his interests.

On June 12, 1945, almost twenty years after he and Mr. Gilcrease took the Mediterranean cruise, from Madrid Bouttier wrote to his Indian friend:

> Dear Tom: I am just thinking there are twenty years we were getting sun in Biskara, in a peaceful time who never will come back, it seems, I mean never the same; I would not let pass this anniversary without sending you a thought.

It was difficult for him to write in English and his conversion of thought is labored. In this communication he became philosophical to the point of sentimentality. He spoke of the new life and hoped that the "injury" to Europe had ended. He commented that the worst was over in France—but that the cost of living had risen. This was one of the occasions when he mentioned his need for funds. He spoke of his two sons and their education in glowing language and ended the letter with sincere wishes and signed it "Numa." The war was over but the economy of the world was still staggering on uncertain footing. Bouttier's optimism had lost luster but he was firm in his faith that the sun would shine again just as it had in Biskara.

Mr. Gilcrease acknowledged Bouttier's letter; then they did not write again with any regularity until May 18, 1947, when Bouttier extended an invitation to his friend, Tom, to visit Madrid. On June 7, 1947, Mr. Gilcrease responded:

> Dear Numa:
>
> It is certainly my wish and my intention to pay you a visit in your own City of Madrid. Upon my arrival, I will expect you to put on a first class bull fight for me. I want it to be plenty wild and bloody. You may remember the first bull fight I ever saw was in Nimes, and I felt as though I were witnessing a Roman Feast Day of olden times when the arena of Nimes was first built. Every minute of that performance I expected to see the lions come out and devour not only the participants but most of the audience.

> I certainly hope that you will see fit to visit me here in Oklahoma and Texas. There is no reason for you to spend your entire thousand years of life in Europe. You can at least afford to give us a few months of your time.
>
> I am becoming wilder every day in every way. I eat my meat and vegetables raw and every day there is another bigger and better hair growing on my chest. I may turn into a grizzly bear some day. Who knows; some say that what we think, we are. I might even become a living dinosaur.
>
> As you suggest, Liberty is a nice name, but my, how good it would be if Liberty could only mean Freedom.

Mr. Gilcrease then commented that his daughter, Des Cygne, had graduated from high school and was entering the University of Oklahoma in September where she would complete her studies. In one of his very rare moods, Mr. Gilcrease told Bouttier that the income from a certain oil lease had exceeded what it was during the war and that he would give him the details in a future letter. Quite obvious it was that Mr. Gilcrease had been able during the years to cast aside some of the domestic memories which had been so acute when he made the cruise with his French friend. His statement that he was becoming wilder every day was his way of conveying to his fellow traveler of yesteryear that time had revived his spirits and stimulated his quest for happiness. He did not fail to impart his hope for freedom and peace in the world.

On the twenty-second day of July, 1947, Numa wrote again to Mr. Gilcrease and indulged in what was perhaps the most lengthy and personal note Mr. Gilcrease ever received from him. It is important to record several of the thoughts expressed by Bouttier because they point up the intimacy of their friendship and the extent of their sentiments toward each other.

Bouttier commented that he was happy to know that Mr. Gilcrease was in "good spirit and humor" and that the only things which were really valuable in life were "plain gold and average honesty." Doubtless his reference was to a stable economy and the reliance of man upon man. Noteworthy are the following lines, which must be read with the realization that he was thinking in the French language and converting his expressions to English.

> Let your hair growing and may be the life of a grizzly bear is better than any kind of human life. If you believe in metempsychosis, as the Indian people, I choose for the next life of that one of the bear in a quiet spot, far from men other than that of a speed bird, something like a swallow, but I am sick about other human life if between 200 men you just find one really good and fair.

His allusion to metempsychosis, the rebirth of the soul at death in another body either of human or animal form, was of course in answer to the comment of Mr. Gilcrease about becoming a living dinosaur. This indulgence in the subject of reincarnation on the part of both men is truly indicative of their depth of understanding of human endeavor and their faith in the Infinite Being. The remaining portions of Bouttier's letter touched upon the progress being made in the education of his two sons. He recalled the remarks of Mr. Gilcrease about the bullfights and said:

> My dear Tom,
>
> I should be happy to see you in Madrid but the good bull races with streams of blood is only during the summer time and the best, with the good "diestros" like Manelete or Arruza are finished. A good race is with plenty sun, strong bulls and cries of sangre, Hombre!!!

The letter is concluded with a request that his friend Tom send him some sheet music of Rachmaninoff, Liszt, MacDowell, and Tschaikovsky. His son was a student of the piano and the music was not available after the war. He then asked Tom to urge the Gilcrease Company to send him more funds so he could buy a house. He wrote:

> I have to buy a house in France where I will dry my bones someday and needs reparations. You understand?

Mr. Gilcrease replied to Bouttier in August of the same year and inquired if they could get together for a visit in Geneva during the month of September. He wanted Bouttier to meet him at Le Mont Blanc. For the first time there is a reference by Mr. Gilcrease to other subjects. He wrote:

> A friend of mine has just returned from Paris and Brussels. He tells me that the political situation in France is not the best but that things are in a very good condition in Brussels. He also says the people are rather hard up in England.
>
> We are working hard all the time and making some progress in our business and at the Foundation here at Tulsa. We expect to open it to the public during the month of October.

Here then is a reference to the opening of the Thomas Gilcrease Museum and an indication that Mr. Gilcrease did from time to time discuss his ambitions for the establishment of a museum with his friend Numa; consequently, it is not difficult to assess the influence their cruise together in 1925 might have had upon the eventual establishment of the Thomas Gilcrease Institute of American History and Art.

In October Bouttier wrote to Mr. Gilcrease and engaged in a long and intricate dissertation about the political situation then existing in Europe. Pertinent excerpts:

> We spent a good time in France this summer with perfect weather. My boys had a good time at the beach, here near S. Sebastian and near Portel which has changed very much. I have been in Belgium. Brussels is exactly as before the war. You could find anything. Except Switzerland, I think in Europa, Belgium and this country are the best in the present time.

He then referred to de Gaulle as being "not diplomatic" but

a good soldier. Bouttier was still anxious for Mr. Gilcrease to visit with him and wrote:

> Maybe you shall decide to come here. I shall reserve for you and Des Cygne something very good. Why you don't come for the Feria in Sevilla in March. And tell me something about the Foundation in Tulsa. Are you satisfied and things are well as you expect? Good health, dear Tom, and come some day here with your girl [meaning Tom's daughter]. Always your very sincerely, Numa.

The several invitations which Bouttier extended to Mr. Gilcrease in which he urged him to visit in Spain and to bring his daughter, Des Cygne, may have been a premeditated pattern of a "matchmaker." His dissertations about his two sons, their accomplishments and their education, coupled with the obvious overtones of their attractiveness, certainly lend credulous speculation to the thought.

The next communication from Mr. Gilcrease to Bouttier told of plans to visit Madrid in 1948. Mr. Gilcrease did not desire to disturb the school year of his daughter and advised Bouttier that she would not be out of high school until the end of the year 1947. He stated that he was completing the building of the foundation before the Christmas season and that the opening would be between Christmas and springtime. He hoped that Bouttier could be present for the occasion. He then mentioned that Chief Standing Bear, a Sioux chief from South Dakota, was visiting with him and that he expected a great number of Indians in Tulsa when the art gallery and library were opened.

In January, Bouttier wrote again and inquired about the success of the opening of the Gilcrease Foundation Museum. He said:

> Tom, you must have taken a lot of pictures, maybe a moving one, in plain colour with Mr. Chief Henry in first class gala dress. Surely something really interesting. Please if you have some, send me pictures. I'd like to see the building. Is it not built on the spot where you lived otherwise? [He continued, after in-

cluding more references to his personal affairs.] I hope you well received my wishes, dear Tom, and 1948 must be the year of our next meeting. What do you think about? Good help, good temper, plenty oil, good success for your Foundation and write me soon.

Tom Gilcrease kept his promise and managed a visit with Bouttier in Spain in 1950. There is very little which research reveals concerning this jaunt into the land of the Spaniards. Tom's knowledge of the Spanish language and his ability to speak the tongue gave him a delightful insight into the country. His appreciation for the mystics, poets, dreamers, and painters should have afforded him and his friend Numa an abundance of subjects to discuss during the sojourn as they walked about the countryside or strolled the ancient avenues where history was always being manufactured. Surely they must have read the ancient parable: "When God created Spain He allowed the Spaniards three wishes. They chose to have the most varied climate in the world, the most beautiful women and the most delicious foods, fruits and wines. God agreed. But after a while they returned and demanded a fourth wish: to have good government." The story is then told that God responded, saying: "That is too much to ask."

Perhaps it was too much to ask. And it is too much, for neither Tom nor Numa left any written impression of the Spanish government. It is probable that they did justice to the foods, fruits, and wines. In later years it is well-known that the Oklahoman was an abstainer, but his quest for culture may have qualified him as a connoisseur of the rare vintage now and then. Whether or not the Spanish señoritas left lasting or temporary mental pictures will always be a good subject for debate, but little would be proved by the speculation.

The Bouttier-Gilcrease episode, as it is applied to the life of Thomas Gilcrease, was like finding a piece of a jigsaw puzzle and laboring to locate the space from which it came. Perhaps this has been accomplished by deciphering the Bouttier notes and the subsequent study of their respective letters. That their friendship ripened into a mutual admiration pact is understandable and was inevitable. That their experiences sparked the interests of Mr. Gilcrease in culture and art cannot be refuted on the record. In later years, Mr. Gilcrease offered his friend Numa a position with the Gilcrease companies if he would consider moving from Portugal, where he then resided. Bouttier declined and discussions ended. Bouttier had returned to Spain and, on May 25, 1964, he departed this life: whether he found the "rebirth" he often mentioned as a believer in metempsychosis must be a challenge to the imagination of man. Mr. Gilcrease had already arrived at the gates when Bouttier died and, who knows, he may have met his friend, the Frenchman, and said:

> I had my choice and I'd rather be a man than a dinosaur, Numa; and I don't like the feathers you selected when you became a bird.

Chapter 2

They Walked in the Garden

By the year 1921, Robert Lee Humber had already earned his Bachelor of Laws degree from Wake Forest College, a Baptist institution founded in North Carolina in 1883. He had been admitted to practice in his home state, but his days of formal study were just beginning. He became a Rhodes scholar in 1923 and earned a degree designated as Bachelor of Literature from Oxford University in England. He had, in the interim years, served as a tutor in the department of government and economics at Harvard University, where he subsequently received his Master of Arts.[1]

Dr. Humber found his way to Paris, France, where he was well-known as a lawyer and business executive. In 1940 he founded at Davis Island, North Carolina, the movement for World Federation which was to bring him international recognition. As his stature grew, the well-earned plaudits were heaped upon him, and in 1948 the American War

Dads Prize was awarded to him for the greatest single contribution to world peace.

After being elected to the North Carolina State Senate, his intense love for the world of art captured most of his attention. The greatest triumph came when the Salmagundi Club of New York City honored him in recognition of his enduring service in the field of art on a national level. His *curricula vitae* is of such magnitude and so diversified that it is little wonder that his name is included in *Who's Who in America.*

> We can never have world peace if we have to destroy nations in order to punish individuals. It is a crime against the humanity and intelligence of man to be summoned to wipe out the entire population of nations as well as their historic monuments that have taken a thousand years to build, because they have momentarily been made the victims of their own despots and criminal leaders.

So wrote Robert Lee Humber when he was reviewing the Conference on International Cooperation when it met in Washington, D.C., in 1965.

Thomas Gilcrease was the antithesis of the gentleman from North Carolina. What mystic forces banded together to bring about their meeting in Paris, France, could, with speculation, be their respective sentiments and love for mankind and nature.

That the memorable meeting occurred in France, often categorically called the cultural crossroads of Europe, is phenomenal indeed and yet, upon reflection, that is as it should have been because the memorials of the past ages still captivate the traveler who ventures on French soil. They were destined to share the searchlight because neither could have charted his courses without the other. Tom Gilcrease had touched his fingers to the spigot of the cultural cask but it remained for Dr. Humber to convince him that there was more to the contents than the aroma and tang. The already acquired wealth of the oil man from Oklahoma may have been an impressive element in the virgin days of their friendship, but it did not remain so for very long. Dr. Humber discovered that Tom Gilcrease was an enchanting storyteller and could enthrall his listeners with the legendary experiences and exploits of the territorial days which had been lived with excitement near the close of the ninteenth century. Recalling the era of their introduction and the days which followed, Dr. Humber says:

> Tom Gilcrease could recount in his inimitable manner the blistering snow storms of the winter season, arriving sometimes even before his parents had been able to clad their barefooted children with shoes to protect them against the rigors of the climate and the severity of the cold. He never forgot the exhilaration experienced by him in shooting his first bird, when his family was away from home. Seeing the feathered creature in a nearby tree, he rushed instinctively to get his father's gun, which he dragged into the yard and, due to his extreme youth, he had to rest the barrel on the railing of the garden fence. Cautiously and deliberately, he took his deadly aim and brought his victim to the ground, but not without being amazed and stunned by the terrific recoil of the gun against his shoulder! Upon the return of his father, there was no parental reprimand but only a sense of pride that his son was learning the basic routine of prairie life and its primitive prerequisites for man's survival.

And so it was that they met — the lawyer from North Carolina who was born in the southern state in Greenville, May 30, 1898, and the oil man from Oklahoma who was born in Louisiana and was eight years his senior. One was destined to work toward world peace and the other was searching for peace of mind. Their paths led them to the realm of art, and each in his own time and way satisfied a burning desire of accomplishment.

During World War One, the American University Union was founded in Paris. The purpose of this organization was to provide facilities for American professors and students to meet and explore their common intellectual interests. When the conflict was over, the work was continued under the sponsorship of the Rockefeller and Carnegie foundations. The program was expanded to embrace the professional and business leaders of France and America who were either sojourning in Europe or who had become residents.

The Union provided the means for study and research in areas of mutual interest and an atmosphere where practical application of their studies could be practiced with congeniality.

Thomas Gilcrease was invited to affiliate when he manifested a desire to acquire a factual appreciation of history; he was motivated by a desire to learn more about the role and significance of history as it pertained to human affairs. He was introduced to Robert Lee Humber, and from that moment their acquaintance became one of mutual intrigue and collaboration. While their approach to each other was one of informality, their salutations remained somewhat formal. Dr. Humber became conscious of the thirst for knowledge evidenced by Mr. Gilcrease and the pangs were so acute that it reminded him of Lord Bacon's youthful motto: "I have taken all learning to be my province." The inquisitive mind and the determination of Mr. Gilcrease to seek out and visit places of historical value, to study epochal crises of the past and to obtain a more comprehensive understanding of their cause and effect was a refreshing stimulus to Dr. Humber. "We spent many evening hours discussing the transcendent aspects of the French Revolution," remarked the erudite Dr. Humber, who was quickly educated to the proposition that Mr. Gilcrease liked the dramatic episodes of history and gave little indication of wanting to suspend the review of what he had captured. Dr. Humber recounted:

> He utterly consumed the history of the Revolution's leaders and fearless men and women of action, such as Desmoulins, who organized the great revolt in the courtyard of the Palais Royal and marched *sans culottes* to the demolition of the Bastille; Mirabeau, who mili-

> tantly defied the King, having sent his messenger with imperative instructions to dissolve the National Assembly, by proclaiming to the royal emissary: "Go tell your master that we are here at the command of the people and that we will not disperse except at the point of the bayonette"; Danton, who immortalized the policy of France, by embodying its spirit in prophetic words: "After bread, education is the first necessity of the people"; Napoleon, the heir of the French Revolution who converted the aspirations of a great people from freedom into a legend of self glory — it was these personalities who left unquenchable embers glowing down the corridors of time and enthralled the mind of Thomas Gilcrease by the very audacity of their leadership and heroic conduct.

Robert Lee Humber married Lucie Berthier on October 16, 1929, and had returned to Paris from his wedding trip when the meeting with the Oklahoma oil man came about. It was January of 1930. Mr. Gilcrease had been in Paris approximately six months where he had taken up a temporary residence with his beautiful Miss America, the first from Oklahoma to be so named. Dr. Humber and his wife were deeply impressed with the devotion of Mr. Gilcrease to his lovely wife and their infant child.

Mr. Gilcrease had been drawn to France by his quest for culture and was at once bewitched by the serenity and charm of the country, and not by the effervescent gaiety which could be found in abundance in Paris. The natural shrines held out a composite welcome where a new kind of social order was within his reach. He yearned to become a studious observer, and the people enchanted him. The sights he saw were the most opulent and magnificent he had yet discovered and the grace of the compact areas excelled anything he had encountered in his former travels. Said Dr. Humber: "He never failed to glow with enthusiasm in describing the splendor of this delectable region of Nature's Kingdom. Whether it was the tempestuous breakers of the Atlantic Ocean at Biarritz, the tranquility of the Riviera at Cannes, the undulating wheat fields of La

Bruce, the radiant friendliness of the Touraine, or the cold sublime grandeur of the Alps at Megeve."

Thirty-two years of intimate friendship may be but an infinitesimal segment of time measured by history, but in one man's life it is a representative experience of inestimable value. Robert Lee Humber and Thomas Gilcrease were so blessed, and from their association longevity, Dr. Humber developed indivertible opinions of Mr. Gilcrease. He has said: "This rare individual was a naturalist, trained from his most tender years in the open spaces of the prairies and in the native haunts of its abundant wild life. He knew intimately the local habitats of animals, the songs of birds echoing through forest glens and the rippling music of mountain streams. He was as familiar with the call of the whippoorwill at dawn as with the plaintive lamentations of the screech owl at eventide. He was a child of the great out-of-doors and carried this authentic credential of his lineage to the journey's end."

Dr. Humber had recognized in Thomas Gilcrease the fondness of nature which was a constant light he kept burning in domestic as well as foreign climes. In all of the aspects of the life of Mr. Gilcrease there was an unbroken link with the direct legacy of his Indian heritage.

Much speculation has been rampant since the establishment of the Thomas Gilcrease Institute of American History and Art concerning the initial interest of its founder in the art world. The conjecture dissolves and factual considerations become apparent when attention is given to the maiden visits to Europe indulged by Mr. Gilcrease several years before he met Dr. Humber. His wealth was the vehicle by which he gained and executed the opportunities of travel. France was not a stranger to him and he found a warmth in the French people which pleased him and gave him a sentimental attachment to their way of life. Several benevolent organizations were the recipients of his charity. In the American Church in Paris, the oldest American church on foreign soil, there is a pew bearing the inscription that it had been endowed by Thomas Gilcrease in memory of his father and mother. Such contacts acquainted him with cultural elements. Art was a part of their lives. Thomas Gilcrease did not imitate or emulate; he was inspired to investigate, and thus he became a novitiate.

The imagination of Mr. Gilcrease was one of his more pronounced assets, and the places which were within his attainment made him a seeker in the absolute sense. With Dr. Humber by his side and well-used books at his disposal, a new kind of hunt occupied the mind of the man who had been famished for history and art. They utilized every spare moment to explore the symbols of ancient tyranny. They sought out the monuments of the battlegrounds, and in due time, everything relating to the historic crusade for human freedom had the assurance of a friendly passport to the mind of Thomas Gilcrease. He had entered the vaults of history and decided to make his life more purposeful by programming a positive future. If, as noted by Edmund Burke, history was a contact between the living and the dead, he was going to make the Indian live again. If he held a secret in his heart, it was a desire to accomplish, to gather, to demonstrate, and to exhibit so that others might look and learn. The simplicity of his pioneer background was actually the springboard for his motivation and for his philosophy of life. He was aware of his potential to a far greater extent than his cohorts, who thought they knew him — and this includes Robert Lee Humber.

"It is not without significance that in naming the Institute, the title of 'history' precedes 'art.' Witness the historical accent of the collection. Willam Penn, negotiating a treaty with the Indians; the portrait of Charles Carroll of Carrolton, the last surviving signer of the Declaration of Independence; the Signing of the Constitution in Independence Hall; the bust of Lafayette; the Lewis and Clark Expedition; the statues of Clay and Webster; Indian Chiefs; earliest sites of well-known government and territorial buildings and American towns and the immutable glory of the Grand Canyon, as only Thomas Moran could paint it," reflects Dr. Humber.

Recounting their years together in Paris, the good doctor observed: "Whenever there was a matter of serious import to be discussed, germane to our association, Mr.

Gilcrease would instinctively remark, 'Let us take a walk in the gardens!' When Thomas Gilcrease took up residence in Paris, he lived in the rue Camoens, and such a comment would mean, at that time, a stroll in the Trocadero Gardens, or later, when he stayed at the Hotel Lutetia, on the left bank, it implied the Gardens of the Luxembourg, or, when he had his abode at the Hotel Majestic, the walk would culminate in the Park of the Bois de Bulogne. The formal creation of Le Notre's great design at Versailles as well as the pristine, unadorned grandeur of the Fontainebleau Forest, with its rendezvous at Barbizon for those who still revere the names in art of the great and the near great, never ceased to fascinate him. Our peregrinations around Paris led us from time to time to visit Versailles, St. Cloud, St. Germain, Malmaison, Chantilly and Rambouillet. Each had its resplendent parks and illustrious history."

The visitations so beautifully described by Dr. Humber contributed in gross measure to the desire of Mr. Gilcrease to explore the beauty of America when he returned home. He never hesitated to go out of his way to visit garden spots of the East and the South, such as Longwood Gardens of Pennsylvania, the Brookgreen Gardens of South Carolina, and Magnolia, Middleton, and Cypress Gardens of Charleston, and the Bellingrath Gardens near Mobile, Alabama. On one occasion he deplaned from a trip to North Carolina for the special purpose of visiting the gardens of Orton Plantation and Airlee at Wilmington. He once remarked, "To leave to posterity a magnificent garden is a legacy unsurpassed." To see the Taj Mahal and roam through its famous gardens was one of his fond desires but the opportunity never arose. He had another burning ambition. He wanted to make a trip around the world with Dr. Humber and indulge in a jaunt of leisure where great centers of art and history could be observed and studied, but like many other dreams he cuddled in his ever active mind, it did not come to fruition. Domestic demands and business interests were the culprits of interference.

The cultural partnership of Gilcrease and Humber did,

however, walk through and visit other gardens. They chartered a plane to Mexico City and visited practically every center of historical interest — browsed through the shops where specimens of handicrafts were in abundance. They studied the Pyramid of Cholula where Mr. Gilcrease evinced a special interest in its adjacent monuments and tombs. Gallup, New Mexico, was on their "must" list where they attended the annual festivals of the Indians, watched the tribal dances and religious rites, examined the work of native artisans so proficient in silver, wood, ceramics, textiles, and figure designs.

Thomas Gilcrease had a deep feeling for the trek man had made across the ages. This sensitive approach might have in good measure accounted for the origin of his now often-quoted expression: "Every man must leave a track and it might as well be a good one." Dr. Humber felt the vibrations of the Gilcrease philosophy with perhaps more certainty than any other person, and it was this keen perception which caused him to comment: "Mr. Gilcrease recognized the man who could create, capture inspiration, and record it on canvas or carve it in stone. Sublime creativity was a part of his being. He liked the kind of art which has as its mission the revelation of the beautiful human experience at flood tide. Sordid realism had no appeal to him in art or in life. He believed that every act of man should be directed to the goal of elevation. Glorification of degradation had, in his mind, no justification. The apex of the pyramid, if it soared, needed a base of virtue and an axis of nobility. He held to the proposition that all human energy should be aimed to improve the human species. Such was his philosophy of art."

The gifted sons and daughters of the human race who had achieved immortality by their accomplishments in the field of art were often the prime subjects for discussion between Gilcrease and Humber in Paris. The museums of Europe were not strangers to either of them and the renowned repositories of art came under definitive study. Mr. Gilcrease, as well as Dr. Humber, dug deeply into the motives and methods of the great collectors and the techniques which they employed to achieve their aims. Whether it was the treasures of the Louvre museum or the Museum of Modern Art, the exchange of thoughts with the learned Dr. Humber, the natural appreciation for the delicate enticements of the masters, will probably never be adequately discovered; but little challenge can be made of the fact that Thomas Gilcrease was determined to let the world see the American Indian in all of his glory, not as a matter of retribution, but as a means of redemption and release from the persecution he felt they had endured at the hands of the white man.

One afternoon in the early part of 1931, Gilcrease and Humber were visiting when, with the suddenness of a well-aimed arrow, Mr. Gilcrease said, "Humber, I want to establish a foundation. I am determined to found a museum, start a library and build a home for orphans." Dr. Humber was astonished but not surprised for he had long sensed that his friend was toying with a thought he had hesitated to express. The suggestion resulted in a request from Mr. Gilcrease that Dr. Humber prepare a charter for the proposed foundation; daily discussions ensued on each important phase of the contemplated entity. The collection of art which the foundation was to encompass was to be universal, especially European. Mr. Gilcrease knew that western culture, which had been transplanted to America, had its origin in Europe and that its inherited art patterns had determined to a high degree its evolution. He reasoned that if the collection was representative of examples of regional development, it would embody a comprehensive survey of western art.

The time was an era of museums. Isabella Steward Gardner had founded her famed museum at Fenway Court in Boston; John G. Johnson had assembled rare masterpieces and enriched the Philadelphia Museum of Art; there was the American Mecca where the great masters of the British Isles could be seen, due to the generosity and tastes of Henry E. Huntington, the founder of the gallery at San Marino, California; there was Joseph Widener, whose flare for priceless art crowned him as one of the three greatest benefactors of the National Gallery of Art in Washington; Samuel H. Kress, who endowed several institutions with treasures and became the modern Atticus of the Roman Empire; Andrew Mellon, the founder of the National Gallery of Art — and many more whose zest for cultural recognition and sincerity enriched the galleries.

Dr. Humber was troubled. Could his friend, Mr. Gilcrease, gain entrance to the gates as others had done? Humber had doubts. The Gilcrease fortune did not place him in the company of barons of finance. *The Mill* of Rembrandt had cost Widener the sum of $500,000; *The Blue Boy* had brought forth $620,000 from the Huntington purse; Mellon had acquired Raphael's *Alba Madonna* for the handsome sum of $1,166,000. The ambitions of Mr. Gilcrease were lofty, and Humber feared that his friend had been carried away by rapturous excitement. He recalled that Mr. Gilcrease had purchased a painting by Ridgeway Knight and one by Thomas Moran, but he felt that the efforts had to be confined to a restricted area where the European subjects would not be a constant temptation to him. He had qualms about the whole proposition and then the idea came to him: Mr. Gilcrease could confine his museum to American art.

To convince Mr. Gilcrease of the wisdom of making a collection of American art was not a simple task. The Oklahoman was still under the influence and spell of the illustrious and influential talents of the master painters. He was somewhat under the spell of the bold innovations of the Paris painters, who for centuries dominated the art history of the majority of countries. The illusion was not a lasting one and Dr. Humber felt that eventually the concept possessed by Mr. Gilcrease would give way to his suggestion. There were many reasons for this projection, none the least of which was the economic consideraton. Dr. Humber reminded his friend that up to that time there was not one museum dedicated to American art. The field was wide open. The conquest of the West had begun to be depicted on canvas and pre-Columbian originals of American art were not to be found in every art market. There had been some very fine paintings of such art sold in Europe where the artists had journeyed to find buyers, and with tender approach they could be acquired and brought back to the United States. Dr. Humber reasoned that it was high time that the vanishing life of the American Indians be relived. The little-known artists who had braved the rugged country where the stakes of the teepee still made landmarks would thereby be encouraged to mix their colors and depict the western skies and the sands of the desert lands. Such paintings, reasoned Dr. Humber, would not be on the market at prices which would present a prohibitive barrier to the collector.

The final decision was that of Thomas Gilcrease. The paths to the eventual establishment of his museum were as narrow or as wide as he wanted them to be. He acquired, he studied, he used his own initiative; and whether there was an entire collection or a single work of art to be had, his philosophy never changed. He did place the word "history" ahead of the word "art" and those who served him, respected his wisdom. He built his museum, and in the well-chosen words of Dr. Humber, "His collection became an ageless monument to its Founder."

Robert Lee Humber once inquired of his friend, Mr. Gilcrease, by what yardstick he measured his personal needs. The response was, "All I need is food, a few clothes, a place to sleep and a car to drive!" Had the interrogation been directed to the challenge he had undertaken to build a museum, he might have answered, "I must not only acquire wealth — I must make it work for me for the betterment of human society."

There was another side to the fraternization of Gilcrease and Humber. The economics of their lives during their residency in Paris was practically as romantic as their escapades into the world of art and museums. Each facet was dependent upon the other. Without finance the acquisitions could not have been accomplished. Without inspiration of purpose there would have been little reason for Thomas Gilcrease to remain in Europe as long as he did or to visit France as frequently.

The conversations were generally informal and occurred at a small sidewalk tearoom, known as the De la Madeleine, facing the church of the same name. The transformation from the potential museum builder to the astute businessman was almost instantaneous for Mr. Gilcrease. His oil interests had made it necessary for him to return to the United States with regularity, and each time there would be further conferences with Dr. Humber. The candor with which the two gentlemen approached their respective problems is summed up in the following statement: "I was profoundly interested in the World Federation, the achievement of world peace through world law, enforceable on individuals, and I knew that Mr. Gilcrease desired ardently to build his own art collection and library. I knew also that he wanted to establish a home for orphans of Indian blood. We were both in need of money and it was only natural that we talked of the oil investments of the company headed by Mr. Gilcrease in the United States."

Mr. Gilcrease related to Dr. Humber the circumstances under which he lost the opportunity to develop Signal Hill near Los Angeles and which subsequently proved to be the richest oil field in the state of California. Day after day, Mr. Gilcrease became more conscious of his confidential status with Dr. Humber and told him of the dry holes and the gushers, of happy days in his early life, and of his domestic problems. Some of these were obvious to Dr. Humber but he never commented about them – he had learned that certain areas of the life of Mr. Gilcrease were gently tucked into a bed of silence, and he respected what was clearly indicated as the proper conduct on these points. The walks in the gardens became more infrequent, and the walls of the American University Union resounded with rumor and sheer gossip about a state in America called Oklahoma where gold flowed from the ground and made people rich. But they could not comprehend much about these geysers of wealth which went deep into Mother Earth.

The brashness of some of the remarks bothered Mr. Gilcrease but he could not stem the tide of events. He was sought out by friends in the Touraine who pestered him about making investments in America. Finally, sensing that there was an opportunity to create additional capital for his company, he agreed to let certain of his French friends become co-owners in oil properties. Equal division contracts were prepared by Dr. Humber in conjunction with the back-home counsel of Mr. Gilcrease. It was stipulated that, as investors, the French citizens would supply capital funds while the company would locate the leases and perform the necessary geological studies and supervise the drilling and field operations, provided that if oil was discovered, any future development of the leases would be shared equally by both parties. The office overhead would be borne by the company and this was made clear to the investors.

To indulge the terminology of the petroleum industry — Mr. Gilcrease and Dr. Humber had gone onto the location and started the drill stem — straight down into the bowels of the earth. The East Texas oil field was discovered. This was 1931, and Dr. Humber officially became the attorney for the Gilcrease Oil Company in Paris. Recalling these fast moving events, Dr. Humber has said: "The new oil field was reputed to possess ten percent of all known oil reserves of the entire globe at that time. Under normal conditions, the major oil companies would have absorbed practically all of the offerings of leases in this area, but the fact that the depression was exerting a potent restraint upon corporate investments permitted small companies and individuals to share in the acquisition of its oil reserves."

The garden walks and the sidewalk tearoom conferences began to wane. The jargon of the oil fields invaded Paris. Oil leases cornered the market and oil paintings remained on the shelves of the art markets in the French metropolis. Dr. Humber's dynamic personality gained momentum, and the assets of the company swelled from the foreign investments. Financial participation was invited from a number of European companies, such as the Comité des Forges, the Raffinerie de la Gironde, the Banque de Paris at des Pays Bas, Banque Mirabeau, as well as Belgian and Swedish firms — all without success.

In February of 1933, the Gilcrease Oil Company determined that the hour had arrived for the organization of a

French subsidiary, the Societé Petroliére Gilcrease. Dr. Humber applied his legal talents to the utmost. The new company opened an office at 44 Avenue des Champs Elysées with Dr. Robert Lee Humber as the Administrateur Délégué. Mr. Edouard Otlet, a Frenchman and colleague of Dr. Humber and an outstanding businessman, was employed and associated with the enterprise. Georges Heilbroner of the prominent banking family of Lazard Fréres was appointed to collaborate with the new company. The Societé Petroliére functioned solely as an investment house; the clientele was of the highest selectivity and there was little opportunity for questionable applicants to participate. Those who were fortunate enough to be selected became copartners in the ownership of the properties.

The ethics of the French company were quickly recognized and the reputation of those associated with it was impeccable. Where there had been restraint in the formative days, the zeal of established concerns and individuals became rather spirited in their desire to invest. Important business houses in Europe suddenly realized that oil meant money. Citizens from other countries, such as Belgium, Holland, Switzerland and England, joined in the venture. The get-rich-quick fever had struck. Caution was exercised in blocking acreage where the highest potential existed. Commenting upon this, Dr. Humber says: "Engineering reports as to porosity, saturation and recoverable oil from the leases were critically examined and reserves with special concern to the longevity of production were explored. The cost of operation and the ultimate net profits to be derived from the investment finalized the studies. The investments paid off and returns were lucrative and beneficial to all parties."

It may be noted that all of the investors have long since been reimbursed for their original remittances, and wells are still producing in the East Texas oil fields which provide handsome returns for those who had faith in Thomas Gilcrease, Dr. Robert Lee Humber, and the officials of the Societé Petroliére Gilcrease and the Gilcrease Oil Company.

In the spring of 1937, the offices of the Gilcrease Oil Company were moved to San Antonio, Texas and established in the Milam Building. The directors had elected Dr. Humber to the office of vice-president of the corporation without his knowledge, but when he was so informed he expressed his gratitude — declined and chose to remain as the head of Societé Petroliére Gilcrease. Seven years had passed since Dr. Humber moved to Paris — he had gathered enduring friends and business associates. Then it happened. On June 13, 1940, like a tornado determined to destroy a people, the Germans entered Paris!

The tragedy of war had befallen a peaceful people. What ensued in the hours of terrorism that followed have been recounted by Dr. Humber in the following enduring and indelible words: "I had evacuated the City three days before — on Monday evening at ten o'clock, along with an estimated two million other people on the public highways, to start my five hundred mile trek, requiring four days, to join my family at Hendaye-Plage on the French-Spanish frontier, where they remained in September after the declaration of war. My relations with the French government, both personal and professional, had always been cordial and wholly satisfactory, but I did not want to remain in the country as the guest of the Swastika! After traversing Spain to Lisbon, my family and I returned to America in July of 1940, on the Steamship *Manhattan,* which had been sent expressly by the State Department of our government to bring the last of the European contingent of Americans home."

The walks in the gardens of Paris had ended for Gilcrease and Humber, but not in the gardens of America. Upon his arrival in America, Dr. Humber was invited to become president of the Gilcrease Oil Company. "Mr. Gilcrease told me that if I would accept the position he would provide me gratuitously with a substantial stock interest. I declined with profound sentimental feeling and explained that world peace through World Law was uppermost on my agenda. With regret he accepted my declination only after making another effort to which he added a year's leave of absence with pay. He felt that such time would permit me to ascertain the reaction of the American citizens to my cause."

Finances for the museum of Thomas Gilcrease appeared

to be secure. He went about making acquisitions, searching out Americana from every art market in the world and in America; taking talented artists by the hand and assisting them in their education. The self-assignment to which he was now dedicated became stronger by the year — he would establish his collection of American art, he would build his museum, equip its galleries, collect rare books, and found a home for orphans. He would guide one of the finest foundations in the United States.

Thomas Gilcrease was determined, and he made one last effort to convince Dr. Humber that he should be a part of his oil company and other interests. They walked, they talked, and they discussed the subject over and over. Neither would yield — Mr. Gilcrease then decided to cast aside his corporate responsibilities and devote his future years to the fulfillment of his dreams. His first acquisitions were placed on exhibit in the Gilcrease Museum in San Antonio.

When Robert Lee Humber ponders the myriad years, his memories catch once again the exciting hours when his friend, Thomas Gilcrease, acquired the now famous collection of Dr. Philip Cole — with its rare group of Remington paintings and bronzes; the William Cary Collection, composed of several paintings, and how the total was purchased so that the desired few would be in the galleries. He recalls the personal contacts with the late Howard Chandler Christy, and his comments that when he painted the portrait of Mr. Gilcrease he had deliberately tried to emphasize the spiritual qualities of the man; his kindness, humility, and unselfishness, rather than his physical features, adding that he saw in Mr. Gilcrease a personality that future generations would recognize to be possessed of rare nobility of character, and a deep sense of dedication to an exalted mission. A touching incident recited by Dr. Humber relates to his friend with whom he walked in the gardens. He says: "It was Friday afternoon in the New York studio of Mr. Christy, following his recovery from an illness of several weeks, when he, Mrs. Christy, Mrs. Humber, and I were visiting and leisurely discussing with him the events reminiscent of his colorful career. Mr. Christy began to allude to the ambitions of Mr. Gilcrease to create a museum of unique and outstanding

Americana and added, 'Let's send Tom a telegram, signed by the four of us, to tell him that we are visiting together and thinking of him!' It was his last telegram."

He also recalls that on one of his trips to Paris, he verified for Mr. Gilcrease the provenance of his bust of Lafayette by conferring with those who had acquired it from a chateau, where it had reposed since the eighteenth century. He was able to obtain a notable example of a "Book of Hours," from one of the French clients, commemorating the marriage of the Head of the Order of Malta in the nineteenth century, and attesting the fact that this exquisite form of medieval art had not perished in modern times.

Then there was the time when he mentioned to Mr. Gilcrease the historical importance of a small volume of geography bearing the title *Cosmographiae Introductio,* by Martin Waldseemüller, published in France at St. Dié on April 25, 1507, and in which the author, referring to the recent discovery of the New World, made the prophetic comment on the reverse side of the fifteenth page ". . . but now that these parts have been discovered by Americus Vespucius (so will be seen in the sequel) I do not see why we should refuse to name it America, namely the land of Amerigen or America, after its discoverer, Americus, a man of sagacious mind, since both Europe and Asia took their names from women."

There is one unhappy recollection which is housed in the retentive mind of Dr. Humber. He was disturbed to the point of exasperation that the news coverage of the opening of the Gilcrease Museum as a private collection for public consumption did not do justice to the efforts of its founder. He protested and was responsible for a rectification of the omission in a subsequent issue of the press.

Dr. Humber speaks with the pride of a brother when he talks of his friend, Thomas Gilcrease, and says: "The Museum which he created, is not a collection of paintings which he acquired one by one, but it is composed of a series of collections, which the owners in some instances had spent years of their lives in assembling. It is for that reason that no museum will ever likely possess the Americana which is housed in the stone building on the Hill." And then he added, "I must liken Thomas Gilcrease to the motto of Marshal Foch, the great French general – 'Action . . . . And tenacity always' – these are the magic words which reveal the secret of the success of this unusual human being from Oklahoma."

It was April of 1956, when Thomas Gilcrease journeyed to Raleigh, North Carolina to be present at the opening of the North Carolina Museum of Art – the culmination of thirteen years of effort by Dr. Humber. It was a crowning ceremony for another great human who knew the meaning of the word action and who possessed tenacity. The physical presence of Thomas Gilcrease afforded Dr. Humber moments of satisfaction he will not again know in his career.

In January of 1962, Dr. Humber telephoned Mr. Gilcrease to tell him that he was coming to Tulsa for a visit too long neglected. When they met, there was a firm handshake and the usual arm-around-the-shoulder embrace. They walked in silence along the shrubbery paths – the trees and the flower beds appeared to whisper to each other that the men from Paris were together again. The eyes of Gilcrease and Humber glanced upon the beauty of the distant hills which remain unspoiled. So very much had taken place. The city of Tulsa owned the collection and preservation seemed assured. The inevitable need for expansion became a subject of discussion. There were a million things about which they might have conversed, but the founder who saw his dreams turn into reality was tired. Dr. Humber wanted Mr. Gilcrease to meet him once again in North Carolina and asked when such a trip would be possible. He told his friend that the dogwood trees would be in full bloom and could be seen from the mountains to the coastal plains. The month of May was considered. Dr. Humber returned home. The dogwoods bloomed earlier than usual in the spring and he telephoned Mr. Gilcrease to suggest that he advance his departure for the southern trip. Mr. Gilcrease said, "I am in the throes of planting some trees I ordered and as soon as I finish I'll be there." It was Friday evening.

Sunday morning Dr. Humber answered his telephone. A

voice said, "He is gone!" A few hours before the call, the invincible warrior had gone to join other chiefs, still reaching out for the ageless quest of human betterment. And in the touching words of Dr. Robert Lee Humber, "He will search amid the happy hunting grounds of Elysian splendor." And so it was — the garden gates were closed.

Chapter 3

The Hill and the Valley

Part I

Miss America Becomes Mrs. Gilcrease

Four years had passed since Thomas Gilcrease and Belle Gilcrease had been divorced. The wealthy but unhappy Mr. Gilcrease sought after and found some consolation in a new role he was playing. His social life had undergone a sudden change and he was neither adept nor capable of meeting the onslaught which greeted him. The gossip spread rapidly that he was a divorced man and fortified. His fortress was, however, subject to attack when on occasion he failed to heed his legal counsel and left the key to his emotions unguarded.

There are elements of speculation regarding several entanglements in which he became enmeshed. If the rumors bore truth, the results were always shrouded in impregnable armor. If Tom Gilcrease had been questioned about his escapades he would probably have answered by quoting Rudyard Kipling's "The Mary Gloster":[1]

> An' a man 'e must go with a woman, as you could not understand; but I never talked 'em secrets. I paid 'em out o' hand. Thank Gawd, I can pay for my fancies!

He continued with his oil speculations and his other business interests, but in the depth of his soul he knew he was not a free man. He would never be. The obligations of his first experience with matrimony had to be met and he was determined to educate his sons and provide for his former wife. There was hardly a day when his wastebasket was not filled with dozens of requests for financial assistance. With every new oil well, he discovered that the organized and the impromptu solicitors were determined to exploit his purse.

Mrs. Alf Heggem, former wife of W. O. Ligon, Sr., was prominent on Tulsa's society register. She was particularly well-versed in the art of sponsoring "coming out parties" and the introduction of the eligible elite to the most promising bachelors of the community. Mrs. Heggem had met Thomas Gilcrease when she and her former husband had at one time occupied the Gilcrease home on the hill. When Norma Des Cygne Smallwood became Miss America of 1926, Mrs. Heggem watched for an opportunity to honor her with a house party and to invite her friend Tom. The opportunity did not come until 1927. The reception was a "Heggem success" in the full meaning of the term. The introduction was very informal but from that moment Thomas Gilcrease was captivated. The beauty and charm of the honoree left him in a state of emotional shock. Mrs. Heggem had placed another social gem in her tiara of sophisticated accomplishments.

Mahala Angela Smallwood and Edward Smallwood married when Mahala was only sixteen. They lived in Bristow, Oklahoma. At the age of nineteen, Mahala was left alone with two children, Lucille and Norma. To support her family Mahala became a cosmetician and gave facial treatments. She later married W. A. Dickerson and then divorced him. She continued with her cosmetic business and then engaged in selling oil and gas royalties throughout the mid-continent field. She was determined that her children would be educated to the best of her ability.[2]

Norma Des Cygne was born on the twelfth day of May, 1909. She was a beautiful baby and at the age of one was declared the winner of a beauty contest of the local infants. As she matured she attracted the attention of everyone who saw her. She attended grade school in Nevada, Missouri, and then her mother moved to Sherman, Texas, where Norma Des Cygne matriculated in the high school division of Kid Key College. Following the Texas schooling, she enrolled at the Oklahoma College for Women at Chickasha, Oklahoma, but did not graduate.

In August, 1926, while she was a sophomore at Chickasha, she entered a contest sponsored by the *Tulsa Tribune* and was chosen "Miss Tulsa." This honor qualified her to represent the Oil Capital in the Atlantic City beauty pageant. In the meantime her mother had established a residence at the Springer Apartments at Sixth and Cincinnati streets in Tulsa. Elaborate preparations were made and, in company with her mother, Mrs. W. A. Dickerson (Mahala Angela had remarried), and her chaperone, Miss Celestia Harrington of the *Tribune* staff, they went to Atlantic City.

Norma had reached her eighteenth birthday. She had a well-rounded body and a delightfully serious face which was graced by long, straight hair which she did up in big buns over her ears. She was buxom and boasted measurements of 33-24-36. Her height was five feet six inches and she weighed 119 pounds. Her oval face was said to be "classically Greek." The judges loved her and the audience gave her a warm reception. She won the bathing suit and evening dress competition, and then by a vote of thirteen to two she was crowned "Miss America of 1926" in the pageant which was built around a King Neptune's Kingdom theme. She had successfully defeated entrants from all over the United States and had become the first Miss America from Oklahoma.

The coveted title won her a number of valuable prizes in money, but the most rewarding compensation was the travel which was provided by the sponsors of the contest. She refused offers from the motion picture industry, but product endorsements yielded her handsome sums.

There was little doubt that she was the most beautiful girl in the United States, and the recognition was fraught with many temptations which had to be overcome by sound parental judgment and her own desire to preserve the title with ethical and moral conduct. The year 1926 was before the advent of television, and radio had hardly made a dent in the air waves. If she had been a candidate of this generation, she would have heard the golden voice of Bert Parks singing "Here She Is, Miss America" and millions of Americans would have fallen in love with her, too.

She had captured the admiration of the citizens of Oklahoma, and was photographed by talent scouts and advertising agencies, and practically every nationally known photographer made an effort to preserve her Grecian features on film. The reporters of the nation typed her as having a Mona Lisa appearance.

Following her achievement in Atlantic City, the victorious Norma and her court of beauties were feted in connection with the Philadelphia Sesquicentennial Exposition and they rode in a triumphant automobile parade to the exposition grounds. On September 30, 1926, Governor M. E. Trapp of Oklahoma, Mayor Herman Newblock of Tulsa, representatives of twenty-seven civic clubs, and the city and county commissioners greeted her as she arrived at the Frisco depot in Tulsa, where 25,000 Tulsans joined in the welcome. Her mother was serving as her manager, and with Armond T. Nicholds, director of the pageant, the reception was the event of the year. The late George L.

Watkins, later mayor of Tulsa, was the chairman in charge of arrangements for the homecoming. On October 1, 1926, she was honored at a banquet at the Hotel Tulsa. The late Charles O'Connor, representative from Oklahoma who served in the 71st Congress; Fred Insull, who was president of Public Service Company; and Colonel Patrick J. Hurley participated in the program. As the months of her reign wore on she became the ambassador without portfolio to the Sooner State, and she joined the Keith-Orpheum vaudeville circuit where her name was flashed in lights across the nation.*

From the outset of their introduction it became obvious that Tom Gilcrease was going to do everything possible to discourage Norma from reaping the benefits of her sudden fame. The *possessive nature* of her suitor was camouflaged by his outward demonstrations of generosity and flattering courtship. Norma was naive and blinded by the anticipation of Tom's fulfillment of his promises.

In company with Norma's mother he took her to Paris, France. Later, his two sons, Tom, Jr., and Barton, joined them, and there was hardly a worthwhile spot in Europe that failed to capture some of the Gilcrease fortune. Tom was not only going to impress his wife-to-be, but he was going to make her appreciate every hour that they spent as they "made the town" in each important city. Norma was young and she was ambitious. She had beauty and she had charm. She could acquire culture, and if there was one

---

* Her last personal appearance in Tulsa was in 1964, when she graciously attended the opening of the Miss Oklahoma Pageant at Tulsa's Civil Assembly Center as a special guest by reason of her distinction as Miss America, an honor which had not come to any other Oklahoman until Jayne Jayroe of Laverne, a student of Oklahoma City University, captured the crown at Atlantic City on September 11, 1966. Norma Des Cygne Smallwood Bruce died on May 8, 1966. She thus ended her career as a devoted wife and mother at the age of 57; she was buried in the Old Mission Cemetery in Wichita, Kansas. The Oklahoma newspapers carried the announcement of her passing, and one Oklahoma paper mentioned that during her life she had figured in a divorce action brought by her first husband, the late Tulsa philanthropist, Thomas Gilcrease. The Miss Oklahoma Pageant Corporation and the Pepsi-Cola bottlers of Oklahoma immediately made plans to establish the "Norma Smallwood Memorial Scholarship Trophy" in her honor.

thing Tom wanted more than anything else, it was a wife who not only possessed culture, but one who could be presented to his local and foreign associates with pride and dignity.

Keeping in mind the youth of Norma and the wealth he had accumulated, Tom discussed his contemplated marriage with his attorneys. An antenuptial contract was prepared and signed on July 7, 1928, which provided that Norma Des Cygne Smallwood was to own, possess, keep, and control all property, both real and personal, which she owned, and Thomas Gilcrease was not to have or claim or receive any interest in such property during the period of the marriage, or after, and he was not to inherit any of her property.

The contract also provided that Tom was to pay Norma, in cash, the sum of $1,000 at the time of the marriage and the further sum of $5,000 per year and a proportionate part of said sum for any fractional year during which they remained husband and wife. In case of divorce, the sum of money agreed upon above was to be payable on the date of the divorce and thereby be a full and complete and final settlement of her property rights, without regard to the one who was at fault or to whom the divorce was granted. There were other provisions in the event of death, and Norma was not to have any claim or receive any interest in the Gilcrease Oil Company, a corporation, or in any of its property or assets by reason of having been married to Tom. In consideration of all of these terms, the bride and groom agreed to marry. There were other refinements to the contact but, basically, it was an agreement to protect each other in the event their marriage was judicially terminated.

Before the contract was signed Tom presented Norma with a valuable diamond of about four and one-half carats, which he had purchased in Cuba – he had paid $7,000 for the stone and the mounting. He told Norma she could wear it as long as she remained his wife.

The period of betrothal had reached the boiling point and it was time for Norma Smallwood to become Norma Des Cygne Gilcrease, wife of the Tulsa oil magnate. September 3, 1928, was selected as the date they would be married. Tom did not belong to any church, although he had at one time been a deacon in the First Christian Church of Tulsa. He did not want a "fancy" wedding and, since they were anxious to leave on their honeymoon, he decided to ask a Tulsa jurist to conduct the ceremony.

S. Morton Rutherford, Jr. was one of the four judges of the Court of Common Pleas of Tulsa County, State of Oklahoma. He was known as a rather stern judge but was respected by all who had legal matters in his court.

It was shortly after eight o'clock in the evening when his residence telephone rang and a voice said: "Judge Rutherford, this is Tom Gilcrease. I want you to marry me. I knew your father when I was a student at Bacone College in Muskogee, and I decided that you could do the job about as well as any preacher."

Judge Rutherford was stunned by this rather frank approach but he had heard of such things and he guarded his reply and endeavored to speak with his usual dignity. He said: "Well, now, Mr. Gilcrease, you see, that is, I should tell you that I have just returned from a hard day in court and it would be my suggestion that you get in touch with a justice of the peace who does these things. . . ." He did not get to complete his remarks when Tom interrupted him.

"Now that is mighty nice of you and we will be right out. Just give me the address and don't bother to get dressed up or anything like that."

The ruffled judge hung up the telephone, turned to his wife and said, "That was some fellow who said he knew my father and he wants me to marry him."

Mrs. Rutherford replied, "You can do what you wish, I am going to retire to my room."

The judge, who was always natty in appearance, took a minute or two for grooming himself, removed his smoking jacket and replaced it with a business coat. There was a long ring of the bell and he opened the door to be greeted by a man and three women. Tom Gilcrease said, "Glad to know you, Judge. This is my bride, Norma, my bride's mother, Mrs. Mahala Dickerson, and Norma's sister,

Lucille." At that moment Judge Rutherford recognized Norma Smallwood as the winner of the Miss America contest because he had seen her pictures in the local newspapers.

He was nervous but retained his dignified approach and asked, "Have you got the license and the ring?" Tom nodded in the affirmative, and then the judge, turning to Norma's mother and sister said: "You ladies will have to act as witnesses." He then reached into one of the bookcases and took out an Episcopal prayer book which contained the marriage ritual. "Do you, Thomas Gilcrease, take this beautiful girl to be your wife and do you, Norma Des Cygne Smallwood, take this man to be your husband?" Judge Rutherford watched them carefully.

Tom smiled and was hardly audible as he said, "Yes."

Then Norma looked at Tom and nodded "I do."

"Is that all there is to it?" interrupted Mrs. Dickerson.

"No," replied the judge. "By virtue of the authority vested in me as Judge of the Court of Common Pleas of Tulsa County, State of Oklahoma, and before God and these witnesses I pronounce you to be husband and wife."

When the ceremony was over, Judge Rutherford was invited to kiss the bride and he did just that. Tom thanked the judge, and the wedding party retired to their waiting automobile. When they had gone, the judge discovered that at some point in the visit Thomas Gilcrease, the oil man, had placed two twenty dollar gold certificates under a lamp on one of the end tables. He could hardly restrain himself as he called for Mrs. Rutherford and said, "Sweetheart, guess who I just married?"

She replied, "I have no idea; come on to bed!"

"Why, that was Miss America of 1926; you remember the name — Norma Smallwood." The judge's wife never forgave her proud jurist for not calling her into the room as a witness. By a strange concidence, a colleague of Judge Rutherford had married a relatively unknown movie actress the day before the Gilcrease wedding. When he told Judge Rutherford about his experience the next morning, he felt rather important, but his chambers became very quiet when Judge Rutherford remarked, "So what? I married

Miss America to Tom Gilcrease last night." Tom never learned that his wedding was the first such ceremony ever administered by Judge Morton Rutherford.

When the pronouncement of the nuptials was over, Tom and his beautiful bride went to Wyoming where they indulged their honeymoon. Just how adventurous the new bride found the selected site for their holiday after marriage will never be known. The Yellowstone country, famous for its trout fishing, hunting, and frontier flavor, had attracted her sporting husband as early as the year 1918. He loved the Hoback River and it held meaningful memories for him. Jackson Hole was his favorite retreat, and, in his judgment, the grandeur of the pine forests, clean air, and fast-moving streams made it the best place to take a new bride. It provided a setting which was magnificent and it was known for being one of the most isolated resorts in the United States. In later years, Tom Gilcrease had more than one memory of the majestic mountains where he had bagged his share of elk, moose, deer, bear, and romanticism. He was in his thirty-eighth year of a life which had, up to that time, been filled with more experiences than the average man could possibly digest with any semblance of comprehension. Norma, who was eighteen years younger, was completely without apprehension of the future and possessed even less understanding of the contract which she had signed at the time of their marriage, and did not anticipate that the time would ever come when their conjugal rights would be disturbed.

Upon their return from Wyoming, they were greeted by their friends, and as soon as all of the festivals of welcome had subsided, they more or less secluded themselves as the newlyweds in Tom's residence on the hill. They found some common interests but Tom would hardly permit Norma to be out of his reach. He watched every new accomplishment and felt that he was one of the most fortunate men in all the world. He had suddenly become aware of a happiness which he hoped would endure. There were moments of tension because Tom had lived alone and some of his patronage was not in keeping with Norma's social desires. He went about his chores on the hill, his business appointments in and out of the city of Tulsa, and insisted that Norma be by his side whenever and wherever he could prevail upon her to join him.

Des Cygne L'Amour Gilcrease was born to Tom and Norma on June 12, 1929. Tom waited until his wife was able to travel and then he took her to Colorado. Norma's sister, Lucille, went with them, and after they were settled Tom returned to Tulsa. Norma and her sister remained in Colorado with the baby until Norma's mother went there by automobile and returned them to Tulsa. They remained in Tulsa but a short time when Norma's mother, at the request of Tom, drove Norma and Des Cygne L'Amour to New York, where they embarked for Europe on October 2, 1929. They arrived in Paris and a temporary residence was established at the Hotel Baltimore, where they remained for several weeks until they arranged for an elaborate apartment at 10 Avenue de Cameron. The apartment introduced Norma to a luxury she had not before experienced. It was composed of a large living room, a small living room, one large bedroom and three small bedrooms, a reception hall, a dining room, a butler's pantry, and a kitchen. There were three servants, in addition to a French nurse whom Tom insisted upon bringing into the apartment to care for little Des Cygne. It was the custom in France to have a French nurse and Tom was not going to forego tradition. The employment of the French nurse brought about the first major argument between Tom and Norma, since Norma contended that she could not communicate with the nurse about the needs of the infant child. She had up to that time attended her daughter personally and, since the infant was still at the breast, she kept her in bed with her until the weaning period occurred. By February of 1930 the French nurse was discharged. The anxious parents cast about to find a nurse who would satisfy both tradition and Norma's demands. They sought the assistance of an employment agency in Bern, Switzerland, and eventually one Martha Wagner, who spoke some German and understood English slightly, was employed. Des Cygne was eight months old when Nurse Wagner came into the lives of Tom and Norma, and in due time she earned the affectionate title of "Nannie." Nurse Wagner literally took over the management of the child. Tom had already forgotten about the infant stage of children, since his two sons by his former wife, Belle, had matured. As for Norma, it was all a new experience for her.

With the baby cared for by Nurse Wagner, the proud parents decided on a trip to Tours where they visited with some friends, the Ouvards. These were truly exciting days, and every place they stopped to enjoy the sights, whether it was in the countryside or the city, the natives would feast their eyes upon the beauty of Norma Gilcrease. She was conscious of her wardrobe and Tom kept her even more aware of her clothing by insisting that she buy almost every garment she tried on or admired. She soon learned the location of the more expensive shops, and when Tom was away on business, she was not at a loss to go shopping with some of her friends who could speak the language.

Recalling this experience, Norma related: "I started to take French lessons in 1929 and also Spanish, art, English, literature, and history. Mr. Gilcrease could speak French and I studied French on his account. I had separate French and Spanish teachers. Mr. Gilcrease then became interested in Spanish and took lessons. Our nurse, Miss Wagner, did not speak English but she had some understanding of it. She could converse in French and a language which I took for a jargon of German. When we would be absent from our apartment, the nurse would also study English. In December of 1929 I started the study of art, and then Mr. Gilcrease made arrangements for my first lesson and I continued to study under Mlle. Mimia until May of 1930. I studied French one hour and a half, starting at eight o'clock in the morning, then I would have a half hour rest period, and then I would take an hour and a half of Spanish. I would take two hours for lunch, then start the art lessons which lasted two hours with private instruction and consume the afternoon with general lessons. This routine kept pace, with English studies added in the evening, until around the first of June in 1930."

It was not easy for Norma to give up her studies, since she did not want to offend Tom, who had written to her from the States and said, "I would much prefer that you do reading and writing because you need these things in everyday life while painting is not a necessity." This was a strange statement from one who was, in later years, to become a nationally recognized collector of art.

Thomas Gilcrease, Jr. went to Paris in June, 1930, to spend the summer with his father and Norma and, joined by Norma's French teacher, they made an extended trip through the Mediterranean and on into Switzerland, then back to Paris. This trip ended all of the studies for Norma, but she did keep up her practice with the brush and the canvas. They left little Des Cygne with her nurse, their maid, and the butler at their apartment in Paris. In September, Tom went to Cherbourg and took the boat to America. Norma remained behind, and some friends, Mr. and Mrs. Umbret, occupied the apartment with her until Norma's mother arrived for a visit. During her stay, they toured more country and visited in Geneva.

The business interests of Tom Gilcrease made it necessary for him to remain in the United States and, on January 4, 1930, Norma, her mother, Nurse Wagner, and the child Des Cygne sailed for the United States. Apparently by this time there were financial reverses taking place in Tom's business life and he wanted Norma to take the *Europa* back to the States. He had always traveled on the *Europa* and it was a bit more economical, but Norma had already booked passage otherwise and she would not alter her plans. Neither of them were strangers to the *Leviathan* or the *Ile de France*. They crossed the Atlantic with such frequency that they had more than a speaking acquaintance with the captains and the other personnel of the great ships.

On one of the voyages, Norma accepted the hospitality of the ship's captain for cocktails, and when Tom heard about the incident he warned her that she was not to so indulge again.

On a previous occasion, while Norma was en route to Geneva with her mother, their automobile needed repairs and two men had offered assistance. Tom, upon hearing about the incident, voiced his objection to such attention and there was a further reprimand.

Life on the hill was resumed and Norma continued with her busy routine. In November, 1931, Norma felt that she no longer needed the nurse for her daughter, and she arranged to have her return to France. There would always be a sentimental attachment for Nurse Wagner. With his family safely deposited in Tulsa, the travels of Tom Gilcrease increased from month to month. During 1931 he was constantly on the go.

Thomas Gilcrease possessed an inner sphere of personality which he vigilantly guarded and which he exposed to few. He was not really aloof but adopted a protective shield by giving the impression that he was a spiritual isolationist. What he could do with the written word for self-expression was difficult with verbal demonstration. He had been exposed to enough of life's manifestations to realize that he was going to eventually find his way to the divorce court. The few threads which remained were delicately suspended over the conjugal bed.

In January of 1931 he returned to Paris, France, ostensibly leaving the impression that business matters demanded his attention. In reality he was running away with the hope that he could find the real answer to his marital problems and the vanishing security which he could not face. During his absence, his wife had become the victim of lonesomeness which she could not justify or explain to others. Whatever her tendencies were for more freedom of thought were accelerated by her youth and beauty and the brief acclaim to which she had been subjected. In the back of her mind lurked the voice of the man who at the age of thirty-seven had wooed her, won her affections, and insisted that she abandon her career and all the engagements she might have known as the most beautiful girl in America. He had promised her he would love her ardently and affectionately. He had, according to her memory, persistently and consistently refused to aid her in entertaining her friends or his friends because of his unwarranted suspicion and unwarranted jealousy. There had been the time when he voiced his displeasure with such temper that he had forced open the door of her bedroom, which she had locked as a precaution against seeing him. He had at no time during their married life attempted to assist her in any entertainment or in social functions with others. He was dictatorial in his manner and would not consult or advise with her with reference to the management and maintenance of the household. She wanted to harmonize their differences and to live with him as husband and wife, even though he had gradually destroyed the affection which she knew a wife should have for a husband. She had accused him of giving credence and credit to the gossip of the servants employed by him at their home, and his false accusations had injured her health and shattered her nervous system and made her life with him intolerable and unbearable. She had either told or intimated all these things to him before he left for Europe. He longed for her letters which did not arrive, except for two or three short notes. The buildup of his emotions was more than he could endure, and finally he wrote to her. The following letters are filled with platitudes of love and sensual implications—with phrases of gentle passion—and might well have been attributed to an adolescent mind but for the searching questions and philosophical and self-serving approach of the depressed mind which conjured them.

Paris

January 31/31

My love darling:

How are you and our sweet baby. What did your Aunt Nellie say when she saw our darling? I sent a message flying to you today and I hope to receive one from you in the morning. I love you and miss you so much that it hurts very much. How happy I will be to have you in my arms again and to hold our little angel on my knee and hear her say daddy I love you and also say je t'aime. Darling don't you think we should plant a nice garden this year so we will have big, red tomatoes, peas, potatoes and all sorts of fresh, tender vegetables? I know you must enjoy our home and find pleasure in doing so many little things to beautify it for your dear baby and daddy. I was happy when there even though you were so far away because every nook of the house, every tree of the yard, every vista and especially our room spoke to me of your wonderful beauty, your precious tenderness and sublime love. Everything there is truly precious to me and in it all lives my darling wife. There she shall always be loved and worshipped by me as my Heavenly sweetheart, my little pal, kind and true, my angel wife and the noblest mother on earth — the darling mother of our sweet baby. Sweetheart, if you tire of my long letters tuck them away for rainy days or for days when you shall receive none because I shall not be able to write so often. My heart is so full of love for you and baby that it just flows out upon paper and I send it to you as my only satisfaction since you are so far away. Dear little wife there is a stream of tenderest love flowing from my heart to you, as big and constant as the stream flowing from Lake Geneva. I am so anxious to receive letters from you. You have been gone almost a month and I have had but one page and two short messages from you. Do you love me? Are you happy and satisfied? Do you doubt my love for you? Do you know that I love you? Do you have something to be happy for? If so, what is it? Do I please you? If so in what manner? Do I displease you? If so, in what manner? Can I do anything to make you happier? If so what is it? Do you appreciate me? If so in what manner? Do I fill your love dreams? If so in what manner? If not, in what manner do I fail? What can I do to fulfill your every dream? Did Daddy give you a sweet baby? Do you want another? If so when? Do I provide well for you? Can I provide better for you? If so, how and in what manner? What are your desires? Can I help you satisfy them all or in part? What do you require in order to be absolutely happy and satisfied? Wherein is your husband strong and wherein is he weak? Do you admire anything about your husband and what is it? Could you change him for a better one? Would you change him? What would you have him to do to improve himself? Is he worthwhile? If so in what manner?

If he would devote his entire life to doing what you would have him do what would it be? Can you make of him something more worthwhile, more noble and more moved? If so how? Darling answer all of these questions thoughtfully and freely. Poke me in the ribs where and when I need it. Only be fair with me. Do you think my love for you is worth protecting? Do you desire thrills other than what I am able to supply? If so what are they? Do you require artificial stimulants? If so what are they and why? Do you think your life can be sweetened and made nobler through anything which I would not approve or through the doing of anything in secret. If so what is it? Do you think you should protect yourself for me with all your life forever? If so are you happy and satisfied to do it? Does it afford you satisfaction to live as you know I would have you live? Do you think my ideas broad or narrow and in what manner? Do you think me refined or not? If so in what manner? If not in what manner? Am I worthy of your love and tenderness? Are you happy to bestow it upon me? Are you satisfied and happy with what you receive from me in return? How can I become sweeter to you? How can I thrill you more? How can I be more in any way to you? Are you satisfied when I do my best for you? Do you know when I do my best for you?

Do you think I love our baby? Do you think I love our home? Are you happy to be my little wife? If so why? If not why? Have you a great love for me or just a love for me? Can I do something to cause your love for me to grow? Do you want to please me in every way? Does it mean something to you to be my ideal love? To be my ideal love do you think you should progress in knowledge and nobleness? Exactly how do you want me to spend my life? My angel don't miss answering one of these questions because they are all of great importance to me. May I hear from you soon and often because my heart longs for you and my soul is uneasy for you. Worlds of big hugs, tender kisses and all my love. Tom

Just one more full page of sweet love for you, my

wonderful lover, beautiful sweetheart, tender gal and sweet darling wife.

love love
kisses kisses
tenderness tenderness

caresses caresses

love thrills

honeyed

My soul's delight and satisfaction kisses My baby's noble mother

love

My angel wife My dream Wife

always My life's sweet-

est belonging.

love

3 hearts in one – Mama, baby and papa.

Paris (no date)

. . . received in Paris. I would much prefer that you do reading and writing because you need these things in every day life while painting is not a necessity. I hope to receive letters which will bring back my inspiration to write you as I have done since you sailed away from me.

My letters have been the overflow from my mind and heart and should indicate to you that they are for you and also what you mean to me. If you will read them thoughtfully you may see deep into the heart of one who truly loves and glimpse the sublimity of the union of two such loves and become thrilled and inspired through hope of attaining the climax of such success, joy, love and contentment. My eyes crave to look up to you – High up into the blue heavens, my heart rejoices in placing you among the angels of distant state and my soul contents to worship you as the queen of knowledge, honor, beauty, tenderness and sweetness. What boundless love and praise liveth in my heart for you — Shall it be rewarded in your heart? Shall it be reflected through your life? Do my letters find a place in your mind and heart? I am more lonesome this evening than ever. Your letter chilled my heart and it pains for warmth of love, praise, tenderness, and sweetness of a little wife so far away.

Heavens of love and kisses,

Tom

February 4/31

Paris

Dear Darling:

Your first letter came this evening and is as cold as you were slow in writing. I have simply lived to receive your letters believing they would be filled with love, praise, appreciation and sweetness. I love you and keep myself thrilled with beautiful harmonious, tender and sweet thoughts of my little wife. I want to love her with the greatest love possible and be inspired with thoughts of her. I want to think of her as being the most beautiful, tender and sweet thing on earth and also the most thoughtful, reasonable, and appreciative darling of all the world. Won't you grant me reason to love you this way, to think of you, to praise you, to be thrilled and inspired with you? Please don't slight my love for you, because, it is a great, tender, sweet and protective love for you. Grant me reason to dream of you and go on dreaming through the days of my life. Grant your life to blossom continually in my heart. Give to my life that which is necessary to keep the love fire burning and give me cause to ever. . .

The reaction of Norma to the foregoing letters was one of complete indifference. On July 11, 1931, she returned to France at the insistence of her husband, leaving Des Cygne in Tulsa with her family. Tom had been in the United States during the month of March and had left again in May. When Norma met Tom in Paris in July, they stayed at the hotel Lutatia and then traveled to Tours and other points of interest. By August, Norma could no longer bear to be away from her child, and on August 11, 1931, she returned to America, arriving on the sixteenth. In September she was stricken with appendicitis and when Tom was advised of her illness he returned home. By this time it was October. But the traveling was not over. He had become a commuter and a lost soul. It was only a short time until he again went to Paris.

Tom came home from Paris on December 24, 1932, and remained until January when he went back to Paris and was gone for approximately three months. Between December 24 and the time he left for France in January, he went to California and was absent from home for ten days. He made three or four trips to France in 1933. He came back to Tulsa in March, was home in May, left again about the middle of June, and then went back to Paris in August. On many of these trips he wanted Norma to join him, but they were too fast, too hectic, and she elected to remain in Tulsa and do what she wanted to do.

The social life of Norma Gilcrease gradually lessened. There were times when she wished that Tom would remain home for longer periods, especially when it was for some special event like Des Cygne's birthday.

There were days when Norma's mind would revert to the stimulation she knew when she and Tom occupied their apartment in Paris. The elaborate rooms, the reception hall, the butler's pantry, and all the other luxuries she had known there. She contented herself with her art, and her first important portrait was an oil painting of her daughter, who by this time was demanding more and more atttention.

Norma's flare for the artistic extended beyond the realm of portraits and still-life subjects. She would spend considerable time perfecting designs and patterns. Her creative mind led her to paint a floral border on the upper portion of the master bedroom walls in the house on the hill.*

---

* This painted border has weathered the years and remained untouched, at the insistence of Tom, even when the lower portions of the walls were

When Tom would come home from his trips he would spend as much time as possible with his daughter.**He took her for long walks in the woods just as he had done with his sisters when he was a boy in the Indian Territory. The open country to the west of the big stone house was like a picture in a storybook. He loved every inch of the ground and had dreams of someday building it all into a great park which he would give to the City of Tulsa. During one of his extended trips away from home, Norma decided to make a studio out of part of the old building near the house. They equipped it with proper lighting, furnished

---

redecorated in later years. The rich color contrast was selected to blend with an oriental rug which is alleged to have graced the floor of the bedroom and which cost Tom the handsome sum of $20,000. The rug remains the property of the Thomas Gilcrease Foundation and will probably be utilized by Norma's daughter, Des Cygne, in her home in San Antonio, Texas.

** Des Cygne, now Mrs. Corwin Denney, is the mother of three precious children of her own and successfully and happily married and residing in San Antonio, Texas. She grew to womanhood never losing a deep-seated admiration and devotion for her mother and her father.

She made three trips to Europe with her "Daddy" and visited every museum, art gallery, and antique shop which was available wherever they traveled. She recalls that her father sought out the famous and historic buildings in each of the cities where they toured for days and days. She recalls that her father once commissioned a painting of a dog cart for her and presented it to her after World War Two when it was shipped from Paris. She saw many of the paintings which went into the museum collection long before they were sent to Tulsa. She was often with her father when he made trips to New York and she accompanied him and Robert Humber to many places.

In retrospect, Des Cygne recalls that when her father started to collect art with a serious intent he consulted many people to be sure that what he acquired was authentic and had value. He acquired rare books wherever he found them. She knew that her father considered America the freest country on earth and that he never lost sight of the plight of the American Indian. She does not believe that her father was aware of the growth he achieved for himself as compared with the things he sought to win for his fellowmen.

"I am confident that the happy time of my father's life was when he was learning French and Spanish and traveling. I do not know whether my father was a supremely happy man. I feel that his most challenging years were when he decided to secure the museum and by 'secure' I mean to make it a permanent addition to his life," recalls Des Cygne. "I know he was careful in his acquisitions and recall that he revisited the same gallery many many times before purchasing *A Cotton Plantation on the Mississippi* by William Walker."

it, and soon had a retreat where she spent many hours. The trophies had been stored in a trophy room by Tom and represented a collection from his hunting trips, and some were acquired from friends and associates, and Norma made use of all these trophies. The birds were mounted on brackets which had been specially made to accommodate the assemblage of feathered friends and animal heads. There was one large door, flanked by windows of equal size on either side, and two windows on the opposite wall with colorful and tinted curtains. The floor was painted and the walls were partially paneled with pine. In the center was a long low table which was generally covered with cured animal skins, and the center of the table was graced with a vase in which fresh cut flowers were always present. Against one wall was an old upright piano and the rotating bench to match. A velvet-covered divan was next to the piano, and several chairs and lamps made up the other furniture. The decor was truly a creation for studio atmosphere and was conducive to relaxation for the talented artist. The low-hanging ceiling crisscrossed with rafters gave the whole place an appearance of rustic endeavor. The walls were what might aptly be called a taxidermist's dream. Hanging on heavy nails and picture hooks were female moose, spike mule deer, mountain sheep, white tail doves, ravens, muskrats, birds of all kinds, gadwal ducks, bull elk, groundhogs, sparrow hawks, badgers, ruffled grouse, squirrels, armadillos, striped gophers, Canada jays, steer horns, deep sea fish, and many other interesting specimens including the head of an eagle. All of these trophies adorned, or cluttered, the interior of the small studio, depending upon whether one was an art lover or a collector of stuffed animals and birds.

And then the stone walls of the old house on the hill suddenly caved in on the lives of Thomas and Norma Gilcrease. The house was too large because it was too empty too long. The emptiness was evident by the fact that there was a gradual disappearance of affectionate gestures between them. Norma occupied her time with such social life as remained for her. Tom, by nature a quiet and unassuming individual, became even more so, and the only comfort he found was with his charming little daughter as he tucked her into her bed, read more stories to her, or told her about what it was like to be happy. The master bedroom was devoid of its master. The oil business became keen competition to the domestic tranquility. Tom became the haunted and not the hunted. Efforts were made to change the ever-changing, but it was all without reward. The inevitable struck the house on the hill just as a tornado gathers from dark overhanging clouds. There was not a cellar to which they might run for shelter. The words of William Shakespeare, which Tom knew well –

> Crabbed age and youth, cannot live together;
> Youth is full of pleasance, age is full of care;
> Youth like summer morn, age like winter weather. . . .*

became more apparent. Friends who meant well became friends who would have been better friends had they remained away. Business associates grew fewer, money became more important than it had ever been in their respective lives and at a time when there was less of it about which to be concerned. Tom no longer encouraged the diminishing wardrobe of his beautiful mate.

When the sun had gone down and blended with the hills of the Creek, the Osage, and the Cherokee nations – another courtship had faded and been made legendary by the uncontrolled hands of man and woman. It had been another safari for an experienced hunter who found the dove of love, but could not keep it.

And then it happened. Reconciliation was impossible.

---

* From Shakespeare's poem, "The Passionate Pilgrim," verse 12.

Part II

The Divorce

On October 9, 1933, Thomas Gilcrease filed a divorce action against Norma Des Cygne Gilcrease and joined as a party defendant his mother-in-law Mahala Dickerson.[3]

Mr. Gilcrease alleged that he was a bona fide resident of Osage County, Oklahoma, and that his residence and homestead was located at Ozark and Osage streets in Osage County, about two miles from the city of Tulsa; that he had married his wife Norma on the third day of September, 1928 and that there had been born of said marriage one daughter, Des Cygne L'Amour Gilcrease, who was four years and three months of age when the case was filed.

Mr. Gilcrease alleged that for a period of two years following their marriage, he and Norma had enjoyed a happy and a harmonious domestic life, but that his mother-in-law, Mahala Dickerson, had moved into their home and alienated the affections of both Norma and his minor child; that Norma had abandoned him, refusing to live with him, had locked him out of her room, refused to eat meals with him and was influencing the minor child to dislike him.

The petition was unusually long and contained allegations by Mr. Gilcrease that he had found it necessary for business reasons to frequently be absent from home, during which time he made trips to New York and Europe on business, and that during his absence Norma and her mother had entertained frequently in their home, and that upon returning from various trips he found evidence which confirmed his suspicions. He alleged that Mahala Dickerson had established a beauty parlor in his home and that, with Norma, she had converted a garage apartment into a studio which was actually located in a barn on the premises about one hundred yards from the house and which contained certain furniture, fixtures, and a refrigerator that had been carried to the barn from his home. Mr. Gilcrease further alleged that his wife was dominated by her mother, that she did not love him, that she wanted a divorce, that she was making enormous and unreasonable demands upon him for money and property settlements, and that she wanted her freedom.

By contrast, the petitioner, Mr. Gilcrease, alleged that he was a temperate man, that he did not drink or smoke or use profane language, and that his ambition during his marriage to Norma had been to live a harmonious life, to properly educate and train their daughter, Des Cygne L'Amour Gilcrease, and to give her the best education and cultural life available. He specifically stated that he was being deprived of this ambition by the actions of his wife and his mother-in-law. He alleged that he was free from blame in connection with the discord that existed in his home; and that he had treated his wife with utmost consideration; and but for the overweening influence of Mahala Dickerson with reference to Norma, that the harmony he had enjoyed would still have prevailed in his home. He contended that his mother-in-law had no right, morally or legally, in his home, but had defiantly refused to leave when ordered to do so, and he requested that the court issue a restraining order keeping Mahala Dickerson from trespassing upon his property and from interfering with his home life.

The petition which Mr. Gilcrease filed then made reference to the pre-nuptial contract which he had entered into with Norma prior to their marriage, and which provided for a stipulated sum of money to be paid and that he would incorporate in his last will and testament that as long as she remained single, he would adequately care for her financial needs. He alleged that from the beginning of his marriage to Norma, he had turned over to her large sums of money to be spent on the household and her personal comfort and enjoyment, but that for two years before filing the divorce action he was in financial distress, greatly involved, and at great sacrifice to himself he had provided

Norma with all the personal money he could acquire and that he had either directly or through money which he had given to her, bought her jewelry and diamonds of the value of approximately $15,000. There were other allegations of unjustifiable expenditures and unwarranted extravagance, coupled with further statements that he had great love for his wife and child, and that if he could be freed from the influence of his mother-in-law, he and his wife could live their home lives in harmony; but by reason of all which had transpired, he had arrived at the deliberate conclusion that the attitude of Norma as detailed in the petition, and in many other respects, amounted to extreme cruelty and gross neglect of duty toward him and that he was entitled to a decree of divorce, but added that pending the litigation he would be content for their minor child to remain in their joint custody.

It should also be noted that the petition prayed that the pre-nuptial contract entered into between Mr. Gilcrease and Norma should be considered as a complete and final settlement of all their property rights.

On the ninth day of November, 1933, Mr. Gilcrease, through his counsel, filed an amended petition in the same case, whereby he added more allegations claiming that he had discovered new evidence, and again seeking to remove his mother-in-law from the premises, which he hoped would result in his wife becoming a *cultured* woman, and alleging that the defendants were determined to overthrow the domestic relations and happiness which had existed in his home. He detailed purchases of clothing and jewelry which he thought to be excessive, and made numerous other accusations contending that certain property had been removed from his home and placed in storage.

After the amended petition was filed, his wife Norma, through her counsel, filed certain legal pleadings seeking to strike portions of the petition filed by her husband, as being redundant, irrelevant, argumentative, and as not constituting a right of action or cause of action in favor of Mr. Gilcrease.

On January 4, 1934, Norma Des Cygne filed her separate answer to the petitions placed on record by her husband, in which she denied each and every allegation made, except that she of course admitted the residence, the marriage, and the birth of their minor child. She defended the actions of her mother in moving into their home and denied that Mr. Gilcrease had frequently admonished her mother to leave the premises. She specifically denied the allegations which indicated that their home was being used for excessive social life. She admitted that she had established a studio on the premises but denied that same was used either by her or her mother for social activities, and said that the studio was provided so that she might pursue her studies in art, and that all of this had been done with the sanction and approval of her husband. She denied that she had frequently told Thomas Gilcrease that she did not love him or that she had made unreasonable demands upon him for money. She did allege, however, that in the month of August, 1933, her husband had made veiled accusations against her and that he persistently criticized her and her actions with respect to her friends and otherwise made remarks which reflected against her; that the insinuations became so intolerable that she did tell him she would refuse to live with him. She defended her actions toward their minor daughter and stated that the child was not being deprived of proper education. She denied that Mr. Gilcrease was free from blame in connection with the differences that existed in the home. She admitted the execution of the prenuptial contract but contended that same had been presented to her without advice of counsel or of friends and without her understanding or knowing the nature of the contract. She concluded her rather lengthy answer by denying that Mr. Gilcrease still loved her, and added that he had made no effort to hold her affections and that her mother, Mahala Dickerson, had nothing whatever to do with the feelings of Mr. Gilcrease toward her, and that he was constant in his criticism of her and in making unwarranted insinuations upon her association with her friends whom she entertained in her home. She denied that she was guilty of any of the acts alleged by her husband and then prayed, by way of a cross-petition, that she be granted a divorce from Mr. Gilcrease, that she be awarded the custody of their child, that the antenuptial contract be set aside and that she be given an equitable and just distribution of the property, funds, and money as the court would deem to be equitable and just.

The trial of the case was started on April 17, 1934, and lasted through the second day of May, 1934. The respective counsels were each accorded two hours in which to argue the case to the court. In announcing the decision in the case the court found that Mr. Gilcrease was not entitled to any judgment against the defendant, Mahala Dickerson, and held that Mr. Gilcrease was entitled to a divorce on two grounds, namely, extreme cruelty and gross neglect of duty, and refused to grant Norma Des Cygne Gilcrease a decree of divorce on her cross-petition. The court in announcing this judgment at first awarded alimony to Norma in the sum of $72,000, to be paid at the rate of $200 per month, with the provision that if Norma remarried, all payments after such remarriage would be eliminated and the judgment for alimony fully satisfied; however, the court further found, after making the order, that Norma Des Cygne Gilcrease had made application for the alimony judgment to be withdrawn because of the remarriage contingency, and to the surprise of all concerned the alimony judgment was reduced to $15,000, payable at the rate of $250 per month, with the first payment to be made on the fifteenth day of May, 1934. There were other portions of the judgment devoted to items of personal property.

The decision of the district court was appealed to the Supreme Court of the State of Oklahoma,* and on January 21, 1936, the supreme court affirmed the decision of the lower court and made reference to the fact that the trial had been long and drawn out and the testimony was conflicting. The justice who wrote the opinion for the supreme court commented upon the fact that the trial judge did not make certain findings, but found that the evidence offered by Mr. Gilcrease was sufficient to constitute extreme cruelty and gross neglect of duty on the part of the defendant, Norma Gilcrease. There was then included in the opinion the following pertinent language:

---

* 54 *Pacific Reporter* 2nd Series, 1056.

> Now, then, the main thing to dispose of and the big question in this case, as has been agreed upon by all the parties, is the disposition of this little girl. It is a sad situation that these people cannot live together and take care of her, but that cannot be done. I cannot give, in this case, a divided jurisdiction as is sometimes done, that is I cannot give her six months to one and six months to the other – that cannot be done, because these people are so far apart that they would never be able to get along. There is no doubt in my mind but that the mother in this case loves this child dearly as she could possibly love a child. On the other hand, there is not any doubt but what Mr. Gilcrease has the same affection for the child. It is as I said a sad situation, but she must go with one or the other of them. I do not think there is any question but what if she were placed in the hands of Mr. Gilcrease she would receive just as good treatment as she possibly could. On the other hand, I feel that if she were placed in the hands of Mrs. Gilcrease that she would receive good treatment – good treatment in either place. But it is my judgment that the little girl would be better cared for in the hands of her father than she would be in the hands of her mother.

The Supreme Court of the State of Oklahoma upheld the finding of the lower court with reference to the reduction of the alimony from $72,000 to the sum of $15,000 and a rehearing was denied on March 3, 1936; however, when Norma Des Cygne Gilcrease later married, Thomas Gilcrease once again sought redress through the courts and endeavored to stop the monthly payments due to his former wife.

This case also went to the Supreme Court of Oklahoma, and on December 12, 1939,* it was determined that the judgment of the first case could not legally be vacated. This latter case became an important point of law in the state of Oklahoma, holding that a husband could not discontinue alimony payments because of remarriage of the wife.

Thus ended one of the most involved and unfortunate

* 98 *Pacific Reporter* 2nd Series 906.

lawsuits in the annals of domestic litigation in the state of Oklahoma. The reporter's notes covered thousands of pages, and as stated by the justice of the Supreme Court of Oklahoma, the testimony was irreconcilable and the conclusion would naturally follow that the witnesses on one side or the other left much to be desired from the point of veracity. Enormous sums of money were spent by Mr. Gilcrease in the procurement of evidence, and portions of the record often went beyond the bounds of good propriety to force or make a point.

Much of the evidence concerned the antenuptial agreement which had been signed before their marriage. In excess of eighty-four witnesses were called to testify. The exhibits were composed of oil company reports, financial statements, estimations, inventories, arguments, photographs of the house on the hill, pictures of the studio, and a little book which was published by Norma's mother, entitled "Magic Power — Beauty," which featured photos of Miss America of 1926 and contained a quotation by John Campbell which read:

> As a white candle in a holy place
> So is the beauty of her lovely face.

When the trial was over there were many mixed emotions, disappointments, and anxious days. The expert testimony dealing with certain exhibits offered in evidence, in an effort to prove some of the allegations brought out during the trial and through the pleadings, created a lengthy case record.

In later years, as in most domestic cases of this kind, the feelings with reference to the minor child, Des Cygne L'Amour Gilcrease, were relaxed, and somehow the child grew to maturity maintaining a respect and love for both of her parents.[4]

The "hills and the valleys" in the heart of Thomas Gilcrease became "the call to art."

Thomas Gilcrease did not marry again.

Book 4
The Collector

Chapter 1

Martin Wiesendanger and The Philip G. Cole Story

The late J. Frank Dobie penned an article for *The American Scene,* a quarterly magazine devoted to American history and art. The issue was devoted exclusively to the art of the American cowboy. Author Dobie's contribution was entitled "The Art of Charles Russell." His concluding paragraph is so significant that it has been selected as the introduction to this chapter, which discloses for the first time the accurate account of the manner in which the paintings of Charles Russell became a part of the collection owned by the Thomas Gilcrease Institute of American History and Art. The inimitable Dobie wrote:

> If the Old West is still important in any way to the Modern West, Russell remains equally important. If

> the Old West is important to far away lands and peoples, Charles M. Russell is important. He not only knew the West, he felt it. It moved him, motivated him, and gave him articulation, as the strong wind on some barren crag shapes all the trees that try to grow there. When one knows and loves the thousands of little truthful details that Charles Russell put into the ears of horses, the rumps of antelopes, the nostrils of deer, the eyes of buffaloes, the lifted heads of cattle, the lope of coyotes, the stance of a stage driver, the watching of a shadow of himself by a cowboy, the response of an Indian storyteller, the way of a she-bear with her cub, the you-be-damned independence of a monster grizzly, the ignorance of an ambling terrapin, the lay of grass under a breeze; and a whole catalogue of other speaking details dear to any lover of Western life, then one cherishes all of Charles M. Russell.[1]

Thomas Gilcrease might have acquired the Russell collection in some other manner than that which is described here as the lines fall away from the eyes of the reader; he might have, but the odds would have been rather slim. He might have been destined to purchase the collection from Philip Cole's estate, from the Montanan who had assembled one of the finest collections of western art in the world, regardless of whether he had met Martin Wiesendanger.

The fact remains that Philip Cole did own a fine collection of Russell's works, that Thomas Gilcrease did meet Martin Wiesendanger, that Wiesendanger was associated with the Kennedy Galleries of New York, and that he did bring the Cole collection to the attention of Thomas Gilcrease. What kind of man was Martin Wiesendanger that he could gain and hold the confidence of the oil man from Oklahoma and play such an important part in the Gilcrease story, and the story of the Cole collection? Well, it all happened like this.[2]

Margaret Wunderlich, wife of Hermann Wunderlich, Jr., of the Kennedy Galleries, had a cousin who was born in Switzerland on February 13, 1908, and who was interned in Germany during the first world war. And so it was that Martin Wiesendanger became the first director of the Texas

Gilcrease Museum. He arrived in the United States when he was thirteen. The year 1921 was one of challenge and confusion for young Wiesendanger. From childhood, he had been imbued with a burning desire to be a biological chemist, and now that he was in America, the opportunity to study was unlimited but funds were not. He sought employment at every agency which would grant him an audience, and finally was offered a job in a telegraph office which he readily accepted. The working conditions were unattractive and the office was in a shabby neighborhood around 23rd Street in lower Manhattan.

Young Martin went from telegraphy to other odd jobs, and then he found work with Fleischmann Yeast Company, which lasted two years. His quest for education and his natural ability as a chemist began to pay dividends. He had reached his nineteenth year and graduated from Columbia University where he had majored in chemistry, and selected art and history as his minor subjects. He found work at the DuPont establishment as a "fermentator," a practical use for his knowledge of chemistry.

Margaret Wunderlich was a niece of Rudolf Cronau. This kinship afforded Martin Wiesendanger his first realistic opportunity. Cronau, a recognized authority on the life of the Indian, possessed a diversified and large library relating to every tribe of Indians on the American continent. He invited Martin to make use of his collection of books on the subject of Indian art, and for many months he not only read dozens of Cronau's books but he studied with Cronau. Cronau was a personal friend of the historic Sitting Bull, whose portrait he drew in Fort Randall in 1881. As an Indian artist he excelled most, if not entirely, in this highly specialized segment of art. He was the progenitor of all Indian drawings, according to authorities, and provided the Indians with crayons and paper, thereby making it possible for them to discontinue the custom of drawing and painting on animal skins. The Museum of Natural History in New York possesses Cronau's works where this innovation is recorded. A number of Cronau's works are now owned by the Thomas Gilcrease Institute of American History and Art. With Cronau's moral and financial assistance, Martin made the break and abandoned his studies in "sugar chemistry."

The depression came in 1929 and again the flowering chemist with artistic leanings found himself in need of work. In 1930 the Wunderlichs of Kennedy Galleries decided to employ him. He was started as a stock clerk and later promoted to salesman. He utilized his knowledge of chemistry in the allied work of being a conservator of paintings. This appealed to Martin, and his career was launched in a new endeavor. When thinking of Rudolf Cronau, he still makes reference to the excellent talents of the famed artist who painted such works as *Kanri-cikala* and *Tananka-Iyotanka,* which appear in a book published in Leipzig, which was entered for copyright in Congress in 1885 under the title of *Von Wunderland zu Wunderland,* or, translated, *From Wonderland to Wonderland.*

Fortunately the Kennedy Galleries specialized in Americana from both sections of the Western Hemisphere. Martin worked long and diligently and earned the title of "customer's man." In the off hours, he found he could earn extra money as a lecturer, and while filling an engagement in Norwich, Connecticut, he met Margaret. She was an art teacher and, while attending one of Martin's lectures, had fallen asleep. His pride was hurt. He made arrangements to meet the backsliding Quaker who had dared to ignore his thoughts of wisdom.

He discovered that her father was a banker; besides, Margaret was most attractive. They were married after a whirlwind courtship. Soon thereafter he was dispatched to western points across the nation to visit museums. Tulsa was on their itinerary where they were greeted by Eugene Kingman, director of Philbrook Art Museum. He sold Kingman a drawing by Fredrich Bodmer and this so encouraged him that he made a tour of the city. The incident is important because Martin and Margaret fell in love with the Oil Capital of the World and vowed that someday they would return and make it their home. And as is written in the storybooks, there started an unusual chain of events which was to make Wiesendanger the first director of the Thomas Gilcrease Museum.

"Hello, Martin, did you see those three people in front of the Wunderlich display windows?" The voice was that of a competitor. It was the custom of the galleries to so inform each other in the hope of bagging big game. The competitor then described the trio as being well dressed but a bit on the rustic side in appearance. Martin thanked his friend and said that he would be on the lookout for them.

Two days later the two men and a woman walked into the Kennedy Galleries. "Do you have any pictures of Indians?" asked the older of the men.

"Yes, sir!" replied the ambitious "customer's man."

"Then I'd like to see everything you have for sale!" replied the man.

"That's a tall order but I'll try to fill it," said Wiesendanger, doing his best to hide his excitement at the possibility of a big sale.

The older man was Thomas Gilcrease; the other was his brother-in-law, Burt Logan, and the lady was his sister, Lena. They carefully looked at everything. Lena and Burt stood by in silence. Thomas Gilcrease hardly talked, but examined every object produced by the bewildered Wiesendanger. They thanked him for his attentive and explanatory remarks and departed as Wiesendanger's hopes faded into the depths of discouragement. In a matter of hours Thomas Gilcrease returned and said, "Young man, I'll take everything you have shown to me; how much do I owe you?" The bill came to $35,000 and the purchaser wrote out a check on a Tulsa, Oklahoma bank. Wiesendanger was so elated that he almost forgot to check the credit references. When he received an answer to his telegram sent to the Tulsa bank, the reply read: "The account of Mr. Thomas Gilcrease is good for seven figures." The Gilcrease-Wiesendanger friendship was off to a quick getaway. Martin recalls that his first purchase by Tom Gilcrease was not all Indian merchandise. One of the pieces was *The Fifth Foolish Virgin* by Martin Schongauer, and several Currier & Ives etchings.

Some time later it happened. Thomas Gilcrease recognized the ability of young Wiesendanger and sought permission of his friend Wunderlich to employ him to assist him in assorting the collection which was to open the museum in Texas. After several months Gilcrease sought permission to employ Wiesendanger on a full-time basis, and thus Martin Wiesendanger became the first director of the museum he was going to open in San Antonio and which was to be operated by the Thomas Gilcrease Foundation. In retrospect Wiesendanger has stated: "I do not recall exactly how we concluded our employment arrangements but I do remember that I went directly to San Antonio with my wife and supervised the opening of the Thomas Gilcrease Museum on March 18, 1943."

The Casino Club of San Antonio was a Texas landmark for social festivity. It was established to provide a larger ballroom, a banquet hall, and kitchen facilities for its members. Thomas Gilcrease was determined to place on exhibit, for the benefit of his friends and for the citizens of San Antonio who were interested in art, his collection of Americana. Whether by predestination or purposeful selection, he had acquired intact what has been described frequently as the most authentic package of western art ever brought together and bought by one individual in the history of art markets. It became known as the "Cole" collection and is the envy of all western museums. This was the arrow which pinned the coup of international recognition to Thomas Gilcrease. His intention was to share with others the paintings, sculpture, and prints with emphasis on the life of the American Indian.

When the ballroom was designed, it was not anticipated that it would be converted into a museum of art; however, the decor of the high ceilings was concave and blended into a pattern of archways, creating an atmosphere of Roman architecture. It was necessary to block out some of the windows and convert the casements into individual arch or roof-like projections or alcoves for the accomodation of art objects. The ballroom became the main gallery of the museum and was bordered by checkerboard and mosaic tile running the full length of the rectangular area. The banquet hall was used for display of the contents of the library, and expensive mesquite wood was used to build the copper screen cabinets to house the books, manuscripts, and other items. The tops of the cases were used to shelve or store the various artifacts. The building was not air-conditioned but was equipped with low-hanging electric fans of the propeller blade type suspended from the ceilings by long tubular attachments.

The main gallery was lighted by a huge chandelier of graduated levels holding various size lamps, delicately shaded and embellished in exquisite design. The library was illuminated by a grouping of circular chandeliers where candle lamps in wagon wheel symbols hung from painted drops. Marble pedestals purchased by Mr. Gilcrease in Europe were distributed throughout the room for the bust exhibits and small statuary, while box-shaped stands were provided for the heavy bronze pieces of the collection. Grey carpet runners were installed to cover the walk portions of the oak floors which were polished to mirror sharpness. The furniture was modest by museum standards but elegant in selection. The library had a large square table which was guarded by four chairs, with one extra for the visitor's comfort. A smaller table was used to display a vase for which fresh cut flowers were supplied daily. The workshop was located in the kitchen section, and it was in this area that the restorative work was done on the paintings.[3]

The opening of the museum under the name of the Thomas Gilcrease Collection by the Thomas Gilcrease Foundation on March 18, 1943, did not attract the editors of the metropolitan newspapers or provide a field day for those who pen critiques in magazines devoted to cultural beginnings. The first visitors were not aware that they had walked into an adventure which was to become an indispensable part of the American art scene.

A multitude of "firsts" can be credited to Martin Wiesendanger, who served as director until 1947 when the museum in Texas closed, and then assisted in opening the museum in Tulsa on May 3, 1949.

He authored the "Foreword" of the first publication of *The American Indian* which was the official organ of the exhibition of paintings, drawings, books, manuscripts, and sculptures. His words, "We are opening the collection to visitors in San Antonio for a period of time," proved to be true. The collection could not have survived the apathy manifested by the people of San Antonio.

Wiesendanger had assisted Mr. Gilcrease in acquiring books on Indian history and introduced the Oklahoma collector to the late Charles P. Everitt, who was known in art circles as "The Treasure Hunter." His delightful book, *The Adventures of a Treasure Hunter*, published in 1951 by Little, Brown and Company, is a standard volume wherever collectors have a bookshelf. This contact resulted in the purchase of rare volumes, manuscripts, and documents which are today in the Gilcrease Library.

The friendship and association of Wiesendanger and Gilcrease was not restricted to the gallery. They hunted together at Pearsall, Texas, on the Frio River. Martin Wiesendanger recalls one experience he had with Mr. Gilcrease: "Tom was a good shot but I'll never forget a near accident. He was sitting on a fence when his gun was accidentally discharged and it knocked him to the ground. Any other hunter might have exemplified fright but all Tom did was to get up, brush off his pants and remark, 'Kicks, doesn't it?' "

During the period when Wiesendanger was employed by the foundation, he personally painted, with the assistance of his wife Margaret, a mural which he titled *Creek Removal,* and which has reference to the Creek Trail of Tears. The painting is in the collection at Tulsa.

The memory of man can be as fallible as the mirage which has brought hope to the parched lips of the traveler in arid regions. The story that is told and retold is embellished with imaginative elements which squeak as loudly as rusty hinges on a weatherbeaten door. The story surrounding purchase of the Philip G. Cole collection from the Cole Estate of Tarrytown, New York, and which is one of the most important representations of Americana in the Gilcrease Institute falls into the category of exaggeration and distortion.

The agreement to purchase bears the date of January 18, 1944, and the consummation date was December 24, 1946. Philip G. Cole, the inventor of the automobile tire valve, had owned the collection for many years. During his life he was a valued patron of the Kennedy Galleries and the nature of his collection was well known to the customers' men and officials of the galleries.

Daniel B. Browne, a resident of New York City, was a "runner" for the galleries in the art world, and being aware of the special interest of Thomas Gilcrease in Indian art, he communicated with Mr. Gilcrease. On November 17, 1943, Thomas Gilcrease sent the following telegram to Daniel Baillet Browne, 42 Fort Charles Place, New York City:

> Confirming conference with Dr. Linus Long Nov. 16 will arrive New York Friday December 3rd to inspect the collection. Our understanding collection withdrawn from sale pending our inspection on about above arrival date. Please confirm.

On November 18, the confirmation message reached Mr. Gilcrease at San Antonio, Texas:

> Telegram received Cole Collection withdrawn from sale pending your arrival on December third arrangements made. Are reservations at Waldorf Astoria agreeable or do you prefer to make your own arrangements. D. B. Browne.

The enterprising Browne did not tell Mr. Gilcrease who owned the collection or the nature of it. Mr. Gilcrease promptly made this bit of information available to his director, Martin Wiesendanger. "I know the collection, Mr. Gilcrease, and it is a good one. We may be able to acquire it if we act quickly and convince the executors that we are really sincere about acquiring it," said the anxious Wiesendanger.

"Then we will leave for New York on the first train we can catch," replied Mr. Gilcrease. Upon their arrival in New York they made contact with the proper representatives and personally spoke with Mrs. Cole. Mrs. Wiesendanger had joined her husband, Martin, and Mr. Gilcrease on the trip. They were received cordially but the meeting was too formal. Mrs. Cole seemed anxious to make the sale but the cautious Mr. Gilcrease maintained his usual straight face. The paintings were badly in need of cleaning and in many instances restorative work was indicated. Preliminary negotiations were under discussion when Mr. Gilcrease decided to return to his office in Texas and give the subject further thought. The requested price was substantial and he knew that there would be trouble on the home front the moment he mentioned what he intended paying for the collection. There began a constant stream of communications between New York and Texas.

The enterprising Mr. Browne was by this time in a state of uncertainty and fearful that Mr. Gilcrease would surrender his desire to acquire the collection. Browne wrote to his friend, Martin W. Wiesendanger, on December 10, 1943, from New York:

> . . . Excepting Mr. Parker, you are the only one who has been given the opportunity to examine the collection. Now that it has been decided to sell, the Trustees are anxious to prepare the amendments to the tax report, which must be filed by the 15th.
>
> Hope that Mr. Gilcrease will decide to acquire the collection as it is the finest of its kind in the United States, and would give your Museum a permanent edge on every Museum in the country.[4]

Tom Gilcrease remained silent and did not become excited to the point of making immediate reply to the letter received by Martin Wiesendanger, and would not permit one to be made. Apparently without the knowledge of Mr. Gilcrease, the ever alert Wiesendanger managed to get word to Mr. Browne that Mr. Gilcrease felt he was being rushed into a transaction. On December 13, the anxious Browne again wrote to Wiesendanger:

> Am sorry that Mr. Gilcrease feels that he is being unduly hurried. This is certainly not the case. In order to facilitate the consummation of an arrangement in accord with your wishes, have waived the payment of

> a very nominal commission during the life of the proposed contract. You must remember that you would be getting title to a collection that cost over a million dollars, and which could never be acquired again at any price, because these paintings are nowhere else available for purchase.
>
> Called the attorney for the estate, after my conversation with you, explaining that Mr. Gilcrease objected to placing securities in escrow with your bank, as security for the fulfillment of the terms of payments, and that he did not wish to advance more than 10% of the purchase price. It is better to keep the matter open, though the discussion be prolonged, and Mr. Gilcrease decide to abandon the collection later, than to close the door entirely by telling them that the deal is now rejected. Mr. Gilcrease may be a proud and imperious person, but so are the Trustees, who said that they would require a deposit in escrow from the Rockefeller Foundation were they the potential purchasers under such an arrangement as proposed.

When it appeared there was going to be a meeting of the minds, Mr. Gilcrease and his director returned to New York and negotiations were renewed. Mr. Gilcrease had changed his mind about the method of payment and told the executors who were in charge that he wanted to pay the bill of $250,000 in four equal installments for tax purposes. The real reason was because of his inability to raise the ready cash as requested. The executors refused to accept his proposition, and he promptly walked out of their offices and returned to his hotel room with Mr. Wiesendanger.

"What are you going to do, Mr. Gilcrease?" asked Wiesendanger.

"They can go to the devil unless they trade on my terms," replied the stubborn Thomas. The telephone rang and Mr. Wiesendanger grabbed it. He was advised to tell Mr. Gilcrease that one of the executors of the estate was in the armed services and that they had sent a cablegram to him to obtain his permission to accept the quarterly payments. When Mr. Gilcrease heard this he decided to wait it out.

Several hours later another telephone call brought the news that a reply in the affirmative had been received from the absent executor. They returned to the offices of the representatives of the estate and purchase was finalized. There was an understanding between the parties that the purchase of the collection was not to be made public for a period of two years. Mr. Gilcrease had two reasons for this stipulation. First, the delay would give Mr. Wiesendanger an opportunity to clean the paintings and do the necessary work on some of the other objects of art which went with the package; second, Mr. Gilcrease wanted to be sure that the bill was paid in full before the collection was placed on exhibit. This was a policy which he insisted upon in all his career as a collector. Until he had a legal right to the property, he would not permit others to see it.

In due course the shipment reached the museum in Texas and Mr. Wiesendanger started the long and intricate job of assorting the artifacts and paintings. He worked day and night to prepare them for exhibit. Some of the frames had to be repaired and retouched, and all in all it was a back-breaking task.

There is a great element of truth in the fact that the associates of Mr. Gilcrease and the members of the family felt that he had gone completely overboard in committing himself to the purchase, but in his usual manner he managed to quell their fears and meet the obligation. Today, the Remingtons, Russells, Sharps, and works of other fine artists are in the Gilcrease Institute partly due to the talents of Martin Wiesendanger, but principally because Thomas Gilcrease was a hard trader and knew what he wanted and how to get it. As for Martin Wiesendanger, he has wondered many times what might have happened if the executor who was away at war had been a casualty at the Battle of the Bulge before the cablegram reached him.

There is not any foundation to the often-told stories about the executors having insisted upon a certified check; or to the rumor that Mr. Gilcrease had left a check with authorization that it be filled in for an amount ten percent above the highest offer; or that after the sale was concluded some art dealer tried to buy the collection; or that the representatives learned that they did not have the right to make the sale and tried to repurchase it from Mr. Gilcrease for a million dollars.

Innocuous rumors have a way of ballooning into matured gossip, and it may well be that the story of the attempt to repurchase came from an actual inquiry which originated with Katharine P. Mills, the former Mrs. Philip G. Cole.

In September of 1946, Mrs. Mills directed the following letter to Mr. Gilcrease:

> Sometime ago you purchased a collection of Russells and Remingtons from the Estate of Philip G. Cole. I am the former Mrs. Philip G. Cole. Included in the collection is a painting which Mr. Russell painted especially for me. It is not well known in the collection as I believe it has never been shown, but it means a great deal to me as it depicts the scene of my birthplace and the country where I spent my childhood. It is called "The Discovery of Last Chance Gulch." Reminiscent of the many happy days I spent in that country I have called my country home Last Chance Ranch; because of this and other sentimental reasons I am very anxious to own this painting.
>
> I hope you will be interested in allowing me to purchase this painting. If you will so kindly communicate with me.
>
> Very truly yours,
> Katharine P. Mills
> (Mrs. Dwight Mills)

On October 2, 1946 Mr. Gilcrease responded by stating that he had just returned from a month's trip to New Mexico and Wyoming and found her letter. He advised her that he expected to be in New York in the autumn and would be pleased to talk with her concerning the painting. Apparently Mr. Gilcrease had no intention of disposing of the desired painting and never held the conference in New York as he anticipated he might do. Four years later he received another letter of inquiry, this time from Douglas H. Bradley, a son-in-law of Mrs. Mills.

I am writing you to make a request I am sure you will understand. However, first of all, I better explain who I am. As you doubtless remember, Mrs. Dwight Mills sold to you a collection of western pictures so that you were able to gather together in one place fine paintings representing American art portraying life in the west.

As you know, Dr. Cole spent many years collecting these pictures and one of them was painted for Mrs. Mills by Charles M. Russell in 1925. This picture DISCOVERY OF LAST CHANCE GULCH has great sentimental value to the family. My wife, Mrs. Mills' daughter, and I would like, if at all possible, to buy this picture and give it back to Mrs. Mills. However, we would be perfectly willing to buy the picture from you with the understanding, written or otherwise, that we would give it back to the Foundation on Mrs. Mills' death.

I realize that this is not in accordance with the original contract of sale but knowing the sentimental value to Mrs. Mills, I am asking you if you cannot make this one exception because this particular picture means so much to her. I would appreciate hearing from you as soon as it is convenient. We would like to give this picture to Mrs. Mills for Christmas, if this transaction is possible.

Sincerely,

Douglas H. Bradley

No further correspondence on the subject of *Discovery of Last Chance Gulch* appears to exist and the painting is still a part of the Russell collection which Tom Gilcrease acquired from Dr. Cole.

There is written evidence in the acquisition files which would indicate that some offers were made by outsiders who had learned or suspected that the collection was for sale, and one dealer mentioned the sum of $500,000, but this was typical of the "feelers" which generally go out after a deal has been closed. It is an old proposition that when an article is not for sale, someone is always ready to say, "Had I known it was on the market, I would have paid much more."

All that has been written here about the importance of the Russell collection which was contained in the Cole purchase applies with equal force and application to the acquisitions of the works of Frederic Remington and Joseph Henry Sharp which were a part of the same transaction. Any attempt to list the masterpieces now owned by the institute would mean authoring a separate book for each of these greats in the world of art. Of one thing there is a certainty: since no other institute contains so many works by such master documentary artists, the modern day historians who are interested in research and facts will find their way to the galleries and the catalogs of the Thomas Gilcrease Institute of American History and Art.

The foregoing is one of many experiences which the "customer's man" of the Kennedy Galleries recalled. His talents have been rewarding and he has been nationally recognized as an artist, writer, print-maker, art restorer, authenticator, photographer, gun collector, and rifle-maker. He was a part-time art instructor for the University of Tulsa while he was director of the Gilcrease Institute. One of his favorite areas of study and research is the pre-Columbian period which includes the Athapascan, Toltecs, Aztec, Mayan, and Incan cultures of pre-1492.

While he was with the Gilcrease Foundation, he and his wife lived in the stone house which in former years was the home of the mother of Mr. Gilcrease and which she occupied until her demise. The Wiesendangers now live west of the famous Gilcrease Institute in the historic hills of the Osage in a house which they personally built. From their porch which overlooks the countryside, there is visible in the distance the three trees alleged to mark the spot where the Dalton boys had their hideout. This is a legendary tale; however, there are some old-timers who feel that it is a story founded upon fact. The antique pieces of furniture in their home are truly art objects, many having come down through Margaret's family. Martin and his wife share much in common. She paints and he loves abstract sculpture. The handiwork blends in with the Dutch prints which adorn their rustic walls.

The most important observation to be made of the association of Tom Gilcrease and Wiesendanger is the influence each had on the other's respective career. Wiesendanger feels that Thomas Gilcrease had contributed much to the discovery of the culture of all Indians, and that historians of the future will find a more profound recognition of these accomplishments. Tom Gilcrease would be the first to admit that a vast amount of the knowledge of restoration and method of selection and search for the genuine came from Martin Wiesendanger. They differed often. They argued, then reconciled their differences only to disagree again, and each stuck to his convictions. This manifestation of independence is reflected in the Gilcrease collection which might not have been successful otherwise. The one who is first in any capacity has much to conquer and it is not always easy to satisfy the untutored.

A fair portion of the biographical data relating to the establishment of the Gilcrease collection comes from the retentive mind of Martin Wiesendanger, and authentic facts supplied by him from personal contact with Thomas Gilcrease have been of extreme value in filling the spaces which otherwise would have been lost.

Bruce Wear, former curator of the Gilcrease Institute of American History and Art, in his valuable book *A Philosophical Approach to Collecting and Decorating*,[5] has struck a chord which vibrates into the heart of Martin Wiesendanger and soul of Thomas Gilcrease, although he did not have either man in mind when he wrote these lines:

> If you wish to possess a sound collection, one which has validity, have a definite purpose in mind. Conduct your collecting in a systematic and organized manner. Before you purchase any item, choose carefully, and establish valid reasons why you desire to possess it. Question the piece. Does it have an intrinsic value, and all the qualities you are looking for? Does it

> express the culture of the age in which it was created? Always question the authenticity of a piece, and have a basis for your belief in its genuineness. Remember, the storage rooms in the museums of the world bear witness to the ability of the faker.

And then he concludes Part One of his philosophy with this gem:

> The ultimate in collecting comes when a person reaches the stage of enjoying and appreciating a work of art, without desiring to possess it.

Perhaps Thomas Gilcrease and Martin Wiesendanger had the same philosophy in their personal foundations. The students of history will have the opportunity to measure their reaches into the world of art. With a spark of wisdom Bruce Wear has written a lesson which comes from the teachers who have arrived and those who are yet waiting for their destinations.

Chapter 2

The Majordomos and the Master

After the resignation of Martin Wiesendanger, Mr. Gilcrease was faced with the necessity of naming his successor. Lester Hargrett, a Harvard student, had been in the publishing business and had devoted intensive study to the Indian laws of the Five Civilized Tribes. He owned reams of material on the subject and in some manner this storehouse of documents came to the attention of Mr. Gilcrease. Hargrett was born in Tifton, Georgia, in the old Creek Territory and was astute enough to make a study of the history and traditions of the tribesmen who were driven from their lands by the encroachment of the early settlers from Europe.

It is not clear whether Mr. Gilcrease was interested in Lester Hargrett as a director for the museum or if he merely wanted to acquire what Hargrett owned. The ever alert master struck a bargain with the new employee and it was determined that as part of the compensation for the material he would make him the director of the museum.[1]

Hargrett's administration was short-lived. At the end of the first year, Mr. Gilcrease became discontented with some of the innovations being inaugurated. The index card system was undergoing a change and Thomas Gilcrease developed a spirit of unhappiness about the progress in certain areas of the collection. The museum building was nearing completion and actually opened while Hargrett carried the title of director. Some purchases were made and a few improvements were instigated in the operation of the museum. One morning the *Tulsa Daily World* carried a headline, "Hargrett Quits as Gilcrease Head." The date of the resignation was September 1, 1949. Tom Gilcrease concluded that he could administer the museum as well as Hargrett had done. The end result of the short association was that Hargrett had come but he had not conquered. He left a few ideas and a limited diary of his activities – he just forgot to record either and Thomas Gilcrease made no effort to search for them.

With the sudden departure of Lester Hargrett, the master became the director and remained in charge until that eventful day when the City of Tulsa became the owner of the Thomas Gilcrease Institute of American History and Art by reason of the gift of the Thomas Gilcrease Foundation. The institute attracted some attention at the local level but there was not any determined effort on the part of the founder to embark upon a program for national publicity. Allied interests occupied the time of Thomas Gilcrease, and step by step he climbed higher and higher up the ladder of uncertainty. As indicated in previous chapters, his personal life had suffered, and he knew that he would not emerge from the shadows of his memory lane unless he applied every muscle in his body to the task of removing the weights which were constantly pulling him into a shell.

The active business career of Thomas Gilcrease had all but come to an end. His keen intellect was no longer burdened with facts and figures about proration and the drilling of wildcat wells. He had a wildcat by the tail and it was not all on canvas. The fever of acquisition still burned deeply into his desire to collect and exhibit. There were not any antibiotics which could be administered to the disease which had overtaken him. He was suffering from pressure of time. He had the same compulsion which overtakes the professional gambler, only his was a moral and cultural pursuit. If what he wanted was underground, he was determined to dig for it. If what he wanted was in a new collection, he was compelled to acquire it in whole or in part. If what he wanted was impossible to get, he wanted to prove that there was a way to get it. Excessive commitments finally consumed him. The one medicine which could cure his ills had ceased to be plentiful on the market. His ancestors called it "wampum." His creditors called it "money." Two and a quarter million dollars had at one time in the life of the founder been but a drop of oil trickling from a drill stem, but Tom's well had run dry. During the uncertain hours when Tulsa was voting on a bond issue to assume all remaining and outstanding obligations which he had incurred in amassing his collections, he suffered from a humiliation which only those who were bosom close to him could sense. He walked softly around the grounds of the museum site or sat upon the old stone porch of his home where the rustic wonderment of his hill faced the skyline of Tulsa and appeared to be in a state of bewilderment; his kind eyes reflected a melancholy he had never known. He was conscious that he had pledged future oil payments to reimburse the City of Tulsa and that eventually every penny would be returned to the citizens. He was caught between third base and the home plate, and rather than be put out he forfeited the game. It was the proudest moment of his life and yet the hardest to face. He was no longer the master. He was the benefactor, and what he did not know then and did not live to fully appreciate was that he had fulfilled his mission in life. In his remaining years he found it difficult to accept — he had parted with the key to the front door, but left a part of his heart in all of the galleries, and on a quiet day the visitors of tomorrow will still hear the rhythm of its beat. It may be in the paintings of the Indian dances of Woody Crumbo or Acee Blue Eagle; in the fleeing feet of Willard Stone's *Road Runners*; in the bodies of *Black Hawk* and *Whirling*

Thunder by John Wesley Jarvis; or in the heart of the cowboy on the horse in Charley Russell's *Trail Boss,* but wherever it is — there will be a calm matched only by the serenity of Albert Bierstadt's *Sierra Nevada Morning* — for the master sleeps.

Majordomo the First

The old cliché that a man cannot serve two masters could have had its origin in the tenure of James Taylor Forrest, who earned and deserved the distinction of being selected as the first director of the Thomas Gilcrease Institute of American History and Art under the proprietorship of the City of Tulsa.

He hailed from New Castle, Indiana where he was born September 22, 1921. His undergraduate days were spent at "Hanover College" where he graduated in 1948 as an honor student with the degree of Bachelor of Science. His master's degree was earned at the University of Wisconsin in 1949 and in 1950 he embarked upon his studies for a doctorate in American history. Jim Forrest is listed in *Who's Who in the West, Who's Who in New Mexico,* and *Who's Who in American Art*; he is a Fellow in the Institute of International Arts and Letters. He is widely known as a lecturer in art and history and is a contributor to the book *Keepers of the Past.* During World War II he served in the Army Air Corps, and his first museum work was with the Wisconsin Historical Society as research assistant.

As a member of the faculty of Sheridan College, Sheridan, Wyoming, he has attracted attention for his methods of approach in the study of history — and his students are generally captivated by his knowledge of the artists of the West, having authored two books on western historical subjects and written many articles on western art for diversified publications. His wife, Carolyn, and his daughters, Mary and Barbara, are vitally interested in history and art.

From the inception of his directorship he stressed the fact that unless the institute emphasized and embraced the concept of education, it would not mature. He said: "I aimed the institution in the direction which I felt would steer it away from its more narrow and limited position as a private collection." In the effort to accomplish what he concluded was a sound and oriented approach, he was confronted with opposition from Thomas Gilcrease. Mr. Gilcrease could not resist, or unwittingly manifested the same attitude toward the use of the collection as a father does toward his son who had reached his majority; he felt that even though he had given his prize possessions to the City of Tulsa, he still had the right to suggest policy of operation. Mr. Forrest knew that he was disturbing the collector's collection and was aware that he would be subjected to critical eyes and contrary-minded opposition. It was not a question of the blind leading the blind. Each had sights and foresights, but their horizons and their visions were blurred by vastly different backgrounds. It was the battle of formal education against self-taught wisdom.

Jim Forrest did not want the books in the library of the institute to remain unexplored. He welcomed the application of researchers and predicted that the day would come when students would seek out the truths for dissertations, and candidates for the doctor's degree would heap glory upon the founder for having made their pursuit successful. There are no debit and credit sides to the operation of an institution with such unlimited potential. While he was concerned with budget problems he was not a businessman and did not so consider himself. He was content to leave the worries about finance to the citizens' committee and other lay people who worked with the officials of the municipality.

Each month of his administration resulted in another breakthrough. He initiated conducted tours which eventually blossomed into a full-scale program for children of elementary and high school levels. He conceived and edited the first issue of *The American Scene* magazine in the spring of 1958. His article, "The Storytelling Value of Art," sounded the call to Indian culture and Americana. He wrote: "The American Scene is a broad concept, but we feel that the material we will 'discover' will warrant the presumption." He then concluded the first segment of his introductory article with the following:

> In the course of our word searching for a magazine name, we thought of many ideas for which we could find no adequate term. Someone mentioned 'picture maker,' which had been used many times, but which has great significance in looking back into the history of Man as an artist and chronicler. Man – apes and parrots notwithstanding – has the distinction of being the only picture-making animal on our planet; perhaps, this is more of a key to his rise up the ladder of human progress than we have given thought. We know that for some 30,000 years man has been a picture-maker; the caves of southern France and northern Spain reveal examples of Aurignacian art which are both descriptive and beautiful. Certainly, the archeologist owes much to the primitive artist; the drawings, the figurines, the picture languages have contributed greatly to his knowledge of the centuries of peoples who lived before written language had evolved. Picture-maker! Fortunately the world has never lost her picture-makers, once they began to work. Much of our knowledge of recent times as well as of the past has been preserved for us by the artist's brush. Often the artist has served as historian, where no other worked. Social historians recently have turned to the arts for documentation concerning other eras and other times. A painting, a piece of sculpture, is treated as any other document, being put to certain tests to judge its relative worth as a document. Treating art works as documents relating to social history, or other aspects of the story of Man, may cause some to cry out, 'But what about art as an aesthetic joy?' Well, what is beautiful will remain so regardless of our interest in it for its story telling value, will it not? In fact, art museums have always known that visitors generally respond best to paintings which depict a familiar theme or present a

known subject. In other words a painting can be beautiful, but can also have documentary value — one value need not detract from the other.

The foregoing gem has been reproduced in part because it set the pattern for future issues of *The American Scene,* which has in these few short years become the most important publication of its kind in the world.

The first three years of *The American Scene* (twelve issues), Volumes I, II, III, feature articles on Will James, William de la Montagne Cary, Robert Lindneux, Bill Gollings, Thomas Moran, Thomas Eakins, the Taos artists, Oklahoma history, Robert Henri, John Mix Stanley, Charles M. Russell (27-page catalog), Joseph H. Sharp, Oscar Berninghaus, Ernest Blumenschein, Irving E. Couse, Vinson Lackey, and many others.

Volume IV features articles on the Arkansas River, Henry H. Cross, Frederic Remington (36-page catalog), Alfred J. Miller, Thomas Gilcrease, and an entire issue devoted to Oklahoma history with articles by many of Oklahoma's best historians, such as Angie Debo, Fannie Misch, Edward E. Dale, Henry Bass, Paula Love, Mrs. Walter Ferguson, Glenn Shirley, and A. M. Gibson.

Volume V features entire issues devoted to the Yellowstone country and the works of Thomas Moran, the dedication of the new Gilcrease Museum facilities, and a review of the library, art and archeological collections, the Catlin Sketch Book, and a special issue on Frederic Remington and Charles M. Russell, the "Titans of Western Art"; with articles by C. R. Smith, J. Frank Dobie, Harold McCracken, Lola Shelton, N. Orwin Rush, Helen Card, Will Rogers, Jr., Ramon F. Adams, and Dean Krakel.

Thomas Gilcrease was a regular visitor to the institute during the early days of Jim Forrest's stewardship. The passing of the museum from a private collection to a public educational institution was something he could neither comprehend nor appreciate during the first few months after he gave away his "dream world." He realized that there would be a more varied program of lectures and a constant revolving of exhibits to show the fickle public, or to use the language of Jim Forrest, "There are too many people who think that one visit to a museum will last a life time."

There was a daring about the relationship between Tom and Jim. They respected each other but neither wanted to give in or completely capitulate to the other's reasoning. The national television programs which were instigated had the approval of the board of directors of the managing corporation, and with some misgiving the executive committee had consented to the promotional activities which brought publicity through *American Heritage* and *Art in America*; however, Thomas Gilcrease remained the old merchant on main street and was not ready to accept the modern. He did not move fast by nature and was not concerned about extending the publicity of the institute beyond the state of Oklahoma.

The demands upon the time of Jim Forrest increased with each new activity instigated. He became vice-chairman of the Administrative Council of the City of Tulsa on August 22, 1956; filled speaking engagements for organizations such as the Federated Women's Clubs and civic groups, and through his industry 4,500 students visited the institute during the school year of 1957-58. He made an important trip with the then president, Alfred E. Aaronson, to New York to interview Dr. Lawrence V. Coleman, prominent museum building expert about expansion plans. He spoke on the subject of "The Role of Art in Education — A Challenge in the World of Super Science" on the opening night of the Gilcrease Fourth Annual Tulsa School Art Exhibit. He fathered the first National Representational Art Show in 1958 to encourage contemporary artists to contribute to the theme so well established in the American school of representational art, and to foster the proposition that restrictions should not be placed on the artist in his creative work, but rather those who wish to create with realistic interpretations should be encouraged.

He wrote an article for the special edition of the magazine, published by the Tulsa Chamber of Commerce, celebrating the fiftieth anniversary of Oklahoma. In this edition, which was called "From Teepees to Towers — 1907 to 1957," he described the Thomas Gilcrease Institute of American History and Art and quoted *Life* magazine as saying: "Thomas Gilcrease has the best collection of art and literature on the American frontier and the Indian ever assembled."

In another issue of *The American Scene,* James Taylor Forrest wrote a stimulating and informative article, "The World of Charlie Russell," and in doing so carried out the purpose of the organ, namely, to tell the story of the artist represented in the collection.

Mr. Forrest knows that the Gilcrease Institute has forged ahead from the years when he argued that it was time to take off the bib and tucker and replace them with garments of development. He has said: "The institute can reach the sky in its field. It is nonpareil in the documentary art of the American West and also fine in other areas. The wisdom of any man who could put it together could never be questioned."

In January of 1961, Mr. Forrest tendered his resignation to become the director of the fine arts division of the Museum of New Mexico in Santa Fe; after a successful tenure in New Mexico he became the director of the Bradford Brinton Memorial at Big Horn, Wyoming, situated in the shadow of Wyoming's scenic Big Horn Mountains and which houses an extensive collection of western art, sculpture, and Indian relics.

The finest attribute of James Taylor Forrest was his frank and positive approach to life. He did not care for sham or camouflage — and his ever present desire for the critical rather than the eulogy did not always make him the most sought after speaker on the podium. Of Thomas Gilcrease he has written:

> Tom was stubborn and very possessive. He never really gave up the collection. He told me a little story once. He knew a collector of Chinese jade and carved ivory who said: "With real fine art the owner never really loses it. That all those who own such articles as 'permanent' objects, hold them as their own forever because they form a sort of link or chain." I watched

him fondle his artifacts and it was obvious that he was hanging onto a possession. He really did not like to have people "gawk" at his treasures. He loved to have people who understood look and love them with him. He told me on more than one occasion: "I wish the 'gawkers' and 'tourists' would go away." He was not impressed with increased attendance except when knowledgable visitors came in and then he was in his glory and he knew what and how to tell the story. I forgave him for his possessiveness because I understood it. There were times when he hurt me deeply because I felt that he should have had more sympathy and understanding for a younger, greener man's point of view. I only hope that I did not hurt him that much, and knowing him, I'm sure I didn't. He had insulated himself from such hurt.

This concludes the experiences of James Taylor Forrest with Thomas Gilcrease. When they parted there were strains of emotion reflected in the face of the first majordomo. The death of Mr. Gilcrease was more than a news item to Jim Forrest. He regretted that they had not met again under circumstances which would have cut away the strings of formality. He would have told the master — "All I ever wanted to do was to carry forward a program which could be constructive and to help you understand why my convictions were just as important to me as yours were to you." Jim Forrest will not have that opportunity but he wrote the following tender words:

You don't like to hurt or to be hurt by those you love with warmth and some understanding. I had a deep affection for you, Tom, and if it is possible for one man to love another — I had that kind of love in my heart for you.

Majordomo the Second

The resignation of James Taylor Forrest had left the institute without a guiding force. The staff members had profited by their experience with their former director and were prepared to keep the doors open until a suitable successor could be employed.

Glen R. Ames, a retired executive of the Phillips Petroleum Company of Bartlesville, was recommended for the position of temporary director. Mr. Ames had been active in the Tulsa Chamber of Commerce and was known locally as a public-spirited individual with a determined and outgoing personality. In February, 1961, he finally consented to serve with the understanding that the services of a qualified director would be engaged as quickly as possible. He was appointed acting director and immediately began a period of orientation. In a few weeks he had in his fashion learned something about the ground rules, but the policies of preservation and lending caused him sleepless nights. He leaned heavily upon the committee chairman of the board of directors and the employees who had been continued in their respective departments.

Glen and Tom were old friends. They talked many times about the operation of museums, and it was a comfort to have the wisdom of the founder so near at hand. His term of office was short. In the spring of 1961 he penned an article for *The American Scene* magazine entitled "Bound for Oklahoma," and predicted that the frontier dream of a navigable Arkansas River would come to pass. His astute business sense brought about some needed physical improvements, and his imagination and native sense of values were responsible for a few budget reforms. In the meantime *The American Scene* magazine had to be published and he suggested a Remington issue, which proved to be one of the most popular of the series on great artists. The service of Glen Ames was a labor of civic pride. He contributed five months of his time and talent without compensation.

Majordomo the Third

Glen R. Ames returned to private life. His service and the work of the other directors had their effect upon the life of Thomas Gilcrease. He had seen the ambitious, the professional, the militant, and the crusader, not necessarily in that order, but surely in fact. The exposure had been good for him, and his own transmutation was a revelation to the members of his family and his intimate friends. They discovered a quality in him that had not existed before he retired from the oil business. They had witnessed what was inevitable – the reaction of man when private property becomes a public trust.

If the collection had been debt free and passed to the City of Tulsa under a bequest from the estate of Thomas Gilcrease, or presented to the city as an unrestricted gift from the foundation subsequent to his demise, the image would have been impersonal and without incident. Certainly his sons and daughter would not have felt so keenly the obligation to protect every wish of their father; they would not have been plagued with the problems of fulfilling the philosophy expressed in the documents of transfer and the other legal instruments which were concluded after long hours of study.

A survey had been made to determine the nature of "operation policy" used in other museums across the nation; however, the executive committee gained but little satisfaction out of the questionnaires which were returned. The laymen discovered that their own ideas were not always practical and they often erred in reaching decisions which were without precedent. The operation of the institute was the business of a full-time, well-qualified, diplomatic professional with previous experience. The publication of *The Journal of The Earl of Egmont,* an abstract of the Trustees' Proceedings for Establishment of the Colony of Georgia, by the University of Georgia Press in 1962 was one of the examples where there was not a unanimity of opinion. Regulations had not been formulated for the release of material for publication. The introduction to the volume carries a credit or acknowledgment to the service rendered by the directors of the Thomas Gilcrease Institute of American History and Art in releasing a prized possession — the *Egmont Journal,* and particular appreciation was expressed to James T. Forrest for his efforts in making the publication possible.

All of the smoke had not settled to the ground when a young and ambitious graduate of Colorado State University, with a bachelor of arts and a master's degree in history, became the successor to Glen R. Ames.

Dean Krakel, a native of northern Colorado, had served on the faculty of the University of Wyoming at Laramie where he taught western history. He came to Tulsa directly from the Air Force Academy at Denver, where he was deputy director and head of their fine arts program. His decision to accept the offer as director of the Gilcrease Institute was based largely upon what he terms a challenge to himself personally, and due to the realization that it would be one of the important museums on the American front in the years ahead.

He assumed his duties on June 16, 1961, and from the first day of his administration it became apparent that there would be changes made in the staff, the table of organization, and the approach to methods of exhibit and management. He put his best foot forward and marched right into the hearts of a host of people. His forte was that of militancy, and by invoking regulations accordingly, he proceeded immediately to alienate some of the civic-minded individuals who were not ready to accept his novel deportment. Dean Krakel was going to be the director, and about that there was no mistake. He had met Thomas Gilcrease on May 12, 1961, although he did not actually take over until June. Between June, 1961 and November,

1964 there was a new and positive majordomo at the helm.

Thomas Gilcrease liked Dean Krakel. He admired his aggressiveness and implementation of security measures. The institute had been fortunate and had not experienced any major thefts from the galleries and Dean was determined that none would take place while he held the whip.

The young and handsome director was schooled in the area of museum work to a greater extent than his predecessors, and it was his experience as an archivist at the University of Wyoming which impressed Tom Gilcrease. He had already authored two books on western history and this afforded him a harmonious and sympathetic relationship with his staff and Mr. Gilcrease.

His first major undertaking was the innovation of "Out On a Limb"; a letter-type inquiry which he mailed with regularity to the executive committee of the institute and by which he sought in advance the opinions and decisions on all matters which were not defined or which were not within his discretion. This medium of communication saved many hours of discussion at formal meetings and provided the civic-minded committee with facts and details they would not otherwise have known.

There were never any serious clashes between Dean Krakel and the board of directors, and his contacts with the Park Department under whose jurisdiction the museum operated were kept on the highest possible plane. If there was an area where Dean Krakel did not make the most of his opportunities during his administration, it was his reluctance to broaden the base of the institute's publicity program at the statewide level.

On October 27, 1963, Director Krakel placed a typescript in the log vault of the institute. This was the first official move to preserve important items of historical value to the museum's founding* papers, indentures of trust, resolutions, proclamations, deeds, including the deed to

---

* Three books containing records of the original transfer of the art collection from the Gilcrease Foundation to the institute. Four books reflecting the archaeological and ethnological material. Four volumes of inventory. One book of assorted papers relating to the other areas of the institute.

the collection of October 27, 1963; a specimen agenda, the U.S. Treasury Department's statement of exemption to Gilcrease Institute as a non-profit educational organization, and other matters.

The preparation of the typescript is an example of the methodical and efficient manner in which Director Krakel pursued his duties.

The negotiation for and the eventual acquisition by the institute of the William R. Leigh collection was the highlight of Dean Krakel's administration.

On November 15, 1964, Dean Krakel resigned his position to become the director of the Cowboy Hall of Fame in Oklahoma City. *The Gilcrease Gazette,* an interim publication of the institute which is printed on the old *Cherokee Advocate* printing press in the possession of the institute, recorded his leaving with a statement that the collection had grown during his directorship. His own feelings about his departure from Tulsa and the institute are most expressive; he wrote: "Mr. Gilcrease was Jeffersonian and had God let him live, I would be there with him because I loved him. In my mind it was and still is his museum. Sometimes we can care too much, and most of my shortcomings there were done in that light. No one was careful enough to suit me, and all activities had to reflect his standards, and that included the magazines. I guess he wound my mainspring too tight. Lord only knows I have missed the Institute and the wonderful people associated with it."

It will always be remembered that during Dean Krakel's tenure of duty, the new addition to the institute was dedicated. In the editorial which appeared in *The American Scene* magazine he wrote: "The Thomas Gilcrease Institute of American History and Art is both a giant and fledgling. Its story is as dramatic as the story of the Indian Territory. Gilcrease is a young museum in an historically rich setting. As a cultural force it is unmeasured – high standards and degrees of restraint always must be conspicuous in the museum's developmental fabric because what happens to the Gilcrease treasures is of national consequence, for there is just one first letter written from the new world, one first book printed in the new world, one Declaration of Independence like ours, one Paul Revere Commission, one 'Wild Turkey' in oil by Audubon, one 'Blackhawk' by Jarvis, one 'James Madison' by Peale; there was only one Charlie Russell and only one Frederic Remington. It is also true — there was only one Thomas Gilcrease."

Majordomo the Fourth

Paul Rossi joined the staff of the Gilcrease Institute on December 1, 1961. His official title was that of curator. He is a native of Denver, Colorado, where he was born on October 1, 1929. From 1930 to 1944 he spent his summers in Aspen, Leadville, and Leydon Junction. His primary and high school education was in Denver where he was a member of the Ski Club and earned letters in football, track, and wrestling. From 1946 to 1950 he worked on Colorado and western Nebraska cattle ranches and followed the wheat harvest from Texas to Canada.

He attended Denver University from 1947 to 1951 and majored in advertising design. His minors were fine arts and anthropology. While attending the university he continued his activities in ski teams, track, rod and gun club, art club work, and he played football.

Mr. Rossi is a veteran of the United States Air Force. As a trained armorer, radar observer, and a member of the 140th Fighter Squadron, 33rd Air Force, he saw active service in Korea. He enlisted in the Active Reserve in 1948 and was in the U.S. Air Force active duty from 1951 to 1952 when he received his honorable discharge.

The Colorado State Historical Society, Museum Division, engaged him as preparator in 1952, and in 1954 he was promoted to deputy curator. In 1956 he resigned his position which had included such duties as designer of exhibits, construction of dioramas, and collecting museum specimens. In 1957 he operated a commercial art studio and worked in all phases of commercial art and museum design research. He was recognized for his special talents in researching and collecting on a contractual and consulting basis and worked extensively in Colorado and Wyoming. He has been a staff artist and has designed for the Rogers Publishing Company of Englewood, Colorado, and worked on design and illustration of aeronautical subjects. From 1959 to 1961 he was senior designer and illustrator for Martin Aircraft and Missile Company.

From 1961 to 1964 Mr. Rossi was curator and deputy director of the Gilcrease Institute and assisted in administration and exhibit designs. He was delegated the important position of associate editor of *The American Scene* magazine.

Following the resignation of Dean Krakel, he was appointed acting director of the Gilcrease Institute on October 27, 1964 and on December 16 of the same year he was named director. He is married to Rita Montoya of Denver and they have six children. Paul Rossi has painted western historical subjects, modern western subjects, wildlife, outdoor subjects, aeronautical and astronomical subjects, dioramas in oil, watercolor, pen and ink, pencil, and wax. He has illustrated books, magazines, aviation, space subjects, and written on the history of American frontier cavalry equipment, uniforms, and horses, including the evolution of the American cowboy.

His brief acquaintance with Thomas Gilcrease is one of his regrets. His position with the institute during the life of Mr. Gilcrease did not afford him many opportunities to know the founder as well as others who had served in the capacity of director. Paul Rossi is not an extrovert. His demeanor in the presence of others imparts the impression that he is blessed with the faculty of giving intensive attention to the speaker, a trait worthy of any individual whose life is devoted to the arts. His talent as an illustrator permits him to see and sense the need for refinement and culture in all he does. He moves quietly but certainly. He is not pretentious in his dress and still clings to the western-style clothing, a carry-over from his Colorado ranch days.

His interest in the Oklahoma Organization of Westerners is affording him a close contact with the business of collecting, preservation, and presentation of history.

November 7, 1964, is the date to be remembered by Paul Rossi. The William R. Leigh Studio Exhibition was completed and viewed for the first time by visitors to the institute. The exhibit was produced from a picture of Leigh's studio in New York and forms a permanent display. The re-creation of the studio is done with such accuracy that one has the feeling that it was always a part of the gallery in which it is housed – and this is a credit line to Mr. Rossi for the accomplishment.

The library of the institute holds a particular interest for the new director. His knowledge of the contents is surprising when account is taken of the work load he carries in his position. If a question is propounded to him, he will look upon the one who asks it with soft eyes and without a trace of expression except for a faint smile – and then proceed to enlighten, instruct and discuss the subject with a calm possessed by few. His favorite expression of astonishment is a simple "Gee whiz!" or "Well, what do you know about that!" or again "That's great!" As a lecturer he can talk for hours without a note and recite the biography of most of the artists represented in the collection.

Paul Rossi had been Tom's guest for breakfast in the house on the hill. They had engaged in a discussion of museum activities and as usual the host was gradually transporting himself into the annals of history. He lived alone in what had once been his castle of happiness.

"May I fill your cup?" asked Mr. Gilcrease.

"No, thanks so much, Mr. Gilcrease, I must be getting back to the museum," replied Mr. Rossi.

"Well, before you go, I want to tell you the story of the mockingbird and a lone tree," he remarked.

"I shall be delighted to hear it," responded the anxious guest.

Mr. Gilcrease then told of the occasion when he was returning with some business associates from a visit to one of the oil leases of the Gilcrease Oil Company. They had been driving for an hour when he noticed a beautiful mockingbird perched on the top branch of a tree. The bird would fly above the tree, circle it, and then return to its perch. The repetition of this unusual performance so intrigued Mr. Gilcrease that he ordered his driver to stop the car. The businessmen protested because it was growing late in the day and they had a long drive ahead to reach their destination before night. Mr. Gilcrease ignored his colleagues, alighted from the vehicle, and sat down upon the ground about thirty feet from where the lone tree stood like a sentinel on the prairie. An hour passed and then Mr. Gilcrease said to his driver, "I am ready to proceed." His associates were tired and disgusted with the delay but said nothing. They did not understand and Mr. Gilcrease did not bother to explain his actions.

Paul Rossi understood and recalled that he, too, had watched and listened to the song of a mockingbird when he was a boy in Colorado. The desire of Thomas Gilcrease to interrupt the trip and provide an audience for the concert of the mockingbird was another demonstration of the depth of feeling which he possessed.

Those who have observed the strides made by Director Rossi are inclined to think that Thomas Gilcrease would have been pleased at his elevation to the position of director.

Chapter 3

Acquisition and the Galleries

Stendahl Galleries

Tom Gilcrease clung to the adage that it is better to seek the source than to follow the streamlets, and a man ought to know with whom he is dealing. He pitted his intuitive knowledge against the adroit salesmen he met in the art markets and, almost without exception, the proprietors of the galleries and studios respected him.

To those from whom he made acquisitions he was more than a "collector" or "customer." He was not always measured in terms of dollars or looked upon as a bargain hunter who would engage in resale if the price was right. His face was as familiar in the foreign houses as it was in the domestic outlets. The dealers knew him as a man with a purpose and they all understood his requirements and expectations. He was as curious and courteous when approaching a one-time acquisition as he was where his credit was recognized from previous purchases. He did not care for superficial embellishments or receptions of welcome.

To praise the achievements of a successful individual is perhaps an exercise of acceptable judgment. The usual is generally devoid of novelty and is sparked with triteness, and yet the simply stated by the educated can become artificial unless the origin is sincere and without hope of reward.

C. R. Smith, chairman of the board of directors of American Airlines and a director of the Gilcrease Institute, is a student of the arts and a collector of western art. Writing of Thomas Gilcrease after the death of the institute's founder, he said: "To see the best in the art of western America, go to Gilcrease Museum. Tom Gilcrease valued the work of Remington, Russell, Schreyvogel, Moran and others before they had widespread recognition. His judgment in paintings was sound and his courage to invest was excellent. He gave Tulsa and the nation a western museum that will never be equalled elsewhere in the world."[1]

Mr. Smith, in writing as he did, has struck the keynote of Tom's success, "sound judgment and courage to invest." Of course, there is the prerequisite of financial ability to carry out such attributes, and Gilcrease was so blessed.

Alfred Stendahl of Stendahl Galleries, Hollywood, California, called Thomas Gilcrease one of the most purposeful men he ever knew and said: "His desire was to preserve the evolution and history of frontier America. I have known personally many of our great collectors of art in many fields and I know of no man who was more devoted to the ideal with which he was imbued. His job will one day be recognized to the fullest."[2]

Stendahl, a conservative individual, did not consider Thomas Gilcrease a connoisseur of art as much as he did a good collector in a limited field. Stendahl based his opinion upon the purchases made by Gilcrease from the Stendahl Galleries and within the bounds of his inventory the criticism is perhaps acceptable. The acquisitions from Stendahl Galleries were mainly in the realm of "Ancient Mexican and pre-Columbian." He, likewise, acquired western American scenic paintings and Indian artifacts from North America, Alaska, and Canada from Stendahl. The important purchase was *The Grand Canyon* by Thomas Moran. Many of the transactions with the Stendahl Galleries were consummated with Earl Leopold Stendahl, Alfred's father. Tom would visit the elder Stendahl about once each year, although their correspondence was limited. Alfred Stendahl considered the Thomas Gilcrease Institute of American History and Art as one of the top ten museums in the world because of the uniqueness of the institute and its possession of important American western and Indian paintings, and he encompasses in his thinking the pre-Columbian and Plains Indian aspect of the collection. Stendahl felt that Tom Gilcrease had a natural curiosity and an acquired culture. This is an honest appraisal and worthy of going into the categorical archives where the lives of men are measured.

Kennedy Galleries, Inc.

Room Three, Number Three, on John's Street in New York was located at the tip of Manhattan Island, and there Hermann Wunderlich, grandfather of Rudolph G. Wunderlich, opened his print import shop in 1874.

The business grew rapidly and four years later the firm, known as H. Wunderlich & Company, established new quarters in uptown New York at 880 Broadway. Another four years saw the establishment move a few doors south to 868 Broadway, and there Hermann Wunderlich branched his activities into special interest items, such as marine paintings, art of the American West, and American miniatures of historical value. He was determined to make the name of Wunderlich represent one of the important sources for authentic paintings and prints. Upon the death of the founder,

Hermann Wunderlich, Edward G. Kennedy, the noted compiler who was responsible for publishing the James Abbott McNeill Whistler catalog of lithographs and etchings, acquired the business. By this time the firm name had been changed to Kennedy & Company, successors to H. Wunderlich & Company. The new century was under way and the new address was 613 Fifth Avenue. When Edward G. Kennedy retired, he brought Hermann Wunderlich, Jr. and his nephew, Otto Tarrington, into the company, and a partnership was formed under the style of Wunderlich and Tarrington and they continued to operate the establishment under the trade name of Kennedy & Company. Upon the retirement of Otto Tarrington, Hermann Wunderlich, Jr. and his wife Margaret assumed control of the galleries. The business is today known as Kennedy Galleries, Inc., and is located at 20 East 56th Street. From the founding date to the current location, the firm moved nine times to accommodate its expansion program and to improve its varied activities of framing and conservation, appraisals, research, and publications.

Rudolf G. Wunderlich, who now functions as the head of the galleries, first met Thomas Gilcrease in 1948 and their relationship was cemented into a monument of respect and admiration which continued throughout the life of Thomas Gilcrease.[3] Rudolf had made a western tour and, being aware of the importance of the Gilcrease collection, he wanted to establish an acquaintance with its owner. What he anticipated would be a strictly business venture ripened into an intimate association, and Gilcrease would often seek the opinion of Rudolf about paintings he had under consideration from other galleries. Commenting upon the proposition of whether Tom Gilcrease was considered a "sharp buyer" in the art markets, Rudolf has said: "I do not know if he could be classified as a sharp buyer, but he had a basic understanding that American paintings would be recognized for what they were in the future, and that even though in some cases the prices of pictures might have been high, by the standard of the time, Mr. Gilcrease felt that such paintings would either appreciate considerably as years went by or become unavailable. I think he foresaw the development in American art much more clearly than most of his contemporaries."

It has been said of Thomas Gilcrease that he would conclude an acquisition regardless of price if he found an object of art which pleased him and he wanted to include it in his collection. Wunderlich had an opportunity to observe such reference to the presumptions which have been attached to Thomas Gilcrease as a collector, and his observations are based upon actuality rather than speculation.

"What Tom Gilcrease did was always within reason with a reason. I do not recall any specific instance where he turned down a painting because of price, although there were occasions when he confided to me that he had done so. Such instances involved 'outer-fringe' dealers, or private artists who, he felt, had over-valued their material. He was by no means an amateur in his evaluation of the importance or price of paintings, artifacts, and books. He possessed a native intelligence regarding the works of the Indian and could detect a 'fake' with uncanny ability. No one sold Tom Gilcrease a bill of goods – he bought because he desired to buy."

While there are as many opinions expressed about Tom Gilcrease as there are questions which could be asked, Rudolf Wunderlich has more nearly supplied a feasible reason why the collection now housed in the institute is representative and how it expanded, than any other person.

"I believe that, like many large collections of a specific type, the collection of Gilcrease evoluted; in other words, he started buying things and before he knew it, the collection had outgrown the space he originally had in mind for it and he had to completely revise his thinking about it. Since his interest in paintings and prints lay in Indians, the West, the pioneer movement, and American historical subjects, he found his way to the Hudson River School of Art and the entire scope of American paintings, running into the twentieth century, and his interest was thereby sustained. The institute has by far the largest collection, or holding, of western Americana, supplemented by American historical paintings, as well as many important early portraits, whose importance lies in the painters, rather than in the subject matter. This applies also to his later acquisitions, such as Homer, Sargent, the Hudson River School, and others. I must comment, however, that the Gilcrease Institute, like other collections, is not yet completed. Thomas Gilcrease was aware of this and tried to fill the gaps in the last years of his lifetime. Perhaps others will justify his apprehension and continue the search," continued Rudolf Wunderlich.

The Kennedy Galleries was the source from which many major acquisitions were made as indicated elsewhere in this book, such as the Alfred Jacob Miller watercolors and George Catlin watercolors of Indian portraits. The association of Gilcrease with Rudolf Wunderlich had a slightly different aspect than other friendships. Rudolf and Tom were known to have attended Broadway shows together, and there were times when they talked over a glass of sherry when at dinner. Rudolf recalls a trip they took together on the Illinois River. Tom had invited his New York friend to join him on an Indian mound dig. "It had been an extremely hot and dry day. At the end of the day we stopped at a local combination bar-restaurant named 'The Apple Tree.' The menu called for country fried chicken. I was aware of the attitude of Mr. Gilcrease on the subject of spirits, and so I asked him, 'Tom, do you mind if I have a large glass of beer? I am utterly parched.' He nodded in the negative and after I consumed the first glass I had another one with my meal. Tom looked at me and said: 'That looks mighty tempting and refreshing but if I drank one glass it would make me dizzy and I could hardly stand up.' I could not help but speculate — was that an inherited trait of his Indian blood?"

M. Knoedler & Co.

Every art dealer, associate, colleague, or art collector who had occasion to transact business with Thomas Gilcrease did so under circumstances unique to the occasion or the purchase. If there was a pattern followed by Thomas Gilcrease in the acquisition of art for his collection, it was based upon a dislike to write letters or engage in any other means of written communication when such procedure could be avoided.

W. F. Davidson of M. Knoedler and Co., Inc., New York City, is considered a dean in the field of the gallery operations.[4] His acquaintance with Thomas Gilcrease spanned a period of twenty-three years, during which their mutual interests brought them together periodically. Thomas Gilcrease and W. F. Davidson met for the first time in 1939, and as a result of Mr. Davidson's knowledge and contacts in the art markets, he was privileged to offer Mr. Gilcrease some of the most important objects of art which are now a part of the collection of the Thomas Gilcrease Institute of American History and Art. The unusual appreciation and discernment of life exemplified by Mr. Gilcrease and his keen and acquisitive instinct, provided many challenges to Mr. Davidson and caused him to marvel at the quiet dignity and innate modesty of his customer. Mr. Davidson considered Mr. Gilcrease to be a front-rank man in the special field of Americana and believes that the collection he assembled and bequeathed to the nation through his gift to the City of Tulsa is incalculable and will increase in importance as the years wear on. Of Mr. Gilcrease, his friend Davidson has said: "The old adage that he is great who has the habits of greatness can be applied with accuracy to Thomas Gilcrease. In the area of western Americana his collection goes unchallenged and unsurpassed. He had foresight and courage which was ahead of his time, and he directed his efforts to preserve the best of the precious symbols of the past glory of the American Indian."

Characteristic of Thomas Gilcrease, his meetings with Mr. Davidson were arranged by telephone. There was a standing instruction to all of the officials and associates of the Knoedler Galleries to be on the lookout for the kind of art which met the requirements of the Gilcrease interest. When an object was located, there was an immediate contact between them, resulting in shipment to Tulsa, Oklahoma, by express, railroad Pullman car, airplane, or any other means of transportation which would assure safety and prompt delivery.

Mr. Davidson relates with almost paternal recollection that it was his suggestion to Thomas Gilcrease which resulted in the acquisition of a group of paintings representing key artists whose works had created what had become a tradition of American art down to the present. Recalling the incident, Mr. Davidson remarked: "I reminded him that the great beginnings of American paintings in colonial times started with Smibert, Feke, Copley, and West; after the Revolutionary War, Earl, Stuart, and Sully influenced the artists of the late eighteenth and early nineteenth centuries; and Homer, Eakins, and Sargent led the development in American art down to the twentieth century." The brief conversation had occurred at the Tulsa Municipal Airport, and Mr. Gilcrease merely made some notes on the back of a scrap of paper he had taken from his pocket.

It was one year later, at the same airport, seated in the coffee shop, that Tom Gilcrease and W. F. Davidson met again. Mr. Gilcrease reached into his pocket, pulled out the very piece of paper upon which he had made the notes the preceding year and said, "You know I think that idea of yours interests me. Let's do something about it."

And so it came to pass that in the non-historical field, he acquired from the Knoedler Galleries the pictures and bronzes which are among the gems of the Gilcrease collection.*

---

* John Smibert (1688-1751) *Portrait of John Cotton;* Robert Feke (op. 1741-50) *Portrait of John Rowe;* John Singleton Copley (1738-1815) *Portrait of Mrs. John Apthorp;* Benjamin West (1738-1820) *Penn's Treaty with the Indians*; Charles Willson Peale (1741-1827) *Portrait of James Madison*; Ralph Earl (1751-1801) *Portrait of Matthew Clarkson;* John Trumbull (1756-1843) *Portrait, Said to be Thomas Wilkes;* Gilbert Stuart (1755-1828) *William Temple Franklin;* John Vanderlyn (1775-1852) *Washington and Lafayette at Brandywine;* John W. Jarvis (1812-1868) *Portrait of Chief Justice John Marshall;* Thomas Sully (1783-1872) *Charles Carroll of Carrollton;* John Neagle (1796-1865) *Portrait of Red Jacket;* Hiram Powers (1805-1873) *Portrait of Benjamin Franklin* (marble); James A. McNeill Whistler (1834-1903) *Nocturne: The Solent*; Winslow Homer (1836-1910) *Watching the Breakers;* Thomas Eakins (1844-1916) *Portrait of Frank Hamilton Cushing;* Augustus Saint Gaudens (1848-1907) *The Puritan* (bronze); John Singer Sargent (1856-1925) *Beach Scene.*

Lionel and Philip Robinson, Ltd.

When Thomas Gilcrease was born in 1890, the noted artist George Catlin had been deceased for eighteen years. When the Honorable C. A. Murray, a young Englishman who had become a good friend of Catlin, armed the ambitious George with a letter of introduction to Sir Thomas Phillipps in 1840, neither could have projected that one day their names would be linked in history with that of Thomas Gilcrease.[5]

George Catlin was an American ethnologist whose parents, Puttman and Polly Sutton Catlin, had dreams that their son would become a lawyer. His legal career started at Litchfield, Connecticut, with misgivings, and he soon discovered that the oriented life of a barrister was not for him. He managed a few months of actual practice in Philadelphia and then abandoned the halls of justice for the world of art.

Young Catlin had been weaned on stories about the Indians. He would sit for hours and listen to his mother recite the experiences she had undergone when she was taken prisoner by Indians at the famed Revolutionary "Forty Fort" when the stronghold was surrendered. The youthful Catlin was consumed by the colorful dress and costumes of a delegation of warriors who visited Philadelphia, and the impressions remained with him as he went about hunting and fishing. As he matured, his imagination took a more mature road. He wrote: "The history and customs of such a people, preserved by pictorial illustrations, are themes worthy of the lifetime of one man, and nothing short of the loss of my life shall prevent me from visiting their country and becoming their historian." He managed to keep the promise.

In 1824, while residing in Washington, D.C., he embarked upon his new career and was soon recognized as an able portrait painter. Among the subjects who came to his studio were Dolly Madison, wife of President James Madison; Samuel Houston, one of America's frontier statesmen from Texas; De Witt Clinton, ace politician of the era; and other famous men and women in high positions.

At the age of thirty-six, George Catlin was determined to capture the ways and customs of the American Indian, store them in his receptive mind, and then execute his God-given talents by placing them on canvas and in pencil sketches. To further his plans he traveled extensively in North and South America. He referred to the Indians as an interesting race of people, who were rapidly passing away from the face of the earth. His summers were spent in painting among the tribes, making copious notes, sketches and memorandums as he lived shoulder to shoulder with the members of the tribes. He learned to speak their language and to interpret their tribal mores. He was completely taken by their simplicity and astounded at their native ability to survive. His artistic mind reeled in excitement, and each morning sun brought a freshness to his instrument of touch.

By 1838 his travels had taken him to forty-eight tribes and he had painted 320 portraits in oil — each of which represented studies from life. He had also produced 200 other paintings, many of which were representative of the Indians as they played their games, indulged in religious ceremonies, and danced to the rhythmical tones of war drums.

The acceptance of his work by American critics, and the success of his exhibits in the United States, gave him an assurance that he had arrived at a high point in the art world. He was determined to display his talents in Europe. His friend, the Honorable C. A. Murray, became so elated and enthusiastic that he arranged for Catlin to have an audience with the queen. The introduction to Sir Thomas Phillipps was rather routine in the beginning but proved to be of inestimable value to everything he considered, accomplished, or undertook from the moment they laid eyes upon each other. When Catlin expressed a desire to publish an account of his experiences with the various tribes of Indians he had observed and studied, Sir Thomas assumed a patron's interest in the young American and not only advised with him, but encouraged the pursuits. Their friendship was at times strained because there was a decided lack of funds in the Catlin treasury.

In 1846 Catlin informed Sir Thomas that he had lost his wife to the grim reaper and was left with four "sweet little babes to mourn for her in a land of strangers." He described the loneliness he experienced with his motherless children clinging around him. He even told Sir Thomas that the remains of his dear wife were embalmed and returned to New York. He wrote: "I am left disconsolate and heartbroken, but bound to labour and protect my dear little ones." A turning point seemed in sight when again he placed his thoughts on paper for the attention of Sir Thomas: "My collection, after completing its Exhibition for 6 months, has been ordered into the Louvre, by the King, where it has been for 6 weeks, exposed to the view of the Royal family solely. The King made 4 visits to it and has been so much pleased as to order me to copy 15 pictures, (enlarging them to double size) and which I am now painting in an attilier [*sic*] offered me in the Louvre. The compliment has been a very high one, but what the emolument will be I don't yet know; probably, like all honour, it will be a costly article."

Catlin then held out high hopes that the American Congress would make an appropriation for his collection. He said: "There has been a bill before the Congress for five years, for giving me $100,000 for it, but there is so much apathy with them and so little soul for works of art or history, that I am now rather anxious to sell the collection abroad to vex them, though I have had until quite lately a different disposition." This statement by Catlin is ironical indeed, considering what eventually became the fate of the collection, which doubtlessly would have pleased the great painter to no end.

But back to the friendship of Catlin and Sir Thomas Phillipps. The financial assistance offered by Sir Thomas and accepted by Catlin set the stage for the acquisition of the works of this great artist by Thomas Gilcrease. Catlin could not repay his loans, and Sir Thomas accepted painting in lieu of pounds. When it was all over, Sir Thomas owned at least 128 pictures bearing the Catlin signature.

The practice of obtaining loans from Sir Thomas did not stop immediately, and Catlin went further and further in debt. Some of his better works were transferred to his benefactor and provided the nucleus of the Catlin Gallery at the home of Phillipps in Middlehill in Worcestershire.

William H. Robinson, Ltd., was one of the major dealers in rare manuscripts and Sir Thomas Phillipps was a valued client. Phillipps was not primarily interested in portraits and other paintings, and the Robinson firm was not anxious to sponsor a gallery collection. Their business relationship broadened as Phillipps gained the reputation of being the greatest collector of rare documents in England, if not in the entire world. One circumstance followed another, and eventually the firm of Robinson was obliged to ascertain if there could possibly be anyone who specialized in buying portraits of Indians and related paintings. They started to investigate and a series of incidents, mostly mouth to mouth recommendations, brought to the attention of the Robinson firm the name of Thomas Gilcrease.

One of their colleagues told them that there was an Indian chief in the United States who lived way out in Oklahoma and he was very wealthy and had oil wells flowing from the ground. The stories reached the anxious ears of the Robinson brothers, and encompassed in the narratives was the fact that this Indian collector was building a museum in the geographical center of the states and was going to fill it with Americana of every type and description. Without resorting to agents or representatives, the Robinson firm lost no time in making contact with Thomas Gilcrease. This was on October 16, 1946. The letter of inquiry is produced *in toto* as follows:

WILLIAM H. ROBINSON, LTD.
16 Pall Mall
London, S W 1
16th October 1946

Thomas Gilcrease, Esq.
Gilcrease Building
San Antonio, Texas U.S.A.

Dear Mr. Gilcrease,

THE CATLIN GALLERY
Original Paintings of George Catlin
of North American Indian Life and
Scenery

I take the liberty of writing to you upon a matter which you may think of great importance and which has the exciting possibilities of a purchase.

It is in regard to the famous collection of North American Indian paintings by George Catlin now housed at Thirlestaine House, Cheltenham, England, and collected personally by the late Sir Thomas Phillipps, Bart., (1792-1872), the friend and patron of Catlin and "the greatest collector the world has ever known." These original oil paintings are fifty-seven in number. The subjects are detailed on the attached sheet.

Sir Thomas acquired the paintings directly from Catlin himself as is shown by correspondence and by notes in the Phillipps catalogue. Sir Thomas Phillipps and his collections are famous and a long account of him is given in our Dictionary of National Biography. This latter account refers to the fact that he possessed a "large collection of pictures by George Catlin, illustrative of the manners and customs of North American Indians."

Although it is too early to say whether the owners will sell these paintings, we have every reason to believe they will, for they have discussed with us the possibility of a sale by auction. My firm, who act as their advisers and agents, are very much against this for the collection would then be broken up and it would never be possible to gather it together again. We have, therefore, received permission to write to you and we very much hope you may consider acquiring the collection for your Museum. We feel you cannot make a definite decision without examining at least a few of the paintings and, if you are interested, and would cable us to that effect, we will approach the owners with a view to sending over or bringing some examples. It happens that my brother, Mr. Philip Robinson, will be coming to the United States early in December and I think it would be possible for him to bring these over with him so that you may be able to make a decision. As the matter is entirely in our hands, we shall not write elsewhere until we receive the favour of your reply and no-one knows that there is even a possibility that the collection may be for sale. As it is the only great Catlin collection in private hands it is the only one that can ever be purchaseable and we submit it is an opportunity not to be missed. The paintings are in fine condition, in their contemporary frames.

We feel it an honour to be able to introduce this matter to you and we should be very proud if the result were that the collection should join your great Indian Museum. So far as we are aware the only other Catlin paintings recorded are in the Smithsonian Institute at Washington and the copies in the Peabody Museum.

I think you may know of my firm by repute for I have had the pleasure of corresponding with Mr. Wiesendanger.

Yours sincerely,

s/ Lionel Robinson

Philip Robinson, recalling the eventful days of the foregoing epistle, says: "In retrospect I cannot help but think that there was some act of God which brought myself and my brother Lionel into the life of Thomas Gilcrease. If we had been picture dealers and not booksellers the collection might not have survived intact because there would have been other competitors for its parts. As it was, the collection was offered as a whole and then offered only the one time. If my memory is correct this was in 1946. It was more than a year after Tom Gilcrease purchased the Catlin collection that we discovered the original of correspondence and other papers between Catlin and Sir Thomas Phillipps and insisted that they should be in the possession of Mr. Gilcrease for his museum. He eventually acquired them from us."

Following receipt of Lionel Robinson's letter of October 16, 1946, Thomas Gilcrease replied, saying: "If you will ship the Catlin Collection of oil paintings to us for inspection and they are found as described in your letter and attached list, we will purchase same. I feel assured, upon arrival, the paintings will be as described by you. Will you kindly forward to us the Phillipps catalogue describing fully the collection?"

On October 30, 1946, Lionel Robinson wrote again to Mr. Gilcrease, confirming a cablegram they had sent and one which they had received from Mr. Gilcrease. In this letter Lionel wrote: "We would like to congratulate you on the acquisition of these historic paintings." He also enclosed a photograph of Thirlestaine House, from which the paintings were shipped, stating: "They were displayed in a special room named 'The Catlin Gallery' — and Mr. Alan Fenwick is the direct descendant of Sir Thomas Phillipps."

The exchange of thoughts contained in further correspondence between the Robinsons from London and Thomas Gilcrease from Tulsa would consume far too much space for this dissertation; nevertheless, there are references which are applicable to the chain of events which cemented a relationship between the correspondents difficult of belief, strange in the annals of art commerce, and practically unheard of in human relationships — to say nothing of the caution exercised in the packing and shipping of the treasures from Europe to American shores.

On April 26, 1947, Thomas Gilcrease wrote a short

letter to the firm of Robinson which typified his determination to state his case when he was sure of his position.

> Dear Mr. Robinson:
>
> We have examined the Catlin paintings which arrived some time ago. We are quite disappointed in that so many of them are only sketches. We expected them to be finished paintings such as we already have here in the gallery.
>
> Is it possible for you to pay us a visit at which time we could talk with you concerning the paintings and other things that might be of interest to us in Europe?

Note that Mr. Gilcrease, ever the shrewd trader, left the door wide open for negotiation.

May 7, 1947, Lionel Robinson responded at great length, and the important excerpt is:

> The great Phillipps collection contained — in addition to the 57 paintings now in your possession — 6 other very fine finished Catlin paintings. These latter are considerably larger than the paintings already sent to you and are very superior to them; they each measure about 2½ feet by 2 feet, exclusive of the old gilt frames. The subjects are fine depictions of Indians hunting the buffalo, Indian war dances, tribal ceremonies, etc. etc. It is probable they are as fine or finer than any of the finished paintings to which you refer as being already in your collection.
>
> I was not aware of these additional six large paintings when I first wrote to you because they had been extracted from the Catlin Gallery many years ago and had been hung in the private house of the principal trustee, and present tenant-for-life, of the Phillipps estates. That they were thus selected is evidence of their quality but it meant that I only recently became aware of them. I rather gather that it was desired that these particular paintings should be preserved in England.

Then followed suggestions by Lionel Robinson that he would endeavor to convince his principals to permit Mr. Gilcrease to purchase the six extra paintings. Mr. Gilcrease did not lose any time in replying to Robinson and he sent a cablegram reading: "Please send six paintings mentioned letter May 7." He followed his message with a letter of confirmation. He also mentioned that the collection of original drawings would interest him. Again he did not close the door because he was determined to acquire the six paintings which had been inadvertently omitted from the collection he had purchased. Robinson wrote again stating that they had been unable to persuade their principals to allow the six paintings to be shipped, but promised that he could rest assured that if they were offered for sale they would be offered first to Mr. Gilcrease and not shown to anyone else in the meantime.

August 15, 1947, another communication reached Mr. Gilcrease. It is also reproduced here in full because of the unusual ending to the story of the six paintings and the composition of expression.

WILLIAM H. ROBINSON, LTD.
16 Pall Mall
London, S W 1
15th August 1947

Thomas Gilcrease, Esq.
The Thomas Gilcrease Foundation
Ozark & Osage Roads
Tulsa, Oklahoma U.S.A.

Dear Mr. Gilcrease,

It was a great pleasure to speak with you on the telephone the other day and I wasted no time in approaching the appropriate persons in regard to the two Catlin Collections of 57 and 6 pictures. I put your views forward in the very best way I could and did not forget to add arguments of my own as to the duty and responsibility of seeing that these pictures went to the best possible museum. In the end it was agreed that the six large finished paintings should be offered to you entirely free of any charge whatsoever as compensation for any disappointment you may have felt in regard to some of the pictures in the first collection. It was felt reasonable however to ask if you would pay the sum of 800 dollars towards the actual disbursements in regard to freight, packing and insurance of both lots.

The collection of Catlin Indian portraits is something I am perfectly sure you will be very pleased with. They are not sketches but finished water-colour drawings. As I mentioned on the telephone our special searches have been successful in locating them. A preliminary cursory examination shews them to be very attractive water-colour drawings and are the actual portraits "painted from the life," signed by Catlin, and with, on the back of each picture, information in Catlin's hand giving the name of the Indian Chief or other person portrayed, the place (and in some cases the date) at which the portrait was painted, and also biographical details or other comments on the person. An example of the kind of interesting information given is on the back of one picture. It is remarked that the person died from small pox two days after the portrait was painted. This occurrance was attributed by the Indians to the portrait and Catlin had to say that he had erased the picture; whilst in fact he had merely covered it with chalk. Catlin's own remarks are frequently supplemented by observations in the hand of Sir Thomas Phillipps.

The portraits are 70 (seventy) in number and are listed as Nos. 13010 to 13079 inclusive on page 230 of the Phillipps catalogue I sent you. You will notice that it is stated that they are painted from the life in full colours shewing the costumes, weapons, trinkets, etc. When found in the Phillipps collection these portraits were bound in two collections between boards and in order to preserve them more adequately we are having each portrait mounted between hinged mats so that the wording on back as well as picture in front is seen. As soon as the work is completed we would propose to send the collection, very carefully packed, for your inspection.

Another Catlin item in the collection is listed as No. 22065 on page 410 of the Phillipps catalogue and described as "Catlin's original drawings of North American Indians . . . Purchased from Mr. Catlin himself by T. P." This collection consists of 50 water colour drawings, each signed by Catlin, of Indian portrait groups (the actual persons identified), tribal ceremonies, hunting scenes, etc. The collection is preceeded by a title written in George Catlin's hand and signed by him, reading "Souvenir of the North American Indians . . . a numerous and noble race of human beings fast passing to extinction and leaving no monuments of their own behind them. . . ." This collection is bound in old boards and we are having a suitable case made to preserve it in transit and this collection will also be sent for your inspection in due course.

I ask you to believe that we have done, and are doing, our very best to assist you and are very happy to be associated with your great work. I hope in the course of some four or five weeks to be able to say that the collections mentioned in this letter have been shipped to you. And we will continue to be on the lookout for other items that may be of interest to your Museum. I am quite sure we will be of increasing use to you over the coming years.

Believe me,

Yours sincerely,

s/ Lionel Robinson

Thomas Gilcrease welcomed the six paintings. His understanding of the purchase commitment was fulfilled.

There were other items of interest purchased by Thomas Gilcrease through the Robinson firm, and on April 7, 1949, Lionel Robinson, at midnight, wrote to Thomas Gilcrease from the Mayo Hotel in Tulsa. He said:

Dear Mr. Gilcrease & Mr. Hargrett,

Just a note to thank you for the courtesy extended to me on the occasion of my visit to the Foundation & to say how much I appreciated the privilege of meeting you. I am proud to have seen the Foundation before its official opening on May 3rd. It is a magnificent and <u>immortal</u> conception & I hope I may have the privilege of assisting in its growth and usefulness throughout the years.

I also hope we may see you in England soon. But whether this year, or next, the whole of the Phillipps Americana remains intact until you see it — and it is greater in extent than the whole of the books available in both the United States and Europe together. Those items I have left with you are, of course, far beyond the average in importance and rarity but I trust they will interest you, for it is the outstanding books that matter & the others may be had at any time.

I will be at the New Weston, New York until May 4th & if it so happens you come East I hope I may have the honour of entertaining you.

With many thanks for all your kindnesses, believe me

Yours sincerely,

s/ Lionel Robinson

In 1948, Philip Robinson and his wife visited the United States, traveled to Tulsa by air, were met at the airport by Tom's daughter, Des Cygne, driven to the museum building, and there received their first welcome in person from the Oklahoma Indian. They had for several months exchanged letters which would have spelled out priceless comments by Tom Gilcrease, but to the great regret of Philip Robinson these communications were destroyed when the William H. Robinson, Ltd., was liquidated in 1955.

The trip from London to America was a most rewarding one for the Robinsons. They were impressed with the museum, its concept, the artifacts, books, and paintings. They learned that not only was Tom Gilcrease a good customer, he was an excellent host who insisted upon their remaining longer than their planned agenda. "Upon my departure, I left with him some very precious Americana in prints and manuscripts which I had brought from London and had earmarked for other buyers. I am sure that his purchase of these treasures was one of the best buys of such material that he ever made, and once again it seemed that fate had intervened to seal the bargain and enhance his possessions," says Robinson.

Shortly after the Robinsons returned to London, they had word that Tom Gilcrease was en route to England and would visit them. It was on this occasion that Tom was presented to Philip's brother, Lionel. Relating this experience, Philip recalls: "They hit it off perfectly, and although Tom generally spent a lot of his time in Geneva he managed to visit with Lionel and me frequently. We never consummated any major transactions after the Catlin purchase but our friendship grew to such proportions that it reached a plane of intimacy, and Tom confided to us that he was for the first time in his career having financial difficulties of some magnitude. At the time, a large portion of our business was with the ancestral families who owned the great historic mansions built in other centuries, and we delighted in showing them to our Oklahoma friend. He was entirely happy and at ease in our company and despite his troubles, he charmed all whom he met. My brother Lionel was particular to accompany Tom on these expeditions which were to such places as Easton Neston, the home of the Lords Hesketh, and Alnwick Castle and Syon House, the ancestral seats of the Duke of Northumberland. It was at Northumberland that the Duke and Tom discussed, perhaps jokingly, the possibility of Tom buying the two magnificent portraits of Brant and his wife, possessed by the Duke whose ancestors took part in the French and Indian War as well as the Revolutionary War. Lionel also took Tom to the vast house of the then Duke of Westminster, Eaton Hall in Cheshire. We later learned that the Duke told his friends that he had not expected to see a person so sweet and gentle and charming as Tom Gilcrease but had rather envisaged a Red Indian Chief complete with feathered headdress."

Among the friends Tom acquired by his social contact with the Robinsons was Sir Louis Sterling. Sir Louis had been a client of the Robinsons for years and was a well-known collector in his own right. He was also a successful financier; he had made money in New York where he was born and then went to England while in the prime of his youth where he remained until his demise. Upon his death he bequeathed his vast library to London University. Tom was often his guest at the society parties in London for which Sir Louis had gained social fame. While attending one of these functions, Tom and Sir Louis solemnly exchanged hats, with Sir Louis wearing Tom's ten-gallon Stetson, while Tom coroneted himself with the English bowler of Sir Louis.

When Tom Gilcrease returned to the United States he did not mention the hat exchange incident with Sir Louis Sterling; however, on November 6, 1952, he requested his friend, Lester Whipple of San Antonio, Texas, to purchase a hat and send it to Sir Louis. Immediately after buying the hat, Lester Whipple wrote to Tom's secretary, Eudotia Teenor:

> Today in accordance with Mr. Gilcrease's direction, I bought at Joske's a XXX "open road" Stetson hat for his friend, Sir Louis Sterling, 7 Avenue Road, London, N.W. 8 England.

November 28, 1952, Sir Louis wrote to Mr. Gilcrease:

> I received a few days ago a wonderful Texas Stetson hat which is a peach and I am the envy of all my friends.
>
> There is no name of the giver and I can only assume it is you as you are the only one I know of the Western States who would be so generous. If I am correct, please accept my best thanks for your wonderful gift

and I hope the next time you are on this side of the ocean we will have the pleasure of your company at our home. Very kindest regards.

Yours sincerely,

Louis Sterling.

If Mr. Gilcrease had mailed the hat personally he would have probably included an appropriate quip and signed the card, "Injun Tom."

Philip Robinson likes to remember his friend Tom as a wonderful raconteur. His homey anecdotes, or parables, were never ending. "The one I shall always cherish relates to his shooting lodge in Jackson, Wyoming, where Tom told me he spent part of each year. He said that Jackson was the land of the 'Bad Men' where civilization had not yet developed, and that during those unregenerate early days, he and his brother would return to their homes for the winter without bothering to lock the door of their cabin, and when they came back in the spring nothing would be missing. He then reversed the thought and said that when civilization eventually came to Jackson it did little good to lock the doors, because when he came back in the spring everything was gone. 'Why,' said Tom, 'I could not even leave my car out overnight without someone syphoning out the petrol, to use the language of my English friends.' "

January 12, 1962, was the date of the last letter from Thomas Gilcrease to the Robinson brothers, Lionel and Philip. He wrote:

12th January 1962

Lionel Robinson, Esquire
Lionel & Philip Robinson Ltd.
16 Pall Mall
London, S.W. 1, England

Dear Mr. Robinson:

Enclosed is check in the sum of $5,500.00 as payment in full for the Catlin material which you sent us.

You will note the check is issued by the Thomas Gilcrease Institute of American History & Art, which explains the reason for the long delay. Museums just don't move along and do things in a hurry as an individual will do. I certainly regret this delay, but am happy the museum has the material and that you now have the "nickels."

Hope it will be my pleasure to visit with you some day and that in the meantime you and your brother enjoy the best of health.

Thanking you again and with best wishes, I am,

Sincerely,

s/ Thomas Gilcrease

Yes, the Catlins, the Robinsons, and the Gilcreases are truly a part of the art history of America and England. The Catlin collection of the Thomas Gilcrease Institute of American History and Art now numbers 75 oils, 137 watercolor paintings, and the library of letters, broadsides, and books which are among the prized possessions of Americana — perhaps the best collection of its kind in the world.

Tom Gilcrease with his sense of history found London and the Catlin works — London in particular — fascinating and a challenge to his every visit.

Chapter 4

The Gilcrease Bibliomania

"I first heard of Thomas Gilcrease through an airmail letter ordering a copy of my catalogue. No one had previously made such a request, so I reciprocated by airmailing my catalogue of the Putnam collection of anthropology. This was the first time I had ever spent thirty cents to send out a catalogue."

Charles P. Everitt did not make a poor investment. His catalog reached Thomas Gilcrease, who promptly purchased several hundred dollars' worth of books and thereafter placed repeat orders. In the months following their exchange of letters and negotiations for hardbacks and manuscripts on Americana, their relationship was one of strictly business and bargain. Then they met fact to face. "Mr. Everitt, I want you to remember that when you send me a book, it must be not only a first edition but a fine copy."

"Evidently you don't know very much about books,"

replied the brilliant Everitt, who was known in the vocation as a treasure hunter.

"Just what do you mean by that?" responded Tom, slightly astonished at the boldness of Everitt.

"Well, Jonathan Carver's *Travels* is one of the great books of western American history. The first edition is of no consequence at all. It's only when you get to the revised and enlarged third edition that you have a real cornerstone book." And then the erudite Everitt proceeded to explain to his guest that while first editions can be fine books, the seventh can be worth ten times as much to anyone who looks past the price mark.

When he concluded his bit of advice, the wealthy Oklahoman smiled and said: "I guess I shouldn't have said first edition. I should have said best edition." This edifying experience left Thomas Gilcrease a much wiser man. He knew how to keep his light a little brighter than the next person from then on when buying books. When *The Adventures of a Treasure Hunter* was published in 1951 by Little, Brown and Company of Boston, Tom Gilcrease was one of the first to acquire a copy and he no doubt read it more than once.[1]

Is a book a personal possession? Why did Thomas Gilcrease embark upon his journey as a collector of Americana? Had he discovered that Americana meant something more than a limited class of rare volumes traded or bartered by a group of odd book dealers? Did he realize that his search for books relating to American history and the Indian would not and could not be limited to the market places of the United States?

What definition did he apply to the magic word of *history*? Did he consider history to be the knowledge of events that have occurred in the past? Professor Carl Lotus Becker, who taught at Cornell University until his death in 1925, authored an essay which he called "Every Man His Own Historian."[2] He wrote: "History is the memory of things said and done in the past. But the past -- the word is both misleading and unnecessary; misleading, because the past, used in connection with history, seems to imply the distant past, as if history ceased before we were born;

unnecessary, because after all, everything said or done is already in the past as soon as it is said or done. History is the memory of things said and done." And then he concluded that such a definition reduces history to its lowest term and includes everything that is essential to understanding what it really is.

Thomas Gilcrease shared Professor Becker's thoughts about history. He learned that he could not restrict his hunt for Americana to the Indian alone. And so, the library of the institute which he founded now houses over thirty thousand books and seven four-drawer file cabinets of documents which are indicative of the things said and done about the Indian and his contemporaries and the events in the life of men who lived with them, taught them, learned from them, and profited by their traditional mores and by their dogma — the red man and the white man and all men. Each book proved to be a chronicle and every chronicle was important to Thomas Gilcrease if it was representative of Americana as he understood the word.

Subsequent to the City of Tulsa becoming the donee of the Gilcrease Museum from the beneficence of Thomas Gilcrease, its name was officially designated as the Thomas Gilcrease Institute of American History and Art. The collection of books, documents, manuscripts, and educational material covering basic information of discovery, exploration and history, became known as the Gilcrease Library.

The collection was more or less a maze of unexplored material. Mr. Gilcrease, in his quest for manuscripts and books, had neglected inventory, preservation, and cataloging. With the formation of the corporate body which was to accept the responsibility in conjunction with the Tulsa Park Board, the supervision at first fell upon certain spirited citizens, who served without hope of reward or compensation.

Martin Wenger was born at Telluride, Colorado. At the time of his birth there were approximately 1,337 souls living in the friendly community, which was not far from Mt. Sneffels, which has an elevation of 14,143 feet, and Mt. Wilson, equally as high. His boyhood was spent at Grand

Junction, and after completing grade and high school he attended the Utah University where his major was in the subject of history. He then pursued his graduate work at Denver University, which was so outstanding that he received an appointment as assistant state archivist for Colorado under Delores Renze, a most capable lady who is now president of the American Society of Archivists. At the time of this important advancement in his career the State Archives was still a division of the Colorado State Historical Society.[3]

Mr. Wenger was fortunate to have the opportunity to work closely with the history library which was housed in the same building where he was employed. He was able to explore the records of the Denver and Rio Grande Railroad, documents on the administrations of Colorado governors, and other historical materials. Western American history held an extreme fascination for him, due to the frontierlike range country where he had matured into manhood. He joined the Denver Westerners, an organization of amateur and professional historians who discussed history over their meals when they met each month to hear scholarly papers written by their members. He met Fred Rosenstock, one of America's truly great book dealers, who recognized the talents of this young and ambitious historian from Telluride. All of these developments increased his interest in the study of history, book publishing, and the mysteries of rare documents.

The curator of the historical society was James T. Forrest, who had been watching the career of Martin Wenger, and in 1955 when Mr. Forrest became the director of the Thomas Gilcrease Institute of American History and Art he urged Wenger to visit Tulsa, hoping that this talented young man would accept a position which would place him in charge of the history materials in the collection. Wenger made an extensive tour of the library and said: "Jim, this is truly an amazing collection. I had anticipated that it would be primarily made up of manuscripts and, of course, I am basically a trained archivist. To my astonishment this is a library of Americana and its magnitude is difficult to assess. It offers a terrific challenge to a librarian!" Jim stood in silence for a moment, looked at Wenger, and then in a sweeping glance surveyed the storehouse which met his eyes and responded, "You could be right, but what we need is someone who knows the collection and what it represents, someone who is willing to develop it and not just process it." Wenger returned to Denver where he carefully considered the offer. He could not forget some of the people he had met on his brief visit. He was inspired by the sincerity and devotion exemplified by Alfred E. Aaronson, as well as the comments of Forrest.

By coincidence he had been offered a position by Dean Krakel who was then in charge of a western history collection at the University of Wyoming Library. Krakel had invited him to accept the position of his assistant. The problem was resolved when Wenger decided to accept the offer of Forrest. This brief summation becomes historically important to the biography of Thomas Gilcrease because the same Dean Krakel was later to succeeed James T. Forrest as director of the Gilcrease Institute.

Wenger was bewildered by the vast amount of material which confronted him when he assumed his post. It seemed that every metal shelf, all the file cabinets, and other containers were filled to capacity with books of different dimensions, many of which were stacked one upon the other. He was fearful that the mere touching of some of the old volumes by unskilled hands would cause irreparable damage to the treasured tomes, and he desired to correct some of the existing practices and to invoke rules for the protection and preservation of what had been entrusted to his care.

The more familiar he became with the collection, the more he realized the necessity for transforming it into an organized library. He recognized the need for funds and man power, neither of which seemed to be available. The bulk of the library consists of books published in the nineteenth century relating to frontier and Indian subjects. There are over five hundred books published before the year 1800, whose aggregate monetary value was said to exceed $175,000; and he was told that the entire library, including the manuscripts, was appraised at well over $1,000,000.

The books range in publication date from 1494 to the present, with practically all having been published before the year 1900, and even those published after that date, for the most part, pertain to the period of time prior to 1900.

There are over twenty legal-size file drawers housing much of the collection, including the papers of John Ross, long-time chief of the Cherokee Indians, embracing the period from 1814 to 1870. There are the papers of Peter Pitchlyn, a Choctaw lawyer and chief, of whom mention will be made later in this chapter; papers of William Burnet, governor of the New York Colony; diaries of General Ethan Allen Hitchcock; and over six file drawers of invaluable early Latin-American documents dating back to the earliest days of the conquest of Mexico (1519-1521). There is also a manuscript dated 1516 relating the first account of the voyages of Columbus. These were only a minor representation of what Mr. Wenger laid his bulging eyes upon when he was formally introduced to the Gilcrease Library.

In the eight years of Mr. Wenger's administration he learned that Thomas Gilcrease knew more about the library than he had imagined. If origins could not be traced through office records, he would often consult Mr. Gilcrease and with dispatch he would have his questions answered. The secret of the retained knowledge of Thomas Gilcrease about the materials remained a soul-searching challenge to Martin Wenger.

In excess of 580 students have made use of the library facilities since it was opened for such purpose under the auspices of the City of Tulsa. There has been some feeling on the part of those close to the library operation that its future use as a repository for source material is difficult to predict because of the current restrictive use of the material for publication; however, it is felt that when the task of accurate cataloging and indexing has been microfilmed completely, or at least to an extent where such reproductions can be utilized, the library will become a nationally sought source for students of history. Since the library became city property there has been a limited number of books acquired and the estimated acquisitions will approach slightly over a thousand volumes.

By 1957 several Tulsans had served in the capacity of committee chairman and co-chairman. It was difficult for them to grasp the actual merit of the library contents, and with this thought in mind Mr. Wenger prepared a statement which appeared in the November-December Gilcrease Newsletter, designed to serve as a paper of current events about the activities of the institute. He wrote:

> A Library devoted to the study of American history is as strong as its documentary collection. Thousands of books have been written about our country's past, but only those which contribute new knowledge or shed new light on past events will survive a long period of time. The Gilcrease Institute Library is particularly fortunate in being able to have at its very beginning a large quantity of significant primary sources materials unused as yet by scholars. The future greatness of the library will depend on the success of the library plan to acquire still many more documentary materials, particularly in the fields of Oklahoma history and the American Indian.

The infant had begun to crawl, and walking days were evident in the distance. Martin Wenger's job called for endurance, ability, patience, and dedication. He possessed these qualifications and understood, as best one could, the attitude of Thomas Gilcrease about the past policies under which the collection had been partly available to the scholars, few that they were, who knew about its existence. They did not see book to book on every question, and there were times when one of lesser strength of faith would have tendered a resignation and moved forward to more fruitful institutions of like nature.

Wenger's talent, his tenacious attitude toward the accomplishment of the work for which he understood he was employed, gave him the impetus to press forward and bring order out of a chaotic situation. Organization was wanting. The books were inserted into the shelves end to end, side to end, and top to bottom. It was a study in confusion and, according to Wenger, resembled a grocery shelf where canned foods were stacked without purpose or relationship.

Recalling the hectic days, he indicated that Mr. Gilcrease was an island unto himself when it came to knowing the contents of the library collection. He could locate any book in which he had a special interest but woe unto others who sought a desired special volume. It was like searching for a precious pearl in a bowl of polished rice.

Wenger was determined to devise and execute a workable card file system of classification. He made a survey which will eventually lead to a positive cataloging program. His foundation material has made it possible for diversified subjects to be located by scholars and researchers, thereby making the institute a veritable paradise for those who would explore the life of the American Indian, western history, and the rustic plains of the hard-riding pioneer of what was once a romantic existence.

He was shocked to find rare and wonderful books in physical surroundings with low-rated, modern fiction which unquestionably had been included in purchases which Mr. Gilcrease had made from other collectors without being aware of their presence. He was equally filled with consternation when he discovered a copy of Bishop Summaraga's *Doctrine Breve,* the first book printed in the New World (Mexico, 1544), said to be valued at $25,000, commingled with other volumes whose value was nil by comparison. Such discoveries led to the erection of a security enclosure, guarded by heavy screen wire doors, as a deterrent to the untutored handling of the precious by the precocious but impractical hands which too often reached out for too much.

Martin Wenger had read somewhere that the basic intellectual virtues are understanding, knowledge, and a willingness to appreciate the efforts of others. The nasty word *policy* had to be defined. There were lay opinions and professional opinions. And then errors of judgment followed experimental rules and regulations. Most of the appointed civic leaders were strangers to all of this activity; nevertheless, it was imperative that a policy-designating purpose be developed. Mr. Wenger was fortunate to have the counsel of Mr. Gilcrease and Mrs. Eudotia Teenor, his long-time and faithful secretary. He was also impressed with a Tulsan who became one of the most dedicated civic assistants to the library. Working with Mrs. W. R. Holway and others, the purpose statement of the library was finalized. It read as follows:

> The Gilcrease Library is one containing basic primary information of a documentary nature of great value as a source for the study of American civilization. The books and manuscripts contain original facts about phases of our past and as such they are the physical link between a time that was and the present day. They are treasured, protected, and assigned high monetary values because of the importance of the information contained in them and not because of their rarity. As such they must be carefully protected and preserved as facilities for the advancement of learning. The only justification for their existence and maintenance is that they will be available for use. At the same time the library must protect itself by limiting its use to competent scholars whose research is for a significant subject and who will use his findings to make an enduring contribution to civilization. This restriction will guarantee the security of the precious materials and at the same time establish a certain respect and dignity that will mark the Institute in the eyes of the world as being one of high caliber.
>
> There are many books of historical value in the library which are not rare. These should be made available to a general patron upon request if that person requires the use of such a book to obtain relevant information. Such patrons would use the books under the same rules and restrictions that are prescribed for the use of the rare books and original manuscripts. The books would not be circulated nor would they be provided for mere curiosity.
>
> The Gilcrease Library is a public trust. Its purpose is to serve the public by being of assistance in studying and interpreting American civilization or phases of it for the public good. It operates on the principle that a free people can remain free only if they are an informed people. The Gilcrease Institute is responsible for providing historical knowledge to patrons or the

general public whenever such information can serve a public good or is requested to do so. As such it is in a position to render a valuable service in the promulgation of American Ideals.

Following the foregoing statement of policy, certain rules and regulations were adopted. They are:

> The application for the use of the facilities of the Gilcrease Institute Library requires that the applicant list his name and permanent and Tulsa address, his telephone number and the subject of the research intended. He is then obligated to detail the purpose of the research, whether it is for a book or article, a thesis or other writing. He is required to set out in detail the extent and use of secondary sources, his publication plans, institutional affiliation, and the date or period for which the privilege is requested. He must then give adequate references and agree to extend credit to the Gilcrease Institute for any use made of the materials and information obtained through the facilities of the library. He then commits himself not to publish in whole or in part such materials without the written permission from the Director on forms provided. Such is the promise of the applicant who agrees to observe the regulations established and governing the use of the materials. As a final gesture of good faith and ethics the applicant must sign the request.

There were soul-searching questions flying in and out of Martin Wenger's potent mind. He would retire at night wondering — was Tom Gilcrease really consumed with curiosity about the lives of people? Did he actually have a craving to learn something about the thoughts and adventures of his fellow Creeks or Indians in general? Did the biographies and memoirs of the writers whose books he acquired teach him, or did he want them so that they would be source material for students of the future whom he would never meet or know? Was Mr. Gilcrease an individual who would not settle for anything less than the whole truth if he could find it? He had watched Mr. Gilcrease in the stacks.

No one else knew the location of the books as well, and when he would seek out one of the rare volumes it would be fondled as if the pages were the tender tresses of a child's long hair. He had a way of opening a book lightly and with such caution that one would have thought every page would disappear when he touched it.

The more Mr. Wenger worked in and out of the cases which had been built to specification for Mr. Gilcrease by Remington-Rand, the more he was convinced that methods, when classified and separated, acquire their true bearing and perspective, as means to an end and not as ends in themselves.

The pattern was set and Mr. Wenger served faithfully from 1955 to 1963, when he was succeeded by Daniel M. McPike. The new librarian, like his predecessor, acquired a good working knowledge of the library and it was only a short time until his services were sought by the researcher and the student.

In the interim, Hope Holway had given of her time and knowledge as a civic servant without compensation except the reward of accomplishment and her natural love for books.[4] This remarkable lady was already known as one of the cultural leaders of Tulsa and had received her education at Radcliffe College where she studied under Edward Channing. Her talents in the field of Oklahoma history and archival work, special studies of the pioneer woman, teachers of Indian Territory, and author of two books and numerous articles, became indispensable to the development of the library policy and its regulations.

The Hispanic Documents

The Hispanic Documents Collection in the Gilcrease Library consists of 26,000 pieces. There are 275 manuscript units of various dates from 1512 to 1857 written in Mexico, South America and the Southwest of the United States as part of the drama of Spanish civilization in the New World. One of the earliest of these is a letter from Hernando de Soto to Ponce de Leon written June 27, 1535. Another is a decree issued by Cortez in 1521 during the conquest of Mexico. Others are letters from Diego Columbus, son of the Admrial of the Seas (Columbus), and from Bartolomé las Casas, the great humanitarian Bishop of Chiapas. Many printed works in the Spanish language supplement the Hispanic collection.[5]

William S. Bailey, Jr., Tulsa, a member of the board of trustees, past president and past chairman of the board, provided a grant with which to compile a catalog of the Hispanic documents. Thus began the ardous task in the spring of 1960, which was completed in the summer of 1961. The part of the collection known as the Conway Papers was kept intact, in the order in which they were first placed in the institute. The catalog reflects that some of the most important documents for the history of Spanish-speaking America are found among the items. They are all important from the standpoint of linguistics and human history for they supply details of daily life not readily available from any other source. The transcriptions and compilations were made by Dr. Clevy Lloyd Stout, Associate Professor of Spanish, Department of Modern Languages of the University of Tulsa.

An official copy of the Declaration of Independence, signed and attested by Benjamin Franklin and Silas Dean, is one of the treasured documents of the library. It is the only one known to exist outside of the Library of Congress.[6] It was acquired on December 14, 1949, from the Rosenbach Foundation through Mr. Philip Rosenbach, together with other important instruments to which reference will be made in this chapter.

The copy of the Declaration of Independence was purchased by Philip Rosenbach in the summer of 1912. He was a guest in the Hotel Adlon in Berlin, Germany, and was visited by a German dealer, one Breslauer. This dealer had three manuscripts for sale, and why they were referred to as manuscripts is most speculative, nor is it known how or when the manuscripts fell into the hands of private dealers.

The facts, alleged to be authentic, reflect that Franklin and Dean had presented the important copy to the minister of Frederick the Great. After the acquisition by Philip Rosenbach, he is said to have sold it to a Mrs. Fishblatt for the sum of $5,000 and later recaptured it under circumstances not revealed. A value of $160,000 was placed on the manuscript.

In 1949, on the fourteenth day of December, Thomas Gilcrease, who had negotiated with the Rosenbach company on prior occasions, began a series of conversations with the Rosenbachs through their agent or representative and concluded a transaction for the sum of $125,746, which included the attested copy of the Declaration of Independence.

Paul Revere

Every school child in the United States at some time in the process of being instructed in American history learns about the famous ride of Paul Revere, the lantern in the church belfry, and how he leaped upon his horse and galloped away. His now historic midnight ride has become legendary and the incident subjected to much distortion because of the temptation to dramatize the hero. The actual ride occurred on either April 18 or 19, 1775. Following the "Boston Tea Party," when Samuel Adams disguised his soldiers as Indians, proceeded to the wharf, boarded the vessels, opened their chests, and threw the tea into Boston Harbor, Commander Gage decided to send a secret expedition to capture or destroy military stores at Concord. His plans were suspected by the insurgents and his movements noted. Then on the evening of April 18 an expedition was sent out. By an agreed plan of signals Paul Revere, waiting at the Charlestown shore, learned the route by which it had started and, on a horse borrowed for that purpose, rode through the country arousing the inhabitants. He was joined by William Dawes, who had left Boston by another route, and by the time the regulars reached Lexington Green, their pathway was obstructed by a small company of minutemen. This was the first armed resistance.

And so it was that he gave warning of the approach of British troops from Boston. His exploit became known throughout the country. He had already enjoyed a good reputation as an engraver and silversmith. He was acclaimed the hero of the hour, and on April 29, 1775 — just eleven days after he made the ride — he was accorded a commission by General Joseph Warren,[7] which certified him to the Commission of Safety and provided that all dispatch and assistance be given to him in all instances, ". . . that the triumph of the Colony may be facilitated. . . ." This now important document is a part of the Gilcrease Library collection where it has been viewed by thousands of school children, adults and serious students of research. Major General Joseph Warren signatured the commission to Paul Revere.* The passage of the Stamp Act had aroused his patriotic sympathy and brought him in close contact with Samuel Adams and other important men of that era. He drafted the "Suffolk Resolves," which urged forcible opposition to Great Britain. Among other appointments, he was an active member of the committee of public safety. On June 14, 1775, General Warren was commissioned a major general, but three days later, and before his commission was made out, he took part as a volunteer, under the orders of Putnam and Prescott, in the battle of Bunker Hill (Breed's Hill), where he was killed. This was forty-six days after he placed his name to the document described herein. Is it any wonder that Thomas Gilcrease wanted to, and did, acquire this invaluable commission where it is now a part of the vast storehouse of Americana he collected?

---

* Joseph Warren was born in Roxbury, Massachusetts, on June 11, 1741. He was an American Revolutionary patriot. He graduated Harvard in 1759 and practiced medicine in Boston.

The First Extant Letter from America of Diego Columbus

"The Spanish expeditionary force had invariably treated the Indians well, but they found that the white man was in bad repute with the Indians, because callous traders had treated them harshly and caused the Indians to look with suspicion upon the Spanish soldiers, and with bitter skepticism upon the Spanish priesthood." This statement is one of the "secrets" revealed to Diego Columbus by Diego de Velazquez. The astute Thomas Gilcrease knew this choice bit of history of the Indians, and when he became acquainted with the contents of the first extant letter from America of Diego Columbus, son and successor of Christopher Columbus, he was determined that the document be a part of his famed collection. The letter is dated January 12, 1512 and the brochure published by Magg's Brothers, booksellers to His Majesty the King, in 1929, carries the following foreword:

> It is an original letter, hitherto unrecorded, which Diego Columbus (son and successor of Christopher Columbus) sent to the famous Cardinal Ximenez de Cisneros, Archbishop of Toledo. The text of the letter, written on two and a quarter pages of folio paper by Diego Columbus's secretary, contains the final words: *"Illustrious Sir, Servitor of Your Very Reverend Lordship whose very magnificent hands are kissed by"* in the autography of Diego Columbus himself, and is signed by him as follows: El Almirante (the Admiral). The letter is dated from Santo Domingo, Hispaniola Island, on the 12th January 1512. (The italics are actual quotations from the original letter in translation.)

The inclusion of this priceless letter in the Gilcrease Library is another instance of the desire on the part of its founder to make available to the searching minds a manuscript of rare quality and content.[8] This is especially true when it is considered that although various letters exist which were written by Christopher Columbus, those of his son, Diego, are very rare, for besides this unrecorded letter only two other extant personal letters are recorded, and but three additional documents bear his signature. This letter is the earliest, and in it Diego Columbus tried hard to influence the king, through Cardinal Ximenes de Cisneros, to abolish the pernicious system of *repartimientos*, or grants of Indians, amongst the earlier Spanish settlers, whose rapacity caused them to work their slaves inhumanly and was not only undermining such good influence as the priesthood might have been exercising in the Indies, but was defeating its own object by causing the destruction of the Indians. Diego Columbus declared:

> Your Very Reverend Lordship, as a Christian and the Light and Mirror for us all, should prevail upon His Highness to give effect to these things which make for the service of God, as this can be better impressed upon them (the natives) now than at any other time.

Bernaldez Codex of Columbus Voyages

Another interesting and rare manuscript to be found in the collection is the account of the voyages of Columbus written by Andres Bernaldez and indexed as the "Bernaldez Codex of Columbus Voyages," or a manuscript volume of an ancient classic. The author was born about 1450 at Fuentes-de-Leon, Spain, and, in 1488, was appointed curate of the village of Los Palacios, near Seville. After the voyage of Columbus, Bernaldez was made chaplain to the Archbishop Diego de Deza, a friend of the discoverer. When Columbus returned from his second voyage and was traveling toward the court of Spain, then in Burgos, he passed through Los Palacios where he was the guest of Bernaldez. Describing this visit Bernaldez wrote:

> He was my guest and left me some of his writings in the presence of Don Juan de Fonseca, from which I copied and abridged them with others which the honorable Dr. Alvarez Chanca and other noble gentlemen wrote, who were with him on the voyage already related, who wrote, what they saw; from which I was informed and wrote this about the Indies as being a marvelous and heroic thing.

Bernaldez then commented that the admiral related to him his adventures, gave him a copy of some of his notes, so that his account is virtually as told by the great discoverer himself.

It is a stimulating commentary that the documents pertaining to the Indian comprise a great part of the entire collection, and approximately seventy percent of the books are on subjects dealing directly or indirectly with the American Indian. There is always human interest in trying to determine the books and documents which are considered the oldest and most important to any worthwhile collection, and such a summation would depend upon the opinion of the one who makes the evaluation. Certainly in the top level would be the original Aztec Codex. The twelve-volume geography of Jean Blaeu, with its decorative and authentic maps (Amsterdam, 1663), the four-volume British Admiralty charts of the Atlantic Ocean known as the *Atlantic Neptune* (1777-80), Pallou's life of Father Serra (1787), Frederick Catherwood's *Views of the Ancient Monuments of Central America,* beautifully colored lithographs (1844), Henry Lewis' rare *Das Illustrirte Mississippithal* (1857), Wharton's *History of Denver* (1868), the original edition of Pat Garrett's life of Billy the Kid (1882), a copy of the first edition of Asa Mercer's *Banditti of the Plains* (1892), and Joel Palmer's *Travels Over the Rocky Mountains* (1847). These selections represent the choices of Martin Wenger.

While there is the ever-present temptation to include in this chapter many other important documents and manuscripts, it is evident that to do so would within itself require many volumes of notes and explanations; suffice it to add, however, that within the stacks of the library are treasures such as the Thomas Jefferson letter on the drafting of the Declaration of Independence, dated July 1, 2, 1776; the *Journal of the Earl of Egmont,* being an abstract of the Trustees' Proceedings for Establishing the Colony of Georgia, 1732 to 1738. This journal has now been published with proper credit to the Thomas Gilcrease Institute of American History and Art by the University of Georgia Press and edited by Robert C. McPherson.[9] This has been one of the few times when a possession of the institute was released for publication. The introduction affords the credit as follows:

> It is with pleasure that acknowledgment is made of the public service rendered by the Directors of the Thomas Gilcrease Institute of American History and Art in releasing a prized possession, this volume of the Egmont Journal, for publication.

The Gilcrease Library has been best described as a non-circulating reference and research library. It reveals dramatically authentic and critical memorabilia of our American heritage and guides the researcher to rusty doors behind which are discovered the struggles and the sacrifices which were indulged by the men who lived by their wits and survived by their faith. It beckons to the sincere student and encourages the curious to probe, interpret, process, and refine the genuine.

There is a great need for a stepped-up budget. The purchase of new and supplemental works is a must and not a suggestion. There cannot be a random or mere chance purchase. The base must be broadened by careful selection and money made available to extend the regions of study where limitation of source material has stopped on the shelves.

The untouched books must be opened, and in the end the rare books will not remain as mere monuments to a forgotten past. The Americana cannot be treated as "sleepy material" – otherwise it might be relegated to the state of keeping company with the tomes of the stacks. Those who are charged with the responsibility of the library must not only remember, but keep, the spirit of the founder in every corner where surely he is watching to see that the safety of the materials must never take precedence over availability and meaningful use.

The rare books housed in the library are of such magnitude in number that the visitor without credentials can grasp but a small segment of what he is told or what he can observe. Among the major items purchased by the Thomas Gilcrease Foundation from William H. Robinson, Ltd., in England will be found *Mexican Imprints,* a collection of twenty-four tracts, the majority of which were printed in Mexico in 1725-27; *The New England Trials of Captain John Smith,* bearing publication date of 1622; *Las Casas,* a memorial to Philip II, written entirely in the autograph of Las Casas in 1555; the manuscript on New Mexico, containing twenty-five eighteenth-century descriptions of very important early sixteenth-century documents, printed in 1788; the original manuscript *Relacion del Descubrimiento del Peru,* written by the Conquistador Diego de Truxillo, 1571; and a priceless document from Abraham Lincoln, bearing his signature, in which the Smithsonian bequest was accepted. This instrument is dated 1862.

William S. Bailey, Jr., acquired and presented other rare works to the library – the acquisition being made from Lionel & Philip Robinson, Ltd. – such as, the original correspondence of George Catlin with his patron, Sir Thomas Phillipps,[10] the renowned collection of books and manuscripts, consisting of seventy-six letters from Catlin to Phillipps and drafts of fifteen replies from Phillipps, of which eleven are written on the blank spaces of Catlin's letters. A forty-leaf book containing anecdotes of Catlin's hunting experiences and a list with descriptions of the twenty-five paintings illustrating La Salle's discoveries in North America, which Catlin executed for King Louis Philippe of France. These are representative of the gift which cannot be appraised today in dollars and cents. The foresight of the donor is the character of augmentation which will make the Gilcrease Library a meaningful and much sought-after repository for students.

The other gems in the great necklace of Americana include the Grant Foreman collection on the history of the state of Oklahoma and the Indian, original editions of works by Catlin, Schoolcraft, McKinney and Hall, Drake, Curtis, and Morgan, all dealing directly with the history of the American Indian. A copy of the book written by Martin Waldseemüller and published in France, which suggested that the New World be named after Americus Vespuscius, is also contained in the library. In a later book published in 1509, Waldseemüller tried to correct his error but the name America stuck with the people and the writers of history. There are books dealing with published and unpublished sources of Cherokee history and, as a matter of fact, with all of the Five Civilized Tribes. Books printed in various Indian languages, such as the Creek, Sioux, Mohawk, Chippewa, Muskogee, and Cherokee. The works of the Bureau of American Ethnology are well represented in distinct volumes, together with many studies and reports issued by the federal government.

A summation of what the Gilcrease Library really means cannot be better phrased than in the closing paragraph on "The Library" which appeared in the dedication issue of *The American Scene* magazine published by the institute in 1963, written by Martin Wenger:[11]

> As time moves away from the colorful and rich frontier period of our culture and we enter the space age of missile and automation, the Gilcrease library becomes increasingly valuable as a permanent repository of the record of that frontier. It not only possesses instruments of that frontier and thus provides physical evidences of our heritage, but it contains

a large amount of basic primary information about our past that yields understanding and appreciation of our heritage. As time advances, the demand for such information will grow and the need to understand our past will continue and intensify. Only then, will the true greatness of Thomas Gilcrease's work in assembling this library become apparent.

Book 5
The Patron

Chapter 1

Protégés

Willard Stone

"Willard, I have a piece of ebony which I acquired from Africa and I want you to carve me a buffalo. I want it all in one piece and I wish you would make it as large as the size of the ebony if you can!" That was the first direct order that Willard Stone ever received from Thomas Gilcrease. Willard looked at Tom askance and would have tried to respond but Tom broke in and said: "This is the hardest material in the world to carve and from the shape of the block I doubt if you can get a good buffalo out of it, but if you can, I'll never worry about your talent, and you need not worry about tackling anything that you want to carve out of wood."

The buffalo came to life out of ebony and is a part of the Thomas Gilcrease Institute of American History and

Art collection with numerous other carvings bearing Willard's signature.

When Willard Stone met Tom Gilcrease in the winter of 1946,[1] he knew little about him except that he was a collector of art and had some kind of a museum where most of the paintings and other art objects were related to Indian lore. Willard was in his studio at his home in Locust Grove, Oklahoma, a small community within easy driving distance of Tulsa. He saw the mailman and made little effort to examine the few letters which had been placed in his box. Mail did not mean too much to Willard. And then he found that one of the envelopes had the return address of the Gilcrease Foundation on it. Willard had been applying some hot linseed oil to one of his statuettes. He dried his hands and in a state of wonderment opened the letter.

"Mr. Stone, I am interested in your work and I would like to have you come to my home in Tulsa. As you may have heard, Woodrow Crumbo, the talented Indian artist, is in residence near my home and we could have a good talk." Their meeting culminated in an arrangement whereby Mr. Gilcrease paid Willard an annual salary of three thousand dollars. It was understood that because of Willard's desire to be with his family—his wife and eight children—he could commute between Tulsa and Locust Grove. There was, however, one stipulation which Mr. Gilcrease placed on their bargain, which had been sealed with a handshake, the customary manner in which Tom Gilcrease liked to do business. All of the wood carvings completed during Willard's tenure at the institute were to become the property of Tom Gilcrease without any reservations or additional compensation. The three-year grant gave him the opportunity he had dreamed of. He could strive for perfection and at the same time be assured that his family would get the proper food and clothing they needed so badly. "I must have whittled a hundred items!" recalls Willard through his ever ready smile and the warm glow which is so much a part of him.

Willard Stone was born in Oktaha, Muskogee County, Oklahoma, on the twenty-ninth day of February, 1916. His parents were George McCoy Stone and Lyda Blanche Headrick Stone. When he was a year old, his father died and the Stone family had to pool their efforts to support a large family. The land was not the best and paying crops were the exception and not the usual. He grew up with a suddenness that would bring fright to the average boy, but at the age of twelve he was in the cotton fields and doing man's work in a boy's world.

The elementary school work of Willard did not leave him too well prepared for high school, but his mother insisted that he attend classes even though there were days when she needed him at home. He used up more crayons than most of his classmates, and every particle of paper around the house fell victim to his marking and his drawings. Mrs. Stone managed to save enough money to buy her young son some art books but he soon used them to the full extent of their space and wanted more crayons and more paper. One day after he entered high school at Oktaha the teacher bought some books which told about a great artist named Michelangelo and another called Rembrandt. The keen eyes of Willard began to pop — he liked to read of their work and the more he read the more he wanted to know about them, especially Michelangelo — and some of the sparks of wisdom from the chisel of the master burned deeply into his youthful brain — such as: "The promises of this world are for the most part vain phantoms, and to confide in one's self, and become something of worth and value, is the best and safest course." Or again — "By sculpture I mean the work that is executed by cutting away from the block; the sort that is executed by building up resembles painting." The latter quotation became Willard's pilot through many long and stormy days and nights. Michelangelo's fantastic ability gave him courage and taught him what the greatest of them all had said: "Genius is eternal patience."

Then came the tragedy which almost ended the world of drawing and painting for young Stone. He had never seen a dynamite cap and when he found several near his home he did what a boy would do — he struck them together and the immovable object met the irresistible force. A blinding flash followed; fortunately instinct caused him to cover his eyes, but it was all too quick and painful. The force of the blast severed three fingers with such devastation that they disintegrated. His right hand was badly mangled. For many weeks it seemed to Willard Stone that the birds came close to him in flight to cheer him, even the howl of the prairie dog changed its cry. Every day for months his mind would flash back to the moment of the explosion and he would relive what he had done. He would recall seizing his wrist with his left hand to hold back the blood, running as fast as his thirteen-year-old legs would take him — to his mother. He would recall the comfort of his mother's devotion and her prayers that his hand would heal sufficiently for him to resume his talent which she knew would someday blossom into a full bloom. She also knew that it was necessary to continue the love pattern she felt for her son without his being aware of her own feelings. She did not want him to indulge in self-pity and thereby become the unconscious victim of deep hostility. She was a wise soul. With these thoughts she encouraged him to use his left hand, hoping that he would eventually conquer the transformation. She knew that the crucial moments had arrived. Would it be frustration or fulfillment? Was her son afraid? Would he continue to live on the dregs of memory?

The catastrophe had matured a boy. He still had a longing which could not be satisfied, and even in his youth he seemed to know that he was growing up and that men are moved by two levers only, fear and self-interest. He would not bow to fear and his self-interest was to be an artist. Commenting on those days of decision and indecision, Willard has said, "Not only did I lose three fingers on my right hand, but the accident blew away my desire to paint and my interest in schooling!" There was only one solution. He commenced to use the injured hand. He recalled that baseball players were known to squeeze rubber balls to strengthen their hands — and so he began modeling with moist clay and any other pliable material he could acquire. This activity led to the discovery that he could hold a knife in the injured hand without too much pain to the stumps which had once been normal fingers. He learned that a sharp knife under his guidance could follow the grain of a piece of wood and that he could tell how the texture would react to his skills.

At fifteen he was known as the boy who could carve a bird or animal out of a block of wood. He had learned something about making clay models of various objects. While his first efforts reflected the need for formal study, he found that he had a natural movement with the instruments he used, so much so that there was a semblance of accuracy to the models which called for a knowledge of anatomy and perspective. The drawing board was useful but his eyes were photographic and the images unfolded before him. He had suddenly developed a creative process instead of a mechanical approach. Muscle structures became a challenge to him. The lurid details of anguish gave way to power and dignity of purpose. An artist was born.

Grant Foreman, the Oklahoma historian, learned about the talents of Willard Stone and suggested to him that his education should be implemented by attending Bacone College in Muskogee, Oklahoma. He entered Bacone in 1936. The transition was not without difficulty; there were many things to consider, none the least of which was adequate financing. He accepted Mr. Foreman's generous offer of assistance, which was not entirely monetary. Through his influence and prominence, several jobs became available to Willard and it was all most welcome. He remained at Bacone approximately three years and ten months.

Willard had already learned that a life of faith enables man to see God in everything and holds the mind in a state of readiness for whatever may be His will.

At Bacone, Willard met Acee Blue Eagle in 1937, and Woodrow Crumbo in 1939. They were members of the faculty. Under their sensitive and sincere guidance he continued to carve, and gradually his entire interest turned to the medium of sculpturing. The painter's brush was given up for the knife and chisel. In his senior year he entered some of his carvings in a national contest and placed second in the competition.

On December 28, 1940, he married Sophie Irene Coger.

The Stone family multiplied rapidly.* Willard calls them his "pebbles" and says, "Until they stop rolling I just can't tell what they are going to wind up doing!"

The human story does not always unfold with the same results as a mathematical calculation, and after Bacone, although encouraged by some of the prizes he had won and by the acclaim of local people and patrons of art, there still remained some hungry children and an understanding wife. His knife became dull and his chisel rusty. He worked at odd jobs. While he gathered wood for the stove and the fireplace, he also gathered blocks of wood which he knew he would never burn. His affinity for the wood which hid behind the protective bark of nature's tall men of the forest was as strong as the prospector's who mined for gold in the unexplored regions of yesteryear.

All of this had already happened when the postman delivered the letter from Thomas Gilcrease. Unlike most artists, Willard wanted his boys and girls around him when he worked. He found that they made excellent helpers and could sand and rub the carvings at the right stage of their production; but more than that, they were his best models, as illustrated by the famous pair of feet for which one of his children posed.

"Tom Gilcrease gave me the chance to find out what I could do with wood and clay and to develop a style of my own. I would not have been recognized had it not been for him, because he gave me the courage to try. His criticism helped me to correct erroneous approaches to my subjects. He had a good eye for art and if I was working on a carving he would not say too much, but when he did voice an opinion he would comment only on the good points. His omission of the bad ones told me what he wanted to convey. Mr. Gilcrease could judge works of art, not only as to subject matter but he understood composition and perspective. If my work or finished carving did not tell a story, he knew I had a dull knife and found a way to let me know without

* Rocky Maloy, Dwight Clyde, Linda Joyce, Lyda Ann, Laura Evelyn, Danny Will, Nettie Carolyn, Jason Monroe and Sophie Irene — ranging in age from two to twenty-four in the order named.

hurting my pride. He was as much an artist as the artist," said Willard.

The humor of Tom Gilcrease was refreshing and intimate. At times it was almost pantomimic manifestation coupled with an inaudible voice. It was bordered by a twinkle of the eyes and the slightest breaking of the smile lines. Willard likes to relate one experience which amused him. When he was working on a certain portrait bust, Tom came into the studio and said, "What happened, did it bust?" He was always uttering something unusual – "I recall when he said, 'If newspapers would stick to the truth, no one would read them!' – and I remember when I introduced him to my wife, Sophie, and he said, 'This must be your favorite squaw, or has she dyed her hair?' "

The three years were productive. During 1947, 1948, and 1949, Willard completed forty-two pieces, all of which are now in the institute, including *Lady of Spring* and *Birth of Atomic Energy*, which he feels are the most important subjects in the collection. The freedom he enjoyed and the opportunity for development of technique and style were the principal benefits he received from his working arrangement with his friend Tom. When he looks back on those fruitful years, he readily admits without reservation that he was a protégé of Thomas Gilcrease. It must be recorded here that Willard did not have formal training in the art of sculpturing; however, he had "that something" which was God given. He loved wood with the same fervor as his idol, Michelangelo, loved marble. He was aware of the grains, colors, textures, and warmth of wood. A block of wood to Willard Stone was something that had once been alive, and he wanted to make it live again. His work smacks of versatility and originality and ranges from traditional and naturalistic motifs to modern and topical subjects.

The practical image of Thomas Gilcrease cannot be erased from the mind of Willard Stone. He has said: "Tom was a businessman and I respected him for his common sense as well as for the wealth he had at his command. He was not generous in the sense that he would shower his employees with extras. He expected a full work day or rather demanded it without being oppressive and dictatorial. The last year of my association with him I was the victim of economic pressure and the money he was paying me would not permit me to meet my needs. I hinted strongly; nevertheless the scholarship grant came to an end. In addition to the forty-two woods, I had completed eight or ten models from clay and a number of drawings. I do not know what value they had then but the market today would demand in excess of $45,000 for respective pieces. It was my impression that someday the institute would cast some of my models in bronze. Tom had made me that promise and perhaps I will yet have that honor."

Willard Stone is by birth a combination of Irish, German, and French, but more Cherokee than anything and by choice likes to be called a "Pot Boiled American." "I am," he said, "a lot of things stirred up together. Some members of the family say a Scotsman was involved way back down the tree and that a famous songwriter was related to us who wrote a song entitled 'For Two Cents, I Would Throw This Penny Away.' According to mouth to mouth information, passed down through the family, I am from one-eighth to one-quarter Cherokee – and being proud of this indefinite information I have accepted the one-quarter version. A twist of fate kept me off of the rolls. When the Cherokees were forced to leave their land in Alabama, Tennessee, Georgia, and North Carolina there was a lot of resentment by many of the families including my own. They would not accept the idea of moving across the plains and mountains to Oklahoma and decided to go to Mexico. There were many hardships along the way; sickness and breakdowns of their wagons. When they reached Parker County, Texas, they held a council meeting and decided that they could fare better if they returned to Oklahoma to join the Cherokees in the West and receive their land allotments. They pressed forward, driving hard through rain and wind some days and burning up in the sunshine of other hours. They were determined to reach Tahlequah in time to beat the closing of the rolls. The country was rough and uncharted and they finally concluded that they could not make it with their wagon train.

A young brave was selected from the group and, armed with a list of the names of the families of the wagon train from the oldest to the youngest, he mounted the best horse they had and they told him to ride hard, ride fast, and enroll them. The name of the rider was never recorded but that is not too important. He didn't make it. Discouraged and without food or funds the train broke up and some of the people settled along the route. Somehow, I don't know the facts, but my family pitched tent in Creek Nation. I was born a little south and east of Oktaha, fourteen miles from Muskogee, Oklahoma.

"My parents tried to prove their rights as Cherokees and did not give up the contest for many years and only then with a keen resentment of the federal government. They thought they had been cheated out of their birthrights. They could not comprehend why some of the renegade whites and others had been enrolled as Cherokees. Neither can I. So you see why I call myself a 'Pot Boiled American.' "

Willard is given to lazy humor when lecturing on his works. His ideas are derived from incidents of everyday life, of circumstances which bring happiness to some people or sadness to others. He has said, "Ideas do not often originate or come to me in my dreams, but when they do, they are important." He respects foreign artists and their culture but he has no desire to copy their works or their standards. He is a firm student of the school that every country should create its own images and set the pace for its own culture. A thing must have a reason for being created. A painting or a carving should transfer thought to the eyes of the viewer, and unless this is done or accomplished there is little compensation for the effort.

Willard does not bear grudges; however, he holds to the proposition that if Thomas Gilcrease had lived he would have fulfilled a promise to him that there would be a separate room in the institute to display his works exclusively and that there would be in existence a special catalog of his works with biographical material.

Willard Stone without hesitation declares that his professor, Woodrow Crumbo, was a superior artist to Acee Blue Eagle. He bases his opinion upon Woody's knowledge of anatomy and structure but he does not underestimate the talents of Blue Eagle. His two years at Bacone as a student in the art classes of Acee Blue Eagle were rewarding.

On the memory side of the ledger Willard recalls an experience with Tom. Willard had handed him a carving of a nude girl and the modest Tom had inquired: "What did you title her?"

Willard responded, "Shame."

Tom turned slowly away from the figure and continued, "Well," he said, "It must be something she has done, she doesn't have anything else to be ashamed of."

From November 16 to December 15, 1962, the wood sculpture of Willard Stone was exhibited at Kennedy Galleries, Inc., at 13 East 58th Street in New York. He had exhibited throughout the Southwest with recognition and acclaim. His work had been shown in Washington, D.C. The *Portrait of Lincoln* has been placed in the Lincoln Museum in the old Ford Theatre. *The Unity of Purpose,* which portrays religious harmony of all the peoples of the earth, representing his belief that there is really only one God and one life in the hereafter, is unique in design.

Of him it has been written, "He typifies the spirit of Oklahoma." His subjects cover such a wide area of thought that a special brochure would be necessary to do him justice, yet here are a few: *Dancer's Appeal, Peyote Bird, Balance of Power, Our Children's Children, Rhythm in Action, Buffalo Bill, Eternal Struggle, Winter, Adam's Rib, Road Runners,* and many more.

His *Turkey Feather Halo* was featured on the cover of the *Tulsa Magazine* in July, 1962, and the piece is now owned by Mr. and Mrs. Thomas Gilcrease, Jr. He has now carved in sassafras and cedar, walnut, ebony, wild cherry, mahogany, and other precious woods.

His most profound regret to date was the absence of Thomas Gilcrease from his showing at the Kennedy Galleries. "I think Tom would have been proud of me. I would have been proud of his being there. I can just see him walking in the door and asking — 'Is there an Indian here named Willard Stone? If so, tell that Cherokee there is a Creek here to look at his whittling.' " What Thomas would really have said — "Willard is something of a genius and the finest wood sculptor of Indian extraction in the United States."

Michael Frome, in his dissertation on "Neglected American Treasures," devoted a part of his analysis of American museums and art to Willard Stone, and predicted that "Stone may be the finest wood sculptor in America." This article was published in the May, 1966, issue of *Holiday* magazine featuring "Travels, U.S.A., 1966." This is one of the finest tributes yet received by Oklahoma's premier wood sculptor.

Thursday, February 17, 1966, was another day in the life of Willard Stone that he will not abandon from his pack of memories. He had worked with patience and devoted thought to make a block of walnut wood come to life. Tom had found the wood during one of his digs in Illinois and knew that it was a seasoned block. He had given it to Willard and said, "What are you going to chisel out of it?"

Willard thanked him for the gift and replied, "Something, I guess I'll have to dream a little!" The dream came and with it the inspiration to convert that block of wood into the image of the one man in his life who had been a faithful counselor to him and had assisted him out of the cavern of discouragement. But Tom was dead. The news of his death was a stinging item which came to Willard while he was in his studio at work. It was Tom's demise which finalized the decision to carve the block of walnut into the likeness of the dearest individual he had ever known in his adult life. The clay model was commenced from memory. Willard used a photograph to guide him, but his talented hands followed the dictates of his impressions which had built up over the years. At the dedication, which took place in the auditorium of the institute, he unveiled what had been the walnut block. He stood silent before his handiwork, turned his back to the large gathering who were there to share in his day of glory and said, "I think it's ready now!" And it was. And it will always be ready to look upon the visitors to the gallery where it is forever enshrined and to be looked upon by them. Willard Stone had offered a prayer that day and the Creek Indian had answered the Cherokee.

The presentation of the bust of Thomas Gilcrease was preceded by another meaningful event in Willard's career. On February 9, 1966 he exhibited his *Cowboy Hero* for the Hall of Fame in Oklahoma City. This was a commissioned piece to preserve the spirit of the Old West. The face is a composite of the heroes from the era of William S. Hart to that of John Wayne. Carved beneath the character is an Indian boy depicted as pulling on the boot which represents the effect of the movies on the youth of America. The block was shaped into a giant boot which serves as the base for the work and exemplifies the tracks the cowboys made during the days when they formed the populace of the frontier country.

And so it came to pass. There is another composite which could be carved from the block of friendship. It would be reminiscent of Acee Blue Eagle, Woody Crumbo, and Vinson Lackey – the sculptor would be Willard Stone. In the background would be a council house of the territory as only Lackey could paint. The mystic beauty would be supplied by Acee, and Crumbo would execute the color scheme with all the richness of his talents. The exhibition would be held in the new auditorium of the institute and it would be dedicated and unveiled by Thomas Gilcrease.

A current visit to the home of Willard and Sophie Stone at the edge of the town of Locust Grove will lend credulity to the wood-carver's statement that he is just a "Pot Boiled American." The residence is everything but stately. The hand-painted sign attached to the wire fence which runs parallel with the highway reads: "Willard Stone, wood-carver." It is a sufficient attraction to the tourists who often stop and express a desire to meet the unusual artist whose modesty is reflected in the makeup of the rural home. It is by no means an architectural model for housing and gives the appearance of having been erected in stages to accommodate the large family of Stones who range in age from the tender years of childhood to the matured offspring.

Willard's studio is a separate little building, duly elevated so that in order to reach the entrance one has to climb up several improvised steps. Once inside the crude cubicle, there is evidence of drawing paper, clay, magazines, various assortments of pencils, chisels, saws, and other implements which make up a wood-carver's vital tools.

Mealtime around the Stone house is something to behold. The aroma is a combination of country fried chicken, fresh garden vegetables, and homemade biscuits, all of which creates an enticement of appetite and makes it difficult to decline the proffered hospitality of Willard Stone to "pull up a chair and eat a bite." Two separate tables are required to feed the hungry mouths of hard-playing children who are unconcerned about guests, customers, or business associates of their easy-going and gentle father. The living room is cluttered with unmatched furniture, and the walls bear evidence that an artist is the head of the family. Etchings and oil paintings are very much in sight on every wall, and Sophie Stone is a busy mother, a gracious hostess, and fully in control of her flock. The unpretentious atmosphere is a welcome sight compared with the other levels of living where sincerity cannot be sensed and wholesomeness is a stranger.

Such are the physical attributes of Willard's castle where his inspiration for individualism springs into being.

Acee Blue Eagle

The late Lee F. Harkins, a Choctaw-Chickasaw Indian, was editor and publisher of *The American Indian* magazine. In May of 1938 he authored an article for the *Rotarian* magazine which he entitled "The Indian Must Face Reality" and posed a very potent question. Mr. Harkins had earned recognition as one of the better-versed Indians relating to the history of his people. He made notable research of their literature and their customs and the ethical significance of their folkways. In his all too brief career he became a serious collector of books of uncommon quality and content applicable to the Indian. The historians have not sufficiently lighted his torch of revelations and the plaudits have been tardy indeed.

"Shall the Indian be kept Indian?" was the provocative query. His comments were: "To keep the Indian Indian you have to turn the clock back. Indian history as we know it is a record of the manner in which he adapted himself to conditions. I glory in the legends, traditions, lore and art of my people. Indian art, yes. Just as we have other 'native' arts in America, but let's not try to do the impossible. You cannot – should not attempt to stop inevitable changes. The fallacy of the sentimentalists, red and white, is to carry the 'restoration of arts and crafts' to the extreme."

It is obvious that Lee F. Harkins was striking at the very hub of assimilation. He sheltered an appreciative conviction for art and the memories of tribal organization and held firmly to the position that the Indian was deserving of the same opportunities for individual development as his white neighbors. He wanted to preserve the past, but he did not want it to consume his people and their lives.

He then reviewed with innocent self-esteem the names of certain of his people of varying degrees of Indian blood who had risen to hear the acclaim of their fellowmen in the United States and beyond its shores; they included such notables as James F. "Jim" Thorpe, the greatest football player of his generation; Dr. Charles A. Eastman, historian and man of medicine; Arthur C. Parker, director of the Museum of Arts and Sciences of Rochester, New York; Charles Curtis, former vice-president of the United States of America; Will Rogers, the favorite son of Oklahoma and ambassador without portfolio to the world; and the artist, Acee Blue Eagle.

Author Harkins felt that there were thousands more of his people who could rise to the heights of professional life and the business world if they would but leave behind their tribal influence and go the educational way of the white man.

Acee Blue Eagle was an ardent adherent to the philosophy of historian Harkins who had undertaken to publish a magazine about the Indian. He, too, felt that assimilation had to come and that if the artistic in the Indian was to live, it would have to come through the outlet for natural talents of man as well as by the preservation of artifacts brought to light by excavation of ancient burial grounds and man-made mounds. Acee was determined to devote his career to the melting of the ways of the Indian into the stream of modern civilization.[2]

At this juncture in his promising vocation he had not as yet met Thomas Gilcrease, who was later to become a devotee to the cause of assimilation by making it possible for the inventive and natural genius of the Indian youth to create and exhibit and thereby exemplify the past to the eyes of the present generation. Thomas Gilcrease would come into his life and be a benefactor without design or hope of reward, except the satisfaction which is known only to such men who breathe with a purpose and die with accomplishment.

Acee Blue Eagle was the pseudonym of Alexander McIntosh, son of Samuel McIntosh and Martha "Blue Eagle" McIntosh. Samuel was part Creek and Scottish. Martha was a mixture of Indian bloods and had some French and English ancestry. Samuel's father, John McIntosh, was the son of the famous Chill McIntosh, who was born in 1775 and died in 1885. Chill was a general under Andrew Jackson and fought at the battle of New Orleans. The name of McIntosh was prominent in the history of the territory, and some of the Creek Indians, under the leadership of Roly McIntosh, moved across the Mississippi and settled as early as 1819 and 1820. This was long before they were authorized to do so by treaty. Some of the McIntosh clan were recognized Creek chiefs.

Acee's mother could have added much to the knowledge

of her son had she lived to really know him. She died when Acee was only four years old and at approximately the same time Samuel McIntosh and a twin of Acee's left this earth. The Blue Eagles are supposed to have been special tribesmen and to have had their name revealed to them by an omen, the falling of an albino eagle, shot by one of the braves and which fell into a crock of berry juice. Color me blue, and so it was.

Samuel and Martha called their son *Che-bon-ah-bee-la* or, translated, "Laughing Boy." The birth date was August 17, 1907, the same year in which the Oklahoma and Indian territories were joined into the state of Oklahoma. When Acee's parents left him, his grandparents took him in charge and cared for him until his eighth birthday when an Indian agent took Acee to an Indian school and started him on his way to education. Acee's playmates called him "A.C." but his tribal name was also "Ah-say" and the contraction became "Acee." In the years of his youth he decided to place the name of "Blue Eagle" on his painting, and thereafter all of his creations were identified by the signature of his adopted last name.

Martha's "Laughing Boy" had shared the life of any other Indian boy. He was not allowed to run away from his community and he was indoctrinated with the legends of the tribe. It was only when he was shorn of his braids and separated from his moccasins that he knew for the first time that he would learn a new kind of discipline in the official uniform of the Indian school. He had already found his way to the creek bottoms where, with the aid of a twig or branch, he would sketch pictures and designs in the sand. The impressions were related to subjects of habit and costumes, of animals and of dancers. When campfires were burning he would take away a segment of charcoal, sharpen it, and use the faces of flat rock or tanned hide upon which to test his photographic mind.

The schools he attended were in Anadarko, Riverside, Nuyaka, Euchee, Haskell, and Chilocco. After leaving high school he was enrolled at Bacone College in the junior division of the school from the first semester of 1928 to 1929 and through the first semester of 1931 and 1932.

Upon entering the University of Oklahoma in the fall of 1933 important things began for Acee Blue Eagle. Several years before his arrival at the university, a group of Kiowa Indians, five in all, had begun their studies with the late Dr. Oscar B. Jacobson. When Dr. Jacobson heard about Acee's enrollment in the School of Fine Arts, he immediately observed that something wonderful had happened to his department. He said: "Acee, I can't teach you the art, the knowledge of the Indian spiritualism and religious symbols, for that is yours and the heritage of your forefathers, but I will help you to concentrate all of your efforts on becoming a great artist." Dr. Jacobson, although perceptive, could not possibly have imagined how much his encouragement meant to this young Indian who was to leave the world a treasure house of Indian dancers who seem to come to life 'midst their sharp and fine lines, their rhythm, and their performance of rituals.

When graduation came, Acee had earned the degree of Bachelor of Fine Arts and heard the call of the footlights. He joined the famous Fanchon-Marco troupe, with which he performed for over three years. There was no end to the talents of the young artist. He discovered that he could paint and lecture at the same time, thereby capturing, captivating and influencing his audiences. Like Will Rogers, he soon discovered that he could do with a brush what Will could do with a rope — hold them and make them appreciate what they were seeing. Acee became a modern medicine man, but instead of a health-giving elixir in a labeled bottle he sold them his dancers on parchment and they wanted more and more. His humor was unusual, his remarks homey, and his punch lines well directed. He would generally conclude with remarks about Oklahoma.

The honors which came to Acee are varied and unique. He was listed in *Who's Who in America, Who's Who in Oklahoma,* and *Who's Who in American Art.* During World War Two he served in the United States Air Force and because of his talents he appeared in over eighteen camps where he entertained the troops, painted and sketched, and endeared himself to his buddies. He was always Acee Blue Eagle the Creek-Pawnee artist from that wonderful Sooner State where he was born.

He was the first Indian artist from America to be presented to the queen at Buckingham Palace and was so accepted by the queen and her sister that the news media of the world caught the story and carried it across the presses of the world. He painted many murals, including one which adorns the post office in Coalgate, Oklahoma, which in recent years was retouched by another Creek artist, Fred Beaver, who is adept in the art of restoration. The original pattern for this mural won first place in the Philbrook Art Gallery competition at Tulsa, Oklahoma and is valued today at over $3,000.

In 1960, his book *Oklahoma Indian Painting-Poetry* was published. He had commenced it before his demise. It was dedicated to his teacher, Dr. Oscar B. Jacobson, in these words: "He has been my inspiration and adviser and because of his coaching, information, and fatherly attitude, I am able to present these works." It was Dr. Jacobson who had made it possible for Acee to attend Oxford and to lecture and travel in many foreign countries. Elsewhere in his book and as a part of the introduction, he wrote: "I am only a friendly Indian telling you of Oklahoma Indian art and poetry as I see it so that the adults and the children will know the cultural and domestic life of the red man and the mystic ceremonial and religious phases which constitute the only true background of this continent."

Acee's painting *Buffalo Hunt* was presented to Captain Wilburn Van Aukin of the U.S.S. *Oklahoma* which was sunk at Pearl Harbor and later raised. The talents of this unusual artist were admired by King Alfonso of Spain, who was one of his patrons. Many Blue Eagle works found their way to the walls of the International Building in Rockefeller Center in New York for the exhibition of 1938.

Acee died June 18, 1959. He had lived a full, fruitful, but all too short, life. He had been married to Devi Dja, the famous Balinese Temple dancer, in 1946. She was known as the Pavlova of the Orient. Acee had a deep affection and admiration for her wonderful talent. The internationally known artist Winold Reiss, the German born portrait painter, left a masterpiece of his work when he painted Acee for posterity.

Before his death he had become a close friend of Thomas Gilcrease, so much so that the first personalized copy of his book was presented to Mr. Gilcrease. Mr. Gilcrease is alleged to have promised to inter Acee's mortal remains near the museum on the hill, if he survived Acee.

May 26, 1946, Acee Blue Eagle wrote to his friend, Thomas Gilcrease, from Muskogee, Oklahoma. The stationery was that of the United States Department of the Interior, Office of Indian Affairs, Field Service. The letterhead reflected the seal of "Chilocco Indian Agricultural School" with the date 1884 within the circular design. The center of the seal is a plow and sheaf of wheat symbolic of the science of agriculture, the primary purpose of the school. Surrounding this theme are the words which make up the name of the institution as above indicated. At the apex is a book indicative of the academic department; the founding date is at the bottom of the circle. The various activities of the school are represented by emblems, such as a brush for the paint shop; a cogwheel for engineering; scissors for domestic art; a horse for animal husbandry; a roller for the print shop; a shoe lathe for the shoe shop; a football for athletics; Indian clubs for physical education; an anvil for auto mechanics and blacksmith shops; a nurse's cap for the hospital; a cow for the dairy department; a rolling pin for the domestic science; a trowel for studies in masonry; and a square for carpentry. The class ring of the school carries the seal and serves as a link of recognition for the alumni of the school.

The foregoing description of the Chilocco school seal has been included here by reason of the postscript contained in a letter Acee wrote to Mr. Gilcrease. There is a contradiction to the statement by Acee that he designed the seal, since the official explanation reads: "The design finally selected was drawn by three students, A. C. McIntosh (later to be known as Acee Blue Eagle), Harvey and William Bedoka." The plow and the sheaf appear to be the art which Acee would produce; however, the point may be subject to debate.

This letter, written in hand, expresses Acee's feelings toward Mr. Gilcrease with more warmth and sentiment than could possibly be imparted by a narrative. It reads:

> Cha-ah-jol-lot: this is a Creek way of addressing endearingly an older person and means "my older one." You have been indeed a grand person to me outside of our business and beyond that connection you have touched my heart with your personal feelings and soul – I have felt closely drawn to you! – a more personal relationship – I think it is both because you are the same tribe and because of your personal self, there's something there that I can't express or explain! I came out of the army with a nervous breakdown, everything in life seemed selfish and false . . . two people have done more to cure me than all others! You and Devi Dja! – some day I hope I can have a long private talk with you and better explain all of this – so often there are too many people around! I do know that the last time you visited me in Muskogee, you gave me the spark of energy to paint that I have not had in four years! You have a spiritual quality about you that is carried over to people of a creative talent! I have been in Chicago for three weeks with Devi Dja – I have told her much of you!! and she loves you as much as I do.
>
> We are going to be married right away – real soon! Nobody knows yet! but you! she is a wonderful person Mr. Gilcrease and I think we need her in the Creek tribe! They were wrong when they said, "East is East and West is West and never the twain shall meet!!" because we are to be married right away.
>
> I need some money for the wedding, so will you please send me $400.00 on my account right away, I have to buy the rings, marriage expenses and a short honeymoon! I am looking forward to you meeting her – I know you will love her for the grand person she is – she thinks you are grand even though she hasn't met you yet! I realize we will have to make our honeymoon short because of the cost of a nice pair of rings – but we have talked it over and realize this!

I hope we will both get to see you before very long—I do hope you will understand what I have tried to express to you, my very dear friend.

I realize that I am very poor at expressing what I sometimes feel in my heart. I hope you can send me the money right away and I do so deeply appreciate your every consideration and personal feeling Cha-ha-jol-lot. All my very heartfelt thanks and every best wishes to you in each and every thing you do!!

With loving feelings,

Acee

P.S. I attended the Chilocco Alumni meetings and was elected president! I designed the school seal in 1937.

Thomas Gilcrease replied to the letter:

Dear Acee:

I have just returned from a three weeks trip to Tulsa and New Mexico and find your good letter awaiting. Mrs. Teenor tells me that she sent you the money requested in your letter and I hope you received it in due time.

Boy, you certainly surprised me by getting married so quickly. I guess you must have felt the same about getting married as you do about a wild horse. You just jump on him, spur him and take off. Well, let me wish for you this:

> A long and happy life together and may you both be inspired to do even better things in life.

I greatly appreciate all the fine sentiments you expressed in your letter to me.

I will be happy to meet your wife and also will be happy to see you again. I will try and contact you on my next trip to Tulsa, which will be in the near future.

Again wishing you and your wife all the happiness in the world and with best wishes for your health, I remain,

Sincerely yours,

Thomas Gilcrease

Tom Gilcrease and Acee had periodic contact with each other during the years that followed. Their friendship had spanned the most productive years of Acee's life. When the end came, Acee saw the rising sun and he was smiling when the darkness of night overtook him.

On June 21, 1949, Wolf Robe Hunt, another well-known Indian, who was later to conduct the official Indian funeral or burial service for Thomas Gilcrease, shot the traditional arrow in the west after first aiming it into the north, as was the custom in the tribal days. The bearers were all descendants of Indians. From Oklahoma were Fred Beaver, Ardmore; Jess E. Davis, Oklahoma City; Roland Whitehorse, Anadarko; Richard West, Bacone; Brummett Echohawk, Carl Woodring, and Louis Ballard, all of Tulsa; and Black Bear Bosin of Wichita, Kansas. The Akdar Shrine Temple assisted in the services with their Indian Patrol, of which Acee had been a loyal member. Wolf Robe played the flute, an instrument which Acee loved and often used to bring happiness to his audiences when he was in vaudeville and when he lectured in Prague, Czechoslovakia, in the early days of his travels. Fred Beaver sang an Indian song and the soul of the Blue Eagle took flight to the happy hunting ground.

The final resting place of Acee was not determined until he was buried with proper honors in the Fort Gibson National Cemetery on September 12, 1962. The plans for a burial on the Gilcrease grounds were interrupted by the death of Thomas Gilcrease in the same year.

The influence which Thomas Gilcrease had on the life of Acee Blue Eagle will be better understood as the fifty-odd paintings acquired from him during his life grow deeper into the hearts and minds of the millions of people who visit the Thomas Gilcrease Institute of American History and Art.

The celebrated artist, Woodrow Crumbo, a contemporary of Blue Eagle, does not feel that Mr. Gilcrease exercised any particular influences upon the kind of art produced by Acee, but it was the encouragement and material assistance when needed that sustained the talents of his genius. Of him Crumbo has said: "He is to be greatly admired for his achievements in the art and lecturing field; his techniques were developed by himself. For the most part he chose to do his programs alone and built a fine reputation as a lecturer, bringing many smiles and good feeling from his audiences toward himself and the Indian tribe."

As the late Dr. Jacobson wrote in his provocative article which appeared in *American Indian Painters,* "Art is perhaps more intimately tied to the life of the Indians than to that of any other people. It expresses and mirrors their intensely spiritual nature and their overwhelming need of beauty. Indian art is very old, as old as the Indians, no doubt; it was related to everything they did, wore, used. Every act of the Indians, from the smallest and most inconsequential gesture, to their stately dances, is a way of prayer. It had to be performed in beauty of line and color, gesture and word.

"The Indian greeted the sun. He thanked the Great Spirit with harvest dance, corn dance, colorful and exactly conceived rituals. In his game and hunting dances to buffalo, antelope, deer, he begged the spirit of the animal involved to forgive the necessity of killing it in order that he might live. He asked the snakes to intercede with the gods of rain that his crops mature. In lovely vigil and fasting he sought the Great Spirit's will for the direction of his life, then he expressed the will in beauty."

Acee Blue Eagle will be remembered for the following important works: *Buffalo Hunt, Fancy Dancer, Peyote Brave, Indian Maiden and Teepee, Warrior with Lance, Mother and Children, Creek Chiefs, Woman Hoeing Corn, Chief with Medicine Pipe,* and countless others which are to be seen at the Gilcrease Institute.

This brief review of Acee Blue Eagle's life has been included because the theme of the Gilcrease Institute is primarily of Indian origin and it is hoped that the reader will thereby grasp a better and more accurate appreciation for the collection.

Rest well, "Laughing Boy": folklorist, lecturer, champion of the assimilation of Indians. The prediction of Lee Harkins was justified.

Woodrow Crumbo

Woody Crumbo, the artist, and Tom Gilcrease, the oil man, met in 1945.[3] The place was the Mayo Hotel in Tulsa. The reason was that Thomas Gilcrease had seen some of Woody's paintings and was determined to acquire as many of them as possible and to also bargain for the talents of the artist as an assistant in the pursuit of his collections.

The formality of their first meeting faded quickly—dissolved by common interests and pleasantries. Woodrow became "Woody" but he could not muster enough courage to address his host by the accepted "Tom," and from that moment on his friend was "Mr. Gilcrease."

"I have been making a lot of changes in my method of collecting art and I would like to have you work for me in furthering the acquisitions I intend to make for the Gilcrease Foundation. Will you consider joining me?"

Woody restrained his innermost reactions and deliberated for several minutes before replying, "I am complimented Mr. Gilcrease but I think you can find other men who are more capable."

The conversation then changed in tenor and tempo. Mr. Gilcrease was determined to acquire the twenty-seven paintings which Woody had on display at his home in Tulsa. His intellectual preparation for the best strategy to employ began to work. He was not a pragmatic collector or one who was given to sinister motives to accomplish the end he sought. Woody placed a price of several thousand dollars on the entire portfolio, and he had hoped for some emotional reaction from the prospective purchaser but none was in evidence.

When the meal had been concluded they adjourned to Woody's home and Mr. Gilcrease made a detailed inspection of the paintings he wanted. One by one he studied the gems which bore the now famous Crumbo signature. Nothing happened. He left and told Woody he would be in communication with him at a later date. At this particular time Mr. Gilcrease was maintaining his residence in San Antonio, Texas, and he commuted between Texas and Oklahoma with as much frequency and ease as the average individual would have expended to walk to the post office in his own neighborhood.

On his very next trip following their meeting at the Mayo, a price was agreed upon and amounted to several hundred dollars in excess of the proceeds Woody had anticipated. When Mr. Gilcrease departed he not only owned the twenty-seven Crumbos but he had employed Woody. There was never a written word between them; like Will Rogers and Flo Ziegfeld, they shook hands and that made the contract binding. Woody's capitulation and eventual employment typifies the bargaining ability of Tom Gilcrease and the faith he had in those he wanted to help.

Mr. Gilcrease had agreed as a part of his bargain with Woody that the entire Crumbo family would live in the home west of the stone house on the hill while he was to be an artist in residence. It was badly in need of repair. With all dispatch the house was placed in shape for occupancy. Mr. Gilcrease insisted upon the installation of a large picture window which would face north. He knew the value to the artist of good light and comfort. When the remodeling was done, Woody felt an exaltation he had not experienced before then or even in later years. He also concluded that Thomas Gilcrease was not eccentric as he was warned he might be. He learned that his new boss had undergone some changes in his social life and that everything he did was rooted with a positive approach. One of the attributes which he recognized from the very start of their association was that Mr. Gilcrease was a very smart man for many reasons, one of them being that if he misunderstood or did not have all the facts, he would immediately change his mind and he could face the necessary change with grace when such a circumstance came to light.

The studio was to be a full-time haven for Woody

when he was not called without notice to join Mr. Gilcrease in a cross-country trip to either acquire or inquire, and he was never sure which it would be when they left home.

At the end of two years his talented brushes and pencils, guided by his positive thoughts, had produced approximately 179 pictures. Mr. Gilcrease paid Woody for his paintings, and the only other commission for which he received an independent sum was for the creation and painting of the "Peyote" bird over the Quonset-shaped entrance to the main building of the institute. He received the sum of $600 and felt that he had been well compensated.

Recalling the "Peyote" bird, Woody relates a fascinating account. "Mr. Gilcrease asked me to paint an appropriate picture to go over the entrance way. I painted a picture with several figures of dancers in ceremony and in full color. I made it to scale fitting the circular design of the Quonset appex. I also made another design in black and white which was to be reproduced in wrought iron and installed on the inside of the building in the Quonset ceiling. Upon completion of the design it was determined that the outside picture would consume too much time and as a practical matter it was my opinion that the finished product would not withstand the elements. It was then decided to place a more modest design outside and mount it on removable frames until a wrought iron production could be worked out.

"With the approval of Mr. Gilcrease I selected the 'Peyote' bird. It was a symbol of the messenger bird, derived from the concept of the peyote ceremony when the winged friend carries messages and prayers to the Great Spirit. In practice this ceremony is beautiful. The whole idea appealed to him and so it was done. I did not feel that the unbleached muslin base would remain in place, but I glued it to the surface and there it has remained to greet the thousands of visitors to the galleries. The other designs were retained in the museum and someday, someone might want to cast them in wrought iron."

Woody's activities while he was an artist in residence

were not restricted to painting. He was advisor to Mr. Gilcrease as he continued to add to his collection of art, artifacts, and books. He assisted in selection and generally his opinions were respected. He traveled to distant states with Mr. Gilcrease where together they searched out certain additions, supplemental artifacts, and paintings on Americana. The intimate association which he enjoyed with Mr. Gilcrease was short-lived but filled with adventure. The three years passed all too quickly. Most of their journeys were by automobile, and if they heard that someone or a gallery had a fine collection of Indian paintings or sculpture depicting the pioneer West, off they would go; distance was not an object and time was not of the essence. They did not make any flights or voyages to foreign countries and all the markets were located in the United States. Woody is the first to admit that Thomas Gilcrease relied upon his own judgment when making a final decision. He was polite and ever ready to hear a sales person expound about the product under consideration. He felt that Mr. Gilcrease was an artist in his own right, and while he did not paint, he liked all his surroundings to be maintained in an orderly fashion. This applied to his home, his garden, and to the trees. He was a lover of nature and nature responded with a courtship of beauty regardless of the season. He was best qualified in western Americana according to Crumbo who said, "He excelled in selecting the things he knew better."

Being the artist to the full implication of the word, Woody did not freely extend encomiums. They had to be earned and he did not expect to be complimented without justification. He had learned to accept the pointed darts of the critic whose judgments were worthy of indulgence. He could bear up under his own injured feeling but he could not tolerate criticism of his boss by untutored and careless-mouthed individuals who were without background or who lacked reason for their statements. Why was Thomas Gilcrease, a calm, cultured, and on the whole a very tolerant and amiable Indian gentleman, a devoted friend of all good artists, subjected to the cutting comments of the unschooled? As incredible as this may sound, when things like this came to his attention he felt like reverting to the tribal days — painting a bow and arrow, have them come to life by some element of magic and embark upon the traditional warpath.

There are many paintings which adorn the walls of the institute or hang in the storage area on the sliding wire frames for future display, which can properly be discounted for technique and craftsmanship. It must be borne in mind that in the arts there are no shortcuts, and that success is not a matter of inspiration but one of patience. Inspiration is important and without it the artist may never be able to reach the heights for which he strives, but all the inspiration in the world will not do any good without conscientious, painstaking, and applied industry. Thomas Gilcrease could not be classed as a specialist in art selections and the spirit of competition was no stranger to him. experience as an oil man had taught him some of his limitations and the spirit of competition was no stranger to him. He liked what he bought, he bought what he liked, he overpaid and there were times when he underpaid; one was the art of bargain, the other was the satisfaction of egoism which he wanted to share with others, and therein he found the justification for his ventures. Just as memory can persist even in the hue of the flame, so can beauty and purpose be found within the frame of a picture if it pleases the eyes of the viewer or the title holder. This is one of man's pleasures and a mark of independence. The particular painting may not have been commissioned or acquired for quality, but rather for its historic and documentary value. While the selections he made may not have always been the works of masters, in most instances they represented the best of the artist for what they were meant to be and if they had any reference to the life of the Indian — they were important to Thomas Gilcrease.

Woody was once asked if he thought Mr. Gilcrease was an avid reader and he replied, "In the three years we were associated together I never saw him read a book, and yet it was uncanny how he could go into the library and take down a volume, blow the dust off the top of it, and then turn to what he wanted to read!"

Tom knew that the long slumber of man on earth was far from over, but he was always alert enough to know that the awakening was in progress. In his later years he was not too concerned with the troubled world. He felt that there was little he could do. He was astute enough to know that one atomic bomb could destroy his entire collection and that the thick walls of the museum building could not withstand the elements of man's destructive curse. If man had reached the moon in the lifetime of Thomas Gilcrease he would probably have been the first to say to one of his trusted employees, "Get me a reservation on the next spaceship and tell Mrs. Teenor to buy a round trip ticket — I am going up there to see if there are any Indian paintings or artifacts which belong down here!" He loved and appreciated the four seasons. He knew that the snow had to melt and the moisture from the flakes had to penetrate Mother Earth before the vernal mysteries would bring foliage to the trees and sweetly scented buds to the stems of the thorned branches.

And so it was that Mr. Gilcrease often chose works of art which were pretty and somewhat sentimental, giving little thought to the value of the painting in relation to history until he matured as a collector and narrowed his search to western Americana. He profited by his errors and gradually became less and less interested in Mexican art and French paintings, which had at one time commanded his attention and tugged at his purse strings.

There was a reflection of the past which Woody detected in the hours he spent with his boss as they rode for miles to reach a predetermined destination to seek out and acquire an object of art, a manuscript or a costume, or even an Indian blanket. He often lived in an imaginary country of his own. Recalling one occasion, Woody related: "We were riding along the highway. He sat for a long time and gazed out of the car window, he viewed the open country and the great plains and with a suddenness which was almost alarming said, 'Look over yonder, Woody, at all those buffalo and Indians. My, my, they must be having a good time — and look at that old Indian sitting on that rock by the teepees — there must be several hundred Indians camped there!' When the mirage was over he smiled faintly as if to let me know that he knew that I was aware of his wonderful dreams."

The economics of art collecting was a constant concern of Thomas Gilcrease. He always created the impression that money was hardly a barricade to the doors of the market-places and the off-main street shops where he would go if he discovered that what he wanted might be for sale. If a painting was offered to him and he felt that it was priced in excess of what his own appraisal dictated, he was inclined to exercise extreme caution by expressing his appreciation to the salesperson for the privilege of seeing the object. He would then turn to whoever happened to be with him and say, "Well, you know if they are too high we will just have to pass them up. That's a lot of nickels." The salesman would follow the customary polite pressure tactics by altering the sales pitch and even go to the extreme of inventing some fictional data designed to catch bigger fish. The stoicism of Tom's Indian nature would then give rise to a superb performance. The salesman would hardly be aware of the mental gymnastics taking place in the customer's mind. The result was invariably the same. The sale was closed at Tom's price – but only when he felt the price was right. This psychological bartering was often witnessed by Woody Crumbo. It was like embarking upon a hunting trip and being the only one in the party who did not know where the leader was headed. It was always a new and exciting experience.

Mr. Gilcrease was deeply conscious of one God and believed in the life-hereafter aspect of religious thought. His sense of respect for humanity made him ever aware of the presence of children. He could not ignore them. It is the opinion of Woody Crumbo, and shared by others, that Thomas Gilcrease felt there should be welfare facilities for all needy children, but he knew only too well that there would always be the "unwanted who want." He often remarked, "You can't feed them all!" He was a skeptic when it came to supporting organized charities, with the exception of the Salvation Army, the organization which in 1953 signally honored him as Tulsa's "Man of the Year." State

Commander Lieutenant Colonel W. W. Bouterse made the presentation.

It is important in exploring the life of any man to slip quietly behind the scenes of his daily pursuits and ascertain how much individualism was present in his personality. Woody Crumbo, being a practicing artist, is gifted with the ability to explore, and he did just that with his boss. He has said: "Mr. Gilcrease held many men in high esteem, Will Rogers, Charley Russell, some of the big men in government, diplomats, statesmen, and ambassadors, but the man he admired most was Charles Page of Sand Springs, Oklahoma. Every Oklahoman knows or has heard of the philanthropy of Charles Page. He made a place for widows and orphans and so imprinted his name in the annals of charitable history that his deeds are sculptured into the foundations he created — foundations with a purpose — foundations which have sheltered, educated, and cared for hundreds of boys and girls who, but for his beneficence, would never have had the one chance. Mr. Gilcrease wanted to repeat what Mr. Page had done. He tried within his ability and fashion. Few will ever know the money he provided at Bacone College and the students who would never have gone there but for the fact that he paid their tuition and gave them expense money."

Yes, Thomas Gilcrease "touched" Woody Crumbo. He broadened his scope in the business of museum collecting. He did with Crumbo what he did with Acee Blue Eagle and Willard Stone and other artists. He touched them too. He helped them when they could appreciate it most.

Woody Crumbo, of the Pottawatomie tribe, was a contemporary of Acee Blue Eagle, and during his teaching career at Bacone, one of his students was Willard Stone. He shares the opinion that Mr. Gilcrease was extremely proud of Acee as an Indian artist whose creativity has contributed much to the pictorial history of the Indians. He feels that Acee Blue Eagle is deserving of admiration for his achievements as an artist and a lecturer. His self-developed techniques were without equal and he brought many smiles and a feeling of joy to those who had the opportunity to hear him and thereby become better acquainted with the Indians.

The sponsorship of Willard Stone by Mr. Gilcrease is one of the cherished recollections of Mr. Crumbo, who feels that without such encouragement the career of Willard would have been delayed in coming to fruition. "Willard is ranked as the best in his field, keeping in mind that his field is wood carvings which depict mostly Indian subjects. He is blessed with good eyes for proportions and designs, coupled with a fine sense of humor. He has the ability to transfer his thoughts to an object of wood, make it come to life, and tell a story," remarked Crumbo.

Woody Crumbo was born January 31, 1912 at Lexington, Oklahoma, and was reared through childhood in the country west of Sand Springs, Oklahoma. He was a student at the Chilocco Indian School in Oklahoma and the American Indian Institute at Wichita, Kansas. His art studies were pursued for three years at the University of Wichita in Kansas, and for two years at the School of Art of the University of Oklahoma.

Woody Crumbo is now the curator of the El Paso Museum where he was formerly director. From 1938 to 1941 he served as director of art at Bacone College; he has been a designer of aircraft for the Douglas Company, a professional artist from 1938 to 1960, and is a fellow of the Julius Rosenwald Foundation for which he was awarded a painting grant during 1955 to 1956.

He considers his best painting *The Burial of Spotted Wolf*, owned by the Koshare Indians at La Junta, Colorado. He estimates that the Gilcrease Institute possesses 179 of his creations.

One of his most popular works is *The Buffalo Dance,* which presents a great lament on the part of the Indian people, a rhapsodic obituary to a once-treasured possession — and a great hope. The Buffalo Dance costume is rich in color tone and consists of buffalo hides complete with horns and tail together with other bits of ornament peculiar to the individual's personal taste. It is written that the origin of the buffalo was for the purpose of furnishing food and shelter for the red man, and it became almost a legend that "when the buffalo disappears from the earth the Indian will be no more." It is therefore understood why the Indian dances his sacred dance of the buffalo while he prays to the Great Spirit for the return of the protective animal.

Fourteen first prizes and six scholarships in six years is something of a record; however, Woody Crumbo knows he lives in a "practical world" too. As a father of a daughter and son, he is aware that the role of the artist is not easy. His son will not succeed his father as an artist who creates, but as one who restores and preserves. He is learning the techniques of materials and methods and one day he may be called upon to direct the restoration of the peyote bird which welcomes the ever increasing number of visitors to the Thomas Gilcrease Institute of American History and Art. If this should occur – he will reflect upon the work of his father and the memory of the man for whom the Great Spirit will call out, saying, "Touch others as you touched my father with your decisive mind, your gentle hands, your kind heart, and your Indian heritage."

R. Vinson Lackey

In his search for Indian artifacts and paintings, Thomas Gilcrease had traversed practically every foot of Oklahoma soil. He awakened to the necessity for preservation of the landmarks before they would be lost forever. He knew that the old government houses where the agencies had served the Indian were rapidly disappearing. Even the photos which had been taken with primitive cameras were becoming extinct. In 1945 he cast about to locate a capable historian and artist who would undertake the seemingly impossible task of research involved in the reclamation project.

Vinson Lackey was his man.[4] Together they engaged in a common cause, aware that they could not reconstruct the buildings which had fallen into decay and become piles of wood ashes in a barren land. The only solution was to provide a pictorial and written record. Lackey, with the financial assistance of Mr. Gilcrease, set out to collect old building plans. He visited the sites of the institutions which still stood and some of them that were only waiting for a stronger wind than the one before. From some of the old-time residents in the respective areas, he managed to reduce verbal accounts to notebook security. Four long years of constant research, followed by months of painstaking, eye-punishing work, and the inspiration became a reality. One hundred and five of the early landmarks were transferred to the canvas by the dexterity of the educated hands of this supremely capable artist. The army quartermaster supplied old army-made plans of forts. The details contained in the records were priceless to him in that they gave the full measurements and architectural drawings of the buildings from which Vinson Lackey reconstructed the physical likeness of the subjects he sought. There were times when he was fortunate enough to locate the remains of an old chimney, in which event the ruins provided him with clues for other research.

In later years he wrote a brief historical description of each of the subjects he had painted, which included schools, missions, business and civic buildings, and military establishments. All of the paintings are now a part of the Gilcrease Institute's collection and, together, the pictures and descriptions create a master record, without doubt unique in museum possessions the world over.

Vinson Lackey was born in Paris, Texas, on the twenty-sixth day of July, 1889 and, with his parents, moved to Hobart, Oklahoma Territory, in January, 1902; later they moved to Muskogee, Indian Territory, in 1904. He attended the University of Oklahoma, from which he was graduated in 1920 with a degree of Bachelor of Arts in history and journalism. His inclination to enter the field of art prompted him to enroll in the Fine Arts School of the University of Oklahoma, from which he took his bachelor's degree in 1922, having studied with Samuel Holmberg, brother of the late Dean Holmberg. The ambition of Vinson Lackey for a career as an artist stemmed from his maternal ancestors.

His great-grandmother, Suzan Tacket, was an artist in London and was commissioned to paint notables in Charleston, coming to America for the assignment.

The student body of the University of Oklahoma was familiar with his drawings which appeared in the campus publications and the yearbooks. Upon graduation, he taught history and journalism for two years before entering newspaper work where he served as reporter, and feature and editorial writer in Oklahoma City. His education was interrupted while he served in the field signal battalion of the Second Division of regulars in World War I. As a captain he was wounded at Soissons, France. During his convalescence he painted a picture of a street in Celettes, France, for which he received an award.

Lackey moved to Tulsa in the summer of 1928 and became affiliated with the Chamber of Commerce where he was manager of conventions and publicity. He remained in such employment for seven years. His next assignment was as field supervisor and editor of the Indian Territory section of the *Oklahoma State Guide*. He became acquainted with the historical and geographical data provided by a staff of 125 who worked under his supervision. When the guide was completed he was appointed state supervisor of the Oklahoma Historical Records Survey, covering all seventy-seven counties of the state. This survey made it necessary for him to employ approximately 200 workers. His next promotion was as state supervisor of the Public Records Indexing project, whereby all wills, deeds, and marriage records of the respective counties were indexed. This service continued until World War II when it was suspended. Some of his other commissions included a brochure on the famous Chouteau family of Oklahoma.

The Douglas Aircraft Company next employed him as template and pattern inspector; however, the ever-ambitious Lackey could not remain away from his love for art and as an avocation he indulged in both commercial art and professional writing. Woodrow Crumbo was an employee of Douglas during the same period and they became fast friends. When the war ceased, Lackey returned to commercial art and professional writing and worked without interruption until 1945 when he accepted the offer of Thomas Gilcrease. His compensation for the paintings was a per-piece project. The actual sizes of the canvasses were 10″ x 12″ for some and 20″ x 25″ for others. The work he undertook for the Gilcrease Foundation consumed three years and ten months, and one wonders as the paintings are viewed how any one man could have done so much in such a short period of time, considering the research, travel, and painting required.

After Mr. Lackey's demise, Mr. William S. Bailey, Jr., then president of the institute, presented his widow Muriel and his son Sam with a certificate of recognition. This posthumous award was the first such award to be presented by the institute. It bore the inscription, "for outstanding contribution toward the preservation of Oklahoma history."

The Lackey collection was one of the favorites of Thomas Gilcrease because he not only knew and worked with the artist personally, but also for the opportunity it afforded him to provide the commission which resulted in these superb paintings. It is hoped that in future years there will be a specially designed historical room where the paintings can be placed on permanent display, not only as a tribute to the artist, but as study pieces for history majors and as a reminder to the visitors that, although many of the structures have gone with the wind, there still remains a visual reflection of the history-making era.

Twenty-three of the representative selections from the Lackey collection were included in *The American Scene* magazine of the winter 1959-60 issue, Volume IV, No. 2. Part of the selections were: *Beck's Mill,* near Flint, Oklahoma, known as Hildebrant Mill, erected in 1838; *Mouille's Salt Works,* near the mouth of Brush Creek, west side of Grand River, five miles northeast of Mazie, two miles from the Old Union Mission which was in use before the Louisiana Purchase; *Old Fort Arbuckle,* which was near Tulsa; *Fort Cobb,* just east of the town of Fort Cobb in Caddo County, which was erected in 1859; *The Capitol of the Muskogee or Creek Nation,* at Okmulgee, erected in 1878;

and *The Capitol of the Choctaw Nation,* near Tuskahoma, erected in 1883.

Lackey's work is architecturally accurate, historically important, and meticulously executed. They are, in fact, miniaturized examples of mastercraft in their reproduction of lost buildings, houses, institutions, and shrines of the territories and early statehood.

Chapter 2

Digging In and Digging Out

On October 22, 1964, a typescript was placed in the log vault of the Thomas Gilcrease Institute of American History and Art by Mr. Dean Krakel, who was then the director of the institute. This significant document reflected the listing of four books containing the gift of archaeological and ethnological items presented to the City of Tulsa by the Thomas Gilcrease Foundation, two of which contained photographic records and film records. The remaining volumes contained basic records and inventories pertaining to the archaeological collection.

The foundation's excavations were conducted in the Mississippi Valley in the states of Illinois, Missouri, Tennessee, Mississippi, and Arkansas; and practically all of the "digs" were made by Thomas Gilcrease in company with Gregory Perino and Dr. David Harner of Springdale, Arkansas. Mr. Perino was employed by the Gilcrease Foundation, while Dr. David Harner joined the expeditions devoting his own time and expenses to the projects. All of the "finds" became the property of the Gilcrease Foundation. Harry McPherson, of Fayetteville, Arkansas, was employed by the foundation for a short time and, during his tenure, accompanied Mr. Gilcrease on a number of important digs. The first excavations were initiated in 1955 in the lower Illinois River Valley approximately fifty miles north of St. Louis, Missouri, where fifteen Hopewell mounds dating from 50 B.C. to 250 A.D. were excavated.

Gregory Perino had been an advanced amateur and president of the St. Louis, Missouri Archaeological Society, where he had devoted ten years of intensive study.[1] Dr. David Harner had met Thomas Gilcrease on an eventful Sunday while visiting the museum. Mr. Gilcrease was looking over some items which had been offered to him by a collector. "Do you think they are authentic?" asked Mr. Gilcrease.

Dr. Harner had replied somewhat tersely, "No." This short exchange of remarks was the beginning of a long and rewarding friendship between Tom and the doctor.

The extent of the excavations, the artifacts discovered and preserved, the inspired activity, and the results can best be understood by learning something of the men who were associated on the digs, who worked with, worked for, and shared the successes and failures of the activities conducted under the auspices of the Thomas Gilcrease Foundation. They were dedicated men engaged in an avocation of adventure.

Tom Gilcrease sought to employ a qualified archaeologist. He made several contacts with applicants; however, most of those who had been recommended did not meet the qualifications or standards desired. Tom wanted an employee who would always be ready to embark on a dig and who could assort and classify the artifacts already acquired which were in storage at the museum. He selected Gregory Perino as that man. The formality was quickly abandoned and his employee became known as "Greg." Shortly after Greg moved to Tulsa and was settled in the workshop area where the digs were examined and studied, Tom said, "I want you to assort my early acquisitions so we can authenticate them." This pleased Greg, who was not long in realizing that his new position offered a challenge and he would have an opportunity to broaden his knowledge of the American Indian.

Greg knew that there was more to the science of excavation than sinking a pick or a spade into Mother Earth with the hope that beneath her garment of topsoil would be found a relic of the people who once considered the site their home. He was also aware that a good pair of eyes was essential to reading and interpreting the profiles of the ground, as was the talent to recognize certain clues which are obvious only to the dedicated and experienced. Tom had remarked to him on an occasion when they were having a discourse about qualified field men, "You know, Greg, I can always hire brains." Greg was flattered and frustrated.

Dr. David Harner had first felt the sting of the archaeology bug when he was only eight years old.[2] By the time he met Tom, the Harner collection was worthy of recognition. The good doctor had conducted his early searches in Illinois, but being an Oklahoman by birth, he felt a keen attachment for the Sooner State and this was the motivating factor for his first visit to the Gilcrease Museum (as it was then known) where he met Tom. Unlike his friend Greg, Doctor Harner had limited his digs to surface hunting and the excavation of mounds and bluff shelters. The first dig with Tom was on May 1, 1955, at a site which had been selected by Greg and Harry McPherson. They all respected Greg's judgment on the selection of sites and particularly in the Illinois areas, although Harry had an excellent background in determining sites in and around the Memphis area.

The indefatigable Tom was unrelenting in his quest for prehistoric culture and the study of antiquity. He often remarked to his colleagues on the sites that day by day a little bit of the past was being destroyed by the ruthless desire of man to increase his economic stature, and if the contents of the mounds were to be preserved for future generations there was no time to tarry. Once on the site, he pushed his men into action; but he never shoved, he shoveled. Greg would keep the crew engaged and the more soil he gathered in the cuffs of his trousers, the closer he felt to the artifacts which the joint efforts of all brought to light. While Greg and the genial doctor had acquired rapport with each other and they both possessed a sympathetic relation with Tom, it was often Greg's impulse to say, "Doc, why are you such an armchair strategist?" However, he never audibly accomplished his purpose but had a good idea that "Doc" could read his mind.

Whether it was Tom's spirited drive for accomplishment, Greg's desire to please Tom and probe with understanding, or Doc's incarnate knowledge of science and theoretical functions of the mind, the results of their digs were fantastic. They discovered new methods of making the excavations, and in a short time some of the university groups began to apply their techniques, and this at a time when the experts shouted "impractical and impossible."

Doc felt that an elementary knowledge of engineering was especially valuable when the excavation was in progress near caves and bluffs. Greg, on the contrary, did not agree and wanted to apply what he called common sense and practical approach with a *feel* for the ground. He often remarked, "If a man does not have a feel for the digs he could put his time to greater use by reading a book or looking at pictures." Greg and Doc could always resolve their differences, and all the while Tom just kept on working because he knew people and he knew Doc and Greg and they were just people and a special kind of folk.

The preparation for a dig was not an easy task. The standard equipment was a sturdy crawler used to remove the soil previously loosened by hand digging to reveal features and artifacts; a pickup truck; sharp shovels; trowels; good brushes; cameras; and well-constructed boxes. The crew of the average dig required six men but by using a crawler, three could do a fair amount of work. With the exception of the necessary clearing to prepare the site, all digging was done by hand. The washouts and natural or man-made depressions always required the use of heavy equipment.

Following the 1955 excavations, Tom and his associates made digs in the Memphis area of eastern Arkansas,

Mississippi, and Tennessee. An entire village of approximately nine acres was excavated on a site known as the Banks' plantation, located at Clarksdale in eastern Arkansas. This venture required three years, but the labors were rewarded when recovery was made of several house patterns, a plaza, 1,000 vessels, and other artifacts, in addition to 600 skeletons of the people who had inhabited the area long ago. Through the use of the facilities of the laboratory of the University of Michigan, a radiocarbon date was obtained from charred corncobs found in this ancient village. The date produced was 1535 A.D. and the multiple overlying house patterns indicated that the village had existed for a minimum of one hundred years. This unusual site was in the area of the De Soto expeditionary route in time and place, making it possible to project that the exploration party of De Soto passed by or remained for a brief stay at the village.

Three large mounds were salvaged at Cherry Valley in eastern Arkansas. These mounds had suffered almost irreparable damage by amateurs and irresponsible treasure seekers. From what remained, Tom and his crew recovered 300 skeletons and many artifacts. From scientific experiments it was determined that, typologically, the artifacts excavated were similar to those found in the important Cahokia site near St. Louis, Illinois. The people of the Cahokia site, according to historic data, had migrated northward into Wisconsin and westward to a short distance from Kansas City, but never southward where the area was overpopulated.

The Banks' plantation, near the Banks Village site, produced a Mississippi mound of an even earlier date. This mound had been constructed to a height of eleven feet and had a diameter of eighty feet, over a small Baytown mound of the Woodland period. Mississippi burials were found only in the eastern face of the mound. The astounding discovery was made that on each side a clay stairway ascended into a crematory fourteen feet in diameter. This stairway had been constructed in the apex of the mound. The date produced on this discovery was 1087 A.D. The artifacts excavated with the burials indicated affiliation through trade with the Cahokia site hereinbefore described.

Subsequent research in Illinois over a period of three years produced some twenty-six mounds where excavations uncovered 2,000 skeletons which were carefully taken from their resting places. To accomplish these feats entire blocks of soil had to be removed for transport purposes. Evidence of this kind of recovery is on exhibit at the Thomas Gilcrease Institute of American History and Art.

Near the town of Kampsville in Illinois, a mound representing the earliest period of mound construction of the late Archaic Culture was located by Tom and his crew, and disclosed the remains of eighty individuals of an archaic culture, and, gruesome as it may be, reflected in print, it was determined that at least half of the population had been cremated in seven crematories.* In each mound where skeletons were recovered there were also repositories of artifacts; and the Kampsville mound produced plummets, charred fabric, copper fish hooks, pearl beads, and other miscellaneous items. The carbon date, gleaned from charcoal and burned bone from the crematories, scientifically established the date of 908 B.C. Dr. George K. Neumann of the University of Indiana, from a study made of the skeletal remains, determined that the human beings which once roamed the area were a migrant group from the south, being indicated with round heads instead of long heads common to the local Archaic peoples. Four miles south of Hardin, Illinois, whcrc more skeltons were discovered, the diagnosis made by Dr. Neumann was substantiated. The vessels which were excavated were identical in style and manufacture to early southern wares.

Across the Illinois River at the Schild site, near Eldred, Illinois, another dig was made which produced physical evidence of acculturation of two different peoples, Woodland and Mississippi groups. The initial excavations of the Woodland mounds, some nine in number, revealed 265 flexed burials and three subfloor tombs. These were dated approximately 900 A.D. On the slope of the west hill of mound nine a cemetery was discovered containing 300

---

* The late Archaic Culture according to a Carbon 14 dating, was constructed about 908 B.C.

skeletons, many of which were of late Woodland and some of Mississippian physical types. It was apparent to the scientific minds that a great many of the skeletons were of peoples who were a result of the mixture of the two races. It was determined that this acculturated group had appropriated to themselves most of the Mississippian customs but retained some of the late Woodland pottery making techniques. Greg Perino fully believes that it is a tragedy that in the later years of his life Tom Gilcrease did not possess sufficient funds to publish the results of his excavations because color slides were made and he was willing to share them with people who were sincere in wanting to use them for educational purposes. It is the opinion of Perino that the fact that Mr. Gilcrease was not able to record with accuracy some of the history of the artifacts he acquired by purchase is said to create a void in the collection, and in many instances the origin of the items has been lost.

The excavations made under the auspices of Mr. Gilcrease were supplemented by collections purchased from Alaska, Central America, the West and the Southeast and contain works of prehistoric art which have never been duplicated. From the Midwest and mid-South collections acquired by Mr. Gilcrease, some two thousand rare works of lithic and ceramic art became a part of his possessions. Tom Gilcrease had a mania for obtaining, if possible, what the archaeologist refers to as a "one of a kind" item. Such relics include rare and well-made early flint blades, gemstone blades and projectile points, bannerstones, birdstones, pipes, plummets, discoidals, stone axes, rare effigy forms of pottery vessels, and shell, pearl, and copper beads. There is an adequate collection of Cahokia artifacts, the Perino collection; Spiro artifacts from Oklahoma, from the Dr. T. Hugh Young collection; Hopewell artifacts, from the L. Gibson collection; and Archaic artifacts from the Dr. P. F. Titterington collection. The largest collection was obtained from District Judge Harry J. Lemley of Hope, Arkansas and contains more than 50,000 artifacts of major significance representing every variety of Caddoan ware and containing a great quantity of rare and unusual vessels from eastern Arkansas. The Poverty Point collection from northern Louisiana contains the greatest assemblage of late Archaic artifacts from that area.

The Man

While there were many facets to the life of Thomas Gilcrease and he wore many hats as a collector, those who were privileged to work with him in the archaeological phase of his career made their own summations of why he was what he was and left the tracks that he did. It was Greg Perino who said, "He was generous with himself and all who knew him loved him for it. He actually spent little money on himself but invested all of his resources in art and archaeology that future generations might know America better. He was never known to have surplus money to give away and no one expected it of him. When he hired a hand or employed a technician he made it crystal clear what the wages would be and the subject never came up again. He had a way of penetrating your skin so that there would be a built-up loyalty beyond all speculation, and admiration for him was surpassed only by the sincerity he generated. He aimed for the best with every given state of circumstances. There was an intentional design for living and this natural trait was inborn. He gave me the opportunity to do what I wanted to do and if I had it all to do over again I would do just that and love every minute of it. And, if I were to measure Thomas Gilcrease the man as compared to Thomas Gilcrease the founder of the museum, I would say that it takes a special person to be both; and he was."

His colleague, Dr. David Harner, has a different summation. Dr. Harner firmly believed that Thomas Gilcrease had a weakness. When he was wrong, it took him a long time to change his mind. He was not a talkative man and only said something when it meant something. Tom often spoke of his mother and took great pride in the Indian blood which came from her. He respected his father but somehow he always left the impression that his father, by reason of having reared a large family, was too busy to divide an appreciable portion of his time among the fourteen children he had sired.

In his quest for prehistoric ware Thomas Gilcrease did not consider himself a philanthropist but rather as an individual to whom God had entrusted a special talent to preserve what had been created.

There has been an abundance of speculative thought as to whether Mr. Gilcrease became a collector of art for the sole purpose of doing honor to the American Indian. His long-time friend and counsel, Lester Whipple of San Antonio, Texas, perhaps more accurately wraps up the package of uncertainty than any other person. He said, "He was very proud of being an Indian. While he was very friendly with the Creeks and was in entire sympathy with them, I don't believe he wanted to be considered solely a Creek. He could have been chief of the Creeks but declined the honor. He accepted the office of honorary Chief of the Sioux Tribe. He was given the name of 'High Star.' He had an avowed resentment to being called 'part-Indian' and would often break a silence after being so addressed with the two words, 'Full Blood.' I doubt if his purpose was to give prestige to the Indian generally."

If Thomas Gilcrease had been privileged to live a more extended life than he did, he would have eventually explored in Egypt, because he was considering a dig in Mexico at the time of his death. He wanted to explore in Greece, Italy and other foreign countries but basically, with the limited time and finances available to him, he was interested in preserving American history. While he was not an extrovert when it came to religion, he was careful with "grave" goods which accounted for his caution in the process of removal of discovered skeletons; and if the burials reflected remains of children he would study the site carefully and his colleagues believed that he uttered prayers which none of them heard. There were no common "finds." All relics were worthy of study. Every people has its culture and Tom Gilcrease knew that each discovery would brighten the history pertaining to the area of the dig.

There was a humorous side to Thomas Gilcrease when pursuing his excavations, and Greg Perino recalls one evening when they were excavating mound eleven of the Klunk group near Kampsville, Illinois. "It was mid-morning; the crew had been working steadily and a young boy had come up to the camp and helped with some of the small chores. As we rested, Tom's eyes caught the boy looking at him and since his eyes always seemed to speak first, there was that twinkling which broke into a faint smile and then he said, 'Young fellow, when I was just about your age we lived in a log cabin with a lean-to built on and a large fireplace. While the fire kept us warm I would sit between my father's knees and he told me stories. It was on one of these nights that a stranger came to our door and my father invited him to come in. The stranger must have sensed the devotion of our home and finally he spoke. "You know, son, I have traveled a long way in my life and once I saw the most beautiful place in all the world; it was a petrified forest. Trees were standing and trees were on the ground. I saw petrified squirrels and petrified birds in the trees. Then all of a sudden I heard the sweetest music and, looking around, I saw that one of the petrified birds was singing a petrified song on a petrified tree." ' The boy looked at Mr. Tom. He looked at me. We went back to work."

Two extremely fine pipes recovered from huge log tombs in the mounds were effigies; one of a raven, beautifully carved from green Ohio pipestone, while the other, also beautifully carved, was that of a beaver made of a gray-colored stone. It depicts a beaver sitting on its tail in a defensive attitude. It has pearl eyes and a section of a real beaver tooth inlaid in the stone for its teeth. These pipes are among the finest in North America. Of all of the artifacts discovered by Thomas Gilcrease these were Tom's favorites. Very often Gregory Perino walks into the storeroom of the museum, gently picks up the pipe with the pearl eyes and the beaver tooth; a faraway look comes into his eyes and he audibly says, "Yes, when Tom went away, he took a little piece of my heart with him."

Chapter 3

The Old Faithfuls

Lester Whipple

Thomas Gilcrease was determined to meet Lester Whipple and wanted him to serve as his personal lawyer. In typical fashion he sent one of the company employees to Whipple's office with a message. "Mr. Thomas Gilcrease said he would like to have you come to his office; he wants to see you," said the timid messenger.

"Well, tell him I'll come over when I get time and be sure you tell just that," bellowed the rustic gentleman.

Lester Whipple is a tall and attractive Texan. His appearance is reminiscent of a prosperous rancher who could easily be cast to portray a western character in a motion picture. He is a descendant of William Whipple from New Hampshire who was one of the signers of the Declaration of Independence. He wears a large hat, cocked to one side, and his bearing is stately. When he shakes hands it is with a positive grip, and one's eyes meet his with a "glad to know you" greeting that makes him one of those unforgettable individuals.[1]

Mr. Whipple was the senior member of his firm, and by referral from Tulsa lawyers he and his associates had performed professional services for the Gilcrease companies. When they finally met as a result of the exchange of messages, an attorney-client relationship was immediately consummated, and ripened into one of the strangest friendships in Texas history. They became *amigos* because they understood each other and could converse in Spanish, although neither of them could boast of having one drop of Spanish blood in his veins. They shared untold experiences as the years brought them closer and closer together. They litigated, investigated, calculated, captivated, and speculated. They criticized each other and engaged in acrimonious debate but they always came out smiling when it was time to leave their respective corners – never looking back and confident that they had both emerged victorious.

While Lester Whipple respected men of substance, he never bowed low to the waist in the presence of a wealthy man; in fact, he never bowed at all. The keen intellect of any individual would sharpen his wits and he found that hob-nobbing with such men was a delightfully stimulating experience. If his perceptive ability warned him that he was to be subjected to a dud, he would retreat from the introduction with such diplomacy that the individual would hardly know whether he had been complimented or castigated.

Tom Gilcrease learned many lessons about living and giving from Lester Whipple. There were moments when he wished that he could match the extroversion in his friend Lester's personality. There were times when he melted before such demonstrations and yearned to be out on a lone prairie where the wonders of nature would offer him a haven of seclusion. The contrary was true with Lester Whipple when he would become so exasperated with the complacency of his friend Tom in trying situations that he wondered why fate had ever brought them together. These divergent attributes made them a dangerous team in business and a winning pair of aces in social circles. Whenever Tom was privileged to be in the presence of Lester Whipple and his erudite and charming wife, Louise, he would assume an air of satisfaction which gave him a feeling of basking in the sunlight of a royal court.

Lester Whipple did not hesitate to throw a verbalism of reproof at Tom when he warranted such subjection. Perhaps the most daring example of this was occasioned when Tom exemplified, by ill-chosen remarks, a somewhat natural prejudice against a minority group. Lester immediately took issue with him, denounced the unfavorable opinion, and then let go with a Spanish idiom which, when translated, becomes, "Don't spit up into the air, some of it is likely to fall back upon you."

The role of private counsel to an oil man is the type of representation which is fading fast from the business-professional scene. A lawyer can no longer expect to share in his client's investments and anticipate compensation from contingency rides of oil ventures.

Within a matter of seconds after Thomas Gilcrease and Lester Whipple met, Tom knew that he had encountered a two-fisted, straight-shooting man – the kind who could look his neighbor in the eye and say, "The next time you water your steers on my pond without permission – there will be barbecued beef in the bunkhouse that night."

Tom related to Lester a brief history and description of the Gilcrease Oil Company which had been organized in Oklahoma and disclosed all of the intimate details of the partnership which he had formed and eventually dissolved in favor of the corporate operation. He advised his new counsel that the majority of the stockholders had sold him their shares and that he owned ninety percent of the company. "Lester, I want to retire from the company," he said. "I will turn the assets over to you and you can organize a new company under the laws of the state of Texas. I want my sons protected and I want them to be stockholders." At the time, his sons, Tom, Jr. and Barton, were attending the University of Oklahoma; one was studying engineering and geology, the other geology and oil accounting. Tom, Jr. was to act as the geologist and Barton the tax consultant in charge of the accounting work.

The astute Whipple discouraged the organization, saying, "Tom, you have built the company. Your name is recognized in the oil fraternity and your sons are inexperienced. I won't do it." Tom reluctantly consented to follow the advice of his attorney, and then confided to him his real reason for wanting to retire from active management of the business was to devote his time exclusively to collecting art.

This statement shook Whipple to the very pages of his Corpus Juris. He did not want to get into the business of art collecting — he understood that Tom wanted a lawyer to look after his oil interests. He learned that he was not only engaged to be counsel for the corporation but was to act as Tom's personal lawyer. The contract of employment was concluded on March 2, 1938. There followed a series of conferences in which the future of Tom's investments and the preservation of his assets were discussed with cautious consideration. Tom had started making reference to his lawyer as "Judge Whipple" and from then on to the end of the trail he referred to him as such. "We never actually signed a contract," said Whipple. "I never had a written contract with him on anything and found I did not need one. His memory was marvelous and he kept his word to the letter," he added.

Later a foundation was organized and Thomas Gilcrease devoted his life to the collection of art. Recalling these formative and thrilling days, Judge Whipple remarked, "The legal matters relating to the collection of art consumed about three-fourths of my time. I would estimate that the greater part of my time during the fifteen years was spent helping him with his collecting, not that I determined what he should or should not buy. He made his own decisions and I was never with him but once when he made a purchase.

"I have reference to an experience which occurred when Tom, Robert Lee Humber, and myself were in one of the major cities of Texas. We had on work clothing because we had gone to visit one of the leases to watch a well come in. We were dirty, tired, and badly in need of a shower. En route to our hotel we passed an art gallery. Tom wanted to go in and browse. Mr. Humber consented and with some hesitancy I agreed. A few minutes after we entered, Mr. Humber spotted a painting of a bull. I do not recall the title of the painting or the name of the artist. Mr. Humber inquired about the price and was told that $1,200 would buy the painting and the frame. He then took eight $100 bills out of his wallet and offered them to the proprietor, which were promptly refused. He laid an additional $50 on the counter. This was refused and the incensed owner told him that nothing less than the quoted price would suffice. Tom then turned to Humber and said, 'Are you all through?' 'What do you mean?' asked Humber. 'Well,' said Tom, 'I just want to be sure that you have finished your bargaining.' With that remark Tom reached into his pocket, pulled out a dirty check book, and with a nonchalance which would have tried the patience of a saint, he wrote out a check for the $1,200, turned to the man, and said, 'Wrap it up and deliver it to the office of Lester Whipple, in San Antonio.' The next day Tom left unannounced on one of his trips. A couple of weeks later a stranger came to my office and said: 'Are you Lester Whipple, attorney for Tom Gilcrease?' I told him that I was. 'Now look here, Mr. Whipple, Thomas Gilcrease bought a painting which was the last one painted by the artist. I am prepared to buy it back and I will pay $30,000 for it right now.' 'Now that's just too bad, my fine feathered friend, but you will have to wait and talk to Tom about that.' 'When will he return?' asked the anxious gentleman. 'When he gets here,' I replied politely but firmly. Another week passed and then the elusive Tom walked into my office unannounced. 'Where have you been?' I inquired. 'Places!' said Tom. I knew better than to press for any further answer so I went right to the meat of the nut. 'You know that painting you bought the other day?' 'Yes, what about it?' asked Tom. 'Well, there was a man in here and he said that it is one of a series of works by the same artist and he has offered $30,000 for it.' I expected Tom to say something. I did not know what his reaction would be because I had not even tried to contact him. He looked at me for a moment and then very cooly said, 'Tell the man it is not for sale.' I was not only amazed but curious, so I inquired, 'Tom, how did you know that it was a valuable painting?' He looked me right square in the eyes and said, 'How did things go in my absence?' That closed the episode."

Judge Whipple's memory has contributed greatly to a better understanding of Thomas Gilcrease, the art collector. His client constantly studied catalogs, talked with art dealers by long distance telephone, visited every museum in every city where he traveled, inspected collections whenever they were advertised. He had a very simple method of buying. First he would locate what he wanted to buy, ascertain the price, and start the search for funds with which to make the purchase. Price was no object and often ranged from $50,000 to $250,000. He knew the trick of obtaining options on what he wanted and he could talk an art dealer into an option by telephone with as much ease as with a written proposal. "He never did it the easy way. It was always the hard way," recalls Judge Whipple.

Another instance where the shrewdness of Tom Gilcrease may well be considered a classic of intuitive collecting is recounted by the judge. "I recall so vividly the purchase he made of some extremely rare books. They were historical and in great demand by the government where the author of the books was born. According to the experts, there was only one printing of the particular volumes, and to prevent them from falling into the hands of foreigners, the country had enacted a very strict law prohibiting the sale under any circumstances. There was only one thing the cautious officials had overlooked. Tom Gilcrease had located the books in a little-known shop where rare documents were for sale and had purchased them for a modest sum the day before the law was passed. They are a part of the treasures in the library of the institute and I doubt if this story has ever been told before."

Lester Whipple's memories of his amigo are as prolific as the repertoire of a dramatist. He recalls a trip which Tom Gilcrease made to Cushing, Oklahoma, where an investor from Paris had come to the United States to inspect certain leases in which Mr. Gilcrease had sold him a substantial interest. When they reached the main part of the town they walked through the business district; Tom wanted his guest to have a good view of the activity. Suddenly Tom heard a commotion and looked back. His French friend had dropped behind and was standing against the wall of a building where he had, without compunction, indulged in one of the customs of his country. The town marshal happened by simultaneously with the completion of the purpose for which he had paused. The Frenchman was threatened with arrest for indecent exposure and he would have been taken into custody but for Tom's adroit explanation of the practice of the French people to perform the act of nature in public places where shelters are stationed. "After all," said Tom to the officer, "we do want him to feel at home in our country, don't we?" The marshal yielded to Tom's persuasion and the Frenchman's charm, and reluctantly agreed to release the poor fellow who could not readily comprehend the reason for having been taken into custody.

Tom Gilcrease did not talk too freely about the traits of his father, and when he chose to do so it was generally to recall some event which made an impression upon him in his youth. His father, like many of the pioneers of the West, was an individualist in the complete meaning of the word. Judge Whipple recalls Tom's recitation of the following example of his father's method of dealing with those who encroached upon his property. "I was at my father's store taking care of some chores when I noticed a wagon pull up across the street from my father's place of business. The wagon was loaded with raw lumber and the man alighted from his buckboard seat and tied the reins to a tree. About that time I called to my father and told him to look outside. The man stood beside the wagon and appeared to be eyeing the land around him. He started stepping off and counting distances. Father walked outside of the store and said, 'Howdy, stranger, anything I can do for you?' The stranger spit a stream of tobacco juice at a lizard which had been crouching near the tree trunk and it struck the poor creature right between the eyes. My father was taken by surprise and said, 'Right good spittin', now what can I do for you?' 'Well, I'm aimin' to build me a house and this looks like a right good spot to build her.' My father looked the stranger right square in the face and said, 'Now that's too bad. This land happens to belong to me and you ain't abuildin' no house here, so I suggest that you just get back on your wagon and move on!' 'Who says?' questioned the stranger. 'I says,' responded my father and with that he turned to me and ordered, 'Tom, go in the store and bring me that log chain and lock that I hung up back of the door near the meat block.' I ran as fast as my feet would carry me and returned with the chain and lock. My father grabbed the stranger and before he knew what was happening he had him pinned against the tree where the reins were hanging. He put the chain under one of the stranger's arms, across his chest, under the other arm, made a chain knot, and slipped the lock between the links. The stranger was there to stay. 'Now,' said my father to the stranger, 'when you make up your mind that this land belongs to me and that you ain't goin' to build no house here, you can call me and I'll come out and let you go.' The sun was sure hot that day and after about thirty minutes the stranger called and said, 'Unchain me, I'm movin' on.' He did. My father watched his wagon as the dust rose up from the road and then he turned to me and said, 'Son, let that be a lesson to you. Don't ever try to take what don't belong to you.'"

Thomas Gilcrease was given many names in the course of his long and colorful career. He was termed the "stingiest rich man" in the world by many of his cronies in the oil industry. To some men he was known as a banker; to others he was considered an art collector. Big businessmen called him a financier.

On the thirteenth day of July, 1946, be became "High Star" and was given the Indian name of "Wicarpi Wakatuya." The official credential was witnessed by George Whirlwind, soldier of South Dakota, and signed by Henry Standing Bear, chief of the Sioux tribes. The text reads: "I, Henry Standing Bear, Chief of Sioux Tribes, on this 13th day of July 1946 by virtue of proper authority invested in me as Chief and in accordance with tribal custom hereby name you High Star and honorary member of our tribe." This simple document written in the personal hand of Chief Henry Standing Bear afforded Tom Gilcrease one of the happier days of his life.

January 28, 1954 was another day of joy for Thomas Gilcrease. The Tribal Council of the Creek Indians gave him recognition and special acclaim for his skill and superior proficiency in the field of "Masterful Book and Art." The certificate bears the signature of J. J. Mingo, executive secretary of the Creek Nation and John F. Davis, principal chief of the Creek Nation. The certification title is the Creek Indian Capital of America, the Creek Council House, Okmulgee, Oklahoma.

Judge Whipple recalls that Thomas Gilcrease was never named honorary chief of the Creek tribe. He was recommended as a candidate for principal chief of the Creek Nation in 1961 but the appointment was not given. Tribal chiefs were, at that time, appointed by the secretary of the interior by reason of the delegated powers from the president of the United States. Before this regulation the appointments came directly from the president. The custom was for the Indian Council of the Creeks to submit five names to the secretary of the interior, and from this list the chief was chosen. Mr. Whipple is of the opinion that the appointment was blocked because of political inactivity. Thomas Gilcrease was a registered Democrat and it was unfortunate he lost out. Regardless of speculation, the events of later years did not alter the decision of the secretary of the interior, and Lester's amigo mentioned his disappointment on occasions, but even the members of his family were unaware of his feeling of despair.

In 1939 the amigos planned a trip to Europe; however, the war forced them to abandon their plans. Judge Whipple has said, "To have made the trip with Tom Gilcrease would have afforded me an even greater appreciation of his ability as an art collector. I had always anticipated seeing him in action with citizens of foreign countries. He had his methods of bargaining which could match any dealer and it would have been educational to watch him acquire what he made up his mind to purchase."

With the same candor as Lester Whipple related most of the events about the business ability of Thomas Gilcrease, he also recited some of his personal recollections about his friend, Thomas Gilcrease. The recitations are not breaches of either etiquette or ethics – they are facts, and justly told so that as facts they will remain wherever the life of Thomas Gilcrease is reviewed.

"Tom Gilcrease had only one real love in his life and that was reserved for Norma Smallwood, the beautiful and talented Miss America of 1926. When his marriage to her was ended, he transferred his affection to his daughter, who became the most important person in his life. He shied away from further matrimony after his marriage to Norma Smallwood ended in divorce. He was wary of female involvement and was cautious not to invite encroachments upon his vulnerable single status. Tom was pursued by artists and women all of his life. Some of them were beautiful and rich and resorted to great lengths to snare him. To know him was to appreciate this fact. He was attractive, cultured, polite, considerate of his fellowman, and possessed an extremely penetrating intelligence and intuition, excelling in every thing he tried, and he could rope a steer with the same ease that he could ride a bucking horse. He had the ability to make the most of every day and would often say, 'I wish we knew just how much more time we have.' Tom just did not want life to overtake him with a job which was not finished and his intense manifestations led many of his friends to think he was an unhappy man; however, I think he was a happy individual and was highly conscious of his success in life. He once remarked to me, 'It is impossible for a man not to pray because every breath a man takes is a prayer.' "

In May of 1940, Lester Whipple received a letter from his friend and client, Thomas Gilcrease. The rarity of a written communication gives sentimental and intrinsic value to the precious document which reflects the incarnate humor and human side of the writer. It was penned in Tom's personal hand on stationery of the Gilcrease Oil Company when the organization was housed in the Milam Building at San Antonio, Texas. The designation "Office of the President" is sharply contrasted with the informal signature it bears. The letter is reproduced in the picture section of this book in its entirety. There was something more to the letter than a demonstration of Tom's ability to write in the metaphor of the Indian. It afforded him the opportunity to mimic the jargon of the Indian. The very fact that he wrote in this vein and signatured the epistle "Indian Tom" bespeaks his devotion to Lester Whipple.

When Tom joined his ancestors it was as if there was really a "bigger well settin other side from sun" – and Lester Whipple uttered two words: "Adios Amigo."

Cephas Stout

Tom Gilcrease had been to town to take care of some business matters. As he drove west on Newton he approached the intersection where the big iron gates served as a barricade to uninvited guests. The road just inside the turn led up to his stone house. His car boy, or chauffeur, was accustomed to his boss calling to him over the talking tube which had been installed in Tom's Packard automobile. As the automobile rolled to a stop, Tom saw a tall young man wearing work clothing come toward the vehicle. The right window was down and Tom said, "Hold it right here; I think that man wants something!"

"Could you use a hand?" said the young man.

"What can you do?" came Tom's reply. By this time the young man was looking into the window, evidently attracted by the speaking tube which was in Tom's hand.

He eyed Tom and the car boy and then replied, "Just about anything anyone else can do, only better, and I'm willing to work."

This forthright reply so impressed Tom that he alighted from the Packard, looked the young man over, appeared to be only moderately impressed with what he saw, and said, "You are hired; come up in the morning and you can join the gardener's staff. Now mind you, there won't be steady work but we will use you as we need you and I'll talk about your wages later."

The young man reported for work the next morning just as the sun was coming up behind the hill. His name was Cephas Stout.[3] He was part Cherokee but he did not tell Tom about his Indian blood until many months later when they became better acquainted. When Tom learned that Cephas had an Indian background he gave him the nickname of "Chief" and that was, perhaps, the last time Tom ever called him by his Christian name.

There was much to be done on Tom's place, as Chief was soon to learn. He lived within walking distance of the hill, and even when work was light, there he was working at something which needed fixing or digging in the garden. More and more Tom learned to depend on Chief for the chores which had to be done right. The hill was a showplace but the only improvements on the land were rustic in appearance and construction. There was the old rock house which had been built by a man named Flowers Nelson, a Tulsa lawyer, who had acquired the property from Grover and Pearl Mackey way back on December 13, 1909. The land was a part of the original allotment of Grover Mackey, an Osage Indian who was on the Indian rolls as number 1499. Flowers Nelson and his wife, Carrie, had built the house out of native sandstone and there was something about the house and the hill which Tom liked. He had met Flowers Nelson in a business way and one day he made an offer. And so it was that the south half of the southeast quarter of Section 28, Township 20, Range 12 in Osage County became the property of Thomas Gilcrease on December 26, 1913.

There was also a garage and a barn on the land. Tom had not done much to improve the house from 1913 to 1927. He was too busy with his oil interests, his hunting expeditions, and many other interests. It was in 1927 that he hired Chief and from that day on captured Chief's heart and hands.

Day after day Chief would dig post holes, plant shrubs, stretch fence, repair tools, make roads, repair roads, help with the planting, feed the stock, build birdbaths, and do a million and one things that no one else seemed to want to do or could do.

In 1941 Tom told Chief that he was going to convert one of the barns into a storehouse where he could keep some paintings and artifacts which he had acquired. It was about that time that he referred to the barn as his "gallery" and the garage as the "library." Tom's second wife, Norma Smallwood Gilcrease, had used the garage as a sort of studio and it had housed a lot of Tom's trophies; however, more will be said about the little studio elsewhere in this book.

In January of 1943, Chief was walking around the premises when he decided to decorate some flower beds which had spread too much. He brought some stone up from below the hill, cut it, and then set it in place in a circular fashion. About the time he finished, Tom walked up to where Chief was standing and said, "Chief, did you do that all by yourself?" He knew that Chief had done so, but his remark was typical. He did not use the direct approach or tell Chief that it was good job, or that it represented what might have been installed by a skilled stonemason.

Chief looked at Tom with his usual worshipping eyes and remarked, "You know something, Mr. Gilcrease, that is the first time I ever tried putting a bunch of stones together and to make anything out of them!" This did not bring any immediate comment from Tom. He had not told Tom that to accomplish his garden design he had driven a wedge into the stone slabs of sandstone and then fashioned them into the desired shape.

They both remained silent for a moment or two and then Tom turned to Chief and remarked, "Chief, we are going to build us a museum right here on these grounds and someday we will have a place where people can come from all over the country to see my collection of paintings and art objects!"

All of this meant very little to Chief and he merely looked at Tom and said, "Yes, I guess so."

Nothing more was said about the museum building until one day Tom came out where Chief was doing some repair work and in a quiet voice remarked to him, "Chief, I guess it is about time that we commenced to think about that museum building." Here again was one of Tom's indirect orders. "And by the way, Chief," said Tom, "better hire yourself some helpers, get the design and the plans all drawn up and the land cleared."

"Well," thought Chief, "the Old Man is really serious." He always called Tom the "Old Man" when he was making reference to him, but he never dared to do it in his presence. He had too much respect for his boss, and although they were the best of friends or as close as an employee and a boss could be, he knew that he could never become real intimate with Tom – no one could do that. The Old Man told Chief to get in touch with a friend known as Vernon "Duke" Ellington, who was considered a reliable engineer, and Legus Chalakee, a stonemason, and it was not too many days until the plans were submitted, approved, and the necessary material ordered sent to the hill.

Alexandre Hogue, a professor of art at the University of Tulsa, was a friend of Thomas Gilcrease.[4] He and Martin Wiesendanger, the curator of the foundation, had visited with Tom on several occasions and the subject of discussion was the building program of the museum. There had been talk about converting the old barn into an art gallery to house the collection which had been moved from Texas to Tulsa. At that time another building on the grounds was being utilized as an office and darkroom for photography. There was not any unification to the suggested plans. The view of Signal Hill as seen from the residence of Mr. Gilcrease was an inspiring sight and he did not want the proposed buildings to obstruct his view. To house everything under one roof and at the same time design a functional, attractive, and well-located entrance was an unsolved problem.

Professor Hogue had detailed some plans he had in mind during a social visit with Mr. Gilcrease and Mr. Wiesendanger. The suggestion appeared feasible and he was delegated and commissioned to prepare the sketches. The talented professor considered the request more of a challenge than an assignment and went to work. The use of Quonset hut beams was to span the space between the two carriage wings which formed a U-shaped design where they joined onto the barn. This idea was reminiscent of the traditional "Indian long-house" and pleased Mr. Gilcrease. The professor had conceived a motif which architects had failed to grasp. The Indian long-house was not unfamiliar to the artist, who had studied Indian history and had painted subjects relating to Indians. His sketch progressed rapidly and embodied the idea of an outdoor mural space recessed in the end of the Quonset arch as well as to the building which would extend to the right, thereby connecting with the office. The old stalls were to be reached by doors to the left and the right with the entrance to the barn area leading to the lower level of the museum. The Quonset was to extend over the barn, forming a hipped ceiling on each side. The arched door was to serve as a lead corridor to the progressive gallery, thereby repeating the lunette formed by the end of the Quonset.

All went well until Chief discovered that there were not sufficient footings to carry out all of the basic thoughts advanced by the professor. The main motif was incorporated in the eventual plans, and Professor Hogue felt that his efforts were rewarded. The contractors made plan-drawings from the artist's sketch. Mr. Gilcrease was pleased. Mr. Wiesendanger was satisfied. The professor was not compensated and did not expect to be.

Chief knew some stonemasons by the names of Wiley and Nick Thornton, brothers, who lived at Tahlequah,

Oklahoma, not too far from Tulsa. He drove to their home and made a deal with them to move up to the hill and remain there until the job was done. While they were not considered cheap laborers, they did receive what was considered livable wages for the price that was being paid about that time. Under Chief's guidance, instructions, and selection, the stone was quarried from a site located about 250 feet west of where the old part of the present museum building now stands.

The Thornton brothers were also of Cherokee blood and they had a mutual feeling for each other and the work progressed rapidly. Hewing the stone proved to be a problem they had not anticipated, since they were not equipped with power tools, but that did not bother the ingenious mind of Chief. The three Cherokees held a pow-wow and devised a method of drilling holes in the stone by using a farm tractor and a compressor. They managed to tool three wedges with which the stone was cracked to specifications, but they still had to resort to chisels and hammers to shape each individual stone, a process which proved to be all too time consuming. Once again the native ability of Chief commenced to activate his inventive mind and he decided that they would have to do some blasting with black powder. A novel approach to the problem permitted them to blast sixty holes with one operation, and the necessary stones were soon evident around the grounds in huge stacks. Each stone had to be from eight to thirty inches in length and exactly nine inches wide.

The electrical and plastering work was contracted, but the steel which formed the roof was the result of hard labor by Chief and his fellow workers. The completed structure was composed of nine rooms including the library stack room and two offices, in addition to an apartment for Mr. Gilcrease who did not like to live in the big stone house alone after his divorce from Norma Smallwood. The fireplace is still evident in the old part of the museum where the director's receptionist has her office.

By adding some rooms on the second floor, Tom established an orphanage for girls in the stone house. Bert and Lena Logan, brother-in-law and sister of Thomas Gilcrease, were employed to serve as supervisors of the orphanage. The stone house which had been the residence of Tom Gilcrease before he moved to San Antonio had been unoccupied for six years. It was remodeled and converted to a "home" for the Indian children of the Five Civilized Tribes who qualified for admission. The upper floor housed the Indian girls and the lower level was the residence of the Logans. A separate building, consisting of three bedrooms and a living room, was erected to accommodate the boys.

The stone building which had been used as a two-car garage, a storage room, and trophy den were to be utilized for the establishment of a technical training center for the boys and girls. It was the intention of Mr. Gilcrease to create a permanent institution. He contemplated the erection of dormitories and library facilities when the second world war had ended, and to make available all of the books and paintings about the Indian which he had acquired. The vast acreage contained native stone and he built a quarry where new stone was cut and stacked for future use. The children were to attend the public schools of Tulsa and have all the freedom any other child would experience. Bert Logan remarked, "If they want to be lawyers, we'll send them to college, but if they prefer to be farmers, we're going to train them to be the best farmers in the country. This is not going to be an institution, it is going to be a home." And then he said, "We're starting in a small way. We probably won't have more than ten or twelve children the first year. We want to start it right. We will expand when the war is over."

The orphanage was the dream of an eighty-acre Utopia. It was only three miles from the city of Tulsa and Mr. Gilcrease had visions of founding a haven of perfectability for a segment of human society which he loved. There would be ample playgrounds and scenic beauty to captivate the young minds and spur them on to higher education. The project became one of experiment rather than reality. He had not provided for a trained staff or anticipated the complications which arise where adequate regulations are ignored. He had also overestimated the number of orphans available in the state of Oklahoma. His enthusiasm lessened with each month of operation and it was inevitable that the foundation which he organized was not going to be functional.

When Mr. Gilcrease gave up his Texas residence he moved back into the old stone house and resided there until his death. The upstairs back entrance has been sealed off and only the outline of a door remains as evidence that young boys and girls once ran up and down the stairs to their quarters. The stone has chipped away in some places, but there is yet a memory to be drawn from a place in the rear of the building where the sons of Tom Gilcrease once made ice cream and the salt has eaten away some of the surface rock. Only one brass ornament still hangs on the front door. The rock rail which runs across the front porch is no longer a resting place for Tom's feet where he sat in his favorite chair and looked at the skyline of Tulsa's budding metropolis and whistled the bobwhites up every evening. The birds still eat from the feeders and fly from tree to tree.

The divorce which was granted to Tom created many situations for Chief, which he had purposefully dismissed from his mind, but he recalls one particular conversation in which he was engaged with Tom. One of Tom's lawyers had been discussing the financial crisis into which the Gilcrease assets had been thrown as an aftermath of the legal complications which nearly always follow such a domestic catastrophe. Tom called Chief into his office and said, "What I am being subjected to is like looking at a pond where you hope to find a lot of ducks. From a distance you see them and you think the flock is large as you move in for the kill, but you suddenly realize that a man's eyes can do funny tricks on him. That is the way it is with human beings when they are dealing with a man like me. Because my name has been dragged through the courts, they think my pond has a lot of ducks, but they have all disappeared into the air."

Another incident which Chief recalls is related to the collection of pre-Columbian gold which is now a part of the institute's precious possessions. Earl Stendahl, a longtime friend of Tom's, had just flown back from the Stendahl

Galleries in Hollywood in Tom's private airplane. It was a Beechcraft Bonanza which had been acquired to accommodate Tom on the many trips he was taking in his search for art objects of the American Indian.

One of the trucks which Tom used for the purpose of hauling cargo returned by plane had just pulled into the Gilcrease grounds. He noticed a somewhat battered and worn satchel which Earl Stendahl had placed on one of the fenders of the truck shortly after it was parked near the hut. Chief, desiring to engage in a practical joke, took the satchel off of the fender and placed it inside of the hut door where it could not be seen. Earl Stendahl went about unloading other artifacts which were a part of the shipment and suddenly he let out a cry of excitement and said, "Chief, did you see a satchel on the fender of the truck?"

Chief felt that he had gone far enough with his prank and in his quiet manner replied, "Why, Earl, I think you will find it just inside the hut near the door." He noticed an expression of relief come over Earl's face and it was a welcome sight, because for a moment he thought that Earl was going to faint from the shock of having the satchel disappear so quickly.

Once inside, he called to Chief and said, "Come in here and I'll show you why I became so frantic." When the satchel was unlocked and opened, Chief discovered for the first time that it contained in excess of $30,000 in pre-Columbian gold. It was all Chief could do to contain himself and he almost fainted. This rare treasure is now a part of the collection of the Thomas Gilcrease Institute of American History and Art.

In the years that Chief was Tom's trusted and respected employee he spent many nights with him after they had been on what Tom called "digs," meaning of course the exploration of Indian mounds in search for artifacts. Only on one occasion did Chief and Tom have an argument, and it came about when Tom wanted him to work at the museum on Sunday. Chief refused and told Tom that he could not and would not do so because he had to take his children to Sunday school. Tom offered to pay Chief a bonus if he would accommodate him, but Chief stood his ground and flatly refused. Later he was talking about "The Old Man" to another employee and made some rather unkind remarks about the pressure which Tom had put on him. What he did not know was that Tom was standing right behind him at the peak of the conversation. When it became apparent that Tom had overheard the entire conversation, he expected to be fired on the spot, but instead Tom just looked Chief in the eyes and said, "How are things?" This ended the episode.

One of the most cherished memories of Chief was his discussion with Tom regarding religion. It was shortly after the divorce and Tom was at a rather low ebb in his relationship with his fellowman. Without any provocation, Tom told Chief to sit with him on the porch of the great stone house. He turned to Chief and said, "Have you ever seen the Holy Spirit?"

They exchanged glances and after a moment or two Chief responded by asking, "Mr. Gilcrease, I respect and admire you but let me ask you one. Have you ever actually seen love and hate?" Chief then said, "Why did you ask that question?" "Well, I'll tell you," said Tom. "I was asked to contribute the sum of $10,000 to a church building fund and when I told the preacher that my income that year would not permit me to do so, he said, 'You are going to send your soul to Hell!!!' and I thought you might have some ideas about the Holy Spirit, but you have answered my question."

In October of 1963 the new section of the museum building was completed.

L. Karlton Mosteller

L. Karlton Mosteller was the lawyer Mr. Gilcrease retained when the Internal Revenue Service filed a substantial tax bill against the Gilcrease Oil Company. This brilliant member of the Oklahoma Bar Association was successful in defeating the claim, and when the hearing was concluded the trial judge remarked, "I found Mr. Gilcrease to be one of the most convincing witnesses I have heard during my long tenure on the bench. His conduct on the stand, his sincere replies, all point to the proposition that the records submitted are correct."[5]

Mr. Mosteller was happy with the victory but it was like trying to kill a centipede by stepping on the rear segment of its elongated and flattened body. The government was not convinced that the operation of the Paris office of the company was free from taxation. They were faced with the "Bank Secret Statutes" which made it practically impossible to reach the resources of the French citizens who had invested in oil and gas leases, it being the contention of the lawyers for the government that those who had purchased interests in oil leases were investors and not owners. Working in conjunction with Mr. Lester Whipple of San Antonio, Texas, and with the full cooperation of the officials of the company, the two lawyers were successful in advancing the theory developed by Mr. Mosteller that the payment of taxes was the obligation of the individuals as owners and not the corporation, and the tax bill was eventually defeated.

L. Karlton Mosteller, son of Jefferson and Ida (Woodall) Mosteller, was born in Bartow County, Georgia, November 28, 1895. He was a veteran of World War I and received his legal education at George Washington University in Washington, D.C., where he was graduated in 1924. On June 22, 1940, he married Helen Briggs.

He does not recall when or where he met Thomas Gilcrease and feels that neither event is important. The fact that he became his legal counsel and served him for many years in tax matters is significant. Their association resulted in a mutually satisfying companionship that was developed largely across the counsel table, and from visitations which were sporadic and generally impromptu. They had not shared expeditions into the hunting fields and they resided in separate cities; their respective vocations were never commingled with like avocations. Tom's art world and

Karlton's tax world were related in only one respect. The money saved on taxes meant that more art would be acquired.

Mr. Mosteller never went abroad with Mr. Gilcrease and all the information possessed by the lawyer was that which Mr. Gilcrease related to him. The establishment of the Paris office on the Champs Elysées was something of an innovation for Americans who were in the business of selling oil and gas leases. The reputation of Tom Gilcrease spread quickly, and it was not uncommon for some of his French friends to cram currency into the coat pockets of Mr. Gilcrease when he was preparing to sail for the United States and to whisper to him, "Buy me an oil and gas lease so I can become rich like you." The Paris money market had been disorganized and inflation had set in. The few who had large fortunes were cautious about making their cash positions known and were on the lookout for investments in America. The French government had exercised some degree of control over the Bank of France. Nationalization had struck at the very heart of the Frenchman; however, some sectors of the industry remained free of direct government supervision. Those who made the acquaintance of Thomas Gilcrease thought that the word "oil" was synonymous with the word "wealth."

"But all of that era is history now!" remarked Mr. Mosteller as he concluded his short review of his experiences as tax counsel for the man who was to found an Indian museum, work at improving the collection, and eventually possess an institute where Americana in all of its aspects would become nationally known and internationally respected.

Tom Gilcrease had often discussed his philosophy of life with Karlton Mosteller. He told him that a poor man's days are numbered and whatever he may be or wherever he goes, it is all just for the wind — and it is difficult for a man to sleep who lies lightly on his pillow. "I am convinced that Tom was the most consistent self-employed individual I have ever known," said Mr. Mosteller. He of course had reference to the boundless energy reflected in everything Mr. Gilcrease undertook in his business life.

When Mr. Gilcrease decided to give the City of Tulsa his vast collection, he sought the advice of Mr. Mosteller and his friend, Lester Whipple. They were both vitally interested in seeing that the gift was properly received and that it would be adequately preserved as an entity. Mr. Mosteller was concerned with implementing the agreements with certain restrictions, and to that end he worked long hours with the lawyers of the City of Tulsa and with private counsel for the "Keep Gilcrease Committee." Following the demise of Mr. Gilcrease when the foundation deeded the additional thirteen acres and gave artifacts and paintings to the City of Tulsa, it was again Mr. Mosteller who devoted his talents on behalf of the foundation and the Gilcrease children to maintain a consistency in the future use of the collection.

On December 23, 1966, "Karl" Mosteller, as he had affectionately been known to his colleagues and associates and to his friend, Tom Gilcrease, died instantly of a heart attack. He crossed the bar to the higher court of men just as he had always said he hoped he would do — with his boots on. He had returned to his country home near St. Michaels, Maryland, where he found respite walking in the beautiful gardens. His wife, Helen, had joined him in the drive from Oklahoma to Maryland and they had planned a delightful Christmas together, as they had done in former years. In keeping with the rugged individualism which was so much a part of him, his request was honored and his mortal remains were cremated in Washington, D.C., and the ashes returned to Oklahoma.

A summation of the association of the Oklahoma lawyer and his Indian friend may properly be described as being founded on talent, preserved upon loyalty and respect. They were content to let others judge for themselves the inward feelings of each toward the other. Their sentiments never came to the surface, but they had been associated in trying situations and emerged with a satisfaction few men know.

The Secretariat

Two secretaries in a period of thirty-eight years of a business career is something of a record. It is more than a record when the "boss" was Thomas Gilcrease.

Charlien "Chic" Steel served in such capacity from 1924 to 1938 when she became the wife of Maurice Sanditen of Tulsa, one of the founders of the Oklahoma Tire and Supply Company. When she resigned her position she was succeeded by Eudotia Teenor who remained secretary to the multiphased Tom until his death.

The gregarious Chic and the demure Teenor shared a common attribute. They were loyal and efficient. They are as vital to the Gilcrease story as the members of the Gilcrease family, and it is a foregone conclusion that they are more aware of the habits of the man served than any living person. Their mental archives house the genuine and authentic data of their years of privileged administrations. A summation of their evaluation of Thomas Gilcrease can be expressed in their individual experiences, following which an agreed quotient will be in order.

Charlien "Chic" Steel[6]

In 1924 Miss Steel was employed by Homer G. Wilcox of the Wilcox Oil Company. It was Homer Wilcox who discovered the "Wilcox Sand," so well-known in the petroleum industry. The genial Chic was addicted to the popular science of working crossword puzzles, and on the day which altered her secretarial life she was searching for a Scotch word. One Lang, an old Scotsman, frequented her office to see Mr. Wilcox and happened to walk in while she was tensely biting the end of a well-chewed pencil as she meditated on her vocabulary. Chic had heard that Mr. Wilcox was going to close his office for an extended leave and she casually inquired of Mr. Lang if he knew where she might find employment. It seems that the affluent visitor possessed information that the Gilcrease Company officials needed the services of a combination bookkeeper-stenographer. He also volunteered the statement that "the Gilcrease officials" would be difficult employers because they were constantly changing their personnel. The determined Chic disregarded the pessimistic remarks of her informer and made application for the job and was accepted. Her salary was $500 per month, and for the era of her employment she was a highly paid individual.

Recalling her days with the company, Chic says, "No one ever had a finer group of bosses; they were so kind and considerate that they spoiled me." There was the occasion when she received a long distance telephone call which she had not anticipated and actually screamed with elation. Tom Gilcrease heard her, rushed to her desk and inquired, "Who was that?"

Chic responded, "My mother!"

"How long since you have seen her?" asked Mr. Gilcrease.

"Two years," replied Chic. Without commenting further he telephoned his chauffeur and ordered him to take her to see her parents who had arrived for a visit with her sister. "I had never been a passenger in a Cadillac and the services of a chauffeur was just too much. I was so happy that I cried," says Chic.

To recapture the peak thoughts of a thirteen-year career as the confidential secretary to a man of the propensities of Tom Gilcrease is not free from effort and invites random sampling; nevertheless, some of them are worthy of recall.

Chic properly includes the fact that Mr. Gilcrease was the only member of the large family who received income from oil runs. He was more than just a son, brother, or wealthy relative; he was "Chief of the Tribe" in the sense that his dollars supported the entire family. His mother, Mary Elizabeth Gilcrease, was residing in Winfield, Kansas, and each month Chic was instructed to send her a substantial remittance for her support. His sister, Mabel, one of his favorites, was often the recipient of expensive clothes and maintained an elaborate wardrobe at his expense, a practice which eventually brought about instructions from Mr. Gilcrease to close such accounts and make them unavailable for future charges.

Chic's sister, Marguerite Joe Steel, barely escaped becoming Mrs. Thomas Gilcrease, and might have been but for the difference in their ages and the divergence of their personalities.

Mr. Gilcrease was generous with his sons, and when Tom, Jr., was either fourteen or fifteen he went on a world cruise with a group of students within his age limits. The cruise was to last about nine months and be equal to one year of schooling. "Tom, Jr., was a champion with the rifle but I do not recall his breaking any scholastic records," recalls Chic. "The cruise was to cost somewhere in the neighborhood of $8,000, but that is what Tom, Jr., wanted and that is what he did," she added.

Chic Sanditen cradles a multitude of tender memories concerning the marriage of her boss to Norma Smallwood, the former Miss America; his numerous trips to Paris where he was exposed to the galleries, museums, and patrons of art. She remembers the Paris office of the Gilcrease Company on the Champs Elyseés, the friendship of Mr. Gilcrease and Robert Lee Humber, and their adventures into the art markets and the society of France. There are reminiscences of the long and much publicized divorce trial with its invective evidence and demonstrative exhibits of documentary material, much of which she was called upon to prepare. She recalls the mental distress visited upon both Tom Gilcrease and his beautiful wife during the contest, and could not avoid the sentiments of despair which took root in the lives of two unhappy people.

With the domestic life of Tom Gilcrease altered by his divorce from his wife Norma, the house on the hill returned to some semblance of normalcy and a few months later one Madame Beaumann, an investor in the Gilcrease Oil Company in Paris, came to the United States with her daughter, Elizabeth, for a visit, their destination being Tulsa by specific invitation. The Madame and Mr. Gilcrease rather unwittingly determined that they would be matchmakers. They directed their attentions to the charming Elizabeth and Tom, Jr., hoping that cupid would step in and cultivate and culminate the suggested marriage. Their designs looked workable, and after what was evidently a whirlwind courtship the wedding date was set – but, alas, and alack – Tom, Jr., had a mind of his own, and the night before the ceremony he eloped with Miss Grace Folsom, who was a secretary to one of the lawyers who had participated in the divorce trial at Pawhuska, Oklahoma, where the case had been heard. The turn of events provoked the otherwise calm Tom Gilcrease, but to the everlasting credit of Tom, Jr., he could not have selected a more devoted wife than Grace Gilcrease. But the Madame Baumann had to be consoled and Mr. Gilcrease said to Chic, "How would you like to take a vacation with all expenses paid?"

She replied: "I don't know where I could get a better offer!" The orginal plans had called for Tom, Jr., and the Madame's daughter Elizabeth to spend their honeymoon in California. Not wanting to disappoint the jilted lady, he requested Chic to drive his car and give both the Madame Baumann and her daughter a tour of the western United States. Chic was aware of the language barrier, but since the Madame was most pleasant and agreeable, the trip got under way.

When they reached the East Texas oil fields, they were met by Mr. Gilcrease and Mr. G. B. Bancroft, who were also en route to California. The party visited the Grand Canyon and introduced the two French ladies to the sport of riding mules down to the Colorado River and up again. They continued on to Salt Lake City, visited the Mormon Temple and other landmarks. At this point in the trip it came to the attention of Chic that a cousin of Madame Baumann's husband had married a widow who had an eligible son and that they resided near Los Angeles. A visit to the home of the cousin must have been predestined, because Elizabeth fell in love with the cousin's son. The parting was difficult but they kept to their planned route of travel, toured San Francisco, stopped at Lake Tahoe, and became thoroughly saturated with all that the West presented.

"I had my fill of shifting gears," said the indefatigable Chic. One month had passed and they returned to Tulsa. Shortly afterward the smitten Mr. Clarke, son of the American cousin, came to Tulsa and he and Elizabeth were married at the Gilcrease home on the hill. Romance, romance, what games you can play with the hearts of God's children!

The chain of events which followed the closing of the Paris office of the Gilcrease Oil Company after the war created unforeseen problems and so altered the lives of the directors that the facts should be reviewed. The determined mind of Thomas Gilcrease could not be changed. He wanted to move the Tulsa offices to San Antonio and, in Chic's words, "All hell could not stop him!" Frank Walling and Pierce Larkin did not desire to leave their homes in Tulsa and sacrifice their friends; consequently, they sold their interests to Tom Gilcrease with the understanding that they would each receive ten percent of the net profits for twenty years, from 1937 to 1957. Charles Lamb had already withdrawn from the company because of a rift between his wife and the wife of another director. Tom Gilcrease purchased Lamb's interest for $150,000. Later he had financial reverses and turned once again to Mr. Gilcrease, whose generosity was forthcoming. Chic has remarked, "Charles Lamb was one of the finest men I have ever known and his departure from the company family was a distressing occurrence to me."

By way of summation and on a personal note, Chic recalls with pride, "For thirteen years I had endorsed and deposited all the income checks for the Gilcrease Oil Company and for Mr. Gilcrease. I checked all the bills, wrote and signed all of the company remittances. I was never bonded." And then she continued, "With the new foreign interests and the added production in East Texas, the office work became too heavy for me. After trying out several assistants, I found one who was efficient and I wanted to keep her. Her name was Eudotia Teenor. When we moved to San Antonio, Mr. Gilcrease asked us to ride with him, so we went family style — Mr. Gilcrease, Mrs. Teenor, her baby daughter and I. One of the last humorous remarks I recall being made by my boss was when we stopped for breakfast en route to San Antonio and he said, 'I'd like two soft boiled eggs and one of them must be good.'

When we arrived in San Antonio I was delegated to purchase the furniture for the offices and otherwise get things going. You know, my boss never dictated a letter to me in all the time I served him — he would tell me in a very few words what he wanted to say and I composed the correspondence. One time I did something wrong of which he did not approve. When he asked about it I said, 'I thought —' He abruptly interrupted me and said, 'I'll do the thinking in this office.' That was the only time in our long association that a cross word went between us. Mr. Gilcrease bought a fine home in San Antonio. His sister Lena and her husband, Burt Logan, lived with him. Lena took care of the home and Burt became the chauffeur. He acquired homes for his two sons and provided a home for his former wife Belle.

"In June of 1938 I told him I was going to be married and would leave my position. It was hard for him to believe. He sat in silence at my desk all morning and then remarked, 'What am I going to do? Who will write my letters and the pay the bills?' But I guess all things have to come to an end. For my wedding gift he bought me a diamond watch. I wanted silverware for our table, and before I left San Antonio I exchanged the watch for the silverware. I still use it and I am very proud to have it. I never told my boss what I had done."

After her marriage, Chic did not see her boss except on a few occasions when someone wanted to visit the museum. One such instance was when Al Friedlander, president of the Dayton Rubber Company, came to Tulsa. He was interested in art collections and Chic telephoned her boss and took her guest to the hill. The meeting ended with reminiscences. He was still the "secretive" individual who guarded his thoughts, and Chic sometimes wonders: did anyone really know him?

Eudotia Teenor

How pragmatic can one be when, with each nostalgic thought which comes to mind, the sentimental overcomes the expected treatment of historical phenomena with special reference to their causes? What are the standards for explicating one's philosophic thoughts? Can the individual apply the tests for determining the value and truths of his fellowman?

The foregoing queries arise in the mind of the seeker of facts when asking Eudotia Teenor the simple question, "What do you recall as the special attributes possessed by Thomas Gilcrease?"

To better understand the responses, it must be borne in mind that "Teenor," as she is affectionately known to her friends, came into the life of Thomas Gilcrease as the successor to Charlien "Chic" Steel at a time when he had just emerged from the holocaust of a domestic tragedy and an economic upheaval. Compared to her predecessor, she is a retiring individual who maintains a quiet silence about the business and social life of her "Mr. Gilcrease" and, unlike the stoical Chic, she gives way to tearful sentimentality if pressed too hard. She never resorts to the use of the name "Tom" even when making reference to what others might term commonplace incidents. It is always "Mr. Gilcrease," and so it will be to the end of her days.

Eudotia Teenor was born in Claremore, Oklahoma, on the third day of July, 1910.[7] Being a native of Oklahoma, she adapted quickly to the philosophy she recognized in her famous boss. She, too, when she took over the reins from affable Chic, sensed that from that moment she would be the confidant to a soft-spoken and cautious man — cautious, because he had a void in his life which was never to be filled again by the love he had once experienced. Teenor soon learned that she was to be more than a typist;

she was to be a secretary in the full sense of the profession, and it became her duty to screen all who sought to have audience with him and especially those who came to seek his favors. Her ability to ward off those who were mere masqueraders in search of fortunes was far more developed than that manifested by Charlien Steel. She was an ace at playing the part of the buffer and not only guarded the physical life of Thomas Gilcrease but, without question, exercised a quiescent effect upon his mental attitude. She inspired him to make the most of his career as a collector and he came to respect her opinions and her talents.

It is a wise secretary who knows the eccentricities of her employer. Teenor was a post-graduate in such knowledge. Several days could pass without extensive conversation between them, and when such days passed there would be a resumption of unfinished discussions without ado. When Mr. Gilcrease was absent from his office or his home, only Teenor knew where he had gone and when he might return. When Mr. Gilcrease was happy, he pressed all about him for results — only Teenor knew what motivated him to action. It could have been a telephone call from a colleague telling him that an art object was available for purchase or that something he had on order was being shipped to the museum. It might have been a letter from his daughter or a communication from one of the officials of the business world — but only Teenor knew and guarded the reason.

Mr. Gilcrease delighted in calling his faithful secretary, Mrs. Teenor, by the name of "She-Row-Kee," a nickname he bestowed upon her as a recognition of her Cherokee Indian ancestry.

The late William Lyon Phelps, Yale University's popular professor of literature, wrote in the preface to his book *Autobiography with Letters* that "the letter giveth life." As indicated elsewhere in this book, Tom Gilcrease was not a prolific writer of letters. When he did indulge in the written word, his communications were brief except when he chose to give picturesque character to descriptions of nature's miracles. On occasion, while in Europe or away from home, he would depart from his usual custom of telephone contact and post his thoughts.

Here then are some of the gems which research has produced and which, as Professor Phelps so ably stated, "giveth life."

From Hotel du Rhone, Geneva, Switzerland, Saturday eve, 1951:

> Dear She-Row-Kee,
>
> After flying a month I'm here in the good Hotel du Rhone—Room 543. James and Margaret met me & brought me home. Today at noon I ate only for you & that was plenty. You should see the mountains with the sun on that snow. It's a sight to remember.
>
> I had a barrel of mail. Everyone is well & o.k. here.
>
> Hope spring stays in Tulsa for 6 months. Say hello to all for me. You might write to me and enclose the Red Bird's song. I'll take a dip in the Rhone River for you—say just at sunrise. Heaps of good luck & the best of wishes.
>
> Injun Tom.

The reference to the "Red Bird's song" was typical of Tom's expressions of longing for the songs of the birds whose nests were as plentiful among the trees on the hill as the varieties of the species whose melodies greeted him each morning and evening. The red bird was his favorite. It was like asking for something ethereal and gaining satisfaction from having done so.

Again, from Geneva, in 1950 he wrote. This time he called her "Teenor," the salutation he always used when addressing her in person, but whether it was "She-Row-Kee," "Teenor," or her given name "Eudotia," it was evident that his complete reliance on her ability to take care of his business affairs and personal correspondence was constant.

Dear Teenor,

It was a shame that we had a bad telephone connection yesterday. I thought we would have a good quick chat but no. The operator thought that I could talk loud enough to be heard around the world.

Have had many desires to set sail for home but I know it's not the best thing to do just now. I'm just getting on my feet & such a long, hard, cold trip might set me back. Then, there's a job to do & as you know I need to stay by James. Something new every day.

When you prepare my personal statement for the coming year you might let me see it before giving it to the bank. You may wish me to sign it.

Please send me 3 of the National Hotel's calendars that I like to carry in my pocket.

Please let me know when you will need more funds & how much. I will need some money by the time you can get it to me.

Wish you, Des Cygne, Thomas & Barton were going to arrive here before Christmas but that's like wishing for my gold mine that's ever in the skies. Well! Each & all of you know where my heart is on Christmas Day.

I'll wish you now a most Merry Christmas & A Happy New Year.

Why don't you put a million or so in the bank, finish your work, grab a plane for Geneva & the bull fights of Spain — Be looking for you.

Give my best wishes & love to all my dear ones.

Thanks for all the good things you have done for me & mine during the year. May the world's best blessings be yours during the coming year. Adios.

T.G.

The foregoing letter reaches into the very heart of Thomas Gilcrease and pours out his devotion to his family and his admiration for his faithful secretary. It also points up the complete longing he had for the house on the hill and reverence he felt for the Christmas season. Such outcroppings of devout observances were topical with the anniversaries of religious events, but the intervening days were reserved for personal supplication of "Inner Light."

Utter restlessness overtook Tom Gilcrease when he was in Europe in 1951. On August 17, he wrote:

> Dear Eudotia,
>
> Happy to receive your letter from Jacob Lake, Arizona. Where is Jacob Lake? That's one on me. Anyway you & Leah are having one big time. Fun from Tulsa to Jackson, then Jackson to Tulsa. That's the life.
>
> Believe this pen is going dry. Leaving tomorrow for Madrid — maybe. I filled the pen & inked my fingers.
>
> Just found in my coat pocket a letter I wrote to you while in Brighton, England so will enclose it.
>
> Weather is perfect here in Geneva. Having luncheon at the Otlet's today. You may have to decipher this letter before you can read it. Wish I had intelligence enough to go to school & learn to read & write — yes & think too.
>
> Thanks for sending the check. Des Cygne wrote that the heat has been drowned by downpours. You know a downpour is when it rains a few drops as the temperature exceeds 103 on ice in Oklahoma.
>
> Say — the baby walks when holding to his mother's fingers. That's some boy — he is my grandson.
>
> Just talked with Sam Ouvrard in La Boule, France. He will meet me in St. Jean de Luz Sept. 1st.
>
> Worlds of good wishes & lots of luck to you both.
>
> T. G.

The luncheon at the Otlet's referred to the home of James and Margaret Otlet. Mr. Otlet was in charge of Tom's foreign office in one of the companies which had been organized to further the Gilcrease interests. Leah was Eudotia's daughter. Sam Ouvrard was a Frenchman who shared many of Tom's travels and from time to time served to instruct "Injun Tom" in the French language. The grandson was the eldest son of his daughter, Des Cygne.

While in Madrid, Tom wrote from the Hotel Ritz on August 24, 1951 and informed Eudotia that he and Numa Bouttier had gone to a bullfight. He said, "Numa & I saw bulls, matadors, picadors & horses all mixed up together. They all got the worst of it. We got back to town safely, not a scratch. Numa is feeling like a Saint on High & looks the part."

From Paris, France he directed a note to "Dear Teenor" on July 19, 1952, and remarked, "I didn't see the London Bridge fall so I left London by plane. Will be returning to Geneva the end of this coming week. I wanted to do a few things while in Europe but time goes too fast. One needs 6 months or a year to do anything worth while here."

August 7, 1952, he again wrote from Geneva and made reference to the extreme heat of Switzerland — "Boy O Boy, what heat! Believe I'll come home to Tulsa just to receive a warm reception," and then he concluded, "We may go to the deer dance in Taos. Many good wishes and may luck be with you."

The tenor of Tom's letter changed with the site of origin. In September of 1956 he wrote from Jackson, Wyoming:

> Dear Eudotia,
>
> It was good to talk with you today.
>
> I may go to Idaho Falls to have my car tuned & brakes adjusted.
>
> River clear & cool & the hillsides are bright and beautiful.

Would you please send me a quart – yes a quart – a quart of that famous hand cleaner.

Ted finished the drawers for the sink in your cabin and is working in Bart's new room.

It may be that I will not go hunting then again I may go – who knows? Perhaps the blind man.

I need 2 good workmen to help me but where can I find them, not here.

Remember me kindly to our friends & dear ones.

T. G.

So it was that Tom's faithful secretary entered into the life of Thomas Gilcrease and was able to capture a part of his personality, his ambitions, his keen insight to all things that have to do with understanding human beings. His letters served to bring forth the incidents that incontrovertibly prove the genius of the man who had visions – put them into reality and awakened an irresistible desire of his friends, his contemporaries, and even his adversaries to know him better.

Why then, it might be asked, would Teenor find it difficult to answer the question about the attributes of Thomas Gilcrease? Perhaps the answer is embodied in one word – *loyalty*. She does not hesitate to remark that the one thing which caused Mr. Gilcrease the most difficutly was his lack of money. This conclusion at first seems fallacious until she enlarges the comment by stating that he could never have acquired sufficient wealth to satisfy his search for the truth about the life of the Indian or, as he so often put it, "the sufferings of his people at the hands of the white man."

There is another reason why the loyal Teenor finds it hard to expose information about the business life of her boss. She became the keeper of the scroll and private archivist to a collector of art, an oil man, a traveler, and an explorer whose bourne was as vast as his quest for Americana.

Since the demise of Thomas Gilcrease, Teenor has remained as secretary of the Thomas Gilcrease Foundation, and the children of the Gilcrease family have entrusted her with the keys to the storehouse of files which house the transactions of their father. Teenor deals in specifics when asked specifics and, with the consent and blessings of the Gilcrease children, has brought to light for posterity a great deal of the material which is encompassed in this biography. She carefully maintained a scrapbook of news clippings covering the era when her employer was underfinanced and overcommitted — the story of the bond issue which assisted in saving the collection — she was the liaison between the attorneys and the citizens' committee when the going was rough.

Teenor was a witness to the Last Will and Testament of Thomas Gilcrease, together with William S. Bailey, Jr. and David L. Harner, dated February 8, 1960. And, while she did not know its contents until after it was offered for probate on the sixth day of June, 1963 in the county court of Osage County, Oklahoma, she was not surprised at what it contained. The instrument of record, after the formal portion, provides:

> Having made such provisions for my children as I think appropriate and sufficient, I do hereby give, devise and bequeath to the Thomas Gilcrease Foundation of Osage County, Oklahoma, all of the rest and residue of the property which I may own at the time of my death, whether personal, real or mixed, and including all property of every kind and character of which I may be seized at the time of my death, irrespective of where located or situated, to have and to hold as its own unconditionally and absolutely; provided, that in the event any of my children shall claim or attempt to claim contrary to the provisions of this my Last Will and Testament, then I hereby give, devise and bequeath the sum of One ($1.00) to each of said children.

The foundation has become Teenor's subsidy, her responsibility, and her love of service. Her office still houses some of the precious works of art which have not as yet been given to the City of Tulsa or to individuals. What the tomorrow of life holds for the foundation or for Teenor will depend upon the trustees. Until that time comes and as long as there is a beat in the heart of Teenor, she will preserve, honor, and respect Thomas Gilcrease and take his memory with her wherever she completes the allotment of her days.

Chapter 4

A Plot of Earth, the Prairie Singer, and the Red Cement Steer

J. Frank Dobie never used his given name of James. William Thomas Gilcrease never used his given name of William.

Frank Dobie was born in Live Oak County, Texas, September 26, 1888. Dobie was the son of a famous cattleman and rancher. Gilcrease was the son of a modest farmer. Dobie was a formally educated man. Gilcrease was an informally knowledgeable individual. Gilcrease never wrote a book. Dobie penned fifteen volumes during his career. Gilcrease acquired every book Dobie wrote and they were personally autographed by the author. Dobie had a wide scope of information about the American West and wanted to know more about his contemporaries. Gilcrease was highly interested in his ancestry and was determined to improve the image of the Indian. Dobie placed his thoughts on the printed pages of history. Gilcrease acquired what others had recorded on canvas, on parchment, and in artifacts. Dobie wrote about the Indians. Gilcrease was part Indian. And when they met in 1938 they each had brought to fruition many of their ambitions. Gilcrease died in 1962. Dobie died in 1964. They were born two years apart — and they died two years apart. In all of their correspondence they were very formal during the first years of their friendship and it was always "Mr." Then they addressed each other as "Dear Tom" and "Dear Frank" but, oddly enough, each signed his letters with his customary signature. It was "Sincerely, Thomas Gilcrease" and "Sincerely, J. Frank Dobie."[1]

To say that Thomas Gilcrease looked upon J. Frank Dobie with a kind of hero worship would not be an overstatement, and to conclude that J. Frank Dobie considered Thomas Gilcrease one of the profound students of nature would be an understatement. A close examination of their intimate letters is rewarding and revealing. They approached each other with the utmost of delicacy. Their association had its beginning by reason of a common interest in books. For Tom Gilcrease, it represented a very tangible introduction to a man of letters and that he would he exposed to a cultural experience which he had never really had in his male acquaintances. For Frank Dobie, a whole new world had opened. He saw in Tom Gilcrease a man blessed with a keen feeling for humanity and one who was unspoiled by the wealth which had made it possible for him to work full time at his ambition to collect art that others might enjoy it. Tom Gilcrease could talk about the works of Charles Russell, John James Audubon, William De La Montagne Cary, George Catlin, Frederic Remington, the Taos artists, and dozens of other men of talent, with the same accuracy and informative quality as he could about a hard and callous-palmed oil well driller or a thinly shod dirt farmer. J. Frank Dobie could match wits with his Oklahoma friend and was sufficiently equipped with memories of his own to know that what "Indian Tom" told him was not exaggeration but factual, although there were times when he knew that he was being gradually pulled into the trap of the most penetrating humor, sprung by an imagination equalled by none.

In 1933 J. Frank Dobie was elected secretary and editor of the Texas Folk-Lore Society. After the publication of one volume the society ceased to exist for some time until it was suddenly revived. Dobie wrote to Tom Gilcrease and told him that with the upsurge of interest, thirteen volumes had been published, all of which he had edited. He assured Tom that the society was not a commercial organization and offered to sell him a complete set of the publications and invited him to become a member. He very naïvely suggested that $100 should be the lower limit for a general membership. He concluded by saying, "I know you are interested in Texas books and have some regard for the cultural background of Texas that our organization is trying to cultivate. Meeting you in San Antonio was a pleasure, and I expect to see you here sometimes."

In the course of events that followed it is safe to assume that Tom Gilcrease acquired a membership in the Texas Folk-Lore Society and, letter by letter, the acquaintance was punctuated by a bit more daring. J. Frank Dobie maintained a qualified but positive allurement. Tom Gilcrease, ever cautious, moved into the arena and tiptoed on the mat. The span of years from 1939 to 1943 was still marked by the high blood pressure of time. The domestic hurricane had disappeared, the news media was no longer concerned with the exploitation of Tom's personal life. The Gilcrease Collection was on exhibition at the Gilcrease Building in San Antonio and the Gilcrease Foundation extended a welcome to the public. A special invitation was mailed to J. Frank Dobie who replied by making reference to Dudley R. Dobie of San Marcos, Texas, a first cousin, who was professor of American and Southwestern history at Texas State College and Sul Ross State College of Alpine, Texas, and who brought Thomas Gilcrease and J. Frank Dobie together. Dudley was a friend of Ed Gilcrease, brother of Tom, and they both resided in San Marcos. When Dudley retired from his teaching career he became a full-time dealer in rare books on Texas and the Southwest. Ed Gilcrease told his brother Tom about Dudley's collection and one day Tom visited Dudley's place of business. It was after this meeting that Dudley introduced his cousin, J. Frank, to Tom. The letter of reply is dated March 12, 1943 and reads:

> Dear Mr. Gilcrease:
>
> Thank you for the invitation to your exhibition. It will not be possible for me to accept the invitation. Dudley told me about some of the fine things you have. It is good to know that you want to share them with others.
>
> Cordially yours,
>
> J. Frank Dobie.

It should be noted that there is an absence of the "sincerely yours," – which was to come later. J. Frank Dobie was taking his time. Tom Gilcrease was not pushing the acquaintance. The melon was not quite ripe and when he felt that it was time to cut the plug to sample the fruit – it had to be cold but firm.

The record is not decisive as to when Dobie first saw the collection, but it was after it had been moved from Texas to Oklahoma. In 1950 Dobie was the recipient of a news article from Tom Gilcrease which carried a photo of the founder of the Gilcrease Museum and a short story about his life. Dobie's letter, written on July 5, said in part – "The hours you made possible for me with Russell and Remington and other artists will always be remembered. Civilized people generations hence will rise up and call you blessed for what you are doing. I enjoyed the company of Robert Lee Humber and yourself very much. Sincerely yours, J. Frank Dobie." Here it is to be noted that the word "cordially" had been suspended and supplanted by the word "sincerely." The melon was about ready to eat.

From 1923 to 1925, J. Frank Dobie served as head of the Department of English at the Oklahoma A&M College in Stillwater, Oklahoma.* He had earned the title of "full

* Now called "Oklahoma State University."

professor" and taught at the University of Texas from 1933 to 1947; however, on sabbatical leave from 1943 to 1947 he was professor of American history at Cambridge. He had overstayed his leave by three years, and this infraction was responsible for the action taken by the board of regents in terminating his association with the university. His severance from the faculty at the University of Texas is probably the most rewarding thing to which he could have been subjected. Had he remained in the teaching profession his writing would not have been as prolific and the world would have been the loser. He died in Austin, Texas on September 18, 1964. When he rode to the eternal ranch where his friend Thomas Gilcrease had already entered the bunkhouse, he mounted his steed quietly and disappeared into the night.

He was among thirty prominent Americans selected to receive the presidential "Medal of Freedom." He had been notified by President Lyndon B. Johnson that the honor was to come to him in July; however, the seventy-five-year-old heart which had propelled him to literary fame was too weak to take him to Washington. On September 14, four days before his ride to eternity, his wife accepted the medal for him as Carl Sandburg, his personal friend, and others equally as well known, looked on. This would have been a proud moment for the bushy-browed Texan, who many times had referred to himself as a maverick and proved his right to the term by his independent actions toward and reactions to people and current topics. His later years as a scholar were a far cry from the job he once had as a foreman of a 25,000-acre ranch in south Texas. A typical Dobie dagger was thrown the time he aimed his pen at the University of Texas and described the cenotaph erected to the memory of the heroes of the Alamo as resembling a grain elevator. He could not adopt an attitude of appreciation to any kind of a monument honoring events that occurred elsewhere.

The *San Antonio Light* was one of Dobie's favorite newspapers. His contributions to the printer's ink were timely and topical but not always tempered. Tom Gilcrease was his greatest fan and collected every article he wrote and managed to purchase first edition copies of all of the Dobie books. He wrote his Texas friend a letter in which he said, "Keeping up with a man like J. Frank Dobie is like trailing a jack rabbit through the mesquite of West Texas. Almost impossible to keep in sight of him."

In the early part of 1952 Dobie wrote a piece which he called "Museums Just Sprout in Oklahoma, It Would Seem." The theme of the article was devoted to a thumbnail review of Woolaroc Museum near Bartlesville, Oklahoma, established by the late Frank Phillips of the Phillips Oil Company; the Will Rogers Memorial at Claremore, Oklahoma; and a discussion of sedge, or bunch grass, which he said cattle did not eat. He commented that next to sedge, the museum development in the Southwest was interesting. The *Pioneer Woman* statue, by the famous sculptor Bryant Baker, was mentioned with some colorful comments about E. W. Marland, former governor of Oklahoma, who had been responsible for adding her to the female citizens of the Sooner State. He said, "She sums up the tears in human affairs of all women of all frontiers. One could travel thousands of miles without seeing any other work of art so powerful, beautiful and moving." The climax of his short pictorial came when he made reference to Wilbur Avery, a wealthy man from Miami, Oklahoma. Dobie wrote: "In time he became obsessed by the tradition of the cowboy. He dressed range style, got him a fancy horse and led all parades. He built a museum room and filled it with trumpery, not knowing the difference between a chromo and genuine art. He probably paid a good deal of money for that cement steer. It is painted red."

On February 27, 1952, Tom Gilcrease wrote to his friend Dobie:

> I notice you did not state your purpose for touring in Oklahoma, but you do mention seeing a red painted cement steer. Now, if you have any intentions of acquiring this steer and you're going to count me in on him I would like some advice as to what you expect to do with him. To breed him to those longhorns of Southwest Texas or to expect him to produce calves

from Tom Slick's million dollar bull seems to me a little far-fetched, however, I'm such an admirer of J. Frank Dobie that I might even be led to invest in this red painted cement steer of Oklahoma, should he ask me to become interested with him in this no doubt fabulously heralded Oklahoma Steer.

The letter is the first indication that Tom Gilcrease forthrightly told Dobie of his admiration for him and also reflects the sharp humor which was not often evidenced by Mr. Gilcrease in the presence of strangers or included in his writings unless he was addressing a close friend.

The "red-painted cement steer" was to ever thereafter be a conversation piece between Dobie and Gilcrease. The trip which Tom's friend had made into Oklahoma, without stopping to visit with him on the hill, brought about a bit of resentment on Tom's part and he chided J. Frank by telling him: "I know that to visit an Indian isn't hardly worth your time, but the spirit of our grand old friend, Charlie Russell, hangs around the museum, and his spirit is always worthwhile to visit with." He then added: "In fact about all this old Indian can do is to maintain a little corner here for Charlie."

Dobie never really understood the last statement, and rather than explore what Tom had in mind—he just did not mention it, either in later correspondence or in their personal visits. Tom wrote to Dobie and told him that he had planted some tobacco west of the museum building on the hill and suggested that when it matured, he wanted him to make a trip to Tulsa and they could have a smoke on the hill. This statement seemed incongruous with Tom's habits because he was never known to use tobacco in any form. He became even more brazen and said: "I can furnish you not only with the tobacco, but a pipe used by the Spiro Mound Indians who lived around two or three thousand years ago at a point where Arkansas laps over into Oklahoma."

The humor of Thomas Gilcrease was growing by the moment as he continued to write to Dobie, and it appeared that he was actually courting the company of the Texas author who had touched off a sentiment which had not before been exposed by Mr. Gilcrease. If he did not have anything in particular about which to write, he did what all men do at some time in their lives — he resorted to observations about the weather, as he did in this choice morsel:

> I am told it rained in San Antonio, so after all, maybe the people took a preacher at his word. I heard this preacher one Sunday some six months ago ridicule the rain makers for not being able to produce rain for West Texas. He said that all one had to do to have plenty of rain when needed was just to take their umbrellas and walk down to church and pray for rain and they would have it forthwith because, he said, the fact that one did take an umbrella with him on a bright sunshiny day would be absolute proof to God that he believed in his prayer to be offered. He said that is just how easy it is for people to have rain when they needed it. Now, I have been listening to see if he would have some simple and easy prescription for one to secure money with which to pay taxes and buy a little cornbread and bluejohn milk from time to time. I certainly could use some such prescription to good advantage.

The words flowed like spring water from a deep well, and Tom ended his greeting to Dobie in a double entendre, not vengefully conceived but avowed with hope of reaction. He wrote, "I used to roll paper for my grandpa to use in lighting his pipe, so you can use this scribbled paper for the same purpose."

J. Frank Dobie was not one to apologize, but he was a gentleman of culture and when an explanation was due he gave it, not to justify his actions as much as to assure the one to whom it was due that the omission was not intentional. He wrote to Tom and told him that he had been engaged in making a series of public talks in Oklahoma, Kansas, Missouri, Illinois, Florida, and Mississippi. His trip had extended over a period of three weeks and his first stop had been Miami, Oklahoma, on the night of February 8, 1952. He had flown from Austin, Texas. His letter was dated March 2; consequently he had discovered Tom's letter upon his return home.

Charles Banks Wilson and Alexandre Hogue had met Dobie in Miami, which was Wilson's home. He mentioned his visit to the Will Rogers Memorial and to the Woolaroc Museum. If Tom Gilcrease had read the article more carefully, he would have noted that Dobie started his piece by saying that he was doing what some people called "lectures," but he called them "talks." Dobie told Tom that he had been limited by the pressure of time or he would have revisited the Gilcrease Museum. His epistle touched upon such subjects as his desire to write an article about Charles Russell and suggested that he would study the collection in the Gilcrease Museum for the material he desired.

The Red Longhorn Steer made of cement did not escape his caustic commentary — he wrote:

> I never have seen any art representation more ridiculous than that cement Longhorn steer near Miami. In a way it's pathetic, too, as representing a man who had means and interest but no taste and no inclination apparently to take advantage of knowledge and taste on the part of other people.

His thoughts then digressed and he informed Tom that the Mint Saloon collection of Russell paintings from Great Falls, Montana, had been exhibited by the Knoedler Galleries in New York and gently hinted that he hoped Thomas Gilcrease would acquire the collection for the Gilcrease Museum. The items to which he alluded were of a personal nature, and yet his fondness and admiration had gradually matured to the point where he made a confidant out of his newly cultivated friend from Tulsa.

> I'm reading proof on "The Mustangs," the most labored-upon book I have written. The most learned part of it deals with the Indian acquisition and dispersal of the Spanish horse. It's being illustrated by Charles Banks Wilson, whom I had not met until the other day. The art director of my publishers, Little

> Brown & Company of Boston, selected him for the job. I saw a good number of his sketches and think that I am going to be happy with his illustrations.

Could there be any connection between this particular incident and the eventual selection by Thomas Gilcrease of Charles Banks Wilson to paint the portrait which is on permanent display at the institute in Tulsa? Such a projection is, to say the least, speculative but not at all unlikely due to the respect Tom had for the critical eyes of Dobie.

Dobie concluded his communication by extending an invitation to Tom to visit him in Austin. He advised him that he had only a few pictures compared to Tom's collection but he did own three or four Russell watercolors. He said: "You might like to look at them and I have enlarged my study . . . it is loaded with books. You can look at them, and we can make medicine." He thanked Tom for his suggestion about the tobacco by saying that he never went anywhere without his pipe and he expected to try out Tom's homegrown tobacco. The last line read: "With good wishes and good memories, I am Sincerely yours — Frank Dobie." Note: He had even dropped the "J."

On May 25, 1953, Thomas Gilcrease again wrote to J. Frank Dobie. He had read more of the newspaper articles, saved them, and told Dobie he was sending them to him. He said that it would afford him great pleasure if Dobie would again visit Tulsa. "As you know, the Indians are rather wild here in the Osage Hills and while I can't promise I'll prevent the Indians from scalping you, I will at least do my best." He added that he had many interesting things that Dobie had not seen.

The invitation brought an immediate response. Dobie thanked him for the newspaper clippings but said it was impossible for him to accept — the note was extremely polite and short. "I don't know when I'll be going your way, but look for me sometime."

On the seventeenth of June, 1953, Dobie again wrote to Tom and imparted the news that he was actually doing a story about "Thomas Gilcrease and his Museum." He wanted verification of the fact that Tom's mother was a one-quarter blood Creek. He was confused but said that his memory plus geography led him to this conclusion. "You need not answer unless you want to, but I'd like to know the year of your birth," he wrote. He called for an airmail reply to meet a weekend deadline and promised to send a copy to the *Tulsa Daily World.* This was the day of realization for Thomas Gilcrease. He answered the very next mail and told Dobie how pleased he was to learn that an article was being written by him about the museum and that he would be on the lookout for the copy. Tom's letter indicates that Dobie had visited him the week before, and no doubt this visit had inspired Dobie to write the article.

Chronology in correspondence can be material to a better understanding of thought exchange. Why Mr. Dobie wrote to Tom on June 17 and told him that he was to write the article and then wrote to him on June 19 to express his elation of having enjoyed the visit in Tulsa is difficult to understand; nevertheless, that is what he did and here is what he said:

> I don't use the word "wonderful" on every occasion, but Saturday afternoon and Sunday were two wonderful times for me. I came away enriched and with a deepened appreciation of you and your extraordinary accomplishments. Thank you very much for your gracious hospitality.

Dobie signed the letter "Frank" and thanked Tom for his prompt reply to his query and said that he would return the "inventory" soon. Apparently Tom had furnished him with some detailed information — without knowing that Dobie was preparing for the article about the museum; otherwise the letter of June 17 would have been unnecessary.

July 2, 1953, he wrote to Tom again and forwarded a copy of the story he had written, castigated the editor of the *Tulsa Daily World* for not honoring him with a reply to the submitted article, returned some manuscripts he had borrowed from Tom, and signed his note very formally — "Frank Dobie."

"Tom Gilcrease and 'The Earth of My Valley' "

The above subheading was the title of the piece J. Frank Dobie wrote, and the copy he sent to his friend, Tom, was inscribed in longhand above the typed sheet in a warm greeting: "To my cherished friend Tom Gilcrease. Frank Dobie – written after a visit to him in 1953."

The summits of the dissertation are classical in concept and represent an insight in what made Thomas Gilcrease one of the most exceptional men Dobie had ever met.

> As time goes on, more and more people who belong to the land are going to find The Thomas Gilcrease Foundation as interesting and enriching as far-traveled experts in art, archaeology, and history already find it startling. Only the ignorant ignore inescapable history; it never argues with or ignores anybody. Only the stupefied and the callous ignore art; it is the response of human beings to their own hunger for the vivid, the significant, the dramatic, the beautiful, the spiritual, the mortal and the immortal, the meaning of life in every form.

> Listening to Tom Gilcrease talk, I am struck by the imprint of the creatures of the earth, plant life as well as birds and other animals, on his nature. He has hunted in Alaska and elsewhere, but in talk he dwells on the way a gunshot one early foggy morning started wild turkeys gobbling on their roosts along the Frio River in south Texas and on the gobbling that went as far up the river and as far down it as one could hear. He loves to linger on a lone coyote's bark that set off other coyotes, and then others, and more and more others, until camp was completely encircled by the tingling cries of the dawn-singers from far and near. . . .

> His home is near the Foundation museum, on eighty acres of ground overlooking Tulsa. Post oak, pin oak, blackjack, red oak, hickory, pecan, walnut, redbud, wild plum and other trees are native, and he loves all of it. He has planted pines, cedars, and holly. Hollyhocks dominate the flower beds – hollyhocks for remembrance. He can point out nests of brown

thrasher, robin, "lazy" dove, oriole, and other birds. At twilight he sits on his wide porch as companion to a pair of woodpeckers that inhabit a hollow skeleton tree. He has boxes for martins and wrens. Chimney swifts live in his chimneys. He expects a fox met twice lately near his house. He recalls a little dog of his boyhood who seemed to detect pregnant jackrabbits from others and could grab the heavily laden ones. . . .

Hanging in one of the museum rooms is a small, unsigned painting from Mexico entitled "La Tierra de mi Valle" (The Earth or Ground, of My Valley. It shows a peasant plowing with a pair of oxen, mountains beyond, a pepper tree casting its shadow in the foreground.) Tom Gilcrease seems especially fond of that picture. The title of it seems to me to express his guiding motive in making the great collection he has made and, also, to express the essential meaning of that collection – "La Tierra de mi Valle". . . .

Here in all varieties of form is "La Tierra de mi Valle." It talks to us about America from times thousands of years before Columbus sailed. It talks particularly of the Southwest and West. It talks in terms of science; it talks human imagination; it talks in terms that people hear gladly.

The article was published in the *Tulsa Daily World* and Tom wrote to Dobie and thanked him profusely for his thoughtfulness in writing it. He told him that the comments were all favorable. There followed another exchange of communications and came October. In the interim, Tom had visited with Dobie at the University of Texas, and it seems that they each took advantage of every occasion to swap yarns and talk about their adventures. And then Tom Gilcrease favored J. Frank Dobie with a gift which was to cement their friendship with such solidarity that only the grim reaper would be able to part their mortal beings; and then they were certain they would meet again. Tom wrote Dobie:

I caught a young coyote the other day and he wasn't

> at all friendly, so I'm shipping the rascal on down to you since you're the coyote's best friend. Maybe you can teach him a few lessons and at least get along with him on a reasonably friendly basis, which is certainly more than I can do. Boy, he howls and snaps at me every time I turn around. Don't let him near your chicken house for his mouth just waters for anything that has feathers on it. Come to see me and the sooner the better.

Upon receipt of Tom's letter the anticipation of J. Frank Dobie went completely out of bounds. He became frantic and wondered what he was going to do with a live coyote. He had been away from ranch life too long to be certain about the best method to keep the animal. His first inclination was to place a telephone call to Tom and tell him that while he admired coyotes he did not feel that a live one would exactly fit in with his domestic tranquility. Due deliberation convinced him that he could not insult Thomas Gilcrease by refusing to take delivery of the animal; consequently he had only one alternative. A suitable cage would have to be either built or located in Austin. The search for such an enclosure proved fruitless and Dobie was distressed. While he was still in the throes of looking for the solution, the crate arrived.

When Dobie finished unwrapping the object which had been so carefully packed, his white hair fell back into place, a feeling of security returned to his tired and worn face and he remarked: "Well, what do you know, that old son-of-a-gun — and to think that I was about ready to abort our friendship." What he found was a handsome carving by Willard Stone, the wood-carver who was a protégé of Mr. Gilcrease and who today is considered the most important wood-carver in America. Tom had approached Willard months before the actual work on the piece began and told him that he not only wanted an authentic reproduction of the coyote but that he knew Willard would produce something creative and meaningful. The animal went onto Willard's drawing board, a cherry wood block was selected, and approximately three months later he was coating the beautiful finish with hot linseed oil, his standard procedure for preservation. When he delivered the creation to Mr. Gilcrease, he told him that he had decided to call it *Prairie Song,* representative of the lonesomeness of the prairie, so often exemplified by the "wolf" family from whence the coyote originated.

On November 2, 1953, Tom Gilcrease received the acknowledgment from Dobie:

> I'm as pleased with the coyote as I was over my first saddle. Your letter scared me though until I thought it over. I thought you were sending a live coyote. I didn't want to keep it chained up and knew if I turned it loose out in the country where I have a little place, the neighbors, all of whom own sheep and goats, would massacre me.
>
> This carving corresponds in a way to one I have on Don Coyote secured in Mexico two years ago. They harmonize with each other beautifully as you'll see when you come to our house. I hope that will be before long. Now thank you very very much.

Two months passed before Tom again wrote to Dobie. The year 1954 started to drop its days from the calendar and each passing hour added new worries to the mind of Thomas Gilcrease, who was spending most of his time on his archaeological collection. He had met Dr. David Harner and was working constantly with Gregory Perino. Tom found it difficult to stay in the house on the hill. He had overpurchased and funds were not forthcoming with which to retire his obligations. He was showing signs of growing weary but these were mere physical manifestations. Those who were in his presence daily were not aware of the strain he was undergoing mentally, and they accepted his minor complaints as normal comments for a man who was placing years on the plus side of his life. They knew that he was like a machine and that a little tuning up would energize and activate his thinning frame.

During this period Dobie was gaining in reputation. Invitations to speak clouded his busy career and he found correspondence more difficult. When he wrote something which he felt would be of special interest to his friend Tom, he sent it on, generally without too much comment or without explanation. When he penned "A Plot of Earth" he dispatched a copy to Tulsa and on January 20, 1954, Tom wrote:

> It certainly was good of you to remember me with A Plot of Earth. I enjoyed reading this little story because of our mutual friendship. Probably enjoyed it more than the average person would because I, too, was born and lived on a plot of earth. These plots of earth give me a keener sense of sight, smell, hearing, taste and understanding of the Creator and the real honest to goodness beauty of nature in its endless forms. I want you to know I fully appreciate and thank you greatly for remembering me and do hope you can arrange to pay me a visit someday. The sooner the better.

This was the third time in recent months of their correspondence that Tom had used the phrase "sooner the better" in requesting Dobie to visit him. He had extended the wishful invitation in July of 1953 and October of the same year. In 1952 he had written about the "preacher and the rain-making" and even suggested that he wished the preacher would formulate a plan which would raise money the same as one prayed for rain.

With all that was troubling him he appeared to gain spiritual momentum when he was writing to Dobie, and his letters were poetic and eloquent. His ability for fluent, forcible, and appropriate use of the English language was never fully utilized. What had by this time changed an acquaintance into a friendship and then graduated into a union of respect and admiration between two men, brought out the expressive talents in Tom with greater impetus than he had ever evinced. His mention of "understanding of the Creator" was surely an uncommon subject in his vocabulary even though it was not a foreigner in his mental mansions.

> The red, black and white woodpeckers of the old snag finally hatched their brood and pushed them out into the open world where they trained them in all the ways of a good woodpecker, and sent them out on their own into far away places. Now the father and mother birds live alone in the old snag where they dream of their young and hope for their future welfare and long for their return of springtime at the mating season. By the way, Charles Banks Wilson painted these birds, the snag and the old swing, and presented the painting to me which now graces the north wall of my living room.

Tom then concluded his letter by telling Dobie again that he was looking forward to his return visit. There had been another transition in their association. The admiration and respect had become sheer devotion. He wrote:

> I remain your friend and a friend to all those wonderful imaginings and stories which you tell through your writings; a first edition of each and all I have in my library here on the hill in Osage County, Blackdog Township of Oklahoma.

Thomas Gilcrease was becoming more aware that he was entering the orbit of his life and that if he was going to fire any retro-rockets to bring him back to the "plot of earth," he would need all the assistance he could find by those who were expert at direction. He was a living Atlas and the world of Thomas Gilcrease was bowing his head with the burden of decisions. He could not and did not desire to pass from the earthly scene without making a suitable disposition of his collection and his museum. As he lay on his bed in the big stone house on the hill he knew he was a lonely man. The story of the woodpeckers was the only way he could tell someone that his own children had left the snag and that he was living alone. He understood that the springtime of the mating season had passed him by and that for all practical purposes his brood were on their own and in far-away places. Sleep, restless sleep, brought little release from the tensions which were taking hold with an unannounced promise to eventually spring their trap — but they were not quite ready. They would grant their host a respite from the impending "reentry."

The absence of personal visits with Dobie brought about a slightly cooler atmosphere. Tom went to Wyoming where he found some therapy for the tensions which had lost part of their tenacious grasp on him. Much had happened in the two years. The creditors had moved in, the Keep Gilcrease for Tulsa Committee had stepped in, the decision to give the collection to the City of Tulsa had been made, and the Thomas Gilcrease Institute of American History and Art had become a reality. There was only one difficulty. Tom had fired the retro-rockets but was not too sure that the capsule would be preserved. His flights into the world of art and artifacts had been scrubbed.

In answer to a letter which Tom wrote to him from Jackson, Wyoming, Dobie said:

> If you are going to stay there through late next summer into fall I might take you up on that invitation to hunt a little. This country (referring to Texas) has been dry so long and the mortality among the trees is so great that my mind is being dried up too. I'm trying to get strung out on another book, however, I am making some attempts at an autobiography. It's harder to be honest on that subject than on some others. Also I find that I'm not so trustful of readers as I would be if I were writing a book of bear stories. I've got a lot of them and am primed to make such a book. Often and often I look at the prairie singer, a carving which you sent me. I like it better all the time. A mighty pleasant thing about it is that it reminds me of you.

The record is not clear whether Dobie ever visited Tom in Wyoming. The next time he wrote was in June of 1958 when he remarked that he had received a letter from Charles Banks Wilson telling him that he was painting a life-size portrait of Tom. Wilson advised him that he was putting all the thought he could muster into the interpretation. He then suggested that Wilson was growing all the time. He mentioned his 1953 visit with Tom and confided to him that he had sent Charles Banks Wilson a copy of the profile he had written about him so Wilson would have a better insight for his portrait. He ended this letter with the words, "abiding appreciation and best regards" — signing his name "J. Frank Dobie."

It was October of 1958 before Tom wrote to Dobie again. He acknowledged an autographed copy of *The Earth of My Valley* which Dobie had sent to him and renewed his invitation for Dobie to visit him on the Hoback River in the Jackson Hole country in Teton County, Wyoming. He said, "I will have a nice cabin at your disposal with plenty of views and a belly full of trout for you daily."

Twelve days later Dobie replied and said, "Yes, it's been too long since we made medicine together. You'll be mighty welcome when you come to my tent this winter. I'm as fond of mountain trout as I am of mountain views. You surely make Jackson Hole alluring." He told Tom he had sent for a copy of *The American Scene* magazine published by the Gilcrease Institute and wished him well on the Wilson portrait. November 1, 1959, Dobie wrote again and advised Tom that he had read the chapter about him in the book *The Proud Possessors*, which had been reprinted and distributed by the Gilcrease Museum. His reference was to the chapter entitled "Thomas Gilcrease" by Aline B. Saarinen.

The paths of J. Frank Dobie and Thomas Gilcrease did not cross again. Periodically they corresponded. Dobie was impressed with *The American Scene* and contributed to its pages. In 1949 he had written at length about Charles Marion Russell, the western artist. In 1961 the *San Antonio Light* published his article on Frederic Remington. He did the piece in serial form in his regular Sunday column for the newspaper. His writing about the Indian horses, the sagebrush colts, and buffalo horses captivated his readers across the country.

When Thomas Gilcrease died in 1962, Frank Dobie could not attend the funeral service. He, too, was under the care of medical men. One cannot help but speculate about the extent of this beautiful story of two men had they met early in life. In Dobie, the Oklahoma Indian found more than he had in his entire career — an introduction to a man of letters — a student of history — an historian — a teacher — someone who understood his philosophy about life and nature — someone who shared his concept of the Creator. In Gilcrease, J. Frank Dobie had found someone who had undertaken to preserve the history of the Indian and had accomplished an ambition — a sturdy man of the West who was glamorous without wearing two guns, a cowboy ten-gallon hat, and chewing tobacco — he had met a self-educated individual with a mind as quick as the streams where he had fished — who increasingly valued what Thomas Gilcrease had done.

J. Frank Dobie did not choose to eulogize his friend Tom, and he could not refrain from transferring his thoughts to parchment; to abridge his tribute would be tantamount to shearing away part of the canvas of masterly skill. He wrote:

> Thomas Gilcrease understood property. Had he not understood it, he could never have amassed the vast, diverse and supernally rich collection housed in the institute that bears his name. Also, had he not understood values beyond property, he could not have made this collection.
>
> Slight of frame, his sensitive features were lighted by intelligence and marked by association with unworldly thoughts and images. The longer I knew him, the more he gave me the impression of having made not only long voyages to lone places on this earth but of longer voyages into deep and lone places within himself. He was one of the islands of humanity. His liberated mind was also a disciplined mind. He was a realist in the best sense of the word, free from delusions and superstitious absurdities often called mysteries. Yet I've hardly known another human being who had the mysteries and beyonds deep inside himself that Tom Gilcrease had. He may have seemed enigmatic to some. What is more enigmatic than sincere simplicity?
>
> I never forget his telling me of the allotment of land brought to the family when he was a boy by his

> half-Creek mother. It was on a stream-engraced prairie near where the city of Tulsa was to grow. The prairie chickens were so thick that when a fence post was put down two or three would try to light on it. When he plowed in the spring, terns would follow his plow, lighting on the handles when he stopped to rest the horses. This land, the birds, the bushes, and the trees on grounds around his home hard by the Institute entered into him. When he went to beautiful medieval Avignon in France to spend a day and remained a month, another world became a part of him. Many of the books, most of the pictures and bronzes and carvings and artifacts of his collection became a part of him. He valued the beautiful. The values of art are also the values of humanity. Now humanity has the meanings that life had for him.
>
> He was my generous friend. I remember him with affection, with respect, and with admiration. I salute his prolonged shadow.

They had shared a plot of earth, laughed about a red cement steer, and listened to the song of the coyote.

Book 6
The Collection Survives

Chapter 1

The Changing of the Guard

Part I

Overcommitted and Underfinanced

Archie Yahola, a full-blooded Creek Indian, is alleged to have been the first known settler in the area which is now Tulsa, Oklahoma. He hunted for game, roamed the hills in the northwestern part of what was then a tented community; but it is extremely doubtful, even though he was far above the average member of his tribe in literacy, that he could have projected his thoughts too far into the future. Certainly it would be rank speculation to recapture any vision which he might have had that a modern city would have its beginnings surrounded by the historical background which he created.

The Lochapokas were a proud tribe who decidedly fell under the influence of the Creek and, like many other of the nomads of the day, they selected their busking ground, a special site where they performed stomp dances and engaged in their gyrations of emotional ritualistic release. Their normal life was not interrupted by too many outside influences, and they recognized the natural beauty of the wooded land where the rivers were not too far distant and where the streams provided ample fish and a water supply for domestic necessities. Archie Yahola was considered exceptionally well-rounded by his fellow tribesman, being somewhat of a champion warrior and a philosopher. These qualifications brought to him the honor of serving as chief of the Lochapokas. One of his successors was a young, virile Indian named Tulsa Fixico, son of Joe Tulsa. There has been much speculation about the name of Tulsa and yet the students of Indian history are certainly not in accord as to why the name of Tulsa was given or used, since it had been a prefix for several tribal communities. Coincidental with the territorial days, "Tulsey Town" came into being. Apparently the business leaders of the early day did not savor the poetic euphony of the word "Tulsey" and Tulsa resulted.[1]

Tulsa's name was derived from Indian language and history, but the exact manner of this adaptation has never been established definitely. It seems, however, to have developed naturally from the old name "Tulsey Town," which, according to the late Chief Perryman of the Creeks, came from the Creek word *tulwa,* meaning "town." The United States Bureau of Ethnology, however, derives it from *Talsi,* said to be a contraction of the Creek word *Tallihasse,* which derivation is given considerable credence due to the supposition that the Creeks migrated to Indian Territory from Florida, the theory being that they adopted the contraction in the new Indian Territory assigned them in the West. The actual location of Tulsey Town was on the banks of the Arkansas River. The original site was chosen by Indians for a meeting place of their councils because of a tradition that there would never be a storm of any serious consequence in that locality. This tradition is said or understood to have been based upon general topography and the course of the Arkansas River at this particular point, and it is a matter of record that, although cyclones have dipped and twisted about all over the country, none have ever come to earth in Tulsa.

It is ironic that Thomas Gilcrease chose the same hills which Archie Yahola knew so well upon which to locate and eventually construct his museum, although at the time he acquired the property the establishment of such a memorial was foreign to his thoughts. As stated elsewhere in this biography, the stone house had already been erected by a previous owner and still remains, sturdy and majestic, just up the hill to the west from the gates which bear the initials TG in artistic wrought iron. "Tom's Place," as it has been affectionately known through the years, is just across the boundary from the city of Tulsa into what formerly was Osage Nation and was ruled by Chief Blackdog, for whom the township was named and is still so designated on the map.

It is a relaxing and sentimental experience to reach the highest point on Tom's place, gaze out into the west, and watch the great ball of fire disappear over the horizon and gently rest the shadows on that part of Oklahoma where the Creek, the Osage, and the Cherokee became known as three of the major tribes of the territory.

Thousands of visitors annually park their automobiles just below the hill and, step by step, walk up in a westerly direction and glance to the south, where almost in touching distance the huge mausoleum declares by its inscription that Thomas Gilcrease is at rest.

Before entering the sandstone building with the oval entrance, the visitor pauses to look to the southeast, and there, nestled just beyond a wooded area, a perspective reaches the eye and indelibly catches a panorama which is unforgettable. The metropolis of Tulsa seems to complete the skyline beneath the canopy of the heavens. The history of the American Indian is about to be explored.

On June 7, 1954, Thomas Gilcrease wrote a letter to the commissioners of the City of Tulsa and directed it to the attention of the Honorable L. C. Clark, then mayor; and in that treasured document he said ever so simply:

> I have spent a great part of my lifetime and personal fortune in acquiring items of historical and artistic value having to do with the discovery and settlement of our country, our Indian heritage, the State of Oklahoma and in particular to Tulsa's area.
>
> It has been my aim and hope that in making this collection I could present it to the citizens of our state and city for the use of themselves, their children's children and succeeding generations to assist them in understanding their heritage and a greater appreciation of fine historical art over the centuries.

It is significant that Mr. Gilcrease, as the founder of the institute, prefaced his letter with the words "Indian heritage." He was proud of the Indian blood which surged through his body, and he was particularly spirited about the genealogy which belonged to his family, although he never at any time in his long life formalized a "family tree" from whose branches he could suspend the many segments of his romantic career.

There is a prelude to the acquisition by the City of Tulsa of the Thomas Gilcrease Institute of American History and Art. The facts recited here had not been disclosed until Dr. Robert Lee Humber, the most intimate friend of Thomas Gilcrease, narrated them for posterity.[2] Says Dr. Humber: "One day I received a telephone communication from Mr. Gilcrease asking me to arrange to visit him in Tulsa for an extended stay. It was evident that he was seriously preoccupied with a question weighing heavily on his mind. When the pleasantries of our meeting were over, he informed me of his problem. I did not know of his financial involvements prior to coming to Tulsa, the unpaid balances and the modality of his payments. He advised me that there was an outstanding sum of two and one-quarter million dollars due on the total purchase price of his acquisitions. The question was how best to handle these obligations. What would be the wisest course for him to follow? The decision was urgent. Certain creditors were exerting an unrelenting pressure upon him for payment.

"I inquired what disposition he had made for the future of the museum, and he replied that his consideration of this subject thus far had been restricted to two basic decisions — that he wanted his collection maintained intact and open always to the public, but that no financial arrangements for its preservation after his demise had been settled. This comment by Mr. Gilcrease obviously authorized a wide range of reflections."

Hours of discussion followed between the old friends, and four solutions were considered: (1) Sell sufficient assets of the Gilcrease Foundation to liquidate all of its debts; (2) return to the former owners the items upon which sums were still due. (3) renegotiate the time schedule of future payments; and (4) choose a permanent home for the collection by giving it to a source which would assume the financial responsibility of discharging the unpaid balance of the purchase price.

Each proposition would be difficult to accomplish and there would be conflicting interests. He did not desire to reduce the income of the foundation below a figure which would enable him to make other acquisitions of art. He did not want to end his career as a collector. He would not consider returning the items for which full payment had not been made. "His collection was like a tasseled fabric whose uniqueness could not be mutilated. It would be like the removal of a structural girder from an edifice whose function would be lacerated by the operation," said Dr. Humber.

There was still another reason why Tom Gilcrease wanted to pay every cent he owed — he was irrevocably committed to its unimpaired integrity — and as so beautifully said by his colleague: "Such was the solemn verdict of the man who was anchored to a dream."

It became obvious that further extensions would be difficult to obtain and therefore the fourth alternative seemed most plausible. The negotiation with some source to acquire the collection in consideration of retirement of the indebtedness seemed workable. A collection estimated to be worth fifteen million dollars in return for an investment of two and a quarter million. The question: Could it be done?

Dr. Humber watched the reaction of his friend, Tom. He had requested advice but in the end the decision would be made by one man — Tom Gilcrease. Privately endowed institutions were considered, tax consequences were discussed, public organizations were mentioned. Finally Dr. Humber posed the all-important query. He said, "If you choose to give the collection away during your lifetime, what public source would you prefer?"

The answer was electrifying: "The City of Tulsa!"

The deliberations had ended without a solution and Dr. Humber returned to North Carolina. After several days, Tom called Dr. Humber to inform him that he had not received any encouragement from the City of Tulsa or the Tulsa Chamber of Commerce. He told Dr. Humber of several approaches which had been made to him, including the University of Oklahoma, Oklahoma City, and the City of Claremore. The project attracted national attention and was aired in the *New York Times* on Sunday, December 13, 1953, headlined "The Gilcrease Collection." Nothing happened. Mr. Gilcrease informed Dr. Humber of the interest expressed by others and how every endeavor had collapsed.

Tom Gilcrease had become a lonely man. He searched for some human understanding of the struggle through which he was being dragged by forces over which he had little control. In desperation he again contacted Dr. Humber and said: "No one here understands what I am trying to do for the people. I am seventy-five years ahead of my time, but the day will come when they will appreciate it. If I should die now, I don't believe that anyone would be willing to put up seventy-five dollars to bury me. They would simply haul me off and drop me in a hole," he said facetiously.

In the latter part of April in 1954, Tom Gilcrease placed an urgent call to Dr. Humber, who was visiting with his son at Newport, Rhode Island.

"I do not think anything will happen in Oklahoma and I want to know if you would be interested in raising the two and a quarter million and adding my collection to the one you are assembling for the North Carolina Museum of Art in Raleigh," said Tom. Dr. Humber was nonplused. "Your collection in Raleigh is predominantly European and my American collection will give it a more indigenous character," said the Oklahoman. And then he added: "You and I have worked together in many ways, and now we will build a museum together. I will pack the whole collection in trucks and take it to Raleigh, and you and I, with the available income of the foundation, will continue to buy works of art until I pass on. I will then leave all the assets of the foundation to the museum to enlarge the collection. In the meantime, I will move to Raleigh, stake out a claim, and raise some camellias!"

The agreement was reached. The proposition meant that Mr. Gilcrease was not requesting a gift of the two and a quarter million dollars but a loan to his foundation for an indefinite period, which could be amortized with the income of the foundation. Dr. Humber was to defer any effort on the project until May 15, at which time an option commitment by Mr. Gilcrease in Tulsa would expire. On the appointed day, Dr. Humber called Mr. Gilcrease and was given the affirmative nod with a wish for his success. Before the week was out, Dr. Humber had made contact with two promising sources of financial collaboration. Mr. Gilcrease called Dr. Humber to ascertain the progress and told him that he had informed a group of local citizens in Tulsa of his Raleigh proposal and agreement, all of which had aroused acute reaction to keep the museum in Tulsa.

The story of how the Gilcrease Museum was eventually saved by the passage of a bond issue could well be termed a saga of Oklahoma history. The foresight, or then, current sight, of two Tulsans share the podium for the narrative. They worked in their respective ways without really knowing each other. Who is to be the judge of whether one is more deserving than the other to be remembered by their fellow citizens? After all, without the cooperation they each had in their pursuits, it is doubtful if either would have accomplished in whole or in part what they had set out to do. Regardless of their individual feelings or the degrees in which each contributed of his time and substance, they are two distinguished Oklahomans by the measurement of civic pride and state loyalty, and to the world of western culture and art.

Part II
Blood Brothers

Thomas Gilcrease was escorting Morton R. Harrison through the Gilcrease Museum. They paused before the painting *Dutchess of Lennox* by Cornelius Johnson, and Mr. Gilcrease remarked: "Now she really rates with me because she was kind of an Indian; you see, she taught Pocahantas to speak English."

The occasion of the personal tour accorded to Mr. Harrison stemmed from a rather sudden friendship. It happened during the summer of 1953; before that time Mr. Harrison had never heard of Thomas Gilcrease, and Thomas Gilcrease only knew of Mr. Harrison by reputation. Mr. Harrison was chairman of the Planning and Resources Board of the state of Oklahoma, and being the imaginative individual that he is, he started an extensive advertising program to attract the attention of the public to many of the outstanding, educational, historical, and recreational sites located in Oklahoma. To accomplish his purpose he erected road signs, and one of the fifty such sites selected was the Thomas Gilcrease Museum.

When Mr. Gilcrease learned of the plan, he called Mr. Harrison at his home in Tulsa and expressed his appreciation. The signs designating the location of the Gilcrease Museum increased the attendance or number of visitors and Mr. Gilcrease asked Mr. Harrison if it would be possible to expand the distribution of the signs. This request resulted in forty additional signs being added to the highways leading into Tulsa, and prompted the Tulsa Junior

Chamber of Commerce to add sixty additional signs for the downtown streets. This episode of the signs started the friendship between Thomas Gilcrease and Morton R. Harrison.[3] Mr. Harrison takes great pride in making reference to Mr. Gilcrease as his "blood brother," since they both boasted of their Indian heritage, Mr. Harrison being part Cherokee and Mr. Gilcrease being part Creek.

Shortly after their initial meeting, Mr. Gilcrease called Mr. Harrison and invited him to his home. He said, "Mort, come on up to the hill and we will have a little powwow over a pot of coffee." From that moment on, all formality ceased and they called each other by their given abbreviated names. This memorable visit resulted in Tom's imparting to Mort the sad story of his financial difficulties and his struggle to meet current obligations and maintain and preserve his art collection.

When Mort left Tom that day he was determined, if possible, to find the means to assist his newly acquired friend. He communicated with General William S. Key, commanding officer of the Oklahoma National Guard, and a friend of long standing. General Key arranged for Governor Johnson Murray to fly to Tulsa for a conference with Tom and Mort. Governor Murray was impressed with the sincerity of Tom to preserve the art collection, and this led to a subsequent meeting of prominent Oklahomans in the Blue Room at the Capitol in Oklahoma City in the latter part of September. The list of invitees, besides the governor and General Key, consisted of: Ralph Casey, appointment secretary of the governor; Mack Q. Williamson, attorney general; Dr. Evans, secretary of the Oklahoma Historical Society; Mr. Milt Phillips of Seminole, Oklahoma, representing the Oklahoma Press Association; J. H. Puterbaugh, industrialist of McAlester and intimate friend of Tom Gilcrease; George Failing, manufacturer of Enid, Oklahoma; Dr. George Cross, president of the University of Oklahoma; Stanley Draper, manager of the Chamber of Commerce of Oklahoma City; William T. Payne, oil man; L. Karlton Mosteller, attorney; N. B. Johnson, of the Supreme Court of the State of Oklahoma; and Mr. Lester Whipple, attorney for the Gilcrease Oil Company of

San Antonio, Texas. Tom Gilcrease, Harrison and Newt Graham, vice-chairman of the Oklahoma Planning and Resources Board, were the only representatives from Tulsa.

Several of the invitees, including the governor, spoke on the matter of finding a way to save the museum from financial disaster, and it was proposed that there was a possibility that the collection could be moved to Oklahoma City where it could be sponsored by the Historical Society, or to Norman, Oklahoma, in conjunction with the university. A meeting was scheduled for Tulsa at a later date and little developed from the Oklahoma City conference.

As the crucial days wore on, other meetings were held with prominent Oklahomans which led to the realization on the part of those interested that the project of raising $2,250,000 from private capital would be next to impossible, and that too few people were aware of the significance of the museum or what was involved. There was discussion of a statewide subscription, but the time and expense involved soon ruled out this possibility. An effort was made to contact national foundations, but this likewise proved unsuccessful. All else having failed, an emergency meeting was held in the governor's office in November of 1953. The attorney general, Mac Q. Williamson, advised those present that in his opinion, a bond issue would be challenged as being unconstitutional, since the art collection consisted of moveable items and he seriously doubted if the land value involved would justify the amount sought, and there was no indication at that time that Tom Gilcrease would include the land or would want to include it in the proposition. A number of other suggestions were made, including the possibility of obtaining a loan from private sources, and Mr. Newt Graham of Tulsa went so far as to suggest a revenue bond, which would have meant placing a mortgage on the property and collection, as well as the establishment of an admission charge to retire the bonds. At the request of some of the interested parties, Tom communicated with the Knoedler Galleries of New York, and Mr. Davidson, owner of the galleries, came to Tulsa for the purpose of providing an appraisal. Mr. Davidson and an art dealer from the West Coast concluded that the collection was worth in excess of twelve million dollars.

Mort Harrison was still optimistic and, being a tenacious individual, he felt that a way would be found to assist his friend, Tom, to raise the badly needed funds. He arranged for a feasibility study to be made by a professional company and was promptly advised that it would take sixty days to receive a report. The company made a preliminary survey and was discouraged because the museum had not attracted a sufficient number of visitors.

On December 7, in the late afternoon, Tom called Mort and told him he had talked with his attorney, Lester Whipple, in San Antonio by long distance. Tom had to raise at least $100,000 and that unless the sum of $10,000 could be forthcoming by nine o'clock on December 8, several creditors had indicated that they would press their claims through the courts. This was indeed a "Pearl Harbor" day for Tom Gilcrease, but it also disclosed to him the generosity and acute interest which his friend, Mort, manifested in saving the art collection for his "blood brother."

Mort hung up the telephone, turned to his wife, Ruth, and said, "Honey, how much money do we have in our personal bank account?" Ruth knew by the expression on Mort's face that he was about to invade the Harrison treasury. "Eleven thousand dollars!" answered the suspicious Ruth. Before eighty-thirty that same evening, Mort Harrison had delivered his personal check for $10,000 to Tom. Mort learned later from Tom's secretary, Eudotia Teenor, that this was one of the rare occasions when she saw her otherwise stoic boss shed tears of gratification.

Mort's check was not enough to satisfy the determined creditors, and without hesitation he sought the assistance of some of his friends. Otha Grimes contributed $1,750 — but more was needed. On the fourth day of January, 1954, he delivered additional funds. Those who responded to Mort's plea, and the amounts they gave, were: George E. Failing of Enid, Oklahoma, $10,000; William T. Payne of Oklahoma City, $1,000; Ralph W. Casey of Tonkowa, Oklahoma, $1,000; and Bryce C. Roby, $1,000; Arthur O. Olson, $1,000; and George H. Parker, $200; all from Tulsa.

The feasibility study had been completed in the meantime, and disclosed that the Will Rogers Memorial at Claremore, Oklahoma, was surpassed only by Mount Vernon in attendance, and that approximately 75,000 people had visited the Rogers Memorial that year. The report further indicated that if the Gilcrease Museum could be established near the Rogers Memorial, and an admission charge invoked, within three years time there would be sufficient funds with which to maintain the museum, and within thirty years enough money would be earned to retire the suggested bonded indebtedness.

The foregoing report was welcomed with enthusiasm and Mort arranged for a number of Claremore business leaders to join with Tom Gilcrease, Ray T. Reed, executive vice-president of First Securities, Inc., of Wichita, Kansas, and himself. They were: Robert W. Love, manager of the Will Rogers Memorial; Ed Livermore, editor of the *Claremore Progress*; Dr. Noel Kaho, representing the Lion Clubs; Harry Hoagland of the Rotary Club; Frank Popdechan of the Claremore Chamber of Commerce; and Joe Marshall, commander of the Claremore American Legion Post. The group elected Dr. Kaho as their chairman. After their initial meeting, a site was selected north of and adjoining the Rogers Memorial. The adjoining tract, 320 feet by 600 feet, was owned by Robert W. Love and his wife, Paula Love, who offered to donate the land to the project. An option was taken on the remaining land for $12,000, and a like amount was to be raised in cash to meet some overdue payments of interest on the obligations which were so badly pressing Tom Gilcrease.

Subsequently, there was a demonstration of civic pride and unusual faith on the part of a few loyal citizens of Claremore,* who responded to Harrison's request for ad-

---

* The names and amounts were: Frank Popdechan, $6.000; The American Legion of Claremore, $2,000; C. W. Arthurs, $1,000; Harry Hoagland, $1,000; Claremore Chamber of Commerce, $1.00; Claremore Lions Club and Rotary Club, $1,000 each. These generous commitments brought additional funds from citizens of Tulsa: Mr. William S. Bailey, $1,000; Black and West Architects, $1,000; Gertrude Clark, $1,000; Alfred E. Aaronson, $1,000; Earl Sneed, $1,000; E. Fred Johnson, $1,000; and N. R. Graham, $1,000.

vancements to assist Mr. Gilcrease. Twelve thousand dollars was raised and Dr. Noel Kaho presented the funds to Mr. Harrison on February 1, 1954.

In the meantime, Mr. C. A. Border, then secretary of the Tulsa Chamber of Commerce, having learned of the progress made by the Claremore group, suggested that a meeting be arranged with the Chamber's board of directors for the first week in March. In attendance were Governor Johnston Murray; N. B. Johnson, justice of the Supreme Court of Oklahoma; Ralph Casey; and Ray T. Reed. Mr. William G. Skelly, president of the Skelly Oil Company, suggested that a "Stud Horse Note"* be obtained and that he would sign for $5,000. Mr. Skelly, who was known for his humorous quips, said, "I don't know nothing about art, but if the collection of Tom Gilcrease is worth fourteen million dollars, it's worth saving for the City of Tulsa." Mr. Jay Walker, also a Tulsa oil man, then proceeded to verbally chastise Mort Harrison with an accusation that he had read in the press that Mort was trying to take the collection to Claremore. Walker was under the impression that Harrison was a resident of Claremore. Mr. Skelly was quick to respond and said, "Jay, don't you know that Mort lives in Tulsa. Now come on, put your $5,000 on the line."

The creditors of Tom Gilcrease became more and more determined to collect what was due to them. Mort Harrison had become so involved with the subject that his determination reached a point of persistency and inescapable preoccupation. He sought out every Tulsan of financial means whom he thought might be induced to make a commitment. His efforts were somewhat rewarded when he accumulated promissory notes in the amount of $28,500.**

---

* A note signed by a group of individuals for the purpose of procuring a loan from a financial institution which might not otherwise have been acceptable. The "Stud Horse" note originated according to tradition and custom when a number of stockmen would band together for the purpose of acquiring a stud horse for breeding purposes. When the horse was sold they would divide the profits or share the loss — between them.

** William G. Skelly, $5,000; Jay Walker, $5.000; William J. Sherry, $2,500; Maurice Sanditen, $5,000; A. F. Keating, $2,500; Louis P. Meyer, $2,000; Julius Livingston, $2,000; Tom P. McDermott, $2,000; Herbert Gussman, $2,000; C. G. Wells, $1,000; John Mayo, $1,000; and M. W. Wolfe, $1,000.

The next few days were crucial ones — Mort and Tom made several attempts to obtain the necessary funds by pledging the notes as security. The leading Tulsa banks declined, and assigned as their reasons — extreme doubt that the collection could be saved and that if the project failed, they would not want to sue the signers, many of whom occupied seats on their respective boards.

March 30, 1954 had come into view on the fast passing calendar. Once again the tireless Mort would not give up. He telephoned Harry Gibson, an old friend who was president of the First National Bank of Muskogee. Mr. Gibson listened to Mort's review of the facts and then, without hesitation, said, "Bring the notes to Muskogee; we are in the lending business and we would not hesitate for one moment to sue Tulsa bank directors." Mort immediately contacted Tom, and by early afternoon they were en route to Muskogee. In a matter of moments after their arrival at Mr. Gibson's desk, they walked out with a cashier's check for $28,500, and were back in Tulsa by 4:30 P.M.

Mort and his friends now had the grand total of $75,200, all of which was repaid by the City of Tulsa at a special occasion which is now a part of Tulsa history and was designated as "Gilcrease Day" by the Tulsa Chamber of Commerce. The date was January 27, 1955.

Part III
Keeping Gilcrease for Tulsa

The sincere and tireless efforts expended by Morton R. Harrison to raise sufficient funds to pacify the creditors of Tom Gilcrease had their impact on all concerned. By word of mouth, as well as press comments, the much-needed interest had been engendered and the possibility of saving the art collection was enhanced.

Tom Gilcrease was still concerned to such an extent that he did not hesitate to converse with anyone whom he thought was sufficiently interested to give him some peace of mind and possible financial assistance. The money provided by the Muskogee Bank, through Harrison's efforts, had been applied to the Gilcrease commitments, but it was not enough and no one knew it better than Tom Gilcrease.

The month of February, 1954, seemed destined to bring another individual into the life of Thomas Gilcrease, who, like Mort Harrison, was so deeply concerned that he embarked upon a plan of approach which eventually reached up, removed the clouds, and let the sun come forth in a burst of glory. That these friendships came to Tom Gilcrease in the closing days of his career can in retrospect be termed "miracles of humankind," and but for the truths which came from experience — the whole subject could be attributed to fiction.

Alfred E. Aaronson and his wife, Millicent, suntanned and fresh from a much-deserved vacation in Hawaii, had just returned to the mainland of the United States, and, as was their custom after being away for any length of time, they reviewed the news items of the Tulsa papers which had accumulated on their doorstep in their absence.

In one of the issues of the *Tulsa World* newspaper, he noticed an item which made reference to the Gilcrease Museum and the possibility of the collection it housed being moved from the city of Tulsa because of its founder's inability to meet his financial commitments brought about by excessive acquisitions and financial reverses in the oil business.

Alfred suggested to Millicent that they make a final visit to the museum so that if the collection was moved from the city of Tulsa, they would at least have a lasting memory of the art and artifacts which it housed.

Upon entering the main lobby of the museum, Alfred saw a rather slender-appearing individual whose demeanor reflected a person who looked quite worn and weary. He introduced himself to this man whom he assumed was Thomas Gilcrease. This, then, was the first meeting of two individuals who were destined from that moment to become colleagues in an undertaking which the most able of the prophets of old could not have predicted. Alfred, in his forthright but kindly manner, turned to this modest man and said, "I understand that your museum is going to be moved from Tulsa or will be disposed of piece by piece because of your inability to meet certain obligations which you have created in your quest for additional art objects and paintings."

Tom, who was by nature a very modest individual, lowered his head, raised his eyes, and slowly replied, "Yes, I am afraid that your comments are correct, because Governor Johnston Murray has been working on my problems for over a year and it looks like everything he has done has failed." The two stood there silently for several moments when Tom remarked, "I must have a large amount of money by March 20, 1954, or my creditors are going to take everything."

Alfred very quietly and with his characteristic smile said, "Mr. Gilcrease, I am not a wealthy man but I would give a thousand dollars to help keep the museum in Tulsa."

Tom looked up rather surprised and said, "Very interesting, but I'm afraid it's too late. Thank you." This historical and eventful but short conversation occurred on February 8, 1954.

Alfred and Millicent continued on their tour of the museum and in one of the galleries Alfred met Mr. Murray Womble of Tulsa. He very briefly reviewed his conversation with Tom, and Mr. Womble was so impressed with Alfred's sincerity of purpose that he said, "Why, it would be a shame to lose this museum and you know, I think I'd give $500."

Alfred responded and said, "Murray, do you know Alf G. Heggem?" Murray shook his head. Alfred said, "I'll tell you what we're going to do. Alf lives across the road from here on Newton Street and on the way home suppose you and I, with our respective wives, stop at Alf's house and talk this matter over with him; and you can't tell — he might even give us a drink." Now Alfred is not a drinking man but he will take a social nip under proper circumstances. They left the museum in their individual cars and drove to Alf Heggem's home; he happened to be out in the yard and, of course, immediately invited them in. Alfred repeated his conversation with Tom as they nursed the drink which Alf had served. Mrs. Heggem interrupted the conversation to say that they, too, would give as much as a thousand dollars to preserve the museum.

En route home from Alf's place, Alfred turned to Millicent and said, "You know, darling, I think I'll write a letter to Alf Heggem and also write to the local papers and see what can be done about saving the Gilcrease Museum for Tulsa." And then he hesitated a moment and said, "No, the word is not *save* but *keep*. That's it, we'll see if we can't keep this tremendous collection for the citizens of Tulsa, the state of Oklahoma, and the nation."

That night Alfred found it very difficult to sleep. There was something about this man Tom Gilcrease that kept returning to his thoughts; he wondered how any man who had been able to assemble so many objects of art had permitted himself to become so involved that all of his dreams were about to be shattered because of financial reverses. What was really behind the overcommitments? Could a man of the apparent background of Thomas Gilcrease get help from local financial institutions? What happened to the oil income which Tom was reputed to have? What kind of friends did a man have who would let him down at a time like this? Tom Gilcrease had a reputation as a banker. What about the local banks — would they help? Would the effort be worthwhile? Would the citizens of Tulsa support any kind of program to keep the museum? These and hundreds of other thoughts raced through Alfred's mind, and finally sleep overtook him and the vision of tomorrow drifted into infinity.

The opportunity for public service and dedicated effort comes to few men as rapidly as it came to Alfred Aaronson. He reached out, took hold of the reins, and decided to meet the challenge.[4]

March 9, 1954, just about one month after his initial conversation with Tom, having noticed in the press a comment to the effect that the state of Texas was bidding for the Gilcrease Museum, he decided to assemble a group of his friends and invite them to his home. Those who received the invitation to this memorable meeting were Newt Graham, a retired banker, well known for his work in connection with the water projects in Tulsa; Victor Barnett, one of the officials of the *Tulsa Tribune*; Morton R. Harrison;* David R. Milsten, his personal attorney and civic leader with whom he had worked on the board of directors of the Tulsa Jewish Community Council; Murray Womble, businessman and personal friend whom he had met at the Gilcrease Museum; Mr. and Mrs. Alf Heggem, business people and old friends; Dr. C. C. Knoblock, Tulsa pathologist, who was prominent in the work of the Salvation Army; Norris Henthorne, one of the officials of the *Tulsa World*; and H. O. McClure of the Fourth National Bank. Of this list of invitees, only the Heggems, Barnett, Harrison, Milsten, Womble, and Knoblock attended the meeting; however, Sid Steen arrived just as the meeting commenced, as a substitute for Norris Henthorne.

In his pleasant but positive manner, Alfred reviewed all that had transpired and when he had concluded his remarks, Mr. Barnett said, "Alfred, you can do it, but it will mean talking to every civic group and business organization in the city of Tulsa and you will have to take charge of it."

Alfred turned to Mr. Barnett and replied, "This ain't for me. I've never made a speech in my life."

At this point in the meeting, Morton Harrison spoke briefly and said, "Gentlemen, an effort is being made to move the museum to Claremore and house it in a building to be erected next door to the Will Rogers Memorial, but there is an urgent matter which should have attention. We are going to have to raise money to prevent some of the creditors from commencing litigation, since some of them have already threatened to sue — we need financial assistance."

Alfred was shocked at this statement, and before the meeting adjourned he wrote out a check payable to "Thomas

---

* Founder of the Will Rogers Hotel at Claremore, then, a member of the Will Rogers Commission, and member of the Planning and Resources Board of the state of Oklahoma.

Gilcrease, Special Fund" for the sum of $1,000, handed it to Morton Harrison, and remarked, "This may be of some help to Mr. Gilcrease."

Morton Harison detailed to the assemblage that he hoped to be able to raise a substantial amount of money from several Tulsans and he had hopes that the balance of the money necessary to complete the project in Claremore would be obtained. Each person who attended the meeting made suggestions and offered comments.

Sometime during the month of April of the same year, Morton Harrison called Alfred Aaronson and advised him that, although a substantial sum of money had been raised and applied to the indebtedness, it appeared that further efforts to move the museum to Claremore, Oklahoma, would prove futile. He stated that the creditors were still pressing Mr. Gilcrease and that any new method of approach would certainly be welcome.

Plans which followed culminated in establishing what was known as the "Keep Gilcrease for Tulsa Committee." A group of spirited citizens joined their hands and hearts and their money. Conferences were held with Mayor L. C. Clark and the proposition of a bond issue explored. What the majority of those who were working on a plan to save the collection did not know, was probably the reason their ambitious program was not thwarted. They were unaware that Mr. Lester Whipple of San Antonio, personal attorney of Thomas Gilcrease, was in constant communication with the president of the University of Texas, Logan Wilson.[5] An effort was made to remove the collection to Oklahoma City. Governor Johnston Murray had contacted Mr. Whipple and invited him to meet with the governor at his office in the state capitol. The plan did not generate. Mr. Whipple then arranged to bring the majority of the members of the board of regents of the University of Texas to Tulsa. They visited the museum and inspected the collection. Following this historic visit, Mayor L. C. Clark called President Wilson at Austin and discussed the subject with him. President Wilson told Mayor Clark: "The University of Texas is interested in acquiring the Gilcrease collection but the University does not at this time have the funds to make the purchase. We are still exploring this aspect of the matter and hope to solve it soon." Everyone knew that Thomas Gilcrease needed two million dollars and without financial aid the entire collection would be involved in litigation. Mayor Clark was determined to gather all possible information. He placed a second call to Wilson, which brought the reply, "Whipple is here in the room with me and we have already bought the collection." They then adjourned to the office of the attorney general of the state of Texas – to complete certain details for clearing the funds with which to make the purchase. Mayor Clark had, in the meantime, been working at a feverish pace to prevent the consummation of the sale.

During these crucial hours, Mr. Philip H. Rosenbach of the Rosenbach firm, one of the principal creditors, dispatched Mr. D. Hays Solis-Cohen to Tulsa. Mr. Cohen, a member of the law firm of Wolf, Block, Schorr, and Solis-Cohen of Philadelphia, arrived in the Oil Capital on Tuesday morning, March 11, 1953. He was met at the rail station by Lester Whipple and they drove with haste to the hill where Cohen and Gilcrease met for the first time.[6]

Mr. Gilcrease, accompanied by Lester Whipple, proceeded to give Mr. Cohen a personally guided tour of the museum and to introduce him to his aides. Recalling the events of that memorable day, Mr. Cohen says:

> Although we met only once, our exchange of views about his problems was a satisfying experience. He recited to me his intimate thoughts about his Indian ancestry and impressed me with the sincerity of his convictions concerning the tribulations and woes inflicted on his people by certain nations of Europe, with particular mention of Spain, Portugal, England, France and Holland and, later, by America. As we conversed he afforded me a personal tour of the museum and I could sense that he found solace in assembling his collection of memorabilia which meant preservation of a historical record of the civilization of the American Indian. His comments extended to the proposition of despoilation and separation of the Indian from his land and his avowed desire to make the white man conscious of

the injustices which had been inflicted on the Indian.

The intensity of the stored up emotion in Tom Gilcrease was manifested by a remark he made when we were looking upon the paintings of Remington and Russell and I had commented on their magnificense and masterful artistry; I told him that they seemed to come alive with action of battle. We had paused for a moment before *The Great Spirit,* the well-known bronze by Remington, when to my utter amazement Mr. Gilcrease said: "Frightful as was the murder and despoilation of the Jews by Hitler, it was nothing as compared to what the white man did to the American Indian." I looked at him increduously, and I am sure my gentle rebuke reached his mind, if not his heart. I said: "My friend, you cannot equate what happened to your people over five centuries of fighting with the white man interlaced as it was with treaties of peace, genuine friendships and inter-marriages with what happened to my people under Hitler in a relatively short span of the second world war. I admit that the white man is certainly not blameless in his relations with the American Indian, and that they as a nation have much to be ashamed for, but at no time in world history, so far as I know, were 6,000,000 defenseless people murdered."

Mr. Gilcrease looked at me and his sober face broke into a faint smile. He extended his arm through mine and said, "Let us go downstairs to the basement; there are some things there I want to show you, and then we can talk more about your mission here."

Upon reaching the basement area, Mr. Cohen was completely taken by what he saw. It seemed that every item which had been purchased from his client by Tom Gilcrease was neatly stored, and the more valuable ones were in a vault. "I cannot and will not put any of these items on exhibition or consider them mine to do as I please until they are paid for," said Tom Gilcrease. If D. Hays Solis-Cohen had needed any assurance of the high integrity of Tom Gilcrease this remark was the capstone.

Mr. Cohen departed from Tulsa with a feeling of inner

satisfaction. He was determined to advise his client that immediate legal action would not be necessary and that he had every reason to feel that his conference with Lester Whipple and Tom Gilcrease would result in eventual payment of the outstanding indebtedness. The extension of time was granted, and the occasion of their meeting had sparked a friendship which caused Mr. Cohen to later comment that he counted the incident a significant episode in his life because the understanding had matured through trying circumstances.

Tom Gilcrease had reached out with facts of history and touched a sentiment with D. Hays Solis-Cohen which brought them together. They both had a torch to bear about man's inhuman treatment of man, and their brief exchange of philosophical conjecture established an understanding that years of association could not have accomplished. Upon his return home, the Philadelphia lawyer wrote to Tom Gilcrease, made a personal contribution to the Gilcrease Foundation, and made it evident that he desired to be a part of a program which had rather ironically brought him to the museum.

And so it was that when the Texas attorney general was in the act of signing the instruments which would have released the funds and sealed the purchase, a telephone call came from Thomas Gilcrease and in his usual composed manner he said: "Call everything off — the collection is going to remain in Tulsa."

Lester Whipple has since commented: "While I know that many spirited citizens of Tulsa worked hard and long to save the collection for Tulsa, they all salute this Philadelphia lawyer whose understanding and sympathetic attitude made it possible for the collection to remain free of litigation until funds could be raised to retire the Gilcrease obligations."[7]

The Tulsa Chamber of Commerce was in the throes of advancing a bond issue to build a civic auditorium, and the key members of the chamber were fearful that the addition of a bond issue to keep Gilcrease in Tulsa would defeat the auditorium election. Efforts were made to procure bank loans, but the local banks would not consider doing so, because of the speculative nature of the project. Alfred's committee went to work to raise the $2,250,000 by a bond issue, but then came the heartbreaking information from Mayor Clark that unless the Keep Gilcrease Committee would underwrite the cost of the election, the bond issue would not be voted on. He charged Alfred Aaronson with the personal responsibility to see that the election cost was underwritten and told him that unless he had such assurance, he would not call it. Once again, Alfred assembled his committee, and one by one they personally contributed and made contacts with interested business people, friends, and associates, and finally a sufficient amount of funds was available to guarantee the cost of the election. The bond issue passed to keep the Gilcrease Institute for the City of Tulsa, but the civic auditorium was defeated.

When the vote was counted on the bond issue which raised the necessary $2,250,000, on August 24, 1954, it was a sad bit of civic commentary that out of the total registered voters, only 12,093 went to the polls to exercise their right of franchise. Of this number, 8,905 were in the affirmative and 3,188 tried to defeat the issue. Relatively, the segment of Tulsa's population which responded to the voices of the Keep Gilcrease Committee was small when compared to the numbers of ballots cast in general elections or on other special issues. A bond issue for "art" had never been attempted before, and many of the voters could not understand why there was any necessity for the city to obligate the citizens for a collection of paintings and other works of art *located in the northwest section of the city, in Osage County.* The "Gilcrease Day" held on January 27, 1955, in appreciation for the creation of the Thomas Gilcrease Institute of American History and Art, more than justified any criticism which had been leveled against so few, by so many.[8]

On Sunday, October 30, 1955, Tom Gilcrease sponsored one of the most unique events in the history of Tulsa. Approximately one thousand persons joined with him on the grounds of the museum where they ate antelope, deer, elk, and bear, personally bagged by Tom in Wyoming and barbecued on the grounds of the museum. It seemed that all of the eyes of the Creeks, the Osages, and the Cherokees looked across the hills at the museum building which, even then, housed in excess of a $12 million collection of Indian art and artifacts. When they called upon Tom to speak, he said, "I'll always be thankful and grateful to the many friends who worked so hard and spent so much effort to keep this museum for the benefit of all our people in Oklahoma and elsewhere. Each and every one of you who had anything to do with keeping this institute here will live on throughout the ages to come, through this wonderful collection that exists here."

The author, as the original counsel to the Keep Gilcrease Museum for Tulsa Committee, was called upon to comment on the occasion and said, "We should tell our host over and over again how grateful we are to him for making the museum a living and meaningful institute in Oklahoma and the world. Tom Gilcrease is above the average citizen and therefore he is a great man."

Alfred Aaronson concluded the formal remarks by saying, "To you good people belongs the credit. Oklahoma always will be grateful to you. Tom Gilcrease knows the way to immortality is to give unstintingly of one's self to others."

To the man whose mind invented the phrase "Keep Gilcrease Museum for Tulsa," there is and will be a special drawer in the archives of human endeavor. His colorful background, his profound religious faith, his love for and of people, his genius, and his sincerity of purpose met the challenge. There was a job to be done and he completed it.

Part IV

The Good "Deeds"

Although the acquisition and financing of the Thomas Gilcrease Institute of American History and Art was begun on August 6, 1954, it was not until July of 1955 that the City of Tulsa, working in conjunction with the Citizens' Advisory Committee, assumed responsibility for the collection.

Speculative though it may seem, if Tom Gilcrease had not overextended himself and the resources of the Gilcrease Foundation, the generous gift he made would have been withheld for several years. These thoughts are predicated upon the premise that there was a reluctance on his part at one stage of the deliberations to make a definite decision. He had toyed with the idea of disposing of the collection for a cash consideration. That he even vacillated in the face of pressure was not due to his desire for "profit," as much as it was to protect his credit and reputation as a solid buyer in the art markets of the world. He had never defaulted on an obligation, and he was proud of his record. The language of "The Deed of Gift and Conveyance"*

---

* "The Thomas Gilcrease Foundation gives to the City of Tulsa the Thomas Gilcrease Collection [consisting] of all art, historical documents, artifacts and personal property now located and situated within the building belonging to the Thomas Gilcrease Foundation. The Foundation represents that the Collection is worth approximately $12,000,000 and that there are debts in connection with its acquisition by the Foundation totaling approximately $2,250,000. That it is the desire and intention to give and donate all of said property to the City of Tulsa for the benefit of the Citizens of Tulsa and Oklahoma, but that grantor is unable to complete that purpose for the reason that it does not have the necessary $2,250,000 to pay off and retire said obligations and deliver said property free and clear. It is, therefore, donating all of its interest in said property,

was authored by Mr. Remington Rogers, then attorney for the Airport Authority and Park Board of the City of Tulsa, in conjunction with counsel for the Keep Gilcrease Committee and the legal department of the City of Tulsa.[9]

The intention of Mr. Gilcrease to donate the proceeds from the oil properties was included in all of the advance publicity given to the proposed bond issue and had a vital effect upon the success of the campaign for favorable votes. The assignment of the oil and gas mineral interests was also an indication that Mr. Gilcrease wanted to see the city reimbursed for the money procured from the bond issue. It was more than a gesture; it was proof positive that he realized the generosity of the citizens who were willing to assist him and his cause, financially as well as physically. In many instances they practically deserted their own business and professional time to assure the officials of the city that everything humanly possible would be undertaken to educate the voters to the reasons why the museum should remain in Tulsa. The assignment, dated January 27, 1955, was pointed and positive.*

---

which includes said entire collection with the exception of the proportionate part or interest represented by said $2,250,000 in debts; all of his interest in said property subject to the aforesaid exception is being bargained, sold and conveyed to the City of Tulsa by this instrument. However, grantor is donating proceeds from certain oil properties described in an assignment bearing even date with this instrument and delivered simultaneously herewith in which certain oil properties are conveyed to certain trustees therein named for the benefit of the City of Tulsa and the people of Tulsa and State of Oklahoma, as fully described herein, in the hope and belief that said oil properties so conveyed will yield to the City of Tulsa and the people of Tulsa and Oklahoma sufficient monies whereby the City of Tulsa, in making this purchase in this manner will ultimately be out no money whatsoever."

* "The Thomas Gilcrease Foundation for the consideration of one dollar and other valuable considerations conveys to the Trustees for the City of Tulsa an undivided one-half of the fractional interests hereinafter stated (these fractional interests vary from 9% to 37%) in and to eight oil and gas leasehold estates, located in Gregg County, Texas. *This assignment is for a limited term and will terminate when there has been paid to grantees herein from the interests hereby assigned the sum of $2,250,000.00* or such lesser amount as the City of Tulsa, Oklahoma, shall advance on behalf of grantor herein to such creditors of grantor now having valid and existing claims against grantor and/or liens against grantor's collection of art, historical documents, artifacts, etc., or portions thereof, collectively known as The Gilcrease Collection."

It was the purpose of the assignment to provide the needed funds, after which the city would not have an ownership in the oil and gas interests assigned. There was discussion of omitting the reversion clause, with the hope that all funds over the necessary amount would remain as an endowment for the operation of the museum. However, this point was not pressed for two reasons: first, it would have evinced an ungrateful attitude on the part of the grantees and, second, it would not have been an equitable request under all of the circumstances.

To be assured that there would be adequate housing for the collection, the Thomas Gilcrease Foundation leased to the City of Tulsa the main building of the museum, together with the ground on which the building was located and the adjacent parking space, for a period of five years, for the consideration of one dollar per year. There was a motive in the execution of this lease which was obvious. Mr. Gilcrease had an undisclosed plan in the back of his mind which he did not make known to anyone until he was ready to do so. This was typical of the man Thomas Gilcrease.

By a trust indenture,* the foundation and the City of Tulsa agreed upon the method of operation and management of the collection. The Park Board of the City of Tulsa, being the governmental agency under whose jurisdiction the collection was to be administered, appointed a group of Tulsa citizens to act as an advisory committee, consisting of N. G. Henthorne, Wade C. Whiteside, and Richard Lloyd Jones, Jr. The instrument was signed by the three trustees on behalf of the Park Department of the City of Tulsa and L. C. Clark, mayor. Thomas Gilcrease executed the document on behalf of the foundation. The principal restrictions contained in the Trust Indenture were:

1. The Collection shall always be kept intact.

---

* August 6, 1954, (amended and executed as amended on January 27, 1955).

2. Ultra modern art shall never be mixed with the collection.

3. The Director of the museum must be in sympathy with the things comprising the collection.

4. Everything in the collection shall be kept properly housed, in good condition, and always displayed for the benefit of the public.

5. The collection shall be maintained under the name of The Thomas Gilcrease Institute of American History and Art.

A special meeting of the Citizens Advisory Committee and the Tulsa Park Board was called for May 1, 1956, at two o'clock in the afternoon. Alfred E. Aaronson, chairman, extended an invitation to the Tulsa city commissioners and informed them that the then mayor-elect, the Honorable George E. Norvell, would be present. The invitees were advised that Mr. Thomas Gilcrease would make a startling announcement that would be of great interest to all the citizens of Tulsa.

He offered to give the museum site, northwest of Tulsa, and the improvements on it to the community in return for its pledge to keep it there – and to construct a new building to house and exhibit more of the vast collection. He also made it known that he would give the greater part of his private collection, including the objects discovered in his excavations. The gift would include part of the land, the museum building, two smaller structures, and the Gilcrease residence. He said: "The institute needs 50,000 square feet of galleries, auditorium, archives, storage space, and offices in a building that is fireproof and air conditioned. If the city will cause such a building to be completed before the end of the present lease on the existing 15,000 square foot building, I will deed the land and buildings there for a park, and my private collection." He then continued and commented that there had never been a survey of the property but he was sure it contained more than twenty-five acres, which compared to just over thirty-five acres in Tulsa's Woodward Park and rose garden combined. He told the officials that parking would always be a problem and he envisioned a modern museum on the crown of the hill, with ample parking facilities, overlooking what he considered "the prettiest sunsets in the Southwest." He reminded those present that in his opinion the executive director should live on the museum grounds and his home could serve such a purpose.*

When he concluded his remarks, Mr. Alfred Aaronson said that the offer amounted to in excess of $20 million, considering the original collection. Mayor-elect George E. Norvell and the other members of the new administration pledged support to the institute and stressed the educational and spiritual value of the offer. Mr. Aaronson assured Mr. Gilcrease that the citizens committee would work diligently for the fruition of the plan. The reception accorded Mr. Gilcrease after he took his seat was a moment to be remembered. The applause was deafening and then all became quiet.

An incident occurred at the conclusion of the remarks of Mr. Gilcrease which will also be recalled with mixed emotions. Mrs. Maud Lorton Myers, widow of the late Barton Myers, and owner of one of the leading Tulsa newspapers, philanthropist, and socialite, immediately rose to her feet. The atmosphere was electric and those in attendance anticipated the announcement of an endowment to add to the proffered gift of Mr. Gilcrease. Mrs. Myers animated her face, looked straight at Mr. Gilcrease and said: "Tom, will you marry me?" The stoic Tom was astounded, his cheeks flushed, and it was obvious that he was at a complete loss for words with which to respond. The unexpected question brought the attorney for Mr. Gilcrease to his feet. "Mr. Gilcrease, don't answer that question!" The remark by Lady Maud was of course intended to be made as a quip to tantalize the modest Mr. Gilcrease. She succeeded in turning a sentimental moment

* This was accomplished in 1967 when Director Paul Rossi moved his family into the house on the hill, at the suggestion of the author, who was then president of the institute.

into one of hearty laughter. The following day the telephone chain of Tulsa's social roster was very busy and the story became a conversation piece for weeks afterward.*

The advisory committee functioned until it was determined to supplant it by a corporation to be known as the Thomas Gilcrease Institute of American History and Art. A meeting of the Citizens' Advisory Committee was held on October 23, 1956, and the Articles of Incorporation, written by George H. Bowen, David Randolph Milsten, and Remington Rogers, were approved.

On October 24, 1956, the Articles of Incorporation of the corporation were filed with the secretary of state, state of Oklahoma.** The incorporators were Alfred E. Aaronson,

---

* Thomas Gilcrease had recognized the whimsical proposal of "Lady Maud," as she was affectionately known, and on May 2, 1956, he wrote to her as follows:

May 2, 1956

Mrs. Maud Lorton Myers
World Building
Tulsa, Oklahoma

Dear Lady Maud:

It was kind of you to attend our meeting yesterday at the gallery. Your presence was appreciated by everyone and you helped considerably in the good cause. You certainly expressed your approval of what took place in a unique and spirited manner which brought joy and applause to everyone at the meeting. I am very grateful for your coming and for your expressions of satisfaction of the meeting. Hoping to see you again and often at the gallery, I am

Sincerely yours,

Thomas Gilcrease

** The purpose clause is long and all-inclusive; however, the initial purpose clause as set out in Article IV, Section 1, reads:

To cultivate and promote through education and otherwise, general interest and appreciation in the traditions, early customs, history and art of our country, and to the origins and beginnings of our people by collecting, preserving and exhibiting books,

Wm. S. Bailey, Jr., Morton R. Harrison, David Randolph Milsten, and Dr. Noel Kaho. The charter was obtained as an eleemosynary corporation pursuant to the provisions of Title 18 of the Oklahoma Statutes, Section 541 to 959 inclusive. The registered agent was Alfred E. Aaronson and the corporation was to have perpetual existence.

The by-laws, following the language of the statute, provided that there could be as many as forty-one directors but there could not be less than twenty-one.

The surprise move which Mr. Gilcrease made was his announcement on October 7, 1958, that the foundation had decided to execute a deed of gift and conveyance to the City of Tulsa, as a gift in perpetuity to the thirteen-acre tract consisting of the museum building and grounds upon which it was located. The permanence of the institute was assured by this conveyance, and for the first time in months, Mr. Gilcrease began to smile and reflect a contentment which had not been apparent previously. He knew that

---

> historical documents, pictures and art objects of every kind and character relating to the conquest, settlement and development of the Western Hemisphere, including artifacts, data, relics, historical objects of every kind and nature, historic and prehistoric, having to do with the origin, culture, customs and civilization of the people of the Western Hemisphere both historic and prehistoric and to advance such interests and appreciation by any appropriate means.

Article IV, Section 3, provides:

> To sponsor, encourage and promote through education and otherwise, the culture, traditions, language, history, handicraft and art of the Indian.

The original directors, whose names are listed in the Articles of Incorporation, represented many prominent citizens of the state of Oklahoma:

> Alfred E. Aaronson; Mrs. Franklin S. Bernsen; Mrs. Walter Ferguson; Otha H. Grimes; Morton R. Harrison; Dr. Noel Kaho; Gen. William S. Key; Mrs. John H. Leavell; Dr. Charles C. Mason; Rev. Patrick W. Murphy; Dr. Clarence I. Pontius; Mrs. Russell S. Tarr; R. K. Lane; Wm. S. Bailey, Jr.; Dr. George L. Cross; Thomas Gilcrease; Mrs. Marshall O. Hardy; Richard Lloyd Jones, Jr.; Hon. W. W. Keeler; Mrs. Edward C. Lawson; George Martin; David Randolph Milsten; Mrs. Maud Lorton Myers; Remington Rogers; and George H. Bowen.

from that moment on, the collection would never leave the hill. It was a day of joy and accomplishment.

The frontal image of the Thomas Gilcrease Institute of American History and Art was not altered when the final plans for the expanded and more spacious building were adopted. The structure which had been erected in 1943 had served the purpose for which it had been intended, but it was neither adequate nor functional for the public consumption of the enlarged collection it housed and contemplated.

As a privately operated museum, the incentive for a broader exhibit concept was exclusively under the control and guidance of its founder, who alone possessed the better knowledge of the potential it offered. Rotation of the collection was infrequent and in many respects it was a "one man show" where the curtain still opened and closed by hand.

The new plans offered sixteen exhibit galleries, covering an area of 35,000 square feet, and provided a horseshoe-shaped traffic pattern, thereby making it mandatory for the visitors to enter and take leave of the premises at the same foyer. There was an acute necessity to centralize the administrative offices and to provide an assembly room where visual education, staff, board meetings and lectures could be conducted without interfering with other museum activities. The northwest extension provided a glass enclosed circular lounge area which was three levels in height, where the visitors could pause to rest and view the hill country where Indians became oil men and where oil men married Indians, where the Osage at one time drove expensive automobiles while cloaked in colorful blankets and where the Indian Agency guarded the wealth of its wards.

The building committee had made an extensive study of the security problems which would be increased with the added galleries. One huge area was designed for storage and workshop facilities and divided by sturdy partitions to provide heavy wire racks on sliding tracks for the storage of paintings. Temperature controls were engineered and a three-door elevator was installed to reach the lower levels, the cab to be activated only by a special key device. Mr. Joseph Koberling, working with Mr. Ed K. Ellis, chairman of the Gilcrease Building Committee, had, it seemed, thought of every practical detail. The price tag was $600,000; the answer — another bond issue. The citizens' committee had profited by the experience of the two and one-quarter million dollar bond issue which had saved the collection in 1954. The year of decision was 1961, and in November the improvement bond issue passed with a comfortable majority.

The unexpected and startling news of the death of Thomas Gilcrease on May 6, 1962, was a painful blow to the members of the Gilcrease family and to the personnel of the institute.[10] Everyone, everywhere, who knew or had heard of Tulsa's Tom Gilcrease, communicated their regrets. The announcement was accorded widespread news coverage. Mr. Gilcrease had personally been a member of the planning committee and had often participated in their deliberations. The ground-breaking ceremonies were, therefore, heartbreaking festivities — sort of a joyfully tearful occasion. Mr. E. Fred Johnson, president of the institute, presided over the event, and Mayor James L. Maxwell turned the first soil with a specially inscribed, gilded shovel while the television cameras hummed and the radio announcers assisted in telling the world that something new was happening in Tulsa. The members of the press were out en masse and the wire services were ablaze with the news.

Months of anxious waiting, limited activity, further planning, and the usual bouts with the weatherman all pointed to a target date which finally arrived on October 27, 1963, when the official dedication was conducted. Mr. Thomas Gilcrease, Jr., and Mr. Barton Gilcrease, sons of Thomas Gilcrease, and Mrs. Des Cygne Gilcrease Denney, his daughter, the trustees of the Gilcrease Foundation, were present. They surprised the dedicatory audience by an additional gift of art, artifacts, archaeological material, and land, all of which complemented the former gifts and which was estimated in value in excess of five million dollars.*

The Gilcrease Foundation conveyed 9.41 acres, being the remainder of the land on the hill, which included the stone house. This was part of the property which is in the extreme southwestern corner of Osage Nation, equidistant a mile from the northern boundary of the former Creek Nation and the western boundary of the former Cherokee Nation.

The nine-member board of trustees had been reduced to three — death and resignation had taken all the others, including Thomas Gilcrease.

The letter of tender was addressed to The Honorable James L. Maxwell, Mayor of the City of Tulsa, and dated October 23, 1963, and in part reads:

> Dear Sir:
>
> The undersigned, being all of the members of the Board of Trustees of The Thomas Gilcrease Foundation, an eleemosynary corporation organized under the laws of Oklahoma, and, acting on its behalf, hereby tender to the City of Tulsa, Oklahoma, gifts of 9.41 acres of land, being a part of Section 28, Township 20 North, Range 20 East, Osage County, Oklahoma, together with the improvements thereon, and the entire collection of Americana now owned by the Foundation and housed in such improvements.

Deeds of conveyance and agreement were enclosed with specific instruction that the documents be officially signed and copies returned to the foundation. The letter then stated that, as the children of Thomas Gilcrease, they were pleased to further the work begun by their father and which was being continued by the City of Tulsa. Words of appreciation were then expressed with gratitude for the

---

* Mayor James L. Maxwell made the announcement from the flag-covered platform where the following were seated, to wit: Henry Bellmon governor of Oklahoma; Robert Lindneux, artist; Gene Gilcrease, son of Thomas Gilcrease, Jr.; William S. Bailey, Jr.; Alfred E. Aaronson; David Randolph Milsten; William A. Baden; Otha H. Grimes; and Gordon T. Hicks.

city for carrying on the work of their father — the progress made, and that they had proved worthy of the trust their father had placed in them. The letter was signed by the three trustees.*

At the executive committee meeting of the institute, held on August 21, 1962, following the death of Thomas Gilcrease, a number of tributes, projections, and sentimental remarks were made. Morton Harrison suggested to the assemblage that the eventual erection of a sarcophagus on the museum grounds should be considered. He turned to the members of the Gilcrease family who were present and said "You couldn't find a better resting place for Tom Gilcrease than on the hill at the museum." In addition to the Gilcrease children, the meeting was attended by the officers of the institute; Mrs. Eudotia Teenor, secretary of the foundation; Mr. L. Karlton Mosteller; and four of the directors, including Mr. Joe Glass, who was later to become secretary of the institute. The staff was represented by Dean Krakel as director and Mrs. Joan Williams, his secretary.

On January 18, 1965, three leading art authorities of the United States appraised the Gilcrease possessions at over sixteen million dollars.[11] The re-evaluation of the collection housed in Tulsa's Thomas Gilcrease Institute, according to Director Paul Rossi, has revealed a tremendous gain over the last evaluation in 1959. The entire contents, with the exception of the William R. Leigh collection, were gathered by the late Thomas Gilcrease. The highest

---

* Mr. Aaronson served as chairman of ceremonies and Mr. W. A. Baden as program chairman. The ribbon was cut and the new edifice opened by Mrs. Des Cygne Gilcrease Denney, assisted by Mayor Maxwell. W. E. "Dode" McIntosh, principal chief of the Creek Nation, gave the invocation by repeating the Lord's Prayer in the Creek Language. The vocal accompaniment was by a group of Indians — Jennie Lee Fife, Cherokee; Frances Spraker, Cherokee-Kiowa; Janice Young, Cherokee; and Lucil Navarro, Creek. Mr. Otha H. Grimes gave a few appropriate remarks. The program was highlighted by the Honorable Henry L. Bellmon, chief executive of the state of Oklahoma. In advance of the dedication, on October 15, 1963, Mayor Maxwell had issued a proclamation which read: "The citizens of Tulsa desire to do honor to the memory of Thomas Gilcrease whose generosity makes the Institute possible," and he referred to the City of Tulsa as the "owner and custodian."

valued item in the collection is a portrait of Frank Hamilton Cushing by Thomas Eakins—valued at $200,000. Others are: *Watching the Breakers* by Winslow Homer, $175,000; *Penn's Treaty with the Indians* by Benjamin West, $175,000; *The Buffalo Hunt* by Charles Russell, $150,000; and *Missing* by Frederic Remington, $125,000. The art collections are valued at $11,760,660, and the breakdown of the important collections and their worth are: Russell, $2,501,759; Remington, $1,283,000; George Catlin, $1,049,500; Alfred Jacob Miller, $733,100; and William R. Leigh, $569,360. The artifact collection, including 212 pieces of pre-Columbian gold work is valued at $1,990,640, and the books, manuscripts, and documents in the library are currently worth $2,656,250. In the library are included the Conway "Cortez" papers, worth $325,000, and a group of papers consisting of the appointment of Paul Revere to the Commission of Safety following the famous "Midnight Ride," and certified copies of the American Declaration of Independence and Articles of Confederation, valued at $186,000.

The art collection was appraised by Rudolf Wunderlich of the Kennedy Galleries in New York City; the South and Central American artifact collections by Al Stendahl of Stendahl Galleries of Los Angeles; and the library collection by John Fleming of John F. Fleming, Inc., of New York City. The evaluations were coordinated by the very talented Bruce Wear, art curator for the institute.

The museum's collection consists of 5,389 paintings made up of oil, watercolors, and prints. One hundred two contemporary Indian artists are represented and 445 paintings of Indian and related subjects were produced by them. The non-Indian artists number 323, many of whom painted western subjects. They are all important limners in the art history of Americana.

Chapter 2

Behind Stone Walls

The first world war had carved its ignominious insignia on the country where Thomas Gilcrease was searching as he traveled. The year was 1925. This was his initial venture to Europe and his itinerary included Africa, Asia, and other major countries about which he had studied at Bacone College. The wanton onslaught of man's inhumanities to man had somehow spared the centers of culture and, being possessed of a burning desire to gather more knowledge about the great artists of the world, he pressed onward to the art markets, to the museums, to the government buildings, cathedrals, and shrines. Before his tour ended, the burning desire had turned into a white flame of inspiration. If the people of the old tired cities could build such monuments to honor their talented ancestors, he could do the same thing for the American Indian.

He returned to the United States with a perspective he had never before understood, with a determination to travel to the ends of the earth to recapture the Indian art which had been painted in America and transported across the seas. He could not at that time have been aware of the enormity of his undertaking or that one day his own portrait would welcome people of all races and creeds to the greatest museum of Americana in the world or that it would bear his name, honor the Indian, and become a repository for the culture of his people.

Thomas Craven, in his Introduction to *A Treasury of Art Masterpieces*, wrote: "We may look upon art as a great tree nourished in the soil of human experience, an organic development fertilized by the fresh energy of young and hardy peoples, and expanding unexpectedly with the enrichments of power personalities."[1] Thomas Gilcrease was himself a product of the soil of human experience by ancestry and environment and, like Craven, he felt that the American artists were a part of the society in which they lived and that they were the leaders of the most exciting and important art movement existing in a troubled world.

There are numerous methods by which paintings acquired by Thomas Gilcrease can be appraised. The connoisseurs of western art can pass critical judgment and measure what they see by their experiences in the art markets. Their price tag is generally one of economic conjecture, keeping in mind that without the profit formula it is difficult to survive. The private collector is often guided by egoism and ups the value by his own selfish desire to acquire, regardless of the intrinsic worth of the work. He thereby creates a base which goes into his portfolio of tax valuations, establishing an unrealistic appraisal.

The intuitive qualities of Thomas Gilcrease were ever present and provided him with a ready apprehension with reference to his acquisition of art. He sought out and obtained the professional services of the world-famed Finlayson brothers. John and Richard Finlayson, of Boston, Massachusetts, were recognized as exceptional craftsmen in the field of restoration by the major museums of the world. Their estimate of the value of the Gilcrease collection was manifested by their willingness to accept repeated commissions from Thomas Gilcrease. Their talents were not available to those who indulged the counterfeit or spurious art.

Perhaps the most accurate estimate springs from John

Pogzeba, the internationally known restorer and conservator of fine oil paintings.[2] A native of Silesia in the eastern part of Germany, he has devoted forty-five years to his creative genius. He started his career by working as an apprentice and later serving an internship in the Doerner Institute of Munich, Germany. His delicate touch and capacity for achievement in the field of restoration has brought him commissions in the important museums throughout the world of art, including the Kaiser Frederick Wilhelm Museum in Berlin and the famous galleries of Italy.

The diminutive Pogzeba was an ardent defender of the constant desire of the directors of the Gilcrease Institute to conserve the collection. They recognized the technical process necessary and sought the services of Mr. Pogzeba whenever availability permitted. In his slightly guttural but soft voice, reminiscent of a neglected German accent, Mr. Pogzeba has said: "Conservation prolongs the life of a painting and restoration repairs paintings which have been damaged. Restoration is not to be confused with repainting. I never resort to the practice because new paint when applied to or on top of colors of long standing will not blend and after several years the black spots will appear where the new painting has been added."

When asked to express his opinion of the value of the paintings in the Gilcrease Institute he said: "I doubt if the citizens of Tulsa or the state of Oklahoma have the slightest idea of the priceless paintings which are housed in the Gilcrease collection. Mr. Gilcrease was indeed an artist and, having done conservator work in every major museum in the United States and the majority of the better ones in foreign countries, I can say without fear of challenge that Tom Gilcrease collected the most interesting and varied works of western art to be found anywhere in the world. No one is yet aware of the real worth or the historic importance of his efforts. He measured art by the standards of the artist. If you took the five important museums in this country and put them all together, they would not make one Gilcrease." John Pogzeba knows what Thomas Gilcrease accomplished.

"The Thomas Gilcrease Institute of American History and Art is a monument to the culture of the American Indian and the western frontier. It is a storehouse of art, the like of which cannot be seen anywhere else in the world. It is an art that is of supreme importance because it is shorn of superficiality and pruned of mannerisms. It is art with simplicity, sincerity, and earnestness. The vast collection is not a plaything for design purposes but rather it is true to its function as the interpreter of life." These were the words of Bruce Wear, former art curator of the Thomas Gilcrease Institute of American History and Art and now president of Gaylord, Ltd., an art consultant firm of Tulsa, Oklahoma.

Mr. Wear, an expert in art analysis and the nemesis of the faker of creative genius, is familiar with every painting and watercolor, every bronze and every wood carving in the Gilcrease collection. His association with the institute extended well over ten years, during which time he was consultant to almost every director and the majority of his fellow colleagues in other branches of the institute's wide scope of material. He has had an intimate acquaintance with the heads of many art markets in America and Europe and has developed a philosophical approach in collecting and evaluating, as evidenced by his new book, *The Bronze World of Frederic Remington.*[3] He is therefore qualified to comment with dependability and firsthand knowledge about the treasures "Behind Stone Walls."

It is Mr. Wear's opinion that Thomas Gilcrease succeeded in acquiring a collection of art that is not based on abstract aesthetic principles that are unrelated to time and space. He earnestly believes that it is an art based on the same philosophies that inspired the friezes of the Parthenon at Athens, which represent a fidelity to the contemporary life of the Greeks. He has said: "Just as this great art of the Greeks is important for historic rather than aesthetic reasons, so the collection made by Thomas Gilcrease is also, for it reveals much of our inheritance and intelligently cherished beliefs. Just as the friezes of Parthenon represent the pantheistic festivity and life of the Greeks, so do the walls of these galleries form a frieze of life of Americans in paint and in bronze."

Mr. Wear also stresses the proposition that in practically every instance the major acquisitions in the collection came from authentic sources. This factor, more than any other, commands the attention of the qualified appraisers.

It would be wishful thinking and impractical documentation to endeavor to record in this volume, which is primarily biographical, the story of every artist, all of the titles of their subjects, and a short history of their respective backgrounds of study and education.

To walk through the galleries of the institute and look upon the paintings on exhibit or those which are in the storage area is to relive for the length of the tour the thrilling scenes of the West when the red man was still mourning the loss of his warriors and the defeats they suffered as they tried to defend the soil they had called their homes for centuries. To have the opportunity to see the original paintings of other phases of life and nature of subjects relating to events still young in history's heart is an unforgettable experience.

The introductory gallery of the museum is the permanent facility for the exhibition of rare documents. This section of the building has been designated as the "Great American Documents Gallery," although it will hold other priceless papers as they come to life through the rotation system under which they are displayed. The addition was a gift of the Junior League of Tulsa and serves to insure the continued safe and effective display of the documents. The dedication was held on February 25, 1967, with Will Rogers, Jr. delivering the dedicatory address. The establishment of the gallery provides the students of research with indisputable data of the past and with the vehicle whereby the visitors can recount with the pioneer builders of the nation the written words which they promulgated, adopted, and put into positive deeds.[4]

An opportunity to view at close range the artifacts and rare documents mentioned elsewhere in this book is a stimulating journey. The repeat visits by those who enter their names on the attendance register is an unsolicited testimonial to the sustained interest created by their initial visit to the galleries.

The searching faces of *Black Hawk and his son Whirling Thunder* by John Wesley Jarvis,[5] extend a welcome to the visitor. The eyes of the painting are hypnotically entrancing. Next in view is the huge oil masterpiece entitled *Sierra Nevada Morning* by Albert Bierstadt. There is a feeling of serenity as one speculates whether the deer are on an exploratory quest for food or have just gone to the water's edge to quench their thirst or are preparing to find a retreat to watch the rolling clouds cover the mountain range in the distance.

There can be no continuity of steps as the visitor goes from gallery to gallery. A party of ten persons go ten different ways, a party of five separate before walking too far, even two visitors part company — and one person finds it difficult to devote himself exclusively to one subject. Such is the magnetism of the collection.

Like a jewel case of unmatched pearls, one painting holds more luster than the other — and the observer commences to wonder whether there is a pot of gold at the end of the rainbow. He can feel the chill in the air as he gazes upon *The Buffalo Hunt on Snow Shoes* by the nomadic craftsman, George Catlin, or looks upon Catlin's self-portrait which resembles a theatrical celebrity. Moving on, the visitor is caught in the stare of *Geronimo* by Henry H. Cross or stops completely enthralled as he views *Jerked Down* by the inimitable Charles Marion Russell and learns that on March 19, 1964, the painting was reproduced and issued on the new five cent government stamp of the United States of America to honor the artist.[6] The permanent Russell exhibit is one of the most important galleries in the institute.

Then there is the horse for which he feels a special pity when he looks upon the *Fight for Water* by Charles Schreyvogel. But he does not tarry; he cannot — his eyes have turned to *Lower Falls, Yellowstone* by the inimitable Thomas Moran.[7] He inaudibly speculates about how tired the prisoner must have been as he marched between the column of horses at gunpoint in *Missing* by Frederic Remington.

Fort Laramie by Alfred Jacob Miller depicts the great entrance looking westward, filled with Indians and traders — a lively and rustic scene where the court area of the fort was guarded by cannons hidden in the towers over the two main entrances.[8] *The Wild Turkey,* John James Audubon's masterpiece, comes into view. Words are not adequate to describe the colorful blending of the feathers, the brilliant colors, and the meticulous detail.

The introductory gallery contains some of the paintings mentioned in the foregoing paragraphs, which is followed by a representative grouping of classical and colonial paintings of Americana, works such as the Frederic Remington and Thomas Moran collections, which are permanent exhibits. The works of the Taos school of artists are temporary exhibitions subject to change; paintings of some of the most prominent western artists, such as Schreyvogel, Leigh, Frank Tenney Johnson, and Olaf Seltzer. Also Indian artists, Acee Blue Eagle, Woodrow Crumbo, and the wood carvings of Willard Stone are included. The creations of George Catlin and Alfred Jacob Miller and hundreds of others fall into the rotating policy of the museum.

The Gilcrease collection also includes thirteen oil portraits of Indian subjects which were once owned by Northwestern University and were presented to the Gilcrease Foundation in 1951. The artist, Kathryn W. Leighton, according to her son, Everett W. Leighton, was influenced by the talent of Charles M. Russell from whom she received personal instruction. Among the better known Leighton portraits are, *Madonna of the Desert,* a portrait of Mrs. Little Plum and son, Blackfoot Indians, used on the covers of *Literary Digest, Widening Horizons* and the *Art Club Bulletin of California*; *Loushanya,* a Chickasha Indian opera star from Ardmore, Oklahoma; and *Chief Two Guns White Calf,* a Blackfoot Indian, one of the models on the buffalo nickel. The Gilcrease Institute became the owner of the Leighton portraits when the collection was given to the

City of Tulsa. They are considered a vital part of the Americana represented in the collections.

The institute offers an educational program for school children or adult instruction. The art exhibitions provide definite information and reveal the important aesthetic significance of the collection. History can be traced by picture arrangement and displays. A portrayal of native American civilization, North, Central, and South American native cultures are explored. Varied subjects come to light for the visitor.

American art without reference to the Indian can also be seen at the institute, such as paintings by Robert Feke, John Smibert, James A. Whistler and John Singer Sargent, W. M. Chase and Robert Henri, along with Thomas Eakin's distinguished portrait of Frank Hamilton Cushing.

It was George Phippen, the artist whose painting *Intruders* is a possession of the institute, who said in a personal letter to Thomas Gilcrease in May, 1952: "I'm looking forward to the day when I can see your collection again. I believe I could make camp in the Russell and Remington rooms for a month and enjoy it, even when the rooms are dark." The visitor concludes that the collection is as vast as the *Grand Canyon* by Thomas Moran; and it is, almost.[9]

Thomas Gilcrease was personally acquainted with many of the artists from whom he made his purchases for his collection. Some of his transactions were concluded by long distance telephone when he had authentic information in his possession. There were, however, a few of the individuals with whom there was immediate rapport and instances in which an exchange of letters would follow. Mr. Gilcrease, while not verbose, nevertheless delighted in conversing with people who expressed an interest in his collection. He knew there was an attic of Americana which had to be uncovered and brought down to the living room of mankind.

Mr. Daniel McPike, assistant director and curator of anthropology, is inclined to the position that the bulk of the Gilcrease collection is anthropologically oriented. He has said: "Thomas Gilcrease manifested a greater pride in his Indian heritage than in his geneologically predominant

Anglo-European heritage. Not that he was adverse to collecting large numbers of books and paintings pertaining to Colonial America, or the Civil War, or the cattle industry, but even in these areas his dominating interest in the life of the Indian is evident. The artifact collection, archaeological and ethnological, is almost universally American Indian. Even the material in the art and library collections from Europe deal preponderantly with Indians.

"The anthropologist has a vast storehouse in what the Gilcrease Institute has collected to study. In one location can be found the archaeological prehistory, the ethnological nonwritten history, and the primarily historical manuscript and imprint material. The thousands of paintings of Indians done in the nineteenth century by Anglo-American artists and the contemporary paintings of Indians by Indians. The collection, found under one roof, is comparable only to the Smithsonian Institute."

It would be utterly presumptuous to endeavor to compile a list of artists and label them as the favorites of Thomas Gilcrease. He recognized in each the quality and substance which gave them greatness. He held in esteem the so-called "Taos" group because, in his opinion, they offered promise for the preservation of the yet unspoiled subjects of the western territory. He considered them to be the remnants of authentic masters of pioneer culture.

To demonstrate the personal relationship between Mr. Gilcrease and the Taos group, four recognized artists will be presented: Joseph Henry Sharp, Bert Greer Phillips, Ernest L. Blumenschein, and Oscar Edmund Berninghaus.

Joseph Henry Sharp

Between the Rio Grande and Sangre de Cristo Mountains in New Mexico lies the town of Don Fernando de Taos, known to artists of the West as "Taos." This fascinating and quaint valley was formerly a trading center occupied by the Indians and the Spaniards. It was the site of the Pueblo revolt in 1680 and the anti-American revolt in 1847. The conjecture might well be that the first people to leave footprints in the sands of its now famous streets were from the school of thought commonly referred to as Taoism, which is alleged to have begun in the Chou dynasty and had as its basic classic the Tao Te Ching. It is probable that they taught conformity to the way of nature (Tao) was the only way to live because such philosophy involved the absence of regulations and the artificialities of civilization. This speculation is as plausible as others which have been advanced. Authentication of any theory should not add to or detract from the mystery of the origin of the name "Taos."

In 1889, Taos developed into an art colony.[10] The beauty and variety of the region, the comforting attraction of the oasis, the shadows cast below the snow-capped peaks, the illusion of a velvet-draped mountainside at nightfall all contributed to the selection.

Joseph Henry Sharp has been credited with being the first artist to pause long enough to explore the country for colonization by the men of brush and palette. The absence of "regulations and artificialities" presented a freedom of body and mind and sparked the intrigue of his love for nature. He was determined to invade the six-story high pueblos which could only be reached by man-made ladders. He wanted to see how the Indians lived and why they tenaciously clung to their primitive method of self-preservation. He loved to watch them loll in the sunshine as they used the bottom rung of the ladders as a place to sit for respite from the torrid sun which baked the walls of their pueblos that sheltered them from the hot winds.

An undated letter in the possession of the Thomas Gilcrease Foundation, addressed to Mr. Gilcrease, which presumably was written during 1945, pinpoints many of the subjects which J. H. Sharp and Mr. Gilcrease had no doubt discussed either by previous correspondence or in person:

Dear Mr. Gilcrease:

From what Standing Bear told you last summer there

must have been two Crazy Horse. The one I painted must have been a relative of another Sioux taking the name for the reflected glory of a great warrior.

There were two American Horse, one Sioux other Cheyenne, both important chiefs. Four Standing Bear — Sioux, Blackfeet, Crow & Taos, all painted at various times. At birth mother or midwife must have seen plenty bear!

About the only data I even kept was the name and tribe, marked on back of margin of canvas — too anxious to get at another.

I should have kept a diary — began one, but like Huckleberry Finn lasted only few days. Some friends think I should retire and write things up — nixy, which I can't paint I die.

My diary was entitled "Teepee Smoke" and was to be wonderfully illustrated by the author! Gee —

First Indians I ever saw, soon after Civil War, were quite a number, side-tracked on old B & O on way to Washington. Later in a 4th of July procession in small town, I had 5 or 6 boys, all painted up by drug store man and on horses — Passing the reviewing stand we gave a whoop, broke ranks, galloped all over town yelling, & stole the show!

Around 1888-1890 my first Indian portrait, "Ogalala Fire," Sioux, was stranded in Custer, on way home. This was purchased by J. G. Butler and now in Butler Art Museum, Youngstown, Ohio. He later bought many of the portraits and pictures for the Museum.

Somewhat later a Comanche or Cherokee from Okla. then in Cin'ti for some weeks, and I painted from him.

These things got me really interested and began planning and saving for the Indian country.

Early, Texas Jack Omahundro and Buffalo Bill shows

added interest & I made some studies & acquaintances –

In the booklet have marked some dates – others are approximate. If you ask more questions maybe more data will come back.

We leave here Apr. 22nd – Taos 24th. I will write Woody about coming to Taos a short time for criticisms and a bit of painting together. I can show him in a short time all I know of painting then it is up to him & experience.

Our very kind regards, always.

Sincerely yours,

J. H. Sharp

Thomas Gilcrease and J. H. Sharp shared a mutual friend in Henry Standing Bear, chief of the Sioux tribe. That Sharp alludes to the fact that some of his friends had suggested that he write his autobiography is a thought he attempted to carry out at a later date. It is a genuine loss to history that he did not pen a definitive review of his career, since the title he selected for his diary is almost romantic in concept, to wit, "Teepee Smoke." The priceless letter does mention the Texas Jack and Buffalo Bill shows; consequently, another conjecture is in order and it would have been stimulating to know whether Oklahoma's favorite son, Will Rogers, knew J. H. Sharp in the days when Will Rogers was a part of the Texas Jack troupe which toured South Africa. The *Woody* mentioned in the last part of the letter refers to Woody Crumbo, and the phraseology of the answer unequivocally reveals that Thomas Gilcrease had requested his friend, J. H. Sharp, to evaluate some of Crumbo's art work and to impart art instructions to him.

The institute owns several hundred of Sharp's oil paintings including the famous *Drum Song*, *Crow Teepees at Lame Deer*, and other varied subjects ranging all the way from deer to bear, from Indian chiefs to birds, and animals to teepees.

Bert Greer Phillips

In 1906, President Theodore Roosevelt created the Taos Forest Reserve. Bert Greer Phillips was commissioned as the first ranger, and at his suggestion the reserve was named for Kit Carson. Phillips could not bear to witness the destruction of the giant trees for commercial use which was turning the Taos Canyon into a barren waste. He knew that if the region was robbed of its beauty, the artists who occupied the colony would soon pack up their kits and seek greener pastures.

Phillips was a product of the town of Hudson, which lies on the Hudson River south of Albany, New York.[11] This was the section of the United States which provided the locale for many novels by James Fenimore Cooper, whose Leatherstocking series are credited with having inspired Phillips to become interested in the life of the American Indian.

While Phillips was studying in Paris at the Academy Julien, he met Ernest L. Blumenschein. When he returned to New York he shared a studio with Blumenschein, and their mutual interest in the culture of the Indian was responsible for their journey to the Taos country.

Phillips was internationally known for his interpretation of the Pueblo Indian culture and the incredible portrayal of landscapes of the Southwest. His mural paintings are considered among the best by art critics and, unlike some of his contemporaries, he had a rare talent for capturing the charm of female subjects.

The Thomas Gilcrease Institute of American History and Art has two of the better works of Phillips in the collection: *Turkey Hunt* and *Corn Maidens.* Thomas Gilcrease was a personal friend of Phillips and they often engaged in anecdotal discussions about the Taos country.

Ernest L. Blumenschein

When the eyes of the Gilcrease Institute visitor look upon the *Enchanted Forest* by Ernest L. Blumenschein, there is an immediate reaction. The artist correctly selected the title, for there is an enchantment about the painting which seems to exude through the pores of the canvas a spiritual invitation. The ritualistic composition jumping out in bright colors creates a peculiar sensation of doubt that nature could have produced such rich tones. The question generally asked is: "Did the artist really reproduce something he had seen or did the imagery of his talents carry him to a state of subconscious visitation with the supernatural?"

Blumenschein has been compared to the French painter Paul Gauguin (1848-1903). Gauguin is credited with being the creator of the "synthesism movement" and the exponent of the theory that to be rid of all that might intervene between the artist's vision and the canvas is to produce what nature displays to sunlight or reveals in the shadows. The combination of separate elements of thought or sensation into a whole was not a new idea with Blumenschein, for it was Gauguin who told his students and colleagues, "How does that tree appear to you?" and if the answer was "very green," then he would say, "Then use green, the finest green on your palette." And if the shadows were blue, he would add, "Do not be afraid to paint it as blue as possible." Blumenschein, like Gauguin, followed the fruitful concept of the plain surface covered with colors put together in a certain order. He knew that every work of art is a transposition, a caricature, the passionate equivalent of a sensation which frees the artist from restraint and permits him to express his own personality.

As a co-founder of the Taos art colony with Bert

Phillips, Blumenschein had first seen the raw country in September, 1889. Phillips and Blumenschein had made the trip to the west for the specific purpose of seeing Taos. He had met Henry Sharp in Paris as a student and recalled that Sharp had told him about the Indian village located at the foot of a mountain in northern New Mexico. The departing was from Denver by wagon, and the story of the broken wagon wheel is now standard fare for scholarly consumption when delving into the life of Ernest L. Blumenschein.

Thomas Gilcrease and "Blumy," as he was affectionately known to him, were good friends.[12] They shared a common understanding, or, as James Taylor Forrest puts it: "They were both vitally concerned with the spirit, the soul, the deep-running and often misunderstood, spiritual life of the American Indian. On the one hand the artist painted his feeling for and understanding of these elemental people who lived in such great harmony and communion with nature. Mr. Gilcrease, the prodigious collector of all things concerned with the Indian, on the other hand gathered together from all corners of the world the whole cloth and the fragments which tell of the natives of this land and from which historians will continue to card, reweave and unfold the fabric of a people, a way of life and a civilization now of the past."

Could it be said, then, that Gilcrease was also a student of a synthesism as a collector? Perhaps so.

Thomas Gilcrease had a profound sympathy for all of the Taos group, and his convincing personality was responsible for having several of them paint their own portraits. Blumenschein responded and the institute owns *Blumy's* which was done by the artist in 1948. In 1951 Gilcrease presented a special showing in honor of the Taos artists and invited his friend to participate. Age had overtaken Blumenschein and he wrote to Tom Gilcrease, "What a blessing to have the great pleasure of painting as you grow older." He then made reference to his friend, J. H. Sharp, who had reached ninety, his friend Berninghaus who had attained the age of seventy-seven, and to himself who was then seventy-seven. They were all absent at the showing but their spirits were there.

Museums throughout the United States possess sundry of his paintings; however, only one museum can boast of *Moon, Morning Star, Evening Star,* which is behind the stone walls at the Thomas Gilcrease Institute of American History and Art together with many others, such as *Taos Pueblo.*

It is fortunate for the world that Blumenschein and Phillips made the trek from Denver and crossed Laveta Pass into New Mexico and on into Questa where, at the edge of a canyon on a narrow curve, the wagon slipped into a deep rut and the wheel collapsed. The view they saw from the Sangre de Cristo and which stretched from the foot of the range was the determining factor that made Blumenschein a co-founder of the Taos colony. The shadows of Blumenschein's artistry can still be seen when one looks up from the valley.

Oscar Edmund Berninghaus

Thomas Gilcrease met Oscar Berninghaus in Taos in 1945.[13] Woodrow Crumbo had joined Gilcrease on the trip and together they spent most of their time meeting their old friends of the artist colony and making new ones. Tom Gilcrease enjoyed the company of Berninghaus largely because his background was vastly different from most of the Taos artists. There was something wholesome about his approach to life which gave strength to his paintings. Some years after they met, the usual request for a self-portrait came from Gilcrease and with the aid of a mirror and a photograph, Berninghaus complied. Oscar Berninghaus, like the male figure in Grant Wood's *American Gothic,* looked like a man who knew the value of hard work. There is somewhat of a resemblance between Berninghaus and

Wood's character with the pitchfork – no doubt coincidental but nevertheless noticeable. Berninghaus, like Grant Wood, painted without aesthetic fears and yielded to the influence that made him a part of the environment he had observed from the caboose windows of the various freight trains where he had worked as a brakeman and from the vantage points of the passenger trains as they sped along pueblo country.

In 1913, he wrote: "I think Taos is a splendid country for an artist because there are more varieties of atmosphere here than I have found in any other place. Up in the hills one can get the right setting for old trapping pictures. There are many varieties of sage and cactus for background, according to the elevation you choose. The Taos Indians are a splendid type; in fact, the best I have ever seen, and if one wants to paint Mexican pictures, he can get a background near Taos, just as picturesque as any spot in Old Mexico."

He was interviewed before his demise and remarked: "The canvases that come from Taos are as definitely American as anything can be. We have had French, Dutch, Italian, and German art. Now we must have American art. I feel that from Taos will come that art." The prediction of Berninghaus has become a truism.

Howard Chandler Christy

There were other artists whose lives had crossed the path of Thomas Gilcrease and whose paintings can be seen in the Gilcrease Institute. With them, as with the Taos group, there was a warm feeling between the artist and the collector. The friendship of Thomas Gilcrease and Howard Chandler Christy resulted in Mr. Christy painting *Hiawatha's Wooing*.[14] It is a bush picture, filled with trees, flowers, and woody undergrowth. The small animals are visible, perched on tree branches which overhang the teepee of Minnehaha's father, if indeed it was the intention of the artist to identify him; however, it is difficult to imagine the outstretched hand of Hiawatha waving a farewell to the Indian sitting cross-legged under the teepee, since he is to the rear of Hiawatha and his bride. The faces of the principal characters are expressive — the sternness of Hiawatha blending into a faint smile. Minnehaha, by contrast, possesses a sadness with a forced gentleness in her appearance. The large deer in the background, with its young, is attracted by the departing pair of lovers whose feet appear to be on tiptoe. They are depicted immobile because their gear is stacked to the left of Hiawatha near a wild bird of unknown species. Surely there was no intention of leaving behind his sheaf of arrows and his trusty bow. The right view of the painting is devoted to a waterfall of great proportion and ducks can be faintly detected on the water below. The bare breasts of Minnehaha are partially covered by her long black tresses which extend to her waist. Her breechcloth is held in place by a beaded belt. This detailed description of *Hiawatha's Wooing* has been included herein because it is the only painting in the entire Gilcrease collection which is a departure from the non-nude standards established for the collection by its founder.

Christy will be remembered for his famous *Christy Girl* and he could hardly be expected to give Minnehaha a homely costume, a rustic countenance, or to wrap her in a traditional Indian blanket.

The beautifully formed figures, locked in a cross-armed hand grip, the muscular, hair-free arms of the warrior, and the facial structures of each of the characters in *Hiawatha's Wooing* demonstrate the imaginative prowess of the artist.

In 1949 Mr. Gilcrease acquired the portraits of Chief Bacon Rind and Will Rogers. They were purchased at the suggestion of Robert Lee Humber. He also acquired *The Signing of the Constitution,* which had been nationally acclaimed. The latter painting accompanied the Freedom Train during the national tour of American cities. In 1949 Christy painted a portait of Thomas Gilcrease and it was on exhibit at the institute until Charles Banks Wilson's portrait was placed in the rotunda of the institute.

Charles Banks Wilson

When Edwin Markham, the poet who wrote *The Man With The Hoe,* was eighty-six years old, a young fledgling made a sketch of him. This event occurred in 1936, and the boy with the pencil was Charles Banks Wilson, a part Peyote Indian. Markham was so impressed with the sketch that he urged young Wilson to study art. Today, Wilson is noted for his paintings of contemporary Indian life in Oklahoma. He is widely recognized for his murals and lithographs and he has illustrated over twenty-two books. His talents have enriched such prize-winning volumes as the classic *Treasure Island, Company of Adventures, Henry's Lincoln,* and the late J. Frank Dobie's personal favorite, *The Mustangs.* He was dean of the art department of Northwestern A&M College in Oklahoma for fourteen years.[15]

The Thomas Gilcrease Institute commissioned him to paint a formal portrait of Thomas Gilcrease. Speaking of the commission, the artist has said: "Tom Gilcrease knew the importance and was aware that I wanted very much to do a good job. I remember a remark he made to the members of the board of directors of the institute, 'I do not know if it will be a good painting when Wilson finishes it, but I do know it will be the best he can do; he's that kind of an artist!' "

When the portrait was completed, it was unveiled by Des Cygne Denney, daughter of Mr. Gilcrease, on January 12, 1959. The pencil sketch, a life study, made by Mr. Wilson in preparation of the painting of the portrait, is considered an excellent likeness of Mr. Gilcrease and is reproduced on the dust jacket of this book. Recalling the event, Mr. Wilson has said: "As with any personality such as Thomas Gilcrease, he was a many-sided man. One of his business asssociates suggested that he be painted as the neat, fastidious gentleman he was. I was anxious to get the opinions of others and talked with one of his gardeners. This man was Indian and knew Tom intimately. He said, 'Don't paint him all dressed up, fix him up in work clothing, comfortable shoes, and paint him like the regular fellow he is.' In retrospect I think both were right."

The portrait is now a part of the collection of the institute and commands a permanent place in the rotunda.

The painting *Oklahoma Melody*, by Wilson, illustrating a scene of modern Indians beating a drum, is in the collection and has been used as a cover selection for *The American Scene* magazine.

Robert Lindneux

Robert Lindneux, at the envious age of ninety-two years, appeared on the speakers' platform and participated in the dedication ceremonies held on October 27, 1963, for the opening of the new building addition to the Gilcrease Institute.[16] He was a close friend of Charles M. Russell, and Mr. Gilcrease derived much pleasure from listening to Mr. Lindneux relate his experiences with the famous Russell. Lindneux's *Shepherd of the Hills* was acquired by the Thomas Gilcrease Foundation as a gift from Northwestern University of Illinois. It had originally been published by John C. Shaffer, a newspaper publisher, who had given it to the university. Speaking of Mr. Gilcrease, Lindneux has said, "He was a very intelligent, studious, and noble gentleman; we had many, many enlightening conversations together." As Robert Ottaker Lindneux approaches his ninety-seventh birthday, he is still painting and has commented that he hopes he will be able to do so to the end of his life. The artist has been toasted from coast to coast and country to country; however, he has said, "Nothing can surpass the feeling gained from having watched America grow into manhood, witnessing transitions, and recording on canvas, in my own way, a small portion of that great pageant."

Olaf C. Seltzer

The late Dr. Philip Cole of Tarrytown, New York, commissioned Olaf C. Seltzer to paint a series of miniatures. In excess of one hundred paintings, five by six inches in size, were completed and executed with such perfection and care that they can be photographically enlarged three times their size and still be sharp and clear in detail. These miniatures represent such subjects as *Lewis and Clark Expedition, Chief Joseph's Surrender, Buffalo Bill's Duel with Yellow Hand, Yellowstone Kelley on the Trial in 1869, Portugee Phillip's Spectacular Christmas Ride, Road Agent's Hideout, Sacajawea, Trumpeter Martin Bringing the Last Message to Custer, The Stabbing of Crazy Horse, Fort McKenzie Massacre, The Duel Between Kit Carson and Captain Shuman, John Colter's Escape from the Blackfeet,* and other historical events depicting the West.

Thomas Gilcrease was captivated by Seltzer's work and treasured a letter he received from him. On October 23, 1949, Mr. Seltzer wrote and thanked Mr. Gilcrease for having sent him an art catalog and a Tulsa, Oklahoma newspaper referring to Joseph Henry Sharp's one-man show – "Mr. Sharp's outdoor scenes of everyday Indian life are very interesting and authentic records of the Plains Indians and their mode of living long ago, and also in part today."

Seltzer has been called the successor to Montana's cowboy artist, Charles M. Russell. James Taylor Forrest, former director of the Gilcrease Institute, has said: "Seltzer's work never reflected distortions. He was sincere about his labors and had a natural love for colors and creativity. He bridged the space between the passing of the frontier and the era as seen today by artists only in retrospect."

The visitor to the Gilcrease Institute will find a permanent exhibit of Seltzer's miniatures.[17] The intricate detail almost blinded this dedicated artist but his work has opened the eyes of the world to one of the best collections of its kind in existence.

William Robinson Leigh

Second only to the gift of the Gilcrease Foundation, the generous and unrestricted presentation of the William Robinson Leigh studio, library, and art collection is the most important addition to the Thomas Gilcrease Institute of American History and Art yet made.[18]

The circumstances which preceded the vesting of title to the properties in the City of Tulsa are storybook in origin and very human in fact. When Rida Johnson Young wrote the lyrics to "Ah! Sweet Mystery of Life," which was set to music by Victor Herbert, it is inconceivable that either the lyricist or the musician could have predicted that the years of the future would make the rendition of the song synonymous with nuptial bliss. It is equally as inconceivable that in 1944, when W. R. Leigh wrote a letter to Thomas Gilcrease in San Antonio, Texas, in future years the name of W. R. Leigh would represent a permanent gallery in the Thomas Gilcrease Institute of American History and Art.

Clarence Canning Allen,[19] southwestern and Tulsa artist, author and caricaturist, was acquainted with Lawrence Tenny Stevens. Allen was the staff artist for the *Tulsa Tribune*, one of Oklahoma's leading newspapers. Stevens was instructor in sculpture at the Philbrook Art Center in Tulsa. They often met to discuss their mutual interests, and during one of their conversations Allen told Stevens that he was going to publish a provocative book on modern art. Stevens, who was a personal friend of W. R. Leigh, remarked to Allen that it would be interesting to invite Leigh to write a chapter for the intended volume, especially since Leigh was a rather severe critic of modern art. Allen thought well of the suggestion and in due time dispatched a communication to Leigh, explained his project, and extended the invitation. Allen knew he would be taking a calculated risk but he wanted his book to be representative of the pro and con views of nationally known men in as many areas as possible and resolved to include Leigh's opinion.

Leigh consented, and promptly wrote and advised Allen that he would contribute the chapter. *Modern Art* was published in 1952 by the Rainbow Press, Tulsa, Oklahoma. Leigh's contribution to the book was entitled "The Evil Called Modern Art" and he wrote in part:

> If a person walks out on a stage to address an audience, it is presumed that the audience expects something worth hearing. Otherwise why did it assemble? If a picture has a right, figuratively, to say to the public, "Look at me," it should possess certain attributes. It ought not to disfigure the wall it hangs on; it ought to be intelligible. The distribution of the masses of form and the masses of color ought to balance. They ought to complement each other and harmonize. Distortions of form or color, the resort to the "abstract," arbitrary drawing (or non-drawing) do not constitute originality. Neither do they hide mendacity, greed, incapacity, or stupidity. Any vulgar fool can do a masterpiece of abstraction, since the more idiotic it is the better it is. The unparalleled imbecilities which our so-called art critics vomit are appalling and disastrous—indeed criminal.

On June 3, 1953, Leigh wrote to Allen that "the fact that the Modernists are against your book does not speak well for them, since they should be able to weather debate and criticism, particularly when so impartially presented. I hope your book meets its deserved success."

In the months that followed, Allen and his wife Loretta made several trips to New York City. They had heard of Ethel Leigh's Traphagen School of Fashion in Manhattan. Of passing interest is the slogan of the school, "No previous art training required but we help the trained to make their present knowledge an asset." Mrs. Allen was interested in designing and they arranged to meet Mrs. Leigh. This meeting launched a stimulating friendship. They exchanged letters on numerous subjects and on one of the trips Clarence Allen engaged in a discussion with Mrs. Leigh about the paintings of her husband.

On March 11, 1955, W. R. Leigh departed from the world of art. His death created a void in the life of his widow and, in due course, she deliberated the wisdom of making a proper disposition of her husband's studio and remaining collection. The Allens returned to New York, visited with Ethel Leigh and expressed their sympathy. She imparted her thoughts to Clarence Allen about the eventual location of her husband's collection and he suggested that the Thomas Gilcrease Institute of American History and Art would be an appropriate place for Leigh's studio, library, and collection. She told Allen that Huntington Hartford had endeavored to acquire parts of the collection for a substantial sum but she had refused to consider his offer. She wanted the studio to have a "home." Allen remarked that it would be wonderful if the collection could be acquired by the City of Tulsa and Thomas Gilcrease.

In a letter written to Allen on June 29, 1955, Ethel Traphagen Leigh enclosed an outline of her husband's career compiled upon request of *Who's Who in America* and she remarked, "You will note he lived to receive at least some of the honors so long overdue him." Allen felt that the time had arrived to make a contact between Leigh's widow and the officials of the Gilcrease Institute, so he wrote to Alfred E. Aaronson, then president, and told him the Leigh story. This was the first time a suggestion had been made by anyone of the possibility that Mrs. Leigh might consider negotiating with the Gilcrease Institute for the sale of the collection. Mr. Aaronson immediately informed Dean Krakel, director of the institute, about Allen's suggestion, and a series of letters followed in which Mr. Krakel expressed an interest on behalf of the institute and promised to meet with Mrs. Leigh in New York to discuss the subject.

On February 13, 1963, Ethel Traphagen Leigh wrote to

Mr. Allen again and advised him that she wanted to keep him informed about the activities between herself and Mr. Krakel and said: "After meeting Mr. Krakel I felt more interested than ever in seeing the Gilcrease Museum that owns so many of my husband's most important pictures, and I would like to see them acquire the contents of Leigh's studio which you and Mrs. Allen, having seen, will understand." She then continued, "As I wrote Dean Krakel, life is short and 'time is fleeting' so I am anxious to have kept in order the various collections of Leigh's studio 'properties' that are collected here at 200 West 57th Street, from his earliest childhood to the painting he finished half an hour before he 'passed on.' "

Mrs. Leigh, in her letter to Krakel to which she made reference (dated January 31, 1963), had told him that she was disappointed in not hearing about a proposed visit he was to have made in early January to negotiate with her about the studio possessions. She wrote: "My lease on Leigh's studio at 200 West 57th shortly expires, at which time it will be turned into business offices, and it will not be so easy to assemble again the props that were Leigh's lifetime possessions."

The eight years which lapsed between the death of W. R. Leigh and the anxiety by Mrs. Leigh in her letter to Dean Krakel of January 31, 1963, was apparently occasioned by a change of directors at the Gilcrease Institute, a multitude of problems which confronted the operation of a museum by the City of Tulsa, and the tremendous cataloging program set in motion following the acquisition of the Gilcrease Institute by the City of Tulsa. During all this time Clarence Allen never passed up an opportunity to mention the Leigh collection, hoping that eventually it would be acquired by the City of Tulsa, either by purchase or gift.

Ethel Traphagen Leigh died rather suddenly and, in due course, the news of her death reached the Gilcrease Institute. Being aware of the possibility that the Leigh studio, library, and remaining collection would be lost unless immediate action was taken, and further realizing the importance which

Clarence Allen had attached to the properties, Alfred E. Aaronson and Dean Krakel, then director of the institute, departed immediately for New York and communicated with John C. Traphagen, who was in charge of the Leigh estate and who, with his wife and son, had the authority to dispose of the personal effects of his late brother-in-law and sister. Relating this memorable visit, Mr. Aaronson has said: "The hospitality of John C. Traphagen was superb. He was not only an understanding gentleman but highly cultured and educated. He took us to the storage area and while making the inspection of the paintings I saw what appeared to me to be a painting by the late and renowned Charles M. Russell. I called Dean Krakel over and whispered to him, 'Dean, am I correct, is that a Russell?' Dean confirmed my opinion and we agreed that it was worth at least $25,000. We did not want any misunderstanding if the collection was presented to the City of Tulsa and we very frankly asked Mr. Traphagen if the Russell went with the collection. He replied, 'Why, yes, Mr. Aaronson, don't you and Mr. Krakel want it?' We were quick to say yes and did not mention it again."

The ramifications which went into the finalization of the gift were not too complicated but there were moments when Aaronson and Krakel actually prayed that all would go well.

The gift of the Leigh Studio collection was concluded during the year when Mr. Otha H. Gimes occupied the office of president of the institute. His diplomatic tenacity and inviting personality contributed greatly to the ultimate decision of the Traphagen family. When the details were completed, the gift was made in the names of the Traphagens in memory of W. R. and Ethel Leigh; the studio was dismantled and, together with all of the collection, shipped to Tulsa. There were five and one-half tons of art and Americana. Dean Krakel had suggested to Mr. Traphagen that if the gift was made to the City of Tulsa, as director of the institute he would see that the studio was reconstructed in exact form and made a permanent exhibit at the institute. This idea pleased Mr. Traphagen and his family. It was carried out to the letter and with the assistance of Mr. Paul Rossi and others of the institute it is today one of the most unique exhibits of its kind in the world. Each article was carefully packed and marked. Photographs were made so that the interior of the studio reproduction would be flawless. Even the artist's smock hangs over the edge of the easel in the exact location where he placed it the last time he worked in the studio. On the easel was his last painting, the famous *Sunset*, completed only thirty minutes before he died.

Neither Ethel Leigh nor the Traphagens were aware that artist Leigh, during his lifetime, had corresponded with Thomas Gilcrease. Ethel Leigh was the second wife of W. R. Leigh and he had never mentioned his friendship with Tom Gilcrease. The significant letter which might have brought about the gift at an earlier date or at least have assisted in the eventual decision reads:

> Dear Mr. Gilcrease:
>
> Thank you heartily for your letter of appreciation of March 21st concerning my book, "Frontiers of Enchantment." Allow me to ask, Have you ever been to the country I described in that book? If you have not, then your estimate is extraordinary, since it exactly parallels those that I received from Englishmen resident in those parts. Hence, it is doubly gratifying.
>
> It is barely possible that I may have occasion to visit Tulsa sometime during this Summer or Fall, in which case I shall be delighted to visit the Thomas Gilcrease Foundation. It will be a very great pleasure to do so.
>
> I am glad you like my portrayal of Indians and our West, for that has been my life work, and I hold that nowhere else in the world are there to be found any finer – if as fine – pictorial possibilities as exist in our Southwest.
>
> Should you chance to be in New York at any time, I

would be most happy to have a call from you at my studio, 200 West 57th Street.

Thanking you again, I remain

Very sincerely yours,

/s/ W. R. Leigh.

It is to be noted that in the first paragraph Leigh expresses surprise and pleasure at the ability of Thomas Gilcrease to describe the country mentioned in Leigh's book. He was gratified that Tom Gilcrease liked his portrayal of the Indian and the West. Here again the eventual permanent exhibit as it now exists seems to have been guided by destiny in all of its spiritual and factual sense. The studio in which Leigh had re-created so much of the life of the Indian and the West found a resting place in the museum which Gilcrease had founded as a repository for Indian culture. Neither man lived to see this romantic culmination of the marriage between artist and collector.

The first public showing of the re-created studio was held on November 7, 1964. In addition to the actual studio, other Leigh works were placed on display, ranging from pencil sketches made when he was six years old, to pen-and-ink drawings made in Africa. Of special importance are his portrayals of the Navajo ponies and burros. It is impossible to look upon one of his burro paintings without having the sensation that the animal is breathing. There is something about a Leigh burro that depicts sadness and contentment.

A list of Leigh's works, his accomplishments, and awards would fill a sizeable brochure, but those who were privileged to know him personally will ever be mindful of his forthright manner of expression, his fearless exemplification of his convictions, and the visions which he turned into reality for the preservation of history.

The Thomas Gilcrease Institute of American History and Art has Leigh's *Close Call*, painted in 1941, a painting of a bear hunt; and *Up Where the Big Wind Blows*, a portrait painted in 1918. There are also eleven other paintings, all acquired by Thomas Gilcrease before he gave his collection to the City of Tulsa.

Paul Manship

When Thomas Gilcrease first viewed the *Prometheus Fountain* in Rockefeller Plaza in New York, he was so impressed that he became determined to meet the sculptor.[20] The critics had credited Paul Manship with having brought forward a technique in which beauty embraced grace of form and purity of lines. Mr. Gilcrease met Paul Manship in 1957. They shared a common interest because Manship wanted to know more about the Indians. This meeting resulted in the purchase by Mr. Gilcrease of *Indian Hunter and His Dog*. On March 28, 1957, Mr. Gilcrease received a letter from Manship in which the sculptor said: "It was nice to see you here in New York. I only regret that our meeting was so limited, but hope that when you come again you will let me have the pleasure of a visit to my studio. Or — if you are in the neighborhood of Gloucester, Mass. — in the summertime, to see you there."

Tom Gilcrease never made the trip to Gloucester but the *Indian Hunter and His Dog* found its way to the hill in Osage County where it is now a part of the Gilcrease collection.

Thomas L. Lewis

Christmas was always a very special day for Thomas Gilcrease. Each year he would select one of the paintings from the Gilcrease Foundation and use it for his holiday greeting cards. His selections ranged from *Fiesta at Cuerna-*

vaca by Thomas Moran to a painting by Laszlo Neogrady which he personally owned and which he used in 1961 as a New Year's greeting. If he was away from home on the day of the nativity he would seek out a western scene, such as *Sundown in the Great West Country*. When the season was over he would spread all the Christmas cards he had received on the top of his large living room table and read them as meticulously as he would a novel. A favorite photograph reveals him in the act of reviewing his cards. He is wearing a red shirt, reading a red-colored card, and a large vase containing brilliant scarlet poinsettias centers the table in all its Christmas festivity.

In 1955 Mr. Gilcrease chose the inspiring painting *Spirit of the Canyon* by Thomas L. Lewis as his Christmas card. He had acquired the painting from Lewis in October of the same year for the sum of $2,500 and was granted permission for the use of the painting on the card. He wrote Lewis on December 21, 1955 and said: "I just mailed out over 1,000 Christmas cards portraying your painting 'Spirit of the Canyon.' This, no doubt, will cause a lot of interest in your painting and you may be obliged to work harder and harder in order to supply the demand. Sorry if it disturbs you. Hoping to visit with you and enjoy some of Mrs. Lewis' A-1 coffee, good enough for a Frenchman."

Tom Gilcrease was introduced to Tom Lewis by their mutual friend Woodrow Crumbo at the institute in Tulsa.[21] They were compatible because of the intense interest Lewis had in western art, and Tom had asked Lewis to paint five places which he felt were worthy of the talents of his newly acquired friend. They were *Devil's Tower,* the national monument in the northwestern part of Wyoming; *Painted Desert*; *Navajo Mountains*; *Black Mesa,* near Estanola, New Mexico; and *Spirit of the Canyon*. Of the five scenes, Lewis completed *Painted Desert* and *Spirit of the Canyon*. Lewis likes to recall that at one time Gilcrease had his painting of the canyon and the famous painting on the same subject by Thomas Moran in the same studio facing each other. Lewis says he was truly flattered and considered the arrangement an unusual compliment to him.

During their association as friends, Lewis spent considerable time with Tom at his Wyoming retreat on the Hoback River. He became so much at home that he made extended visits to the beautiful Wyoming country. He painted Tom's favorite fishing place, Blue Hole on the Hoback, and in 1956 sold it to Tom, who wrote Lewis on October 18, 1956 and asked him to bring the painting with him when he visited Tulsa on November 8, together with four other paintings Gilcrease had purchased from him, including his famous *Shiprock*. The fishing scene remains a part of the personal collection and is in the possession of the Thomas Gilcrease Foundation. In 1957 he presented a reproduction of aspen trunks to Mr. Gilcrease with his compliments.

June 24, 1907, was the date and Bay City, Texas, was the place of the birth of Thomas L. Lewis. His childhood was that of any normal boy except that his grade school teachers recognized that he possessed a talent for painting and encouraged him to foster such a career. As his "eye for color and design" came to maturity he yearned to place the mysteries of the swampland on canvas, the South-beech and cypress trees held a certain fascination for him and from it all he found that he could apply deep warm tones and bring out the mosslike apparition which nature provided. He was adept at capturing the charms of the Southern people and reproducing the cotton fields, river-boats, and shanty life existence which they represented. He actually lived in their villages and from this experience became self-indoctrinated with their customs and mores. The techniques and originality of other painters provided him with practical knowledge and he sought them out to learn and earn.

The critics for a time wanted to call him the mixed-up artist when they were exposed to his ability to mix all colors together and create an effect which has been described by his friend, Woody Crumbo, as a warm overlaying tone as of late evening. Of him, Woody has said:

> He started painting pictures in grey tones, using color seen only on very grey days. He worked on this idea for some years and produced some very startling effects, but they were not exactly what he was after.

With the continuing of experiments, he arrived at the idea of using all warm tones such as one sees on a clear sunlit day at a distance. The idea brought about a more satisfying effect, and he found that people in general were much surprised and pleased with his new found way of expression. Paintings created in the warm sepia tones sold rapidly and much of his time was divided between painting in true color and sepias.

The Taos artists recognized Lewis as a new talent and he worked with many of them in the Sangre de Christo Range near Taos. He now owns the "Taos Art Gallery" and does his best to keep up with the commissions which come to him.

On January 9, 1956, Tom Gilcrease wrote to Lewis and told him that the letters were many praising the Christmas card portraying his *Spirit of the Canyon.* He mailed Lewis twenty-five of the reproductions.

The association of Lewis and Gilcrease was not long lived but it will be long lasting in the memory of those who view the art of Lewis and remember that it was recognized by Thomas Gilcrease for its lasting qualities long before time so branded it.

Alexandre Hogue

When recalling his tenure as director of the institute, Mr. Wiesendanger beams with pride and satisfaction realized from having introduced his friend, Alexandre Hogue, to Mr. Gilcrease.

Alexandre Hogue was born in 1898, the only son among five daughters, of the Reverend C. L. Hogue, a Presbyterian minister. His mother, an artist in her own right, recognized her son's talents and encouraged him to study. His early instruction was with Miss Elizabeth Hillyer of the Teachers College at Denton, Texas. His work has earned for him the title of "The Painter of American Natural Resources." It has been said of Hogue that his paintings speak louder than countless pages of humanistic novels and have been a principal factor in soil conservation. He could prove with the brush what scholars had failed to do with the pen. His studies led him to the Taos colony and then he became a professor of art. He became head of the Art Department of Hockaday Junior College, a post he held from 1936 to 1942. In 1945 he became director of art at the University of Tulsa.

On February 5, 1959, the Thomas Gilcrease Institute of American History and Art held a one-man show of his works and the exhibit remained during the entire month. At this event he lectured on the captivating subjects of "I Remember When" and "Experiences That Shaped the Artist."

As the friendship of Professor Hogue and Mr. Gilcrease ripened, they exchanged comments about art. The following comment from Professor Hogue is somewhat provocative.[22]

> He loved to bait me about "this crazy art" and I can truthfully say that he did not rule out all modern art. I was able to show him the similarity between the Indian paintings, which are very abstract, and the work of an artist like Raymond Jonson. I recall that in company with Woody Crumbo, Mr. Gilcrease made a trip to Albuquerque to visit Jonson's studio and liked what he saw so much that he acquired practically everything on exhibit. It is a tragedy for the Gilcrease Institute that one of the Directors persuaded Mr. Gilcrease to part with Jonson's works by giving them to colleges in the southwest area. One of them is currently owned by the University of Tulsa.

In later years when there was a possibility of the Gilcrease collection being lost to the City of Tulsa, Professor Hogue invited Mr. Gilcrease to speak to the Art Students League at the University of Tulsa. The invitation was extended in support of the bond issue which was then under consideration. This was perhaps the only time that Mr.

Gilcrease personally spoke in public about the necessity of keeping the collection in Tulsa. The students conducted an open forum question period for nearly two hours following the principal address, and subsequently Mr. Gilcrease confided to Professor Hogue that the experiment had been a turning point in his understanding of the vital workings of the bond issue and what it could mean to the destiny of the collection.

Professor Hogue is a student of the internationally known Frank Reaugh, famous for his paintings of bulls and Longhorn cattle. The institute now owns six of Reaugh's paintings including *The Herd* and *The Intruder*. Strangely enough, it was *The Intruder* which provided the story as it appears in the chapter on "Amigos."

The Stone Walls Endure

Each year that passes, the traffic count at the Thomas Gilcrease Institute of American History and Art increases. The ever growing flow of young people who make their way from gallery to gallery is a source of gratification to the officers and staff who constantly strive to make the exhibits attractive and achieve a greater educational interest in the entire collection.

Since the founding of the institute as a municipally owned project by reason of the beneficence of Thomas Gilcrease, it has been conservatively estimated that every item behind the stone walls has enhanced in value and that the appraisal now exceeds fifty million dollars.

The building of a definitive catalog of the collection cannot be defined in point of time. The anthropological and archaeological articles number more than 350,000. The varied items include pottery, basketry, fabrics, tools, weapons, clothing and ceremonial paraphernalia. In recent years the research made has brought to light over 70,000 specimens of primary and secondary source materials relating to history, exploration, and settlement in this hemisphere.

The stone walls will stand with the ages, and what is to be found behind them will nurture those who are hungry for knowledge.

Epilogue

Chapter 1

The Fleeting Arrow

Part I

"Let not my departure in the flesh trouble you, my sons, and doubt not that I shall serve you better dead than alive!" These words are attributed to Saint Dominic. They could have been the words of Thomas Gilcrease. Whether his children would have accepted such terminal advice is speculative to say the least. There will always be the quest for inner peace. If their father knew happiness and resolved his emotional conflicts which in later years, as well as in his early years, were fraught with economic insecurities, domestic memories, and the dilemma of coping with sudden fame, then perhaps Saint Dominic unlocked the vault to let the sun warm the cold recesses of mystery. There can then be what Joshua Loth Liebman heard from a wise elder in whom he confided when he made up his inventory of the "goods" of life, namely, the gift that God reserves for His special protégés — peace of mind.

G. Mallet Prevost had been in Tulsa for only a few hours when he was invited to visit the Gilcrease Institute of American History and Art.[1] He had heard about the incomparable collection of Indian artifacts, paintings, and rare documents. He had visited the Smithsonian frequently and was a noted collector of old firearms. He walked through the exhibit rooms and became intoxicated with all that met his eager eyes. As he turned the corner to enter the office of the director, Dean Krakel, he saw a man he will never forget. There was something familiar about him, and there should have been because he had, only moments before, walked away from viewing the famous painting of Thomas Gilcrease by the celebrated artist, Charles Banks Wilson. His friend with whom he had made the visit introduced him, "Mr. Gilcrease, this is our Washington liaison attorney. He is a member of the patent bar and also assists us with copyright protection matters." Tom extended his hand. There was a determined smile on his lips. He did not appear as vigorous as usual. After a second or two he spoke and his words were almost prognostic in their simplicity. "Glad to know you, Mr. Prevost. That is a French name, is it not?"

"Yes, sir," replied the attorney.

And then Mr. Gilcrease let go of the arrow which pierced the quiet of the room. "You say you are a patent lawyer. Now, what I want to know is this. Can you get me a patent?"

Prevost was somewhat abashed. He turned to his friend, who was a colleague, and then looked at Mr. Gilcrease and said, "On what?"

"A tired old Indian," responded the institute's founder.

On May 8, 1962, Mr. Prevost airmailed a letter to his colleague in Tulsa, in which he enclosed a news clipping with headlines appearing in bold type. "Thomas Gilcrease, Oilman, Dies; Gave Millions in Art to Tulsa." Mr. Prevost, like thousands of Americans and citizens from almost every country in the world, was struck by the news, but he knew it was too late, and all he could do was close the file and mark it "Patent Pending, applicant deceased."

The "tired old Indian" had called to Chief (his trusted employee and friend, Cephas Stout) and asked him to sit in his automobile with him.[2] This was on Friday. They sat facing the Osage Hills just to the west of the museum building. "It was just like the Old Man knew this would be the last time he looked at the beauty of those hills," said Cephas.

Mrs. Eudotia Teenor had observed her twenty-fifth year as private secretary to Thomas Gilcrease.[3] It had been a wonderful week for her – until she contracted a virus infection which made it necessary for her to remain in bed for several days. Her residence is located several hundred yards from the house on the hill and faces south, from where she can look out upon the vast open country to the west and to the north, take in the vista of the institute building and the stone house next door where Mr. Gilcrease's mother had died and which has been converted into the office of the Gilcrease Foundation.

It was May 5, 1962. She had recovered from her illness; she went about the preparation of her breakfast, fed her dog, and decided that it was time to walk over to the house on the hill. Mr. Gilcrease had not been in the best of health and she was determined to be as cheerful as possible in his presence and, anyway, it was good to be out of bed and to have recovered from her bout with "that awful bug." Mr. Gilcrease, as usual, was happy to see her and to know that she had recuperated. She told him she had much to do even though it was Saturday, but he insisted that she remain and visit with him. They talked of various things, and in his typical manner he commented about the season and how the flowers were already in bloom. She went to the window and looked out. He walked to where she was standing and pointed to some of his favorite trees and discussed their beauty at that time of the year. He watched the birds gather at the feeders, listened to their songs, and for a moment she thought she detected a few tears in his eyes.

It was lunch time and he invited her to partake of the meal with him. The television set was on; a baseball game was in progress and, since it was his favorite sport, he watched. He did not care for most of the programs — his tastes ran to news and sports. Before they were aware of the hour, it was nearly three o'clock in the afternoon and the announcer said that the Kentucky Derby was about to be run. Together they viewed the race and when it was over she returned to her home.

The intuition of woman, no doubt prompted by apprehension of her observation of her long-time employer, caused her to return to the house on the hill at approximately five o'clock in the afternoon. As she approached the back door she indulged her usual signal to Mr. Gilcrease — and whistled her "bob-white" call to apprise him of her return. His failure to come to the door created immediate concern and she entered the house. A quick glance into the breakfast room — he was not there; then the south living room — nothing. Excitement overtook her and she ran to the door, heard a commotion in the bedroom, and went in. Mr. Gilcrease was trying to walk but was having difficulty remaining on his feet. She quickly asked him what was wrong. "My feet, my feet, they are heavy and I cannot lift them." The faithful Teenor assisted him in reaching the bedside where he fell limp; she removed his shoes and turned him lengthwise as far as her strength would permit.

Dr. Earl I. Mulmed of Tulsa was summoned. He arrived as quickly as the traffic would permit him to cross the heart of Tulsa to reach the heart of one of his favorite patients. During the dragging minutes, Mrs. Teenor exerted every effort to make Mr. Gilcrease as comfortable as possible. She found that she could not lift him alone and she called to Cephas Stout, who, joined by Dave Wilson, another employee, offered what assistance they could give. When the ambulance arrived, which had been called during all the excitement, Mrs. Teenor rode in the ambulance and asked the driver to avoid the use of the siren, knowing how her boss disliked the noise of such things; however, en route, a second severe attack occurred and the ambulance driver had to press for speed and take every precaution to avoid an accident.

Immediate notification was given to the children of Mr. Gilcrease, and his sons, Thomas, Jr. and Barton, were able to be at his bedside before he expired, having flown by private plane to connect with the Braniff Airlines in Dallas for a direct flight to Tulsa. Gena and Grace, their respective wives, arrived by automobile early the following day.

Mrs. Teenor did not learn until after it was all over that when Chief reached the room in answer to her call Mr. Gilcrease looked up and said to his trusted friend, "Thank you."

There will ever be a voice saying to the lady who whistled the bobwhite call: "My feet, my feet, they are heavy and I cannot lift them." These were his last distinguishable words to her and he had said: "Thank you." He had told them farewell. Those tireless feet would not have to leave any more tracks — they were already made in the hearts of those who served him — loved him — and were with him to the end.

Thomas Gilcrease, Jr., brother Barton, and their sister Des Cygne Denney gathered in the old stone house the day after their father died and discussed the burial arrangements.[4] Thomas Gilcrease was not a member of any congregation and did not profess to be a church-going man. He had believed with all the faith of which man is capable that one did not have to attend church to be a good Christian. This was his credo in life and he knew his children would respect his wishes. All he ever wanted was a decent and Christian-like burial suitable to his circumstances and condition in life; no fanfare and no professional people to participate in the services. He wanted the expenses to be modest in amount.

On May 9, 1962, at three-thirty in the afternoon, the Reverend Guy C. Tetirick, a retired Tulsa Methodist minister and former president of the Tulsa Ministerial Alliance, officiated at an outdoor service held on the museum grounds, sometimes referred to as the bower of nature where the master had planted roses, azaleas, chrysanthemums, soulangeanas, magnolias floribunda, American hollies, dogwoods, and fruit trees of select varieties — the garden spot where the new shrubbery welcomed the old. Approximately five hundred persons composed of friends, business associates, relatives, representatives of the City of Tulsa, Indians from numerous tribes, and state officials gathered on the hill to extend their silent homage to Thomas Gilcrease. A large tent had been pitched just east of the stone house and those who were unable to find chairs were seated in a semicircle on the lawn or stood on the long porch, which extended from the north side of the house across the front to the south side.

In the stillness which settled over the hill Tom Gilcrease must have heard the voice of his friend, Dr. Robert Lee Humber, whisper to him: "Do you recall our leisurely walks through your gardens while I listened to you tell me about the variety of flowers and trees which are even now all about us? Do you recall, and I am certain that you do, the time you discussed with me your desire to landscape the ravine and to create a lake nearby — our walks in the early morning when the dew still glistened on the leaves or in the cool of the evening, when the prismatic beauty of sunset had just painted both sky and hills with a brilliant iridescent glow — or when we wandered among the flowering shrubs, and you would stop, scan the sky, discern a flock of birds winging their way southward to warmer climates and how, without a moment's hesitation, you could identify the species even though they were flying through clouds remote from your observing eye?"

The sons and daughter of the deceased were with their respective families and occupied the first rows under the tent. Belle Harlow Gilcrease attended the service, sitting with her sons. Her stoicism belied her genuine feelings, for she remembered her life on the hill with Tom and her devotion for him had remained positive through the years. Tom, Jr., Barton, and Des Cygne looked often at each other as if to reassert their mutual affection. Perhaps Des

Cygne would have found comfort in having her mother by her side but she did not attend the service.

Eudotia Teenor, Cephas Stout, and their respective families occupied the rows immediately back of the family section. The mockingbirds were evident as they flew from tree to tree and joined the soft and appropriate music which came from the ensemble on the porch. It was as if the whole world had suddenly stopped on its axis, for there would be many changes on the morrow and then life would go on.

The service was simple and included a eulogy by the author who said, in part:[5]

> On this 9th day of May, 1962, we gather under a May sky in our glorious Oklahoma, where the skyline of Tulsa beckons to us in one direction and where by the mere turn of our heads we can see the Blackdog Township in Osage County close to the common boundary of the lands of the Creeks, Cherokees, and Osages. Here we pause to extend our thoughts to the memory of a man who practiced moral soundness, devotion to all the wholesome attributes of man's pursuits, and whose body encompassed a heart that was divided only by the many sparkling facets of love which made up his total personality. . . . He was a man whose nature would not permit him to destroy nature. And even the birds and other fowls of the air recognized him daily as he constantly gave attention to the birdbaths and the bird feeders which he erected so they could be viewed from his window. When the snow was on the ground there was food for his feathered friends who made their homes near him; . . . perhaps the best remembered portion of his philosophy — and he had a philosophy which consistently gave him courage to press forward — he summed up by saying "A man must make his tracks."

He then concluded with his poem which has been reproduced in various publications since it was authored:[6]

> Man must make his tracks
> As he searches out the years,

To learn the truth of living
    And become immune to fears.

He must grow with all the suns,
    And by moonlight learn the glory,
As they plot the course he travels
    And unfold his earthly story.

If genius be his destiny
    He must challenge and create,
Inspiring those about him
    With knowledge so innate.

And when the rivers overflow
    And bring him back to shore,
The grains of sand will sparkle
    And keep him evermore.

Part II

The wishes of Thomas Gilcrease for a simple funeral service without fanfare were observed, if the pageant of the Delight Makers can be accepted as ancient ritual rather than a colorful ceremony.

Chief Wolf Robe Hunt, full blood Pueblo, was a good friend of Indian Tom.[7] "When I die I want you to conduct the traditional ritual at my funeral service," was the request of Tom Gilcrease to Wolf Robe Hunt. Such a request meant that a pledge had been made, and so it was that the Indian friends of Tom had gathered on the hill near the great stone house.

Chief Wolf Robe Hunt came to Oklahoma from the Acoma Indian Reservation in New Mexico, the home of the Pueblo tribe. His Pueblo name is *Ke-Wa-Tse-She*, meaning "Growing Plant." It was the custom of his tribe for young men to hunt the mountain lion, the bear, the wolf, and the eagle. He had killed a wolf and had taken the hide home; he used it for a robe and his father called him Wolf Robe. He was designated chief by his father, who was known as "Dawn Boy" and was a member of the Delight Makers. The honor is handed down from father to son. Those who gathered to witness the rites and pause in tribute to the man who lived on the hill sat on the ground on the front lawn while the immediate family and close friends assembled under a tent which had been pitched to ward off the hot sun. When the biblical passages had been read and the eulogy concluded, the Delight Makers (Waldo Emerson "Dode" McIntosh, chief of the Creek Nation; Shelly Taylor, Cherokee; Kenneth Tiger, Creek; Jeff Whisenhunt, Cherokee; Albert Johnson, Cherokee; and Bessie Sorethumb, Creek) formed a circle. As the son of Dawn Boy of Acoma, Wolf Robe then gave the call of the Delight Makers and his voice rose in a high pitch as his hand opened and closed over his mouth to create the vibratory effect of what is sometimes referred to as the war cry. He then sang the sacred song and by so doing made his gestures sacred so the Indian gods would watch and listen. This was followed by a short prayer in the Pueblo tongue, at the conclusion of which the participants sprinkled the corn meal, to provide food for the departed, as they danced around their own circle. Wolf Robe's supplication told of the passing of an Indian with a request that his soul be protected as it went back to *She-Pa-Po* or the "Great Spirit" from whence the mortal had come. Wolf Robe then reached for an arrow and placed it in his bow. Symbolically, he shot the arrow into the sky to the north, the south, and the east. He then aimed the arrow high into the sky and shot it into the west where it disappeared. As the arrow sped on its way it became a protective weapon to seal the spirit against evil on the way to She-Pa-Po, or the happy hunting ground.

The spell was almost broken when a young boy retrieved the arrow and offered to return it to Wolf Robe who declined it, saying: "I cannot accept it, my son, because to do so would violate the ritual of the Delight Makers.

Go, go and keep it for yourself or give it to Wicarpi Wakatuya's museum." The boy and the arrow disappeared. Who he was or what he did with the arrow will probably never be known.

The arrow should have been shot into the north sky but Wolf Robe wanted its flight to be in the direction of the Indian lands, where the nations of the Creek, Cherokee, and Osage converged in the beauty of the day.

Those who witnessed the ritual will always recall the full ceremonial dress of the Indians; and when the service had ended, hundreds of Indian Tom's friends walked down the hill from the big stone house. The casket bearing the mortal remains was removed to the Rose Hill Mausoleum in Tulsa, there to await the building of a permanent resting place.[8]

The birds flew into the trees to hide their tears. Darkness fell upon the hill. The lights went out in the great stone house. Wicarpi Wakatuya had reached the She-Pa-Po.[9]

Chapter 2

At Rest in the Rolling Hills

Part III

They walked carefully. Their heads were bare. Firmly, but surely, each step brought them closer to the sarcophagus where they would entomb the mortal remains of their friend Tom. They should be remembered as the bearers, for one day students of history will seek their identification — Alfred Aaronson, William S. Bailey, Jr., George Bowen, Otha Grimes, Morton R. Harrison, and David Randolph Milsten. With hearts as heavy as the bronze casket they carried, step by step they walked from the top of the hill to the mid-lower level, around the semicircle which leads to the entrance of the mausoleum. A sextet of Tulsans who, from the beginning, had supported the movement to make the institute a part of their great city; dedicated men whose vision had inspired hundreds of others to participate in the call to art and but for whose persistence and faith there would not have been a greenish blue limestone memorial to the memory of the founder who was to rest forever when their final act of love was accomplished.

On August 21, 1962, there had been a meeting of the executive committee of the institute with the mayor of the city of Tulsa and members of the Gilcrease family and of the Gilcrease Foundation. Morton R. Harrison vice-president of the institute, and member of the Will Rogers Memorial, had listened carefully to those who spoke before him and he said: "It's a privilege to me to have known these children. I so state to you three children, as I did to the three children of Will Rogers, you couldn't find a better resting place for your father than the place on the side of the hill he loved so much." This remark prompted Mayor James A. Maxwell to contribute these words: "The time will come when you children will make a decision on a location of final resting place for your father. As a spokesman for the people of the city of Tulsa, I hope you will keep the museum grounds in mind. It would be a fitting place."

Mr. L. Karlton Mosteller, long-time friend of the family and one of their attorneys, remarked: "Someday the 'things' on the hill would be together in time." His remarks were silently interpreted to mean that a location of a mausoleum on the grounds where Tom had lived would be the desire of Tom's family. All eyes were toward Tom's daughter, Des Cygne, and his sons, Thomas, Jr. and Barton. It was obvious that they approved, and the tears which moistened their cheeks gave evidence of the appreciation they felt in their hearts for what the citizens of Tulsa had done and were willing to do.

Many months and meetings later a report was made by Morton R. Harrison to the executive committee and board of directors. Otha H. Grimes had succeeded E. Fred Johnson as president; Gordon T. Hicks was present representing the Tulsa Park Board. Mr. Harrison's report reflected that a decision had been reached. He had walked over every inch of the hill and presented the plans to Mrs. Eudotia Teenor, the faithful and efficient secretary of the foundation and Tom's personal secretary in his lifetime. The initial sketch was displayed. The east, or top, would face the city of Tulsa and the west, the institute. The structure would be thirty-eight feet across and rise fourteen feet from the slope of the hill. There would be a crypt for the remains of Thomas Gilcrease, one for his mother, and another for his father. It was to be built of reinforced concrete and faced with limestone to be selected by the members of the family. The architect was to be Bob West. A resolution prepared by David Randolph Milsten was then introduced and adopted. The memorial would be built.

A light rose pink Tennessee marble was selected for the interior with a black Verde antique marble strip around the entrance, and the floor and patio to be of Virginia greenstone. The epitaph was provided by Thomas, Jr., who found appropriate lines among the papers of his father.

The Hanniford Construction Company of Tulsa was awarded the contract on August 9, 1963, in the amount of $44,000.

In the early days of 1964, Mrs. Teenor and Mr. Harrison visited the family cemetery northwest of Mounds, Oklahoma and located the grave markers of Tom's parents.[10] The gravesite was marked by a life-size replica of a tree. The monument had been made from a granite block and shipped to Oklahoma from Georgia. The tree was so located that its branches were supposed to designate the respective graves. This unusual monument would have been the subject of a prize-winning photograph. After the death of Mr. Gilcrease and the decision to relocate the remains of his parents to the mausoleum, the granite tree was removed from the little cemetery where Tom had placed it. It now stands in the front yard of the stone house where Elizabeth Vowell Gilcrease lived until her death. The workmanship on the granite tree is so lifelike in appearance that a close inspection is necessary to recognize that it is not one of nature's offsprings. In due course, arrangements were made to disinter the remains of William Lee Gilcrease and Elizabeth Vowell Gilcrease so that they could be interred in the mausoleum. They now rest forever in the same crypt with their son, Tom.

If this were a novel instead of a biography, the writer of fiction might eliminate from his manuscript several characters from his story before writing "finis" to his efforts. The biographer is confronted with the same problem, but for natural reasons. Therefore, it is ironical that it must be recorded that four principals in the life of Thomas Gilcrease followed him in death: Norma Des Cygne Bruce; L. Karlton Mosteller; Jewel Willard, sister of Tom, who deceased on March 18, 1967 in Muscatine, Iowa and was buried in Winfield, Kansas, having died at the age of fifty-four; and Thomas Gilcrease, Jr., who died on March 16, 1967 in Nacogdoches, Texas, following a heart seizure. He was survived by his widow, Grace; a son, Gene; his mother, Belle Gilcrease; his brother, Barton; and his sister, Des Cygne Denney.* He had moved from San Antonio and acquired a large ranch in Nacogdoches where he was determined to live out his days. At the time of his demise, he was an active member of the Gilcrease Foundation and keenly interested in the Thomas Gilcrease Institute of American History and Art. He was buried in the Nacogdoches cemetery, with the author of this biography officiating and delivering the eulogy.

From somewhere on the Hoback River in Wyoming, during September of 1956, Thomas Gilcrease wrote the epilogue for his biography.[11] He addressed it: "To: The

---

* Des Cygne (Mrs. Corwin D. Denney) was killed in an automobile accident on March 30, 1968, in San Antonio, Texas. She was riding alone at the time of the accident when her car apparently missed an exit on the San Antonio expressway. She was a member of the Gilcrease Foundation and of the board of directors of the Thomas Gilcrease Institute of American History and Art at the time of her demise. She was a gracious and intelligent person who was extremely appreciative of what the City of Tulsa and the Gilcrease Institute were doing to preserve the image of the museum her father founded and gave to the City of Tulsa.

Gilcrease Tribe." It is reproduced in the exact language, for no greater beauty or choice of words could better journey into the soul of this Creek Indian whose devotion for his beloved America was profound and real.

> Turning Leek Curve the towering Tetons, to my surprise, growled almost in my face. These great mountains seem furious – a more menacing appearance I've never witnessed upon the profile of this wonderful mountain range – Nothing less than cold, grey, wolfish snarl, swirled about their bosom as pent up anger of one hundred million years – I winced, my blood chilled as long lost souls on Arctic seas. Why, O stately mountains, such venom portray and cast over vale and brook, so peaceful, beautiful and enchanting. This uncontrolled anger shall descend upon summer's fleeting days, autumn shall blush with a thousand glorious colors, warmth of returning sun shall, for a spell, dissipate this icy thrust. Angry winds, may again, before winter blast, uproot age old firs, break and crush golden, cottonwood at Ben Goe's bridge. Sunset dreamy in pastels rare, moody in purple and cobalt blue, thrilling in pink and rose, charming in silver and gold, once again linger in western skies. Mountain maple and prim rose aflame. Northern lights of rainbow hues play among the stars. On hilltop and over valley a silvery moon glows with softness of velvety blue. In distant stillness of frosty night, coyote from hillside cold, calls his kind. From mountain side and canyon deep, bull elk bugles to his mate, buck deer proud, alert and ready to vie for his choice. In valleys along winding brook, moose browse among red willows. Bears feasting on mountain ash berries readying for winter's hole up. Chipmunks scurry here and there. Pine squirrels chatter, cut and store cones for winter's food. Blue Jays call from fir and balsom trees. Snow birds, chickadees and finches grouping for long southern flights. Nutcrackers feeding on pinon nuts. Blue and ruffed grouse bunching for winter protection. Geese and ducks feed and rest on lake and marsh land ready for autumn's migration to southern climes. Snowy owls hoot from cedar snags on cliffs high at evening time. Cutthroat trout leap in pools deep and blue up and

down the silvery Hoback River. Frost came and blushed the aspens, breezes fresh wafted away their golden garments, deserted they stand in nude and beauty of venus. Indian paint brushes gone with summer's flight and wild daisies droop with autumn's tang. Equinox blustry and howling, rolls southward. Day shortens and goes with sunset. Night chills and lingers. Candles flicker. Work and play rest, and are tenderly enfolded by dream world. Tomorrow may come with blossom full, fresh and fragrant or with blossom faded and falling — Tomorrow will tell, yes, tomorrow will tell.

Thomas Gilcrease

Tomorrow will tell, "Wicarpi Wakatuya"; you are the "High Star."

Day after day visitors walk down the hill, and through the iron gates of the memorial can be seen the inscriptions:

Thomas Gilcrease, 1890-1962

William Lee Gilcrease, 1868-1913

Elizabeth Vowell Gilcrease 1873-1935

On the huge stone at the upper level they read these words:

AT THE FEET OF THE ROLLING OSAGE HILLS
WILL I WORK AND THINK UNTIL MY TROUBLED
AND WORN BODY SHALL BE CALLED.

Bibliographic Notes

BOOK 1

Prologue

1 *History and Legends of the Creek Indians of Oklahoma.*
2 Robert Louis Stevenson, apothegm.
3 *A History of Oklahoma* (San Francisco: Doub & Company, 1908), p. 3.
4 *Ibid.*, p. 107.
5 *History and Legends of the Creek Indians of Oklahoma*, p. 2.
6 *Ibid.*
7 *A History of Oklahoma* (San Francisco: Doub & Company, 1908), p. 33, note.
8 *Ibid.*, p. 190.
9 *Ibid.*, p. 33.
10 *Ibid.*, p. 199; C. L. Thomas, *Five Civilized Tribes and Osage Nation, Annotated Acts of Congress* (Columbia, Missouri: E. W. Stephens Publishing Co., 1913); Stanley Vestal, "The First Families of Oklahoma Come From Many Tribes," *American Indian Magazine*, Vol. 1, No. 4, p. 10, Jan. 1927.
11 Creek Roll. Card No. 456. Field No. 458. Final Roll of Creek Citizens. Department of the Interior. Commission to the Five Civilized Tribes.

Chapter 1

1 Letter from Thomas Gilcrease (hereafter referred to as "T. G.") to Lester Whipple, signed "Indian Tom," 1940, in possession of Thomas Gilcrease Foundation (hereafter referred to as "Foundation").
2 Letters of E. E. Dees and Charlie Howell, Robeline, Louisiana.
3 "El Camino"; from State Historical Records on Natchitoches and Robeline, Louisiana.
4 Author's interviews with members of the Gilcrease family.
5 Original note, Foundation. Author's interviews with members of the Gilcrease family. Correspondence with Mrs. E. W. Morris, Vowell's Mill, Louisiana.

Chapter 2

[1] *A History of Oklahoma* (San Francisco: Doub & Company, 1908), p. 256.

[2] *Gilcrease v. McCullough,* 162 P. 178, Case No. 5775, Supreme Court of Oklahoma, October 10, 1916. Rehearing denied January 9, 1917.

[3] Prudie Patillo, "Alexander Posey, Creek, Was Promising Poet and Satirist," *American Indian Magazine,* Vol. II, No. 7, April 1928. A paper written for an American history class at Bacone College. *The Poems of Alexander Lawrence Posey,* with a Memoir by William Elsey Connelley, (Topeka, Kansas: Crane & Company Printers, 1910).

[4] Questionnaire to Dr. Roger W. Getz, president, Bacone College, Bacone, Oklahoma. "The Beginnings of Bacone College," a brief sketch of early Bacone life prepared for Founders' Day Service, February 9, 1960, on the 80th anniversary of the college.

[5] Gilcrease letters in the Foundation files.

[6] Questionnaires to members of the Gilcrease family.

Chapter 3

[1] C. L. Thomas, *Five Civilized Tribes and Osage Nation, Annotated Acts of Congress* (Columbia, Missouri: E. W. Stephens Publishing Co., 1913), p. 330.

[2] Author's interviews with Belle Gilcrease.

[3] Author's interview with Tom Gilcrease, Jr.

[4] *Belle M. Gilcrease v. Thomas W. Gilcrease,* Case No. 2622, filed in Tulsa County District Court, April 4, 1911, and dismissed same date.

[5] *Outdoor Life,* Vol. LIV, No. 6, December 1924.

BOOK 2

Chapter 1

[1] *American Indian Magazine,* Vol. I, No. 1, October 1926, Lee F. Harkins, editor, Tulsa, Oklahoma.

[2] Article by Paul S. Hedrick, *Tulsa Daily World,* November 24, 1935. "Observe 50th Anniversary of Glenn Pool," *Tulsa Daily World,* November 13, 1955.

Chapter 2

[1] Foundation files.

[2] *Encyclopaedia Britannica,* Vol. 22, p. 258 c.

[3] Transcript of *Gilcrease v. Gilcrease,* 54 P. 2d, 1056.

[4] Author's interview with Tom Gilcrease, Jr.

[5] Author's interviews with H. L. "Red" Branscum.

[6] Author's interviews with Lester Whipple, attorney.

[7] Foundation files. Correspondence with E. L. Ames, Jr., of Venus Oil Company, successor to Gilcrease Oil Company, San Antonio, Texas.

Chapter 3

[1] Foundation files. Authentic documents on file in office of secretary

of state of Oklahoma. Author's interviews with Martin Wiesendanger, Tulsa, Oklahoma.

2 Martin Wiesendanger, "An Indian Foundation," *The Southwest Review*, Vol. XXXI, No. 4, Autumn 1946.

BOOK 3

Chapter 1

1 Notes of Numa Bouttier, originally written in French and discovered in the Foundation files during research for this book. Personal letters between T. G. and Numa Bouttier. Correspondence with Monsieur N. Bouttier, Versailles, France.

Chapter 2

1 Factual data and material compiled by Robert Lee Humber, Greenville, North Carolina, especially for the author in connection with this book. Letters in the Foundation files. Author's interview with Eudotia Teenor (hereafter referred to as "E. T."), secretary to the Foundation. Questionnaires to various members of the Gilcrease family.

Chapter 3

1 *Rudyard Kipling's Verse*, Inclusive Edition 1885-1918, (Doubleday, Page & Co., 1921), p. 147.

2 Questionnaire to Norma Des Cygne Bruce. Questionnaire to Des Cygne Denney. News items and author's interview with S. Morton Rutherford, Jr., attorney, Tulsa. Facts contained in divorce record of *Gilcrease v. Gilcrease*, 54 P. 2d, 1056. Letters of T. G. reproduced in case record. Author's interviews with Cephas Stout, employee of T. G.

3 *Gilcrease v. Gilcrease*, 176 Okl. 237; 54 P. 2d, 1056, and transcript of the evidence contained in said case. 186 Okl. 451; 98 P. 2d, 906; 127 A.L.R. 735.

4 Author's interview with Des Cygne Denney and other members of the Gilcrease family. Author's interviews with long time employees of T. G.

BOOK 4

Chapter 1

1 J. Frank Dobie, "The Art of Charles Russell," *The American Scene* magazine (hereafter referred to as *A.S.*), Summer Issue, Vol. III, No. 2, 1960, p. 3.

2 Author's interviews with Martin Wiesendanger, Tulsa.

3 Description taken from old photographs of the Thomas Gilcrease Collection as it existed in San Antonio, Texas. The *Tulsa Tribune*, September 23, 1955. The *Tulsa Daily World*, August 24, 1956.

4 Old letters and documents in the Foundation files.

5 Bruce Wear, *A Philosophical Approach to Collecting and Decorating*

(Tulsa: Commercial Publishers, 1958). Author's interview with officials of Kennedy Galleries, Inc., New York. Author's interviews with members of the Gilcrease family. Foundation files.

Chapter 2

[1] With the exception of the facts with reference to Lester Hargrett, the source material for this chapter is based upon questionnaires with the subjects and from the author's association with the majordomos, from various articles contained in the early issues of *A.S.* and from James T. Forrest, "In the Museum," *Trends in Collecting,* Summer Issue, Vol. XLVI, No. 2, 1958.

Chapter 3

[1] *A.S.,* "Titans of Western Art," Vol. V, No. 4, p. 1.

[2] Questionnaire to Alfred Stendahl provided necessary information for Stendahl Galleries.

[3] Questionnaire to Kennedy Galleries, Inc., New York, from answers supplied by Rudolph G. Wunderlich, president. Kennedy Galleries brochure of May 1966.

[4] Questionnaire and author's interview with W. F. Davidson, executive vice-president of M. Knoedler and Co., Inc., New York.

[5] Author's correspondence with Philip Robinson, 16 Pall Mall, London. Dr. A. N. L. Munby, *Phillipps Studies* (Cambridge University Press), Chapter III, 1840-1860. Correspondence between T. G. and Lionel Robinson from the Foundation files.

Chapter 4

[1] Charles P. Everitt, *The Adventures of a Treasure Hunter* (Boston: Little Brown, 1951).

[2] *Prose Readings,* edited by William M. Sale, Jr. (New York: Rinehart & Co.), p. 79.

[3] Author's interview with Martin Wenger, April 26, 1966.

[4] Article in the *Tulsa Daily World,* January 18, 1958. Martin Wenger and Mrs. W. R. Holway meet with Bernard Karpel, librarian of Museum of Modern Art, New York.

[5] Martin Wenger, "Gilcrease Library," *Oklahoma Librarian,* published by Oklahoma Library Association, Oklahoma City, Vol. XVI, No. 1, p. 12.

[6] Aline B. Saarinen, *The Proud Possessors* (New York: Random House, 1958).

[7] *Encyclopaedia Britannica,* Vol. XXIII, p. 371 B.

[8] The First Extant Letter From America of Diego Columbus, son and successor of Christopher Columbus, dated January 12, 1512 – description of manuscript Maggs Bros. Booksellers to H.M. The King, 34 & 35 Conduit Street, London, 1929. This brochure also contains biographical data on Diego Columbus.

[9] *The Journal of The Earl of Egmont,* Abstract of the Trustees Proceedings for Establishing the Colony of Georgia, 1732-1738, edited by Robert G. McPherson, (University of Georgia Press, 1962).

[10] *Supra,* note 5, p. 311. Data supplied by Mrs. H. H. Keene, library assistant, Thomas Gilcrease Institute of American History and Art (hereafter referred to as "Institute").

[11] *A.S.,* Vol. V, No. 2, 1963, p. 23.

BOOK 5

Chapter 1

[1] Author's interview with Willard Stone, January 30, 1966, and subsequent visits and exchange of communications, February 17, 1966. Article on Willard Stone, the *Tulsa Tribune*, February 16, 1966. The *Tulsa Tribune*, July 26, 1966. The *Tulsa Daily World*, February 18, 1966.

[2] Author's interview with Willard Stone, contemporary of Acee Blue Eagle. Author's interview with E. T. of the Foundation. Letters from Acee Blue Eagle to T. G. "Acee Blue Eagle" from an article in connection with Memorial Exhibition of Blue Eagle works, Institute. *A.S.*, Vol. IV, No. 4, 1962, "Tempera," by Acee Blue Eagle.

[3] Questionnaire to Woody Crumbo, April 25, 1966. Author's interview with E. T., Foundation.

[4] Author's personal acquaintance with Vinson Lackey. Undated letter from Vinson Lackey to T. G., in the Foundation files. Author's interview with E. T., Foundation. "Last Pages of History, Institutions of Indian Territory," *A.S.*, Winter Issue, Vol. II, No. 4, 1959-60. "R. Vinson Lackey, Artist, Dies," the *Tulsa Daily World*, August 9, 1959. "Tulsa Art and Artist," the *Tulsa Tribune*, January 26, 1953. *Short Histories of the Early Institutions of Indian Territory*, Founded By, For, or On Account of Indians, as pictured in a series of 105 paintings by Vinson Lackey, Institute files.

Chapter 2

[1] Questionnaire and author's interview with Gregory Perino. Letter of February 11, 1966, from Gregory Perino.

[2] Questionnaire to Dr. David Harner, intimate friend of T. G. First *Gilcrease Newsletter*, Institute. Gregory Perino, Archaeologist with Foundation, "Archaeological Collection," *A.S.*, Gilcrease Dedication Issue, Vol. V, No. 2, 1963.

Chapter 3

[1] Author's interviews with Lester Whipple May 5, 1966, and August 23, 1966. Questionnaire to Lester Whipple.

[2] "Injun Tom" letter, in the Foundation files and Lester Whipple personal files. Author's interview with Tom Gilcrease, Jr.

[3] Author's interview with Cephas Stout on various occasions. Open letter, "Dear Mr. Gilcrease," *A.S.*, Dedication Issue, Vol. V, No. 2, p. 7.

[4] Author's interview with Alexandre Hogue, professor of art, University of Tulsa. Letter to author from Alexandre Hogue dated May 26, 1966.

[5] Author's interview with L. Karlton Mosteller, May 26, 1966. Biographical sketch supplied by Robert B. Milsten of law firm of Mosteller, Andrews & Mosburg, Oklahoma City. *Memorial Services*, booklet containing remarks of The Honorable Alfred P. Murrah, chief judge of United States Court of Appeals, Tenth Circuit, December 27, 1966. E. T., professional service facts, the Foundation. Minutes of Executive Committee, Institute, August 21, 1962.

[6] Author's interview with Charlien "Chic" Steel, now Mrs. Maurice Sanditen, Tulsa. Questionnaire to Charlien "Chic" Steel, long time secretary

and one of the most authentic sources for material on the Gilcrease Oil Company.

[7] Author's interview with E. T. Author's interview with Charlien "Chic" Steel. Foundation files. Author's interview with Tom Gilcrease, Jr. Letter in the Foundation files. Personal correspondence between E. T. and T. G.

Chapter 4

[1] J. Frank Dobie, "He Projects a Long Shadow," in the Foundation files. Author's exchange of letters with Dudley R. Dobie, cousin of J. Frank Dobie. J. Frank Dobie, "Thomas Gilcrease," *A.S.*, Vol. IV, No. 4, p. 3. Personal correspondence between J. Frank Dobie and T. G., in the Foundation files. J. Frank Dobie, "Tom Gilcrease and the Earth of My Valley," *Austin American* and *Fort Worth Star Telegram*, June 28, 1953.

BOOK 6

Chapter 1

[1] *A Pocket Directory of the City of Tulsa, Oklahoma,* Souvenir Edition, compiled and published by W. T. Wood, Noel, Missouri, and containing an article by Dr. Fred S. Clinton. Author's interview with Jim Kennedy, pioneer of Tulsa. Angie Debo, "Tulsa Metropolitan Force," *A.S.*, Vol. IV, No. 4, 1962.

[2] Special article written to author by Dr. Robert Lee Humber. Letters from Foundation files. "Saving a Vanishing Frontier," *Life* magazine, March 8, 1954, Vol. XXXVI, No. 10.

[3] Author's interview with Morton R. Harrison.

[4] Author's interview with Alfred E. Aaronson, March 6, 1966. "Keeping Gilcrease Museum for Tulsa," *A.S.*, Dedication Issue, Vol. V, No. 2. Minutes of Executive Committee Meeting of Institute, August 21, 1962.

[5] Personal letter to author by Dr. Logan Wilson, president of American Council on Education, formerly president of University of Texas.

[6] Author's correspondence with D. Hays Solis-Cohen, Letter of December 25, 1953, D. Hays Solis-Cohen to T. G., in the Foundation files.

[7] Author's interview with Lester Whipple.

[8] Remarks of author at Gilcrease Day dinner, "The Creation, Development and Fruition of Thomas Gilcrease Institute of American History and Art," January 27, 1955.

[9] Authentic legal documents on file with City of Tulsa.

[10] Martin Wenger, "Thomas Gilcrease," *Chronicles of Oklahoma,* Summer Issue, Vol. XL, p. 98.

[11] "Gilcrease Appraisal Tops $16 Million," the *Tulsa Tribune,* January 18, 1965. Authentic documents on file with City of Tulsa.

Chapter 2

[1] *A Treasury of Art Masterpieces,* edited by Thomas Craven (New York: Simon and Schuster), excerpt from Introduction.

2 David Jones, "Cleaning Protects Gilcrease Art," the *Tulsa Tribune,* November 25, 1965.

3 Bruce Wear, *The Bronze World of Frederic Remington* (Tulsa: Gaylord, Ltd., Art Americana, 1966).

4 "Great American Documents," special brochure available at Institute gift shop. The *Tulsa Daily World,* February 25, 1967. The *Tulsa Tribune,* February 24, 1967. Remarks of author at Dedication, February 25, 1967, in the Institute files.

5 *A.S.,* Vol. V, No. 2, 1963, p. 18.

6 "Titans of Western Art," *A.S.,* Vol. V, No. 4, 1964, p. 47. *A.S.,* Vol. III, No. 2, 1960, p. 27.

7 "Yellowstone Country," *A.S.,* Vol. V, No. 1, 1963.

8 *A.S.,* Vol. IV, No. 3, 1962, p. 12.

9 "Yellowstone Country," *A.S.,* Vol. V, No. 1, 1963.

10 *Gilcrease Newsletter,* November-December, 1957, Institute. Letter from J. H. Sharp to T. G., Foundation files. The *Tulsa Daily World,* January 13, 1957. "First Artist to Visit Taos," *A.S.,* Vol. III, No. 3, 1960, p. 4. Reflects self-portrait.

11 Foundation files. *El Crepusculo, De La Libertad,* Taos, New Mexico, June 21, 1956. "To Capture Beauty," *A.S.,* Vol. III, No. 3, 1960, p. 3.

12 Biographical data, Foundation files. "The Deep Running Spirit of the Indian," *A.S.,* Vol. III, No. 3, 1960. Reflects self-portrait.

13 Biographical data, Foundation files. "For the Artist, Taos Had Everything," *A.S.,* Vol. III, No. 3, 1960, p. 5. Reflects self-portrait in Gilcrease Collection.

14 Author's conference with E. T., Foundation files.

15 Author's exchange of communications with Charles Banks Wilson. *Gilcrease Newsletter,* Vol. IV, No. 1, January 12, 1959. *A.S.,* Vol. IV, No. 4, 1962. Article by Maurice DeVinna, the *Tulsa Daily World,* Fine Arts Edition, January 16, 1966.

16 Author's interview with Robert Lindneux. Correspondence, June 8, 1966. Robert Lindneux, "The West of Robert Lindneux," a special exhibition by the cowboy artist, chronicler of the West, 1959. News Bulletin, May 1964, Institute. *A.S.,* Vol. II, No. 2, p. 6.

17 *Gilcrease Newsletter,* January-February, 1958, p. 7. The *Tulsa Tribune,* December 17, 1957. Letter from Olaf Carl Seltzer to T. G., October 23, 1949, Foundation files. Philip G. Cole, *Montana in Miniature* (Kalispell, Montana: O'Neil Printers, 1966), illustrated by Olaf C. Seltzer; co-editors Van Kirke Nelson, M.D., Kalispell, Montana, and Cato K. Butler, Missoula, Montana. "The Old West Revisited, The Private World of Philip Cole," *A.S.,* Vol. VIII, No. 4, 1967.

18 Grand Central Art Galleries, New York, "90th Anniversary Roundup of William R. Leigh's Paintings," 1963. "William R. Leigh Studio Exhibition," *Gilcrease Gazette,* Vol. I, No. 4, December 1964. David C. Hunt, "W. R. Leigh, Portfolio of an American Artist," *A.S.,* Vol. VII, No. 1, 1966. Dean Krakel, "Mr. Leigh," *Montana,* the magazine of western history, Summer 1967.

19 Author's interview with Clarence Canning Allen. Review of correspondence.

20 T. G. correspondence, March 28, 1957, Foundation files. Article, "An Appreciation," by Thomas M. Beggs, Director, National Collection of Fine Arts, Foundation files.

21 Author's interview with Thomas L. Lewis, July 6, 1966. Woodrow Crumbo, "Biographical Sketch of the Life of Thomas L. Lewis, Artist."

Foundation files. Letters from Foundation with T. G. and others.

[22] Author's interview with Alexandre Hogue, May 26, 1966.

Epilogue

[1] G. Mallet Prevost, Patent Attorney, Washington, D.C., liaison counsel for the Institute.

[2] Author's interview with Cephas Stout.

[3] Author's interview with E. T.

[4] Author's personal participation in the event.

[5] Author's complete Eulogy on file with the Institute.

[6] *A.S.*, Vol. V, No. 2, p. 8, October 1963.

[7] Author's interview with Chief Wolf Robe Hunt, February 20, 1966. "Gilcrease Bade Twofold Adieu," the *Tulsa Daily World*, May 10, 1962. Photo of Chief Wolf Robe Hunt.

[8] *Gilcrease Newsletter*, Vol. VII, No. 4, April-May 1962, on death of T. G.

[9] Original document presented to T. G. by Henry Standing Bear, chief of Sioux tribe of Indians, naming T. G. "Wicarpi Wakatuya," in the Foundation files.

[10] Author's interview with E. T. and Morton Harrison.

[11] Foundation files.

Index